CALLOW BRAVE AND TRUE

A Gospel of Civil War Youth

by Jay S. Hoar

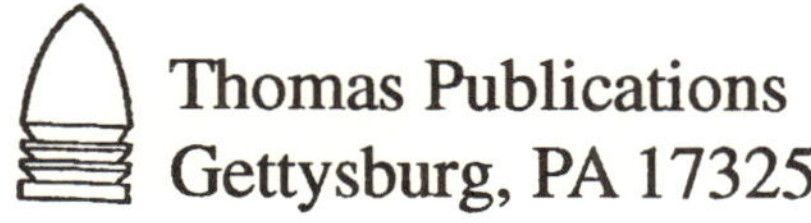
Thomas Publications
Gettysburg, PA 17325

Callow Brave and True

A Gospel of Civil War Youth

Printed and bound in the United States of America

Published by THOMAS PUBLICATIONS
P.O. Box 3031
Gettysburg, Pa. 17325

ISBN-1-57747-45-1

Cover design by Ryan C. Stouch

"Little Reb" by sculptor James Nathan Muir, Greer, AZ.

Charles Morrison's headstone in Madrid Village Cemetery, Madrid Maine. The author's grandmother was the niece of this young casualty.

In Memoriam

Grandmother Augusta Emily Hinkley Hoar's
Uncles of Madrid, Maine

Pvt. David Morrison
1840-July 27, 1862
Company A, 11th Maine
Mortally wounded at Fair Oaks, Va., May 31, 1862
Grave #3027, Soldiers Home Nat'l Cemetery
Washington, D. C.

&

Pvt. Charles Morrison
Feb. 1, 1848-Sept. 1, 1864
Company E, 32nd Maine
Company M, 31st Maine
Died of Disease - 16 yrs. 8 mos.
Madrid Village Cemetery

Impressive Little Grown-Ups

Drummer, mascot, marker,[1] monkey,[2]
Little Boy Gray, Little Boy Blue,
Little Girl Nurse of either hue,
Just what did you do in our sad fray?

Was it Uncle Jeff's urgent call? Or Uncle Abe's?
Did you carry a message? Play a tune? Act the spy?
Stand guard? Mark time? Were you foe or ally?
Yours were billets suitable for babes?

Weren't you *really* older?
Could glory-hunger so smoulder?
Your such few years seems unfair.
Were grown men all *that* rare?
Your service was based on need?
Why—you could barely read!

Tender soprano, all too willing,
You, Cherub Face, on aching feet,
What hateful, hurtful, haunting sights
Stole your peaceful slumber, nights?

Regimented Innocence martially schooled,
Beardless brave youngster partially fooled,
We honor you--the fledgling Fair,
The faithful Forgotten. We honor you.

J. S. H.
1990

1 The soldier who forms the pivot of a wheeling column, or marks the direction of an alignment.

2 A powder monkey (esp. 19th century) a youth aboard a warship among whose duties was carrying powder bags from the powder magazine to the gun crews beside the cannon on the gundecks.

Contents

Preface

Across the thirteen decades since "the Late Unpleasantness" passed on into history, one of its most fascinating legacies has remained substantially under a shroud of mystery. The issue over *who* were the youngest military figures to have rendered plausible or direct service to the Confederate States Army or to the Union Army has often been broached, and has sporadically been treated in far-flung articles by a variety of freelancers and historians—some of real prominence. These chroniclers have commonly attempted to present convincing articles and stories on one or several youngsters, either from their own locale or from a wish to extend recognition to them. In the century and a quarter now concluded, these worthy chroniclers have produced a body of interesting "literature" about the youngest on each side; however, these writings have always been widely scattered and in varied periodicals, usually rather brief, and, though of merit, inclined to draw erroneous conclusions.

Quite understandably, any serious, book-length effort to discover and draw conclusions on this challenging facet of American studies has largely been"written off" as impossible to achieve. The wistful rewards of such a study have been unfairly equated to the proverbial failure one may anticipate while looking for a needle in a haystack. Such dismal prospects spawned by this defeatist attitude toward our wide open field for so long explain the until now non-existence of any reference book or comprehensive tabulation on the child soldiery of the war. The idea itself is old, has been lying fallow a century, originated a century before me. But the responsibility for pioneering a major exploration of this virgin territory has fallen to me. And I accept. Keenly aware that whatever contribution I make will fall short, that little known discoveries will later surface, that some worthy child soldiers (especially those who died early of wounds or disease) will never be known, I harbor no pretensions about being definitive. Nor ought we to consider that to be the goal. I can only candidly hope to be comprehensive enough to be meaningful, or to permit Americans today an opportunity for amply appreciating the extent of the great contribution made by youngsters during our saddest war.

What success I have enjoyed rests chiefly on two realities: (1) the humble realization that I alone was nowhere near being equal to the task of obtaining and assimilating requisite data; that I must depend upon a network of talented and generous individuals to provide tips, leads, suggestions, out of the blue offerings; that I, in fact, be thankful how much of my author's role is that of coordinator, director, sifter, and organizer; and (2) my unique vantage point of operating with a full knowledge of details on most of the nation's eldest and last Civil War veterans of the 1940s and after. This resisting and irresistible knowledge, 25 years accruing, has conferred upon me a solid cadre, Reb or Yank, of those among our last surviving veterans who some eighty years earlier had been only boys age 15 or well under.

Courtesy of Wm. C. McKenna

Another young unknown drummer boy of the Civil War

Acknowledgments

I said it of *The North's Last Boys in Blue* and I'll say it again for *Callow Brave and True*— "No one person could even so much as claim to have written this book. It has taken the understanding, cooperation, talents, and generosity of scores of key individuals who have initiated or responded with vital data." These source-persons, whether scholars, descendants, local historians or family genealogists, have, by their respective expertises, made this present national study possible, a reality. Regrettably a percentage of these priceless contributors are no longer with us. But they have left behind choice tokens of their having once passed this way. The three children of David Wood come to mind for example—David, Jr. (1890-1982) of Montrose, Colorado; Frances and Dorothy Wood, of St. Petersburg, Florida. Or Hilda Ogletree (Mrs. Ray G.) Kempt, of Nacogadoches, Texas, in 1982 for her father. Or Virginia L. Carpenter (88 in 1993) for her grandfather, Chas. J. Orrick, of Fullerton, California. Or Eleanor G. R. Furnace (88 in 1993), of Murrieta, California, for her father, Mancil V. Root. Or David Easterly (1891-1989), of Englewood, Colorado, for his father, "The Baby of the Civil War." Or Victor J. Hinton, 82 in 1976, (who was delivered by Dr. Robert B. Tyler in 1894), of Joplin, Missouri's Historical Society. Or Miss Kathleen Moore (during 1971-83), of Selma, Alabama, for her father, James W. Moore, last (life) "C-in-C" of the U.C.V. These are but a mere representation of their fellows. I especially thank them all, for they are already gone. Some conception of the writer's indebtedness to others may be readily apparent at the concluding of individual notes where a Nota Bene (N.B.) is often posted. But we ought surely to give further visibility to numbers of long-term encouragers who bore offerings, suggestions, leads. Their identities? Hunter Phillips, S.C.V., of East Gadsden, Alabama; David Sullivan, of Rutland, Mass., C.S.A. Marine Corps scholar; John Rix Seibert, II, of Akron, Ohio; Jerry and Lorraine Orton of Syracuse, New York; Seward R. Osborne, historian of Olivebridge, New York; Cmdr. Charlie Lott of Forrest's Escort Camp 1239, S.C.V., Villa Rica, Georgia; Col. Jack W. Rudolph, of De Pere, Wisconsin, a 1933 West Pointer, and knowledgeable on Civil War youth; Marion M. Pliner, genealogist-historian at Fort Dodge, Iowa. Raymond L. Collins of the Medal of Honor History Society (& Alexandria, Va.) has been a stout source for augmenting the list of youngest awardees. Valuable support has emanated from Barry A. Price of Fancy Gap, Virignia; from Robert M. Coch, researcher-sleuth, of Flat Rock, Michigan; from Baron T. Smith, an authority on California Rebs, of Nipomo, California, and from Jerry Wildenhaus, of Dayton, Ohio, and LeRoy Barnett, strategically located at the Michigan State Archives in Lansing. Charles L. Sullivan, S.C.V., 30-year educator and author in the Social Studies Department at the Perkinston Campus of Mississippi Gulf Coast Community College, gets high marks for his able contributions/supports. Thanks to sculptor James Nathan Muir for the photos of his limited edition sculptures, "Little Major" and "Little Reb." These two bronzes are an allegorical tribute to symbolize all the "children" who have marched off to beat the drums of war. Acclaimed by collectors and a member of the prestigious Society of American Historical Artists (SAHA), Mr. Muir specializes in Cavalry subjects and Civil War. Some of his works reside in the U.S. Cavalry Museum at Fort Riley, the Gettysburg Battlefield Museum, and at the Atlanta Historical Society. The scores of testimonials interspersed throughout this study convey their own eloquence to the truth that this writing process is the result of a network of cooperation nationwide. Of immense value to the cause of *CB&T* have been the appearances of special notices for research assistance so generously tolerated by *Confederate Veteran* magazine's Editor-in-Chief James N. Vogler, Jr. Taken together, these are the wealth and essence of this investigation that completes our trilogy in Civil War biography. As long as anyone reads this book, at least so long will my gratitude to these providential authorities endure.

Introduction

That our American Iliad should have occasioned the emanation of many hundreds of youngsters eager to achieve military importance was, at the time, taken pretty much in stride. That our struggles for nationhood(s) {U.S.A. & C.S.A.} and the mortal glory that went with these should have permitted preteenagers to become musicians throughout the regular ranks on so large a scale, while well less than extraordinary in the 1860s, remains highly eligible for comment.

There had been a tradition from the Old World and its centuries of warfare all along that child soldiery, under certain conditions, was acceptable, even understandable, though we are prone to believe these extremities were a rare phenomenon. Uncommon perhaps, but not so rare as we suppose. To offer instances of young teens on duty in European armies is no real chore. Sergeant Donald MacLeod (1688-1791) of Skye, Scotland, became at age fourteen a soldier in the British Army for seventy-four years, retiring at age 88! He served under Gen. Henry Clinton in the attack on New York when he was 87. Upon his death at 103, his eldest son was 84 while his youngest was 10![1] James Christian (1692-1807) of Cullercoats, England, was wounded at age eleven while a cabin-boy aboard Sir George Rooke's flagship during the capture of Gilbraltar in 1704; happily, his wound was less than severe, for James survived as a war veteran 103 more years to reach age 115—admittedly not your typical example.[2] The Marquis de Montcalm (1712-1759), the defending French general who was mortally wounded in the Battle of Quebec during the French and Indian War, had joined the French Army at age twelve and became a captain at seventeen. Johann Friedrich Krieg (1730-1793), whose surname is German for *war*, joined the French Army at sixteen, and, before his retirement as a general, sustained twenty-four battle wounds.[3] John Paul Jones (July 6, 1747-July 18, 1792), a native of Kirkbean, Kirkcudbrightshire, Scotland, did at age thirteen cross the Solway Firth to Cumberland, England, and become an apprentice aboard the merchantman *Friendship* out of Whitehaven, where he filled out his papers. He became a 3rd Mate aboard the slaver *King George* at sixteen; he achieved 1st Mate aboard the slaver *Two Friends* at nineteen.[4]

The Count de Custine of France, who would achieve renown as "General Mustache" while serving with the Continental Army in the American Revolution, had entered the French Army *as a lieutenant* at age seven; but he had a few privileges going for him, to be sure.[5] Gebhard L. Von Blucher

(1742-1819), who helped win the Battle of Waterloo, had begun his career by enlisting at fourteen in the Swedish Army; however, captured by the Prussians, he changed sides and became a Prussian field marshal.[6]

Gregg S. Clemmer, S.C.V., of Germantown, Maryland, reminds us of his great-great-great-great grandfather Rev. Eleazar Clay (Aug. 4, 1744-May 2, 1836), who, at 13 years 7 months, entered the French and Indian War in March 1758 and served several years.[7] We should be mindful that American lads of some six or seven generations learned marksmanship early for food procurement and protection from the Indians.

The well known logo-like American Revolution depiction that epitomizes "the spirit of '76" is more historically and demographically accurate than most Americans today are likely to be aware of. The youthful percussionist at the right, the old man drumming away at center, and the middle-ager, to his left, playing the fife or piccolo are "right on" for accuracy as to who the soldiery were in all our earlier wars. Ironically, the real-life men who first posed for this famous threesome were actually three Civil War recruits in civilian attire.

Many youths were musicians in the Revolution. One of the eight Elijah Kelloggs in that war was the future Rev. Elijah Kellogg, Sr. (1761-1843), who enlisted from South Hadley and, at fourteen, was a drummer boy at the Battle of Bunker Hill; he was at Valley Forge and fought at Monmouth. An alumnus of Dartmouth College, a trustee of Bowdoin College, a minister for Portland, Maine's Second Congregational Church, he fathered a son of the same name who became a famous Maine author of boys' books. Kellogg served seventeen months as a drummer and twenty months as drum major until discharged Dec. 16, 1779, having provided cadence respectively in Capt. Noadiah Leonard's Company of Col. Benjamin R. Woodbridge's 25th Regiment and in Capt. Oliver Lyman's Company of Col. Dike's Regiment.[8]

James Forten (1766- 1842), a great-grandson of a slave, as a youth had run away from his Philadelphia home at age twelve to be a drummer boy in the Continental Navy.[9] Private Josiah Pascal Tucker (Aug. 5, 1767-Nov. 9, 1845) of Amesbury and Norton, Massachusetts, joined Capt. Moses Knap's Company of William Shepard's Third Regiment, Continental Army, on May 1, 1777, at age 9 years 9 months, but *reputedly* 11. One reason Josiah had signed up was to help his brother, perhaps as assistant, a doctor who got killed in the line of duty just a little later. Josiah remained with this schoolmaster and grew toward early manhood in the service of his country during a three-year tour of duty until discharged May 1, 1780. He died at Granby, New York, and rests in the Lewis Cemetery.[10] Another youngster was Samuel Andrews (1764-Jan. 1, 1822), who enlisted in 1775 at age eleven and was with the ill-fated Arnold Expedition that fall.[11]

William Anderson (Jan. 8, 1763-May 6, 1841), a Buckingham County, Virginia, native, enlisted at age fourteen from old Wilkes County, Georgia, to serve in Capt. Burrell Smith's Company of Georgia troops and served thirty months, guarding the frontier and outposts at Gourd Vine Station and at Cherokee Corner in Georgia. He re-enlisted as a rifleman in the Georgia Line under Gen. Elijah Clarke and was at the Siege of Augusta.[12]

Numbers of 1812'er musicians, ages twelve to sixteen, were in uniform during our Second War for Independence; perhaps a full score of them returned for service, again in their old capacities, as sixty-plus-year-olds during the Civil War. A prime example of a youthful 1812'er would be that war's last known survivor, Hiram Cronk, of Ava, New York, who died May 1, 1905, at 105 years. He is said to have lived and died at Hillside, near Rome, and, after years of neglect, was honored by a massive parade in Brooklyn after his death.[13] Of relevant interest to our theme is the fact that William Woolson (b. 1778)—a native of Weston, Massachusetts, and grandfather of the nation's last known Union Army soldier, Albert H. Woolson, of Duluth, Minn., was a private in Capt. Josiah Farrar's Company of Lt. Col. Christopher P. Ballinger's Regiment of New York Militia. Private William Woolson took his older son, Roswell (July 24, 1803-Feb. 16, 1882), with him as a drummer boy. Roswell served the identical War of 1812 tour that his father William served, from May 12 to Aug. 30, 1812. Hence, Musician Roswell Woolson was precisely 8 years 9 months 18 days old on his initial day of military service, arguably the youngest 1812'er.[14] Owen Thomas Edgar (1831-9/3/29), last known veteran of the Mexican War, who died at age ninety-eight in Washington, D. C., was only fifteen on his earliest service.[15]

Probably the youngest recruit to achieve enlistment in the U. S. Marine Corps was a lad named James Buckner of Connecticut. Born in the 1830s, he enlisted at age seven as an apprentice Marine, obligating himself to serve until his 21st birthday. Buckner died Aug. 27, 1887, in his fifties, a Mexican war veteran.[16] Our famed short story author of the mining frontier, Francis Bret Harte (1836-1902), had a brother in the Mexican War at age thirteen.[17]

In summary, there had long been a tradition that youth be accorded their decided and legitimate place in martial endeavors when our Civil War came along. From the vantage point of this present study, we arrive at an overwhelming conclusion: that the American Civil War proved to be their heyday. We would like to believe that, ever since, in our Western world, extreme and early teenage youth are rarely drawn upon. But, even in the late 20th century, several of the current and especially internecine wars in eastern Europe and farther east still rely noticeably—they are seen toting weapons on TV occasionally—on childlike and barely adolescent boys.[18] In fact, today, youngsters bear weapons consistently. "An estimated 250,000 children *under* 18—some as young as 5—have served in 33 conflicts in 1995 and 1996, the Save The Children group reports. Most were with armed opposition groups carrying out dangerous tasks—mine detection and spying."[19]

Biographical Essays

John Converse Elmendorf

Oct. 4, 1848 – June 8, 1861

The tragic early loss of such pre-teenagers as New York State's Elmendorf and McKenzie in June 1861 well before major battles, as indeed the mortal wounding of William Montgomery, 15, 155th Pa., who died Apr. 12, 1865, at Appomattox, may be taken, at least poetically speaking, as the alpha and omega of our immediate topic. Southern boys shared the same fate, of course, as we shall notice. One of the purposes of this study is to remove any hesitations or wonderments over this whole issue of whether or not little fellows, musicians, or youngest privates were subject to dying during the performance of their duties. Accordingly, we begin our detailed inquiry for the youngest identities by presenting those whose lives were abruptly, shockingly sacrificed. To this end, *Soldierboy Casualties* (*scarcely* comprehensive) occupies Appendix C, the better to disarm some of the current (since 1975) rampant glorifications, romanticizations, idealizations, commercializations (particularly the grand color prints of battle scenes that equate to gross taxations of "the real thing") of the war and those caught up in it. It is well, then, that we should begin our investigation with these sobering portraits, the likes of whom seldom become subjects for Civil War artists.

One of the earliest casualties in those opening weeks of the Rebellion was John C. Elmendorf of Kingston, New York, which was to have its full share of youngsters in uniform—Girard L. McEntee, William Vallette, Joseph S. Schepmoes, Henry Clay Durham, *soon* accounted for. Certain of John's ancestors were known to have answered their country's call, to have risked life itself for the national good: Great-granddad Petrus Elmendorf had fought in the American Revolution; Granddaddy Cornelius had been an 1812'er. They were New Yorkers just as both his parents were—Peter P. and Elizabeth Converse Elmendorf. Little of John's brief childhood is known these 150 years later. Their first born, he had by April of '61 attained a firm grasp of his three R's (reading, writing, reckoning). But mighty excitements all that spring—states seceding, the onset of war, Lincoln's first call—fanned the contagion of patriotic fires within both Peter and John. To Seward R. Osborne, a historian who lives in Olivebridge, New York, goes credit for preserving what we have of musician Elmendorf's slim story. In his "The Little Drummer Boys—Kingston's Youngest Volunteers," Osborne has written:

Father and son enlisted in Company F, 20th New York State Militia (Ulster Guard) on Apr. 23, 1861. Peter was a line private, while his son John became a member of the regimental drum corps. However, only Peter marched with their unit from the Academy Green to Rondout Creek, where they boarded the steamer MANHATTAN bound for the war zone. John was absent sick at home. Having recuperated by early May, little John "went along with a patriotic zeal commendable in a much older person" and joined his father and the 20th at Annapolis Junction, Maryland. Taking his proper place as a drummer, he "rigidly performed all his duties during the march and in camp" and rapidly became the pet of Company F. One soldier described the lad as being "remarkable for his aptitude and skill as a drummer and remarked (upon) for his manly deportment and self-possession"—all at the tender age of 12.

On May 22, John accompanied his father on a sick-furlough home to Rondout. Here among his kindred, "enfeebled by exposures and fatigues of service," John suffered from disease. On the night of June 8, 1861, John C. Elmendorf "fell a speedy victim" to inflammation of the lungs at age 12 years 8 months 4 days. On Monday afternoon, June 10, he was buried with full military honors in the Houghtaling Cemetery on Pine Street (a street no longer there). In a Resolution of respect to the grieving parents, Col. George Pratt said, "Death comes to us in many painful forms, but it is most distressing when it takes from us the young just as they are giving promise of future usefulness." Fortunately young Elmendorf died at home where he received comfort from his mother.[1]

Clarence David McKenzie

Feb. 18, 1849 – June 11, 1861

Where else to begin this manifestly American epic than at Brooklyn, New York! And what more appropriate personality than that of a twelve-year-old from a humble Christian home? Surely one of the earliest fatalities among soldierboys in "this cruel war," McKenzie's accidental death by a stray bullet was merely one of hundreds of such pathetic flukes that happened in camp and elsewhere. In fact, only the day before (June 10) had Pvt. Cesar Meisel, also of Company D, 13th New York, died of a gunshot accident.[1] But McKenzie's transparent innocence, his unadulterated unworldliness, his integrity of purpose overwhelm us. He personified a cosmic discrepancy, that perennially outrageous human paradox: children as warriors, as purveyors of death by violence, as victims of regimented mayhem, murder.

His little life story began in Brooklyn, where he spent his brief childhood with both parents and siblings, their first home a fourth floor tenement on Bridge Street. Strangely, though an entire memorial biography *The Little Drummer Boy, Child of the 13th N.Y.S.M. & Child of the Mission Sunday School (1861)* by Luther Goodyear Bingham (1798-1877) details our subject's character, personality and tragic end, Clarence's parents, obviously dutiful and model, remain nameless. The pervasive theme of this sketch is how Clarence came to be a Christian and a beneficent influence of Sunday school upon young folks. We are assured that his introduction to such training was "singularly providential."[2] On a bright Sabbath a Mr. Plummer of the John Street Mission was out seeking scholars for his class and met a brother, age 8, of Clarence at the street pump. Together they went to the nearby McKenzie tenement home where they sought and got the father's approval. "Yes, Willie may go, and Clarence and Martha and Charlotte may go too," consented the paternal voice in the matter.[3] Clarence, six, proved "one of the most punctual, orderly, best behaved, and interesting boys there." He continued three years at this John Street Mission School until his folks moved to Brooklyn's extreme south end, where he attended the Hanson Place Sunday School. After this move to No. 23 Liberty Street at age nine, Clarence evidently enrolled in the Sunday School of Rev. McClelland, pastor of the Lawrence Street Presbyterian Church. Clarence was a member here when in April 1861 he left for the war. We know that as a civilian "The Little Drummer Boy" developed into a musician and percussionist of some note. In fact, as early as July 9, 1860, at age 11 years 4 months 21 days, he enlisted in the Thirteenth Regiment Drum Corps—"The National Grays." His first parade with his regiment took place on Oct. 12, 1860, at the reception for the Prince of Wales (the future Edward V).[4] All during this earlier, more pleasant martial tour in percussion with his National Grays, Clarence fine-tuned his skills. When in mid-April 1861 it became rumored Clarence was going to the front with the Thirteenth Regiment for a drummer, anxiety and interest for his welfare escalated, spread swiftly. Some had trepidations he would never come back alive. It seems that a certain Bible had, *providentially*, been awaiting two years the right moment to be presented to the right person.

The Little Drummer Boy, Child of the 13th Reg't., N.Y.S.M.

Clarence David McKenzie, at age 12.

The giving of this Bible was made a special occasion when the whole Lawrence Street Presbyterian Sabbath School was gathered by Superintendent J. S. Madrid. He it was who gave it. And Clarence read it often. This bestowal was a great comfort to all concerned, for scarcely a week later, with his father's approval and his mother's foreboding anxiety, he enlisted April 23 for three months. So, right there in Brooklyn Clarence, well experienced for his new soldierly assignment, became a member of Company D, 13th New York State Militia. On that day he was 12 years 64 days of age, or six years under 18—the age he was officially set down at.[5] Before departing with his comrades by steamer on April 30 to Annapolis, Maryland, Clarence once more showed the Bible to his folks, saying, "Mother, I wish to read one chapter to you before I go." It was the last she would hear him read.

The Thirteenth was distinctly a Brooklyn unit, particularly Company D, in which Clarence's brother Willie (William), 14, was also a musician; their regiment was locally regarded as an elite group of exemplary men, many of them devout church members. Clarence and Willie were thus quite at home with those who respected their religious upbringing. Clarence's Bible proved a veritable vade mecum, while often his habit of praying to God shamed some elders into attempting its merits. Letters signed, "Your Clarry" were faithfully written to his parents; recorded in his Memorial Story, their composition dates are May 10, 14, 24, 26, and 28.

The regiment arrived at Annapolis Tuesday, May 28.[6] Clarence slept in Captain Balsdon's tent.

The precise circumstance of young McKenzie's tragic death occurred so suddenly—like a roll of thunder and bolt of lightning out of a cloudless, azure sky—as to shock all. A soldier in Company B, Wm. L. McCormick, lacking a musket, borrowed one from a comrade then assigned as a cook. Unknown to the borrower, the piece was loaded. Anticipating an approaching drill, McCormick (said to be best friend of Clarence) was practicing his manual of arms in McKenzie's quarters, when, coming to "Charge bayonet," his hand barely struck the hammer of the weapon, releasing it—[McCormick believed it only half-cocked]—and discharging it. The lead ball struck McKenzie in the back, passed through and out at the stomach, striking a brick wall and chipping the brick.[7] This was at 2:00 p.m. June 11, 1861.

Conscious, Clarence lived but two hours, some of that time unable to speak. He was seated beside another drummer on a pavement, his back toward the wall and but a short way from it. The first thought he uttered on receiving the mortal wound? "Oh, what will my poor mother say?"[8] Initially embittered by the fatal, unwise handiwork of McCormick, Clarence shortly forgave the whole thing, upon further reflection. He drew his final breaths in his Captain Balsdon's arms. Ladies from Annapolis brought flowers. The body was laid in an ice coffin and made ready, under an escort of that Captain with four men and older Brother Willie.

They arrived at the two-story frame McKenzie home at 23 Liberty Street late June 12.[9] His funeral took place from St. John's Church on the corner of Washington and Johnson Streets at 4:00 p.m., June 14. Children of Public School No. 8 and the Lawrence Street Presbyterian Sunday School were present. Streets adjoining were packed with spectators. Under Captain Balsdon, of Company D, members of the 13th Regiment and a reserve corps escorted the flag-draped coffin to Greenwood Cemetery. Four fellow drummers rolled the funeral march. To nearly conclude, we cite a passage in Chapter VIII, Bingham's *The Little Drummer Boy:*

> *"Jack," the Little Drummer's faithful dog, followed the hearse to the grave. When the coffin was lowered into it, he went forward and looked attentively down to see where they had laid his young master. When the volleys were fired Jack ran away. After the procession retreated he remained, and after the grave was filled, he laid himself upon it. For many nights he was in the habit of spending long hours till toward morning he went home.*[10]

Jack's feelings reflect those of the other mourners, for the melancholy passing of Clarence McKenzie elicited widespread emotional gloom at the time. His name came up on at least three occasions in the Fulton Street Prayer Meetings by various Brooklyners. Public curiosity was satisfied only when later in 1862 his *Memorial Tribute*, edited by Luther Bingham, appeared. We are gratified to learn that one of Brooklyn's thirty G.A.R. posts was named C. D. McKenzie Post 399.[11]

But, for us who now discover him some 130 years later, McKenzie stands in for several hundred other callow innocents like himself who, in the four years immediately after his own demise, were to be cruelly cut down and forever denied their promising birthrights.

Charles Edwin King

Apr. 3, 1849 – Sept. 20, 1862

When news of the tragic battle death of Charley King swept over southeastern Pennsylvania in the aftermath of Antietam, a tangible, visible melancholia descended upon the land. Entire counties of citizens young and old were invested with lamentations, were plunged into grievous sorrow. Historical accuracy would be served well simply to announce that *this* youth was *the* most famous of all the soldier-boy musicians who went to the war and never came home. His very name soon became (and has since remained) a by-word for the heroic youngster who sacrificed his life for the welfare of his country. How many others like him were required to make so costly a price? *Soldierboy Casualties* is a token effort to answer this haunting question. See Appendix C.

West Chester, a borough since 1799 and some 23 miles west of Philadelphia in Chester County, had from birth been home to "Charley." In the June 1860 census the Kings were recorded as Pennell, 33, a merchant tailor; Adaline (Bennett), 33, homemaker; Charles, 11; Lewis, 9; Theodore, 6; Ella, 4; William, 3; Anna, 2 months, and living on the 100 block of Barnard Street. By 1861 West Chester had 4,757 citizens.[1] Though little of this lad's earliest years has been preserved, we know he lacked not for playmates. We are quite certain, too, that by age ten he was into percussion. In fact, we (Dennis C. Roussey, of nearby Downingtown, Pennsylvania, Civil War aficionado and sleuthing authority on King, and the writer) strongly suspect that *he* is the smallest musician 9 or 10-looking centered in a locally known West Chester photograph of 1859 vintage: a quintet of finely uniformed fife-boys and drummer boys posing with their drums.[2] One suspects that Pennell King, a merchant tailor, might well have had a hand in such sartorial excellence and elegance. Unidentified also, the other four musicians *look* ages 12, 13, 15, and 18. With the onset of war, Charley King, aflame with patriotism and well practiced, having the good fortune to be twelve already, felt fully qualified for a military tour. We shall see from dozens of youngster-musician cases like Charley's—Tommy Hubler (1851-1913, 12th Indiana); Charlie Scott (1st Vt. Hvy. Art., 1849-1901); Abram Springsteen (1850-1930, 35th & 63rd Indiana); Johnny Clem (24th Ohio? & 22nd Mich., 1851-1937)—that they faced stiff opposition from "the old man" (not mentioning, mind you, "the old lady") who stood adamantly in the way. In this our epic study of those youngest caught up (ensnared?) in America's lachrymal extravaganza, we shall become familiar with the ploys of such boys—nagging, arguing, reasoning, drumming at all hours, earning money drumming for local recruiters.

During August 1861 recruiting efforts were afoot near West Chester for a Company F of a 49th Pennsylvania Infantry. Young King spent considerable leisure that summer at the recruiting quarters, usually with his drum in tow. "So impressed was Captain Benjamin H. Sweeney with his drumming skills and eagerness to enlist," wrote the distinguished battleground photographer, William Frassanito in his *Antietam* (Group III: The West Woods), "that the captain agreed to intercede on the boy's behalf."[3] Capt. Sweeney, 32, visited the Kings and presented clarifications on predictable duties of a drummer boy; in short, he recruited persuasive arguments as many another such officer was known to do across the land—how that musicians did not (*officially)* go into combat, how they remained back to help wounded or acted as surgeon's assistants. As other inspired recruiters, Sweeney employed his coup de grace: "I will personally take responsibility for Charlie to guard him from peril." Pennell and Adaline, surely with *some* misgivings, consented.

On Sept. 9, 1861, Charles E. King enlisted for duty with Company F, 49th Pennsylvania Vols. That day he was 12 years 5 months 9 days. From the start he was a hit with all his older comrades who thrilled to his renditions during drills, marches, battles, and evening serenades. It got so they were clamoring that *he* should be their Regimental Drum Major—nothing less than. And it came to pass in fairly short order. Musician King hosted the pleasant novelty of drawing pay regularly and sending it home for savings. His Civil War? He served in these Army of the Potomac commands —Hancock's Brigade, W. F. Smith's Division to Mar. '62; 1st Brigade, 2nd Division, 4th Corps, to May '62; 1st Brigade, 2nd Division, 6th Corps, thru Sept .'62. Charley's program was the 49th's:[4]

-Organized at Lewistown, Pa., 9/10-9/20/61
-Duty near Lewinsville, Va. & D.C. Defenses until March 1862
-Advance on Manassas, Va., 3/10-3/15
-Return to Alexandria. Embark for Va. Peninsula
-Siege of Yorktown, 4/5-5/4
-Lee's Mills, Burnt Chimneys, 4/16
-Battle of Williamsburg, 5/5
-Pursuit to the Chickahominy & picket duty until 6/25
-Garnett's Farm, Golding's Farm, & Savage Station, 6/27-6/29
-White Oak Swamp Bridge & Malvern Hill, 6/30-7/1
-In works at Centreville, Va., 8/27-8/31
-Assist in checking Pope's rout at Bull Run, 8/30
-Covering retreat to Fairfax C.H., 8/31-9/1
-Maryland Campaign begins, 9/6
-Sugar Loaf Mountain, 9/10-11
-Crampton's Pass, South Mountain, 9/14
-Battle of Antietam, 9/16-17

Once we peruse this summary of Charlie's full year of heavy service, we lose all thought and focus on his usually forgotten initial de facto Civil War contribution: his having in May 1861 provided percussion for a three-month company of enlistees from West Chester departing for training at Harrisburg.[5] And now, sixteen months later, he was to be the youngest life of some 2108+ federal soldiers "taken out" at the grim harvest called Antietam. To appreciate the immediate circumstance of Drum Major King's mortal wound, we defer to Mr. Frassanito's detailed account:

At Antietam, the 49th Pennsylvania was placed in support to the immediate right of Capt. Andrew Cowan's First Battery, New York Light Artillery, on the Miller Farm just north of the East Woods. There was little going on at the time the unit reached the field (shortly before 1:00 p.m.) and several members of the 49th took the opportunity to talk with those of the 125th Pennsylvania, remnants of whom were located nearby. The two units had been recruited from the same part of the state and many of them were old friends.

The fighting for all practical purposes had ended on the northern portion of the battlefield by the arrival time of Hancock's Brigade and the 49th Pennsylvania, but the men were occasionally subjected to scattered artillery fire. Essentially, the Southern gunners wanted to show Union forces that they were still ready to meet any renewed attacks against the Confederate left flank.

During one of these artillery salvos, a shell exploded amidst the ranks of the 49th Pennsylvania, wounding several soldiers, including 13-year-old Charles King, who was hit "through the body" by a piece of shrapnel. With great care and affection, members of Company F carried the bleeding boy back to a field hospital where, three agonizing days later...he died from his wound.[6]

Many battle units, not then engaged, were fatally close to the fighting, as at the infamous Cornfield nearby. Again, in a passage chosen by Dennis C. Roussey (Vice President, Page 1 Publishers, Inc., Downingtown, Pa.), citing Sgt. Robert S. Westbrook's *History of the 49th Pennsylvania Volunteers,* we learn that, despite cautions, musicians' lives were, at times, in jeopardy:

Gen. Hancock...ordered us to fall back twenty paces out of range, which was done just in the nick of time, for the rebels ran some batteries out and opened fire on us.... Bullets and shells filled the air, claiming victims in units not actually fighting.

Gus Heller, of Company C, lost a foot on the skirmish line, and Charley King, of Company C, was pierced through the body and fell into the arms of H. H. Bowles of the Sixth Maine.

The quick-witted response of Musician Henry H. Bowles, 21, (1841-June 4, 1916) of Cherryfield, Washington County, Maine, and Company C, Sixth Maine, gentled Charley's shock, preventing his being thrown to the ground. It was Bowle's brief brush with history, and a grievous week for him and scores of comrades nearby. Bowles, a "cloth dresser" by trade, who had enlisted Apr. 19, 1861, lived to be discharged Aug. 15, 1864, and go home.[7]

At the fatal hour of Charley's mortal wounding of a lung, his father, Pennell King, a private in Company D of an Emergency Militia regiment hastily assembled at Gov. Andrew Curtin's urgent request, was only ten miles away, offers Dennis Roussey. But Pennell did not learn of his son's fate until returning home on or about September 26; in fact, the boy was already laid away.[8] West Chester's *Village Record* that October 7 remarked, "Daily are we called upon to record names of brave men who have fallen a sacrifice on their country's altar, that gives us pain, but how much keener the anguish when tidings reach us that a child of such tender years has been a victim.... He was a true little hero." *The Jeffersonian* report on King ended, "We should be glad, if we were able to write his epitaph—'Very young, quite small, yet manly, kind, affectionate, quiet, trusting, yet proud and ambitious, and a superior musician.'"[9]

One of the few tangible links to this martyred musician are six silver spoons smithed from melted down coins withdrawn from Charley's bank account. A fruitless search for the hero's grave in the early 1980s led to their discovery in a corner dining room cupboard at the Charleston home of Samuel and Dorothy Detwiler, daughter of Franklin King, son of Charley's brother Harry. Mrs. Detwiler was presented these spoons from a cousin years before, with a card briefly noting their background and concluding that Charley King was "buried in an unknown grave."[10] Regrettably, it must be reported these 135 years later that an enduring mystery shrouds the actual when and where of Charley King's burial. Placed in a temporary grave at Antietam, the body was quite certainly transferred, whether to West Chester or to the National Cemetery at Sharpsburg appears impossible of establishment. Having to accept that he is one of the 141,000+ Civil War unknowns is galling. He is practically in his own category—famous as an unknown. His drum and a few of his effects on display at the Antietam Battlefield Visitors Center Museum *are* increasing King's identity daily, for our current much younger America is steadily discovering him. His presence here among so many soldierboys like himself will prove to be the caliber of memorial he has always deserved. War and childhood innocence are a cosmic discrepancy so mutually disparate, so at cross-purposes, so incompatible that we wonder aghast at their co-existence. No matter how prettily we dress it up, human combat remains a dirty business growing dirtier with each passing age; as a contagion, it has proven a perennial stigma on our human condition. War is the pesky pestle in the mortar of human life, daily grinding away the innocent, relentlessly pulverizing to an early death many of the best among us.

Henry Clay Durham

Nov. 19, 1849 – July 8, 1863

This Kingston, New Yorker, was the fifth of eight children born to Elisha (b. 1798) and Adaline Osborne Durham. A gardener by trade, Elisha was overseer of Wiltwyck Cemetery, according to the 1857 Kingston Directory. Somewhat physically disabled, Elisha, nearly sixty, was unable to work full time. This situation fairly (a tad *un*fairly, with 8 youngsters "underfoot") compelled Adaline to open a boarding house. By winter-spring 1861, Henry began gainful employment under Elisha, who drew wages for him. By mid-1862 Elisha's disability was approaching 100%, for he now had to hire a work crew, *his* capacity being their supervision. Money was short. Partly to alleviate fiscal pressures, Henry enlisted at Kingston on Sept. 6, 1862, for service with the 156th New York Volunteers, "the Mountain Legion." He was 12 years 9 months 18 days. That November 17, he mustered in as the Company A drummer. Henry's percussion was so effective that in short order he was promoted to Sergeant of the Drum Corps. His Civil War career is no secret:[1]

-Depart New York for New Orleans, 12/4/62
-Into Camp at Carrollton, La., until 2/11/63
-Expedition to Plaquemines, 2/11-2/19
-At Carrollton until 3/6
-Operations against Port Hudson, 3/7-3/27
-To Algiers, 4/1, thence to Berwick City 4/9
-Operations in Teche Campaign, 4/11-4/20
-Fort Bisland (near Centreville), 4/12-4/13
-Vermillion Bayou, 4/17
-Exped. from Opelousas to Alexandria & Simsport, 5/5-5/18
-Operations against Port Hudson, 5/22-7/9
-Expededition to Clinton, 6/3-6/8

Literate from sound public schooling, this approaching teenager enjoyed the boon and catharsis of writing letters home to his folks. Henry's Jan. 5, 1863 "good news" from Camp Kearney (near Carrollton) proudly announced, "I have been paid and I gave $40 to Lt. Peter Elting to send to Kingston. It will be Father's name on the envelope." The little Kingstonian kept but $6.00 for himself.

On June 6, Sgt. Durham was admitted at the Arsenal Hospital, Fort Williams, Baton Rouge, ill with typhoid and malarial fever. His surgeon, William H. Mather, of the 173rd New York, was moved to write Elisha and Adaline:

> *I remember well the day when Henry entered the hospital. His straightforward manner and intelligent answers to all questions propounded, and beautiful and innocent features at once attracted my favorable attention. Late last evening I called at his bedside, and he was talking to himself in an unintelligible manner, but on bending my ear toward him I could hear, "I am sorry, I am sorry," repeatedly. I strove to quiet him and started from his side, when he raised his emaciated little hand and said "I am going to die in eight hours," then resumed the broken, unintelligible speech...He called for his mother and friends, but, alas, they could not come.*

At 8:00 a.m. on Wednesday, July 8th '63, at 13 years 7 months 19 days the end came.

> *"By foreign hands his dying eyes were closed,*
> *By foreign hands his little limbs composed."*

Monetarily poor, Elisha and Adaline Durham were not able to have their son's remains sent home.[2] Far from his native Ulster County these 133 years, little Drummer Boy Durham rests at the National Cemetery, Baton Rouge, Louisiana, in Section 19, Grave No. 1216...*not quite* forgotten. Too, he is memorialized at Wiltwyck Cemetery, Kingston, New York, on his parents' gravestone.[3]

Charles Howard Gardner

Feb. 1848 – Dec. 21, 1863

"Celebrated" as one of the more widely known pathetic instances of a youth losing his life in the battle maw, while our lachrymal extravaganza was yet in full swing, deaths of young Gardner's caliber sent out shock waves of sobering reality to the Northern press and populace. His mother's sad plight (a poetic irony attends absence of her name from existing available accounts), his own naive innocence, and his ultimate tragic end plunged many a Michigan family into mourning for weeks. At the time (December 1863-June 1864) Gardner's death along with those of dozens of other youngsters' fatalities—among these Joel Closson's (Co. A, 14th Maine—4/22/62) at age 13-4-26; Patrick Howard's (Co. A, 1st Vt. Hy. Art.—6/25/64) at 15; Charley E. King's (Co. F, 49th Pa.—9/20/62) at 13-5-17; Freddie Painter's (2nd Conn. Hy. Art.—6/1/64) at 14; Cyrus F. Snell's (Co. C, 19th Maine—6/12/64) at 16; Elnathan Smith's (Co. E, 3rd N.J. Inf.—July '64) at 15—weighed heavily upon the conscience of Secretary of War Stanton. Attuned as he surely was to morale and the damaging toll on civilian sentiment (so destructive to the popularity of the administration & war itself), it weighed sufficiently to cause him to issue a General Order to Union generals in the notorious, gory Atlanta Campaign to forthwith discharge any and all soldierboys known to be under age. Thus, at length, Johnny Clem's rather sudden discharge whereby he was sent home. Private Gardner's sacrifice may well have been a factor in the survival of Clem and other "clemesque" soldierlings.

Of Flint, Michigan, for apparently his entire civilian life, Charley Gardner, 13, at the firing upon of Fort Sumter, was one of many Wolverines then just entering "teenagehood" and enthralled by the momentous crisis of civil war. Within the limits of greater Detroit there would be shortly (4' to 5' tall) several more such musicians—Robert H. Hendershot, William H. Dennison of Oronoko, John Hamley, and William Young. Then, too, Flint, Michigan's own most visible personality among musicians on parade here would be its late surviving Corydon E. Foote, 13-0-1 on enlistment in the 10th Michigan—Foote, who died at ninety-five in 1944.

In mid-May, 1861, Charley saw his father leave home in response to Lincoln's first call; he enlisted in the 2nd Michigan Infantry organized there in Detroit May 25, where they trained into early June— "The first three-years Regiment from Michigan." That made Charley the man of the house that summer, since he had a sister and little brother. Likewise, upon Lincoln's second call, Charley's favorite teacher, Simon C. Guild, soon (9/21/61) consented to join the 8th Michigan Infantry. The loss of his two closest role models reached into the boy's very conscience, into his morale, his reason for living. He reasoned with Guild (promised a captaincy) about his qualifications as a drummer. Such a service would free up an extra man, went his plea. At the same time he began "to work" on his mother. "I think it my duty to go, especially, as you, Mother, do not greatly need me at home."[1] How Charles H. Gardner wangled himself into Company A of the Eighth Infantry, as musician at Flint for three years, at fourteen (if actually that)[2] is told rather well in several early sources, among these that footnoted by Jonathan Robertson, (Michigan) Adjutant General, in his comprehensive compilation *Michigan in the War,* 1882. We follow Robertson's entry at the conclusion of his chronicle of the Eighth Michigan's service record, where he states, "The total regimental enrollment was 1,792 officers and men, while its losses were 9 officers, 131 men killed in action; 3 officers, 64 men died of wounds; 2 officers, 195 men died of disease."[3]

The poor mother who had already surrendered her husband, reluctantly consented, and her boy joined Co. A, 8th Michigan, with Captain Guild, ordered to Port Royal. On the way, Charley met his father in Washington; he saw him a little way off, and forgetting that he was in the ranks, broke and ran to his father's arms. It was their last meeting on earth; the father died soon after in Alexandria. After his father's death Charley wrote:

> *Dear Mother,—I am near broken-hearted. I try to be cheerful, but 'tis of no use. My mind constantly runs in the direction of home, a fresh gush of tears comes to my eyes and I have to weep. But, Mother, if this is so hard for me, what must it be for you? Don't take it too much to heart, for remember that you have me left, and I will do my best to help you. I shall send you all my money hereafter, for I really do not need money here.*

And this promise he fulfilled to the letter. His Captain [Guild] guarded him like a father. At the terrible battles of James Island (6/16/63), Va., the Captain, while on the parapet of the rebel works, was struck by a shot and he fell over the wall into the rebel hands, and was seen no more. Charley, so bereaved, his captain and dear friend gone, in his agony of soul murmurs *"Oh, how I pity his poor mother!"* Charley passed through many severe engagements, often escaping death as it were by a miracle. Still, he kept with the regiment; was at Vicksburg, and with Burnside in the East Tennessee Campaign, in the mountains, and at Knoxville. But during its siege, a chance shot struck him on the shoulder and entered the lung (12/1/63). Their surgeon wrote to his mother, "He has been in a dangerous condition, but is fast recovering." Next tidings, the regiment on the way home on veteran furlough;

heard from at Louisville, at Indianapolis, at Michigan City, and last at Detroit. "He may be here tonight—he will be here tomorrow," said his devoted and loving mother. Every summons to her door was Charley. Everything was in readiness for a happy meeting—mother, sister, and brother waiting for him. The suspense is great and trying. A knock at the door! All start—all cry "It's Charley!" All rush to the door. No! A telegram: "The regiment has arrived, but Charley is dead."[4]

Thus our memorial to Charles H. Gardner (& his family) these 130-odd years after-Charley, who attained about age 15 years 10 months. It is well we should know his story, the better to squelch the myth that youngster-soldier casualties were extremely rare, and to underscore the abject and absolute insanity of warfare as a solution to religio-geo-political problems.

Frederick D. Painter

Feb. 1850 – June 1, 1864

Just here, we raise an undeservedly small monument to an all-but-forgotten Connecticut drummer boy. He was killed in his line of duty June 1, 1864, on the battlefront at Cold Harbor, Virginia. While providing a heavy percussion to drown out cries of the wounded, as several of his fellow musicians (Chas. N. Baldwin of Woodbury; Myron Ferris, Chas. Henry Pine, Philip Stabell, Henry Van Deusen, and Wilson B. White—all of Winchester)[1] were doing, he bravely moved forward with the Second C.V. Heavy Artillery's disastrous assault on earthworks defended by Longstreet's seasoned veterans. Fred never came home. What ever did become of him is not known today, if indeed his hastily prepared burial spot ever was temporarily marked. Wooden crosses were tempting kindling to those shivering nearby that winter of '64-'65.

Frederick was the second of five children born to his parents, who during the late 1840s to mid-1850s, were living in nearby southeastern New York. We know this from the local 1860 Census Record, kindly provided by Joseph C. Sweet, vice president of the New Canaan Historical Society. This record reveals that the father, Rev. John H. Painter, then age 48, was a native of England and a Methodist minister, and that the mother was Elizabeth, age 45, a native New Yorker. The five children—Ann E., 12; Frederick, 10; Mary M., 9; George H., 6; and Thomas, 3—were all born in New York. About 1858, then, the Painters moved to New Canaan in very southwestern Connecticut. A copied portion of an 1867 New Canaan Map (sent by Mr. Sweet Mar. 24, 1993) pinpoints the "Rev. J. H. Painter" home as adjacent to "Rustic Arbor School No. 9" in "District No. 9" on Comstock Hill Road and his "M. E. Ch." (Methodist Episcopal Church) just a three-minute walk southward on the other side of the road which runs parallel to the south-flowing Silvermine River that lies only 150-400 yards to their east. Here, little Frederick for nearly five years played with brothers and sisters, learned Bible verses and music, attended Sunday School and the Rustic Arbor School and did his chores. Exactly what led to his joining Mr. Lincoln's Army cannot be precisely reported. We do know that this lad responded to recruiting efforts by Lieutenants Marsh, Knight, and Hosford for the newly organizing Second Connecticut Heavy Artillery, ordered by the War Department Nov. 23, 1863, to be built around the old Litchfield County 19th Connecticut (orig. Org. July 22, '62) as its nucleus.[2] Frederick, of his own will and heart, volunteered in mid-December, presumably with reluctant consent from his folks.

On Dec. 19, 1863, Frederick, not yet fourteen, enlisted and was mustered-in the same day. By March 1 the new 2nd C. V. H. A. were 1800 strong. They drew garrison duty at the Washington, D. C., forts—Worth, Williams, Ellsworth—during March and April. On May 17 they were ordered to join the Army of the Potomac and did so at Fredericksburg. Here they were assigned to Gen. Emory Upton's 2nd Brigade, 1st Division, Sixth Army Corps. They were at Spotsylvania Court House May 19-21.[3] On May 22 they crossed the North Anna River; while skirmishing they lost their first soldier to a Southern bullet. In the ensuing week they strove mightily to destroy railroads at key points and they also completed probably the hardest march of their entire tour. On May 29 they were at Hanover Court House; May 30 saw them on picket near Totopotomy Creek. Then, the next day, near Cold Harbor, two more of Pvt. Painter's comrades were killed and five wounded.[4] His own last two weeks of life, as indeed the day he died, are well documented. What led to his untimely and swift departure from all earth's offerings? Captain James N. Coe (late of Co. H) supplies the answer on Page 173 from his *History of the Second Regiment C. V. Heavy Artillery:*

> *June 1, under command of Colonel Kellogg, the regiment was disposed in three lines, under Majors Hubbard, Rice and Ells, and advanced in that order, the objective point being the heavy earthworks defended by Longstreet's veterans. It passed at double-quick, to the first line, capturing it and sending to the rear over 300 prisoners; forward again at double-quick, with intervals of less than 100 yards between the battalions, to and through a stiff abattis, within twenty yards of the enemy's main line, where it met a most destructive fire from both its front and left flank, but pressed on, some even to the top of the main line of earthworks. Nothing could withstand the murderous fire that now met them, and the First and Second Battalions crept back to the somewhat less exposed position held by Third, but leaving on the field 323 of Litchfield County's bravest sons, 129 of them dead or mortally wounded—a record [said to be] unsurpassed by any [other] regiment of the Union Army during the war. Among these were the ideal soldier, Colonel E. S. Kellogg, who fell riddled with bullets in the advance with the First Battalion, Capt. Luman Wadhams, who was mortally, and Major Ells, who was severely wounded.*

As with nearly all who died that day, our lad's name went unmentioned in history and biography. Surely, though, word of Frederick's personal sacrifice got back to New Canaan's District No. 9 and the bereaved Painter family. But their community had no newspaper then. So, no known obituary for him. Now, some 130 years later, perhaps a kind poetic justice may be in evidence here in the 1990s for *this* drummer boy: our present account—sadly more focused on his heroic death than on his humble life—is, verily, Pvt. Painter's long delayed obituary!

Edward Black

May 30, 1853 – June 30, 1872

One of *the* youngest on either side was Hagerstown, Indiana's Eddie Black. He was one of the three sons of George H. (Feb. 6, 1828-Sept. 1889) and Lydia Ann Beck Black (July 1832-Feb. 24, 1903). Lydia Ann was a native of Hagerstown, Maryland. Edward's twin brother Edwin died Mar. 17, 1854, at less than a year old. But he already had another brother, Charles H.

It is well known that Eddie first entered Federal service on July 24, 1861, at age eight years one month and twenty-four days. On that early day in the war this lad enlisted as a drummer boy with the 21st Indiana Infantry, under the command of Colonel McMellen. (This outfit became the 1st Indiana Heavy Artillery in February 1863—after Eddie's tour had expired.) What did Musician Black's Civil War consist of during his first tour? With the 21st Indiana he gave cadence through these operations:

-Departure for Baltimore, 7/31/61
-Expedition to Maryland's Eastern Shore, 11/14-11/22
-Move to Newport News, Va., 2/19/62
-Sail on steamer Constitution *to Ship Island, Miss., 3/4-3/13*
-Operations against Forts Jackson and St. Philip, 4/14-4/28
-Occupation of New Orleans—arrive at Camp Algiers, 5/1
-Expedition to New Orleans and Jackson RR, 5/9-5/10
-Move to Baton Rouge, 5/30
-Support role at Battle of Baton Rouge, 8/5
-Evacuation at Baton Rouge. Move to camp at Carrollton, 8/20
-Action at Bayou des Allemands, 9/4-9/5
-Skirmish near St. Charles Court House, 9/7-9/8[1]

Eddie was captured at the August 5 encounter at Baton Rouge and held prisoner for a few days, one of his more memorable adventures. Another had been their regiment's marching into New Orleans that May 1 as he assisted their band with playing the tune "Picayune." Two other brushes with the Southern forces impressed Eddie—the 21st Indiana's part in the action at Bayou des Allemands and the skirmish at St. Charles Court House. A general order at about this time abolishing certain military bands apparently precipitated Eddie's release from duty, and he was discharged on Sept. 11, 1862, at 9 years 3 months and 12 days of age, making him one of the very youngest veterans (upon discharge) of the entire war. At this point he had served 1 year 2 months and 5 days.

Eddie, according to family tradition and that of the First Indiana Heavy Artillery, rejoined many of his senior comrades in the fall of 1862, to serve in Company L under Lt. George H. Black, his father. It appears young Black's total army time was nearly forty-four months.

Eddies's drum has been carefully preserved in his family down the years, first by his mother, who gave it to her surviving son, Charles H. Black; thence Charles, who eventually passed it on to his daughter, Anna Black, of Indianapolis; then by Anna, in 1943, who gave the drum to Alice May Beck Mawson, of Indianapolis. On Oct. 23, 1963, Mrs. Mawson gave it to Mrs. Elliott (Beck) Mount, a first cousin (once removed) from Edward Black himself. Upon Mrs. Mount's passing, Dec. 25, 1969, at Fort Worth, Texas, the historic drum was presented by her son Allen Wade Mount, Sr., to the Children's Museum in Indianapolis.[2] This museum has authenticated this drummer boy's exceptional service with copies of his army war record and his mother's petition for a "Mother's Army Pension."

A number of local historians believe that when Edward Black died on June 30, 1872, just a month beyond his nineteenth birthday, he did so from disabilities incurred from his battle service. He was buried at Crown Hill Cemetery in Indianapolis, beside where his parents would be buried—one of the earliest youngest to die after "The Boys' War." His grave marker proudly asserts:

DRUMMER BOY of the 21st INDIANA REGT.
At 8 Yrs. 6 m.
The youngest Soldier of the Rebellion.

And he was...for one month and twenty days during July 24-Sept. 12, 1861, the day before Charles Knecht was enlisted by Gen. Henry Wager Halleck. (See Appendix G.) Black apparently was the second Union Army soldier to enjoy this rare distinction, second only to Thomas L. F. Hubler, from whom he unwittingly had removed that distinction. Drummer boy Black, at inception of his service, was a full year and five months younger than Drummer boy Hubler had been. Hubler's great claim is that he was the earliest of the Union Army's child-soldier drummer boys. Black, however, may well be entitled to his claim of having been the youngest P.O.W. of the war.

Zachariah Taylor Lamb

Jan. 1849 – 1882

Georgia's Gray legions (110,000), like those of other Confederate States, attained their numbers, whether grizzled or green, by stretching eligible age limits both up and down. So right, so deep-felt were their causes (a strict interpretation of the Constitution, for example), that males *anywhere near* service age—even pre-adolescents—clamored to be in the C.S.A. Yes, schooled to states' rights, boys knew why their South had left the Union. Modern-day Americans have little conception of how eagerly and seriously boys of five and six generations ago volunteered to serve in the Southern armies.

"Zach" was born at Bear Creek, Henry County (s.s.e. of Atlanta), Georgia. His parents were Jacob (1802-1873) and Julia Jordan Lamb (1830-1915). Jacob, 45, and Julia, 17, his second wife, had married in Henry County on Nov. 11, 1847. Already wealthy in half brothers and sisters born in North Carolina and Georgia, Zach became eldest of five brothers and a sister in Jacob's second family. Zach's siblings were all eastern Alabama natives. For a while at least, it appears he had playmates aplenty. Fortunately, we may learn more of the family and situation he grew up in from a Sept. 3, 1996 letter of Robert E. Lamb, 71, of Cave Spring, Georgia:

> *Great grandfather Zach was less than a year old when in 1850 Jacob moved west to northern Russell County, Alabama, which was to become, after the war, Lee County—one of the few by that name honoring Robert E. Lee rather than "Light-Horse Harry." As a planter and land speculator, Jacob did well in buying then newly available public land(s) cheaply and selling at a profit...the recent domain (homeland) of the Creeks, Chickasaws, Cherokees. Zach matured on his father's plantation(s) in eastern Alabama. Jacob would live his senior life on the plantation that fronted along Hospaliga Creek in Russell County (Lamb Creek today). By 1861 Zach was living in Russell County.*

On Mar. 18, 1862, Zach, at about age thirteen and two months enlisted at Griffin, Georgia, becoming a member of Company G, 44th Georgia, "the Huie Guards" which had just started organizing.[1] He traveled all the way back to this point, a few miles south of his birthplace, it is believed, to be closer to his half-brother John M. Lamb (b. 1828), who was (conscripted?) a private in Company C, 53rd Georgia—"The Fayette Planters." Zach was enlisted by R. L. Henley for "3 years or the war." Very often the nearness of a relative rendered possible the presence of a youngster volunteer.[2] They would both serve under Jubal Early part of their time and in the A.N.V. But the duty was hard and army life grim with grime and grief.[3] On Sept. 3, 1864, 3rd Sergeant John Lamb was killed at the Berryville, Virginia, engagement. Twenty days later at Mount Jackson Zach was captured and forwarded to Point Lookout, Maryland, where he became acquainted with a prison routine. None too soon he was exchanged at Camp Lee, Virginia, Jan. 25, 1865. Whether he ever did further duty with this 44th Georgia is uncertain. Of ex-Pvt. Zachariah T. Lamb's later life—at 16+ years he had already lived half of his total days—we return to thoughts from his great-grandson, Robert, who served in the Air Corps of World War II:

Zach married Miss Mary T. "Babe" Baker (1849-1907), a native of Salem, Ala, on Nov. 13, 1866. They had 3 boys and 2 girls before he was 30. Their son, Julius E. (1874-1953) was my grandfather, whose son, Henry A. (1897-1943) was my father. Father, who married Elizabeth D. Meisel (1891-1965) and was an engineering officer in the U. S. Merchant Marines, while with [the] James Pinkney Henderson *on the Murmansk, Russia, run, also lost his life. In attempting to avoid a Nazi U-Boat off Nova Scotia, the* Henderson *collided with another merchantman.*

Zach was a stone mason and well known for his trade. He was employed in Cullman, Alabama, when his untimely and rather mysterious death occurred. He was working on St. Bernard's Monastery (now a prep school), when he was taken ill and died of a disease, rumored contagious. He was buried in Cullman as there was some sort of epidemic and bringing back his body to Lee County wasn't allowed. The body was stolen "they believe" by medical students within hours of the burial. Nobody knows what became of it. When I handled the estate of his granddaughter (a daughter of Pearl Lamb {Mrs. James T.} Newton East 1881-1978, Zach's youngest), I found a small cloth bag with 72¢ in it and a note—"This was the money that was in Daddy's pocket when he died." This keepsake had been passed down to the granddaughter by her mother Pearl. I obtained a C.S.A. marker for Zach, which stands beside his wife's stone in rural Lee County, Ala. I believe I have about 20 ancestors who served the Confederacy, counting uncles and cousins, but Great-granddaddy Zach was the youngest of them.

Nathaniel Mcl. Gwynne

July 5, 1849 – Jan. 6, 1883

Utterly unique in "Congressional-Medal-of-Honordom" is the story on this Urbana, Ohio, native. Because he died so young, because he often relocated, because he left minimal progeny, and because fate essentially decreed he should lie forgotten an even century by the world, Gwynne's rediscovery and renewal are remarkable. For this achievement we are primarily indebted to two individuals—"Sonny" Wells of Liberty, Missouri, a Civil War aficionado and authority on Gwynne; and John Reichley for his write-up "Youthful Civil War Hero Identified as Civilian," in *THE ANNALS* [official publication of the Medal of Honor Historical Society Dec. 1985 Vol. 8, No. 2].

As early as late January 1864, Nathaniel, then 14, was trying repeatedly to enlist in a Buckeye regiment. After several refusals because "You're too young," he did at length persuade a 13th Ohio Cavalry captain to permit him to "accompany" that command as a "camp private" who would water the horses, fetch firewood, and run errands. Elated and "igknighted" by this qualified acceptance, young Gwynne no longer felt he was a civilian, his actual status, nonetheless. This permission would have occurred in early May 1864 when the 13th O.V.C. was organizing; accordingly, on May 11 "camp private" Gwynne left Ohio by rail with "his" regiment and arrived shortly at Annapolis, Maryland. A week later they marched into White House Landing, Virginia, where they were until June 5. During June 8-August 10 they were in the 1st Brigade, 3rd Division, 9th Corps, Army of the Potomac, after which they were re-assigned to 3rd Brigade, 2nd Division, Cavalry Corps.[1] In early June the 13th was in operations at Cold Harbor, then they were before Petersburg all during the nearly ten-months siege. The fighting was heavy and frequent. It was in late July (but before the infamous Mine Explosion), as the two armies were counterattacking each other, that Gwynne, whose unit was called forward to the battlefront, jumped on a horse and joined his comrades. Within the hour Nathaniel saw the colors—the 13th O.V.C.'s unit flags and U. S. Stars & Stripes—captured by the Confederates then withdrawing. As if by instinct, the lad, then 15 years 3 weeks of age, charged forward astride his mount in the wistful hope of retrieving the 13th's Old Glory. "You might say this 15-year-old had hair on his chest," Sonny Wells reminds us, "for seemingly everybody in a Gray line of about 1200 Rebs were shooting at him, plus four cannons." [The few known accounts of this incident concur in a distressing absence of mention of any covering fire from his comrades, though it is reasonable to assume they gave him some.] A cannonball crushed Gwynne's left arm, the arm that held the just-rescued colors. The arm was later amputated. One account states, "He dismounted, held his horse's reins in his teeth, re-retrieved the sacred flag, and climbed back into the saddle. He suffered two leg wounds on his ride back to safety."[2] Wrote Reichley, "Belatedly, the Captain placed Nathaniel McL. Gwynne on the cavalry's muster roll, backdating the documents to the day he first tried to enlist. Thus, we have a case of a civilian earning the Medal of Honor and then being fraudulently enlisted." On Jan. 27, 1865, Gwynne, then 15, became one of the youngest recipients of the nation's highest decoration. [Willie Johnston, of the Third Vermont, and John E. Anglin, of U.S.S. *Pontoosuc,* are known to have been younger. See Appendix E].

Private Gwynne was finally mustered out with the 13th O.V.C. in Powhattan County, Virginia, on Aug. 10, 1865. The 13th's casualties were 65 killed, 52 died of diseases.[3] His own death 17 years later from nerve damage suffered at Petersburg was not, of course, figured as a casualty officially. Relatively little of Gwynne's post bellum years has come down to us today. The sparse record affords some facts: attracted to the midwest, he soon settled in or near Kansas City; he married one Niva Carter in Putnam County, Missouri, in 1873; they had a son, Nathaniel David, born the following year in Memphis, Missouri; he and Niva were divorced in 1882. As a struggling family they lived about six years in Fairmount, close to Independence. From 1881 on he had a real estate license. Known to have been living with his son in Bonner Springs, Kansas, late in life, he died there at age thirty-three and left little Nathaniel orphaned at age eight. The hero's last descendant, a granddaughter, is said to have died in the early 1940s.

Only in the 1980s did Kansas City historians begin to learn about Gwynne, a true hero-type buried in their midst. It was Sonny Wells who found his grave in Union Cemetery, Kansas City, Missouri, and who brought due recognition to this neglected patriot-soul. After considerable planning and arranging, on Veterans Day 1985, some 102 years after his burial, a special Medal of Honor headstone was placed on his grave during Memorial ceremonies. This event was the climax of a parade in Kansas City led that morning by the color guard and U.S. Army band from the First Infantry Division at Fort Riley, Kansas.[4] Given his century-long low profile, it is most fitting that Gwynne should grace this reunion of the callow, the brave, and the true.

William "Willie" Johnston

July 1850 – 1887?

What ever became of Willie Johnston? For some 125+ years since 1866 a mystery surrounding this drummer boy has stubbornly endured. His unaccountable disappearance defies scholarship, frustrates Civil War studies, and distressingly so this past quarter century. Of all our youngster musicians in The American War, South or North, Willie is arguably *the* most intriguing, significant and strategic to *this writing field. It is plainly disturbing that such a hero could simply drop out of life unnoticed.* "Unsolved Mysteries" of TV popularity is bantam weight or relatively tame compared to this case. Why? Musician Willie Johnston, age 12, of Company D, Third Vermont Infantry, for "gallantry in Seven Days' Battle and Peninsula Campaign" (June 25-July 1, 1862), was awarded the Congressional Medal of Honor by Secretary of War Edwin M. Stanton on Sept.16, 1863, at age 13 years 2 months (approx.)...one of the truly *early* recipients of the nation's highest decoration and *the youngest ever* awardee.[1] Of Vermont's 21 Medal of Honor awardees, Willie Johnston was the earliest by over thirteen months.[2]

Even from his earliest, controversy attended this lad's life. Both Morristown and Warrentown, New York, claim to be his birthplace. The identity of his mother, who reportedly died from her son's birth complications, theoretically, may be recorded *somewhere,* since the name Eliza does get a rare mention. Then there is the unfortunate matter of his last name—spelled Johnson (minus the t) in several, certainly a minority of, documents. That the name is Johnston is clearly recorded, a telling instance being statements witnessed by Caloris Morrill, Recruiting Officer and Notary, Feb. 6, 1864, at St. Johnsbury, and signed by father and son, whose signatures include the t. Also, son Willie says here that his age is 13 years 7 months, thus fixing his birth in July 1850.

Willie's father was William H. B. Johnston, a native of Nottingham, England, and an engineer. Precisely when he came to America is indeterminate. We may be reasonably certain he arrived in the New World with his first wife, for he stated on Apr. 29, 1898 (Certif. #418 795, Reply Form 3-402-Nat'l Archives), "I was married in England 61 years ago. My wife died in Morristown, N. Y. We (referring to his 2nd wife, Theresa) have six children—the youngest is thirty." Presumably, by the mid-to-late 1840s William and his first wife (Eliza?) were settled in upstate New York, where Willie was born and lost his mother. Shortly after, William with his infant son removed to Montreal. The second marriage, at an Episcopal church in Montreal, united W. H. B. J. with one Theresa Martin in 1853.

By the late 1850s the Johnstons were living well north of St. Johnsbury, tradition specifying Derby or Salem as the locale of their farm. Probably four of Willie's eventual six step-siblings were born there by 1861, among them Reuben Frank Johnston and Nellie Johnston.

Records concur that Father Johnston (Wm. H. B. J.), age 40, first enlisted June 1, 1861, at St. Johnsbury, in Company B, Third Vermont Infantry, and was there mustered in on July 16, as a private, where the regiment organized. He would be promoted to corporal and served for quite some time as "Captain of Engineers."[3] He would reenlist *as a veteran* at Brandy Station, Virginia, on Feb. 15, 1864, and finally muster out July 29, 1865.

Initially, like many another unmonied recruit, his incentives for joining were increased by bestowal of bounties; in his case, $500 from the United States and $187.50 from St. Johnsbury—greatly supportive to his growing family. *Just be-*

Hartford, New York Historical Group

Willie Johnston, 13, with his Congressional Medal of Honor.

fore the Third Vermont departed for Washington (7/24-7/26/61) or about July 21, son Willie appeared, responding to an announced regimental shortfall—a need for one more drummer. He proved, to the satisfaction of those judging, he had percussional skill(s). Since his father "*would be there for him,*" he was allowed in and set down as age twelve (in the minds of those above him—everyone). Archivable documentation for his first 4 1/3 months of (f)actual duty remains mostly in the spiritual realm, for Willie was considered a civilian until his Dec. 1, 1861 enlistment at Camp Griffin in the D. C. defense perimeter. Even then, a "mythconception" that he could not draw pay deferred his mustering-in until May 1, 1862 or *after* his battle service at Lee's Mills! The writer, however, credits Willie's unofficial, yet de facto, service by noticing his age in late July 1861—11 years *and a few days.* One suspects that, as with a few other "pre-teeners" in this study, his donning of the uniform was also a birthday concession. Since Willie was nominally a civilian during his earliest service or greatest trial period, military records on him for 1861 essentially do not exist or are cryptic enough to defy being (re)produced. Consequently, what authority would seriously acknowledge his first 131 days? Probably none. Yet, *this* study does. Plainly, as week after week went by and Johnston performed up to expectations and beyond, his non-military status proved increasingly outrageous, untenable. Men of the 3rd Vermont in growing ranks beyond Company D began to campaign for the boy's enlistment, pressuring the elder Johnston. Behind this impetus was the popular conviction that their youngster comrade deserved pay. On day 132 recognition won out. We observe too that as of June 1, 1861, fellow musician Julian Scott, 15 1/4, fifer, technically under age, was performing in Company E.[4]

In March 1862 the 3rd Vermont was rotated to the Virginia front and fought their first action at Young's Mill on April 4. They were in the Peninsula Campaign integrated with the Vermont Brigade (2nd, 3rd, 4th, 5th & 6th):

-Lee's Mills, 4/16/62
-Battle of Williamsburg, 5/5
-Garnett's & Golding's Farms, 6/27-6/28
-Savage's Station Battle, 6/29
-White Oak Swamp Bridge, 6/30
-Battle of Malvern Hill, 7/1 [5]

Throughout this gruesome battle week and earlier—the boy at times marching near his father, reportedly in the color guard as at Lee's Mills (4/16)—Willie was surely often at risk. "He was a brave little fellow who held to his drum and brought it safely off in the frantic retreat to Harrison's Landing."[6] Varying accounts concur that during the finale of this tragidrama, when grown men were throwing away their weapons, knapsacks, and blankets, the faster to scurry from danger, musician Johnston chose not to panic nor to sacrifice his equipment (more awkward than average) amid the mood of the moment. [Let us not be deceived. The Vermont Brigade with New Hampshire, Massachusetts, New York, Pennsylvania, Michigan, Indiana and New Jersey regiments especially, fought bravely in these gory contests, yielding terrain stubbornly, usually. Adjudged a Confederate win, the Seven Days were essentially a stand-off, with McClellan's forces firmly entrenched, but Richmond remote as ever.] After these Vermonters and other blue-clads reached Harrison's Landing, Virginia, and order was restored the ensuing day, a discovery surfaced. When Brig. Gen. William Farrar "Baldy" Smith requested drummers for use at his Division Parade, the only drum available was the one Willie had clung to. Impressed, Gen. Smith gave the small boy (barely 4' 7" or so) the honor of drumming for this formal "parade" (inspection/accounting).[7] He, as others, shortly offered testimonials to the lad's bravery, much desirous his exemplary behavior should merit a tangible commendation. Their witness statements went all the way up to the White House. Lincoln himself was reported to be so impressed as to recommend to War Secretary Stanton that this boy should be eligible for the newly instituted military decoration. Under just what circumstances (ceremony?) or precisely where conferral of this award took place is no longer known. But Stanton himself presented it on Sept. 16, 1863. We do presume that within hours the ought-to-be-famous, only-such portrait was taken of Musician Johnston, 13, *wearing his Medal* while uniformed with his drum. (Notice Willie's still rather diminutive size to his drum and to the chair!) Our final note pertaining to this key episode of his life is an observation: During his valorous week this boy was *probably not quite twelve;* on bestowal of his medal, not more than 13 years 2 months! John E. Anglin, of Portland, Maine, the second youngest recipient, earned a Navy Medal of Honor at age 14 years 2 months 18 days.

Musician Johnston's Company D Muster Roll reports reflect extensive sickness for the rest of 1862. He was admitted at U.S. General Hospital in Hampton, Virginia, for July-August; at General Hospital, Fort Monroe, for September-December. His health complaint is not revealed in these records, but, one would assume he convalesced and regained his strength. On January 22, 1863, he was rotated to the General Hospital at Baltimore and assigned largely indoor work as a nurse, while living at Lafayette Barracks near Jarvis Hospital. On detached service from his regiment, he was thus occupied until October 7 when he was transferred to 60 Company, 1st Battalion, Invalid Corps. His extensive nursing chores were, after all, an alternative standard use of young soldiery in need of relief from daily exposures and harsh conditions. The Invalid Corps unit was re-designated as Company D, 20th Regiment, Veteran Reserve Corps, and for much of 1864 Willie drummed daily with the 20th's Brass Band. Eventually, recognition came his way when he was elevated to being head of the drum line. However, just prior to this assignment, he was discharged (2/14/64) at Brandy Station and the next day reenlisted as a veteran volunteer, with his father, by a Lt. Bowker. Because Willie was "to have a furlough of at least 30 days in his state *before expira-*

tion of his original term," he was furloughed home immediately, it is believed, with his father, to visit their family. By late March he resumed duty.[8] Special Orders #175 of May 12, 1865 at length transferred him from his 20th Regiment V.R.C. unit back to Company H, Third Vermont. "On paper" the reason may have been so that Willie could be with his original comrades (those living, that is—371 of the 3rd Vt. had died) to share their march to Washington (5/24 - 6/2), their Corps Review (6/8), but not their mustering out (7/11/65).[9] Studying Willie's final muster "Returns," it looks like he performed again at Baltimore in a military band until August 12. He was mustered out on August 31 at Brattleboro, Vermont, having received the same size bounties as his father. At that time he was 15 years 1 month "or so" and had nearly fifty months of Union Army service. Given his youth, this lengthy set of enlistments almost certainly was some kind of record.

In his April 21, 1987 letter Roger D. Hunt of Rockville, Maryland, a researcher-author of Civil War books, found a thrilling article in a G.A.R. journal called *Grand Army Review,* published in Boston, (Vol. 4, No. 1, June 1888) stating that Johnston's drum with the inscribed Medal of Honor attached was found with a note in an old house in Chelsea, Massachusetts, on May 9, 1888. "The note," offers Mr. Hunt, "bore the words 'Willie Johnston, aged 13 years, Company D, Third Vermont Regiment. Presented with a medal by Secretary Stanton for carrying this drum through the Seven Days Fight before Richmond, being the only drum carried the last of June and 1st of July.' This drum to which the medal was attached was found by a tenant who intended to pawn it. But another tenant secured it, and it now awaits the claim of the owner or his friends at the office of the Sergeant-at-Arms at the State House." One postulates that William "Willie" Johnston lived quietly in Chelsea for a stretch of years, perhaps a loner. Whether he ever married is moot. His leaving no progeny heightens the difficulty. His never requesting or drawing a pension only deepens the mystery.

Only a few isolated facts remain. Willie's father and stepmother with a few of their children went west. W.H.B.J. (WC 590, 171) and Theresa successively resided in Soldiers' Homes—in the late 1870's, Danville, Illinois; in 1881, the National Military Home, Brookville, Kansas; in 1889, at La Junta, Colorado; later at Solders' and Sailors' Home, Monte Vista, Colorado. In 1899 Theresa and William separated and she became a resident of Denver. None of these V. A. Centers (today) have kept their old records. Father Johnston died Mar. 7, 1902, very likely in a Veterans Home. Colorado's Bureau of Vital Statistics deny he died in that state. Teresa died in Denver Oct. 4, 1915, and is buried at Crown Hill Burial Park (Block 26, Lot 142) at 2600 16th St. Several of *her* children, including Reuben and Nellie, are there, but NO Willie. His ultimate fate—indeed, much of his life—endures as a tightly kept secret.

Somewhere, somebody in America must have some information on this missing person of the old 3rd Vermont Infantry. Somewhere, somebody must have Willie's drum and inscribed Medal of Honor.

Berry H. Binford

Oct. 1852 – Sept. 2, 1889

His full name was (Richard) Littleberry H. Binford. His parents were Dr. (Richard) Littleberry H. (Aug. 1, 1826-Nov. 6, 1891) and Sarah Elizabeth "Sallie Bettie" Richardson Binford (Mar. 5, 1831-Feb. 17, 1856), daughter of William and Ann Richardson. Berry's paternal grandparents were James Addison Binford (b. 1786) and Sarah Bell Binford. An early colonial family, the Binford lineage was first recorded in America when Governor Berkley granted acreage in 1665 to Anthony Binford in Lower Norfolk County, Virginia. Anthony's son James bought land in Charles City County (later Prince George), Virginia, paying two pounds of tobacco per acre. James' grandson, James Binford, married Margaret Mosby in 1745. Their son, John Mosby Binford, moved to Alabama before 1820 and after marrying Eliza Frances Hardiman of Charles City County. In fact, John and Eliza first moved to Northampton County, North Carolina, which he represented in the state legislature during 1788-1807. When they resettled in Lauderdale County, Alabama, they brought at least three of their children with them: James Addison, Abner (b. 1794), and Eliza F. Hardiman Binford.[1]

Berry grew up with two older brothers and playmates, William A. and John, on their folks' plantation on Anderson Creek in eastern Lauderdale County just north of the Tennessee River. At least two accounts exist that credit Berry with rendering C.S.A. service at an unusually early age. The first and less accurate appeared as an obituarial tribute Sept. 12, 1889, in *The Alabama Courier.*[2]

> *Memphis: Sept. 3. Berry H. Binford, who was the youngest soldier in the Confederate Army, died yesterday while on a business trip to Monroe, La. His father, Dr. Binford, was a surgeon in the Confederate Army. The boy, when about 9 years old, struck out to find his father and reported to Gen. Wheeler, who took him for a Federal spy sent in by some of the Union people. The General kept an eye on the little chap, and, finally turned him over to Col. Josiah Patterson, who knew Dr. Binford, and at once assumed the boy's care. As he would not go back home, a pony was secured for him, a gun was sawed off the proper length, and he was recognized from that time on to the end of the war as a soldier. It is stated that young Binford and another boy, not much older, undertook to do a little special service once. They went out between the lines, somewhere up in North Alabama,*

threw up some small breastworks, and awaited the advance of the Federals on the opposite side of a small river. The column came in sight and the boys opened fire as if backed by an army which the Federals naturally supposed to be a fort. The two held their "fort" a whole day and when night came on, they scampered off to rejoin their command several miles away.

Binford was the famous suspicious case that caused a panic in this city last summer and subjected several distinguished physicians to a perfect avalanche of chaff when it turned out to be a case of alcoholism instead of yellow fever. Berry Binford's mother was a native of Athens, Ala., where he has relatives.

One W. E. Vasser (an Athens, Ala., citizen) hand wrote an 80 page booklet entitled *The Youngest Southern Soldier,* circa 1907, in five chapters: I. Scene of the Boy Soldier's Services, II. A Runaway from Home Enlists, III. Stories of the Fifth Cavalry's Services, IV. A Brilliant Raid Under Forrest, V. Fall of Selma and Surrender.[3] From Chapter II Vasser's text, more tightly reported here, offers:

In September 1864, while Roddy's Command was encamped near Decatur, no little surprise was felt at headquarters when a lad, 11, presented himself with the declared intention of joining the army. Tall for his age, of a wiry build, hair and eyebrows as the raven's plumage, he displayed soft black, anxious eyes in a face of alabaster whiteness. Name? Berry Binford...He'd run away "to fight the Yankees." His intelligence and determination so wrought upon the officers that they consented for him to remain in camp while they sought his father's wishes. Dr. Binford crossed the river at once, and arriving at Decatur camp, at length gave his consent for Berry to be a soldier, fearing Berry might run away again and join an outfit that would take him far away. Capt. John A. Steele, now (1906) with the U. S. Marshal's Office, at Birmingham, wrote the following reply to the author (Vasser) requesting details of Berry's enlistment:

Mr. W. E. Vasser — *Birmingham, Ala. July 8th 1906*
Athens, Ala.

My dear sir:

Berry Binford is the son of my old friend Doctor Richard Binford, deceased. In September 1864 he came to my Company F, Burtwell's Regiment, 11th Ala. Cavalry, when we were in camp near Decatur. He remained with me, doing a soldier's duty, going out on the skirmish line nearly every day until we left for Tennessee. Then he joined a company in Col. Josiah Patterson's Regiment of Alabama Cavalry. Though very young, Berry did duty as a soldier...I consider Berry as much entitled to recognition as many Confederate soldiers who now wear the Cross of Honor.

Respectfully,
John A. Steele
Capt., Co. F, 11th Ala. Cav.

Berry was provided a pony, a musket to the proper length with trimmed stock to fit his shoulder. A saddle was adapted to his use. At bugle call, in the crisp air of dawn or dusk, the boy trooper would mount his horse with a veteran alacrity and display in frequent skirmishes with Federal marauders as steady an aim as he ever took at a squirrel in the hickory growths of Lauderdale. Col. Patterson, a Scots-Irish-Huguenot, was to comment on B.H.B. in a letter to Mr. Douglas Anderson of Nashville, a friend of the boy soldier:

Mr. Douglas Anderson *Memphis, Tenn. June 26th 1897*
Dear Sir—

... "Binford was certainly the youngest soldier I ever saw, and I take pleasure in saying he performed the duties of a soldier with alacrity. He was a child in arms and bore himself in an astonishingly manly way."[4]

Berry, often at regimental headquarters, sometimes enjoyed privileges, like sleeping in a tent or eating at the officers' table, but, often he had only the food he could gather by the wayside. More often he slept in the "Tavern of the Stars," with leaves under his blanket, and his head on his saddle. Among Binford's comrades (or C.O.'s) was Lt. Col. Jabez Lamar Monroe Curry, later a noted educator, writer of fine books, and powerful platform speaker.

While much of Vasser's account is given over to exploits of Generals Forrest and Roddy during 1863-64, Binford, it is understood, soldiered throughout all, either in the 11th or in the 5th Alabama Cavalry. He surfaces again in Chapter V:[5]

During winter '64-65 when Gen. Hood maneuvered in Middle Tennessee, a disastrous campaign that ended in retreat from Nashville, one day Pvt. Binford was with another young soldier named Pippin of Courtland; as they were foraging in the countryside near Corinth, Berry came upon a farmer making syrup from sorghum cane. While filling the young soldiers' canteens with sorghum, farmer Jesse Cobb felt he recognized Berry and inquired his name. Mr. Cobb had been an overseer for Dr Binford. Learning Berry's identity, he threw his arms about his waist and drew him from his horse in a paroxysm of joy to meet the son of his old friend under such romantic circumstances. He had Berry re-

main with him that day and night...Cold weather had set in, and Berry was thinly clad. He wore a blue federal cape and for greater warmth had wrapped his feet in pieces of blanket. Mrs. Cobb cut out a suit from homespun cotton jeans, dyed with copperas. She and her daughters sewed the garments rapidly. Brass buttons were found for the coat—this was all the uniform Berry had during the war. He was given a pair of stockings (girl's) and though he blushed at such dainty hosiery in his rough boots, they were thick and warm and came up well above the knee. Before the happy young trooper left, the next day, Mr. Cobb also gave him a fine pocket knife of his own and $10 in money.

Private Binford's military career was waged in his own sector, northern Alabama and under General Roddy, J. L. M. Curry and Col. Patterson. In 1865, he was in various phases of the culminating Battle of Selma (4/2/65), an important C.S.A. Depot and largest remaining arsenal. Berry, for nearly all his service, was with the 5th Alabama Cavalry. He was at Ebenezer Church, "one of the hottest fights of the war."[6] After many staunch defense maneuvers the 5th Alabama Cavalry "made its escape, but without horses, food or ammunition...under the leadership of Berry's honorable C. O., Jabez L. M. Curry."[7] It was well into May before an escaped remnant of the 5th Alabama (incl. Col. Patterson) surrendered upon orders from Gen. Roddy. Private Binford, ultimately a prisoner, had then but recently surrendered with scores of his comrades, within sixty miles of home.

Vasser's key account ends on a eulogizing note: "No glory of conquering heroes can utterly obliterate the service of this child soldier. In his trustful boyhood he had followed paragons of practical knighthood—Patterson, Kelly, Curry, Roddy, Forrest, Wheeler."[8]

Nothing of Binford's twenty-three post bellum years is available for reporting, such as whether he ever married or left descendants. His too-brief life closed just as he neared his 37th birthday. He was living in Memphis, Tennessee, at the time. He was not ill for long, dying as he did at Monroe, Louisiana, while on a business trip. His parents are buried at the Athens (Ala.) City Cemetery, Section I, Lot 91 (approx.), and nearby he too came to his final rest. The engraving on his stone reads:[9]

Youngest Confederate Soldier

In 1915, Miss Mary Mason and her local U. D.C. compiled comprehensive listings of northern Alabama CSA veterans (mostly with, but also, of necessity, sometimes without service records) and sent these to the sacred Confederate Battle Abbey in Richmond, Virginia. Among those names they sent without benefit of an orderly service record was that of "Berry H. Binford (Youngest Confederate Soldier)"...which, if we insert *combat* to modify *Soldier,* would surely come mighty close to the truth.[10] Apparently, this present attempt to place Pvt. Binford in the history of the C.S.A. is overdue and most justified.

The Scott Brothers

Lucian Scott (b. 1842)
Julian A. Scott (b. 1846)
Charles W. Scott (b. 1849)

Second only to the legendary Johnny L. Clem (1851-1937, 22nd Mich. Infy.) in attaining fame or national standing of all the Civil War youths marching across the pages and years of this study, Julian Scott, like Clem, was to enjoy near-celebrity status early on from his unique contributions to our Civil War legacy. Scott triumphs as Vermont's noted soldier-artist; he remains justly renowned for his intimate battlefront portrayals of soldier life. He is a reminder of at least one other Vermonter who as a young man went off to "This Strange Sad War" (Whitman) and handily recorded on canvas, paper, pad, or poster details of army life all around him—Pvt. William Henry Jackson (Apr. 4, 1843-June 29, 1942—Co. K, 12th Vt.) of Rutland, whose talents at sketching camp life and personnel were rewarded by his being made regimental staff artist.[1]

The Scott family, ancestrally Scottish Presbyterians, were among Connecticut's early Europeans. By succeeding generations they tended to settle farther inland and northward. A distinct military tradition had come down in the family all the way from the 1637 Pequot War, to Julian's great-grandfather Jonathan's lieutenancy with the Bennington Militia in the Revolution, to his 1812'er grandfather's determined role against the British at Plattsburgh in September 1814, and to an uncle's service in the Mexican War.

Julian's parents, Charles Winfield (b. 1815 in Hartford, Vt.—d. 12/29/1872 at Dover, Ill.) and Lucy Kellum Scott, had married July 14, 1840, and left her hometown of Barton, Orleans County, Vermont, to settle some twenty-five miles off to the southwest at Johnson, Vermont. Here, at the confluence of the Gihon and Lamoille Rivers, their small acreage fronting on the east-west main street (present day Route 15) overlooked the latter, larger waterway, good for powering mills though not for traveling. Here Charles prospered as a watchmaker and jeweler; here they became members of the Congregational church; here Charles and Lucy (until her demise Apr. 26, 1855, from childbirth) added eight Johnson natives, six of whom would reach adulthood—Lucian (1842), who aspired to journalistic tendencies for *The Lamoille Newsdealer*; Cleora (1844), who crafted hats, pioneered a "fonetic

Robert J. Titterton

Julian Scott, age 30, in 1876.

spelling system," liked to go by "Kle," and became Mrs. Ladd-Davis of Brooklyn, New York; Julian, who, with his natural gift for drawing, learned as a pre-teener to make pencil portraits and paint signs; Julia, who took in sewing and became Mrs. Z.L. Carpenter of Kansas City, Missouri; Charles Walter (1849), who would become a physician; and (Henry) Percy Scott, who fulfilled himself as a practicing attorney in Kansas City. The collective achievements of the Scott children were not won by accident.

Rural Vermont communities, as indeed most New England towns of 150 years ago—1840s & '50s—evinced an ethnic solidarity, a close-knit public spirit, acquaintanceship with and respect toward neighbors, and a vital Christian heritage. Johnson was outstanding for another key trait in its unpretentious abecedarian character—the worth of a formal education.

Few counties then had anything approaching higher learning. But Johnson had Lamoille Academy with its widening reputation for excellence. Reputedly, its most famous alumnus would be Admiral George Dewey (1837-1917), *the last* active duty (unretired) Civil War officer commissioned or noncommissioned.[2] Anyway, the Scotts funded at least five of their six children through Lamoille Academy to the annual tune of $250.00 per student—truly a commitment.[3] Though Julian took a drawing course at Lamoille, the privilege of visiting art museums remained remote from his isolated world until after he left home to enlist. Late in the 1850s Father Scott remarried, providing their household with a kindly stepmother, Susan Pollard or "Mother Pollard," as they deferentially and eventually even fondly, came to address her. His health broke in 1857 under an ambitious work load to support the eight of them. But each child pursued gainful skills that eked out the straitened income. Lucian assisted at watch repair. The interdictive onset of civil war effectually abbreviated the Scott brothers' boyhoods.

While Julian is our central, most visible personality (for purposes of this epic biographical review) with his qualifying credentials as a youthful standout quite in order, this account is essentially about the three oldest Scott lads, each willingly drawn into our tragic Boys War of the Sixties. Integrity, perspective, and romantic curiosity require detailed comment on both Lucian's and Charlie's own military "tours." Julian's story and theirs intermesh, and interdepend. All three would sustain severe woundings that directly or indirectly foreshortened their otherwise natural longevities. All three enlisted as soon as they could.

Lucian (Oct. 21, 1842-Aug. 19, 1894), already 18, upon learning of Lincoln's opening call, could not abide the predictable plodding pace (compared to what he had in mind) of state volunteer organizings. Despite frustratingly untoward travel conditions (alias mud season), he reached Albany, New York, within an incredible three days. Here, he enlisted April 18 for three years service with Battery F, Fourth U. S. Artillery. That very day of Lucian's arrival in Albany his unit arrived in Washington, D. C., where within hours he caught up with them. In early June they moved to Carlisle, Pennsylvania. Lucian's lengthy letters home and to Hyde Park, Vermont's *Lamoille Newsdealer* inflamed his brothers' zeal and that of 147 other young men whose names, since 1921, are memorialized in bronze across the street today from where Lamoille Academy stood. Julian, 15 1/4, meanwhile just concluding his academics at Lamoille, got himself enlisted as age 16 and a painter (then more fantasy than fact). In stature 5' 4", of hazel eyes, a dark brunette, he joined on June 1, 1861, as a fifer, the *official* qualifying age for fife-boys being sixteen.[4] On July 16 he mustered in with Company E, Third Vermont Infantry, then organizing at St. Johnsbury, and entrained to Washington during July 24-26. They drew duty at Georgetown Heights and at Camp Griffin on the capital defense perimeter until their march to Alexandria (3/10/62); during these tenderfoot months Julian's 3rd Vermonters became part of Brig. Gen. W. F. "Baldy" Smith's Vermont Brigade (the 2nd, 3rd, 4th, 5th, & 6th Vts.) and early on guarded the Chain Bridge near Camp Lyon and fought (9/11/61) a skirmish at Lewinsville, Virginia; here Julian began pen-and-ink sketches, authenticating better than words the life, death, and landscape of warfare around him.

But, to return to Lucian's "foughtunes," mainly to confirm him as the Scott brother who partook of the largest dosage of unpalatable tragidrama...before resuming Julian's own Civil War. Lucian's Battery F was initially in action at Falling Waters (7/2/61). As a battle unit, they served successively in the Armies of the Shenandoah, of the Potomac, of the Shenandoah, of Virginia, of the Potomac, of the Cumberland.[5] However, Lucian's worst injury came early—at Ball's Bluff (10/21/61)—when a double-charged cannon kicked farther back than allowed for, knocking Lucian a wallop on his head. Ordinary men would have justified and wangled a swift return home for good. The injury subjected him to epileptic seizures no less. Even so, he soldiered on in the Shenandoah, at Middletown, Newton, Winchester, Cedar Mountain, Second Bull Run, Antietam, "the Mud March," Chancellorsville, Gettysburg, and finished his obligatory (as he saw it) triennium doing guard duty at Bridgeport, Alabama, and other points along the Chattanooga Railroad until his discharge at Nashville in April 1864.[6] Lucian went home to Johnson and recuperated for nearly five months. But on Sept. 9, 1864, credited to nearby Eden, he reenlisted for a year to serve in Company M, First Vermont Cavalry.[7] He joined them in time for the Battle of Opequan (9/20) and much of Sheridan's Shenandoah Valley Campaign—Cedar Creek (10/19 & 11/12). He was taken prisoner at Rude's Hill, near Mt. Jackson (11/22/64). During the next ten weeks he was confined at Libby Prison, where he came close to actual starvation by February 15. That day Lucian was paroled in an exchange of prisoners. This harrowing Gehenna contributed to his ever after semi-invalidism and myriad recurrences of "the 1000-yard stare." Hospitalized that spring of '65, Lucian was mustered out

June 21, in health a mere shadow of the 18-year-old of some four years earlier. His war injuries may well have burdened his marriage to one Sarah B. (?). Their daughter Alice M. Scott (b. 12/12/67) was almost ten upon her parent's divorce in 1877. Lucian devoted himself to Johnson, where he was known, beloved, and respected. He was a member of the local Good Templars Lodge, being a non-drinker and espousing sobriety. During the 1870s and early '80s he was proprietor of a Yankee Notions Store where he sold, rented, or repaired firearms, violins, eyeglasses, watches, jewelry, silverware, etc. Very much a homebody and invalid in the care of family and friends his final decade, Lucian died at home, not quite age 52. He was laid to rest beside his mother at Whiting Hill Cemetery in downtown Johnson.

Musician Julian steamed with his 3rd Vermont across Chesapeake Bay (3/23-24/62) where, near Fort Monroe, they disembarked to become a pawn in Gen. McClellan's Peninsula Campaign. They fought a modest action on April 4 at Young's Mill. As part of the Vermont Brigade, under orders from "Baldy " Smith, they were encamped along Warwick Creek quite to the south of the month-long siege of Yorktown. Company E and three others of the 3rd Vermont—200 men—were chosen to attack a Southern stronghold across Warwick Creek. Led by Captain Samuel Pingree (Vermont governor 1884-86), Julian's comrades captured a strategic rifle pit and held it tenaciously for one of their longest hours against several C.S.A. regiments; their signals for support that shamefully never came were witnessed by many who would have gone to support them. But McClellan lacked the will to escalate this engagement at Lee's Mills (4/16/62) into a major confrontation. These valiant Vermonters, of necessity, retreated back across the Warwick (Appropriate name or what!) as dozens acquired their first or second bullet wounds. Musicians weaponless were expected to aid wounded and get them to safety or a field hospital, however makeshift. Accordingly, Julian saw the mini-disaster developing, sprinted into the water, waded all the way over twice and part way numerous times under "terrific fire" of blazing musketry, repeatedly risking his own probable fatality. He rescued no fewer than nine comrades. As Robert J. Titterton, of Elmore, Vermont, states in his 1993 master's thesis, *Julian Scott: Special Agent to the Eleventh Census* and in his 1996 biography, *Julian Scott: Artist of the Civil War and Native America:* "For this action Scott drew the first citation of an individual act of battlefield bravery in the Civil War leading to a Congressional Medal of Honor."[8] Perhaps the sheer novelty of this award accounts, in part, for an ostensible delinquency in its bestowal upon Pvt. Scott—a 34-month hangfire—in February 1865.[9] Ironically, the youngest ever to earn and receive this highest U. S. decoration was the 3rd Vermont Infantry's own William "Willie" Johnston of Company D, who a few weeks later at the Seven Days' Fight (6/25-7/1/62) qualified for *his* award (in Abraham Lincoln's personal estimate and recommendation to Secretary of War Stanton), which bestowal actually took place fairly promptly on Sept. 16, 1863; it was the earliest of an eventual twenty-one such Civil War decorations awarded Vermonters. Julian on his day of valor was just 16 years 2 months.

Later, in the same "Battle of the Seven Days Retreat" (Day 6 or 6/30) during a rearguard engagement at White Oak Swamp (Bridge), while the Vermont Brigade was "in the thick of it," Pvt. Scott sustained a mean minie ball wound in the hip. In time it would contribute to rheumatism. Official records state that he was initially detached from his 3rd Vermont on July 4 to perform nursing duties in the camp hospital.[10] But he went there as a patient, for, clearly, the hip wound rendered him nonambulatory for a few weeks. Standard policy then dictated that all musicians would have been assigned as nurses; accordingly, the clerk simply did not realize that Julian Scott was one of the patients. By August 13 he was officially detached as a patient at General Hospital on David's Island in New York's Long Island Sound. As he slowly recovered from his own injury, Julian performed menial tasks Walt Whitman-like in service to dozens about him. For his amusement and the morale of others as well, he allowed himself to succumb to a favorite temptation and pastime: sketching hospital scenes. His talent attracted notice of a visiting philanthropist, Henry E. Clark, who gave him art supplies and a key friendship. In fact, Clark, an 1821 native of Hartford, Vermont, was himself a turning point in the mid-teenager's life. (Categorically, we are assured by Robert Titterton that, although Hartford was Julian's father's birthplace also, this isolated fortuity had NO bearing upon Clark's generosity.) Private Julian Scott obtained his discharge for disability Apr. 28, 1863, at David's Island.[11]

Robert J. Titterton affirms in "A Soldier's Sketchbook" (*Civil War Times Illus.* Sept./Oct. '91):

> *Clark immediately secured him an enrollment at the National Academy of Design in New York City and promised to pay all of his expenses. His destiny, now clear, Scott dedicated himself to his vocation. He also got private tutoring from prominent artists, including Emanuel Leutze, known for "Washington Crossing the Delaware." Leutze, trained in the Dusseldorf school of painting, held that artists should become intimate with subjects they depict. This ideal required trips to actual scenes and great attention to detail.*

After a year of formal study Julian was enabled to do exactly this. Clark deliberately arranged his protégé's week-long visit with Washington officials. Letters of introduction paved our artist's itinerary into war-torn Virginia, for Clark orchestrated Scott's sinecure (a godsend) as honorary aide-de-camp to his former division commander, "Baldy" Smith, now a major general in charge of XIII Corps, Army of the James. It was mid-May 1864, in time for the Drewry's Bluff battles and for the Bermuda Hundred Campaign right afterward. Julian sketched three solid weeks to great authentic advantage, both for these drawings themselves and for their becoming the basis of his many future paintings. His forte was the common soldier's perspective. Adeptness at facial features and capturing known individuals' identities in details in battlefield scenes were already within his talents. He included his own identifiable face in several paintings. Among his famous Civil War paintings and portrayals are:

"The Drummer Boy"
"Civil War Drummer Boys Playing Cards"
"A Game of Freeze-out"
"Civil War Battle Scene: A Moment of Decision"
"Colonel Robert Potter at the Battle of Burnside Bridge, Antietam"
"Portrait of General Hancock at Williamsburg" [Smithsonian]
"Major General George B. McClellan"
"The Battle of Golding's Farm"
"The Rear Guard at White Oak Swamp"
"The Vermont Brigade at the Battle of Cedar Creek" [Montpelier]

Julian Scott closed out his Civil War endeavors—again, via Clark's "pull"—by visiting embattled Richmond's ruins and war-torn environs shortly after Lee's Surrender. There he harvested his final hands-on crop of original drawings inspired by the war's ugly destruction...his accommodations being at the Governor's Mansion.

The youngest Scott enlistee—Charles Walter (Oct. 31, 1849-May 13, 1901)—offers irresistible credentials for our central theme. Although the least robust, "Charlie," despite his obvious value at home, lived for the day he could join up. That day was July 6, 1863, at Morrisville, where he reported his age as sixteen and his occupation, jeweler. He was exactly 13 years 8 months 6 days. Five days later he mustered in as bugler for service in Company L (Org. 7/11/63), First Vermont Artillery (Orig. Org. at Brattleboro as 11th Vt. Infy. 9/1/62).[12] Since Company L drew mundane duty at Fort Lincoln on the D.C. defense perimeter, Pvt. Charlie Scott spent a quieter, more sheltered tour than he had ever preconceived. After six months of the rather rigorous military routine taxing his physical capacity, he was given an early discharge Dec. 30, 1863. The physician noted: "Said Charles W. Scott is, in my opinion, wholly unfit from tender age to perform military duty...he has not yet arrived at the age of puberty being only thirteen and feeble of constitution." Charlie went straight home and recuperated on two months rest and home cooking. Abruptly on Feb. 29, 1864, at Sharon, Massachusetts, he re-enlisted as bugler for Company I, 28th Mass. Infy.[13] Now, all of 14 years 4 months, he got himself set down as "18" and joined many new comrades at Stevensburg, Virginia. This time Pvt. Scott saw plenty of up front fighting at the Wilderness (5/5-7/64), at Spotsylvania (5/12-21), Assault on the Salient (5/12), North Anna (5/23-26), Cold Harbor (6/1-12). He built up a soldierly reputation and attained popularity beyond his own regiment. A confirming account of the fourteen-year-old "written from camp Mar. 30, '64, to *The Lamoille Newsdealer* by a member of the 19th Mass. Vols." offers:

> *There is only one man here with whom I was acquainted in Vermont and he, Charles W. Scott, of Johnson, is a fine fellow. Anything in his power he will do for a brother soldier; and in any enterprise, however dangerous it may be, he is not afraid to engage. Only this morning a Lieutenant of my regiment who had been out on picket came into camp with the following report of him: He said that on the previous evening, as a few of the men were gathered near the Rapidan, they saw approaching them from the opposite shore a boat in which were two men who appeared to be Union prisoners trying to escape. When they had reached about the middle of the river, a squad of rebels appeared on the other side in pursuit, firing upon them as soon as they got within reach. One of the men was wounded so that he could not swim, and the other jumping overboard swam toward the Union shore. The wounded man followed his example, but we saw that he must perish, unless someone volunteered to save him; who would it be?—it was a moment of fearful suspense. Charles W. Scott came forward, stripped off his coat, swam to where the drowning man was, drew him to the shore and saved him. A few shots were fired at him but to no effect. Fifteen minutes afterwards you might have seen him drying his clothes by a neighboring campfire, as if nothing had happened.*[14]

On June 3, 1864, at Cold Harbor an exploding shell blew Bugler Scott off his mount, causing him to strike the back of his head on the ground, stunning him and effectually ending his usefulness to the 28th Massachusetts. (For the rest of his life he had a "divot" or wound there deep enough to insert two fingertips.) He required hospitalization and was initially sent to an army hospital on Blackwell's Island, a human dumping ground in New York Harbor, notorious for its lunatic asylum, penitentiary, and almshouse. Here, Charlie was wasting away, if anything, getting rather little restorative care. In these few crucial weeks before space for him became available at General Hospital on David's Island, his brother Julian, already living by spells in his prospective "hometown" (N.Y.C.), quite certainly visited Charlie as often as possible. This would be most likely, for in early January Charlie and Julian learned sad news from home—their youngest sibling, George, 8, had died that Dec. 28, 1864. Soon brother Charles was transferred to General Hospital, where on Mar. 15, 1865, he was discharged for disability. Julian got him aboard a train to Essex Junction, Vermont, whence Charlie could reach Johnson. Home again, at 15, he returned to the superior care of his sister Julia, 17, and Mother Pollard. By their ministrations he regained strength during five months of R & R (rapture & rejuvenation), being newly reunited with Brother Lucian, who was also unfit for further military duty. That the Scott menfolks were keeping their womenfolks busy nursing would be an understatement. At mid-summer, though the War had ended, Charlie believed he was psychologically and physically ready to return to duty, perhaps disappointed that he had not done enough. What mixed emotions must his family have struggled with! We are amazed, again, to learn that on Aug. 14, 1865, Charlie, 15 years 9 months, enlisted a third time. He joined Company F, Eleventh U. S. Infantry (2nd Battalion).[15] Private Scott, still in the role of bugler-musician, joined his unit then at Richmond, Virginia. Here, the regiment were committed to various occupation duties until October. Indeed, this major post bellum errand at several Southern points was their chief function all during Scott's third tour of 11 months which, for him, ended July 29, 1866, when he became a Civil War veteran three times over at age 16 years 9 months—likely some kind of record in itself.

After leaving the army Charles resolved upon a medical career, challenged, it seems, by vicissitudes of his own battle-scarred condition. He apparently attended a medical school in or near Hartford. He married Miss Susie M. Kidder, who died Dec. 27, 1878, leaving him their son, Charles Walter Scott, Jr. For years Dr. Scott was corresponding secretary for the Society of the Army of the Potomac. Much of his medical practice—some twelve years—he spent in Kansas City, Missouri, where he could be near his brother Percy and sister, Julia (Mrs. Z. L.) Carpenter, who may have had a hand in helping to raise the young Charles Jr. Another remarkable fact emerges from Dr. Scott's brief life; his second wife, Anna M. Scott (Nov. 2, 1861-Dec. 18, 1954) survived him by over 53 years—one of the longer Civil War widowhoods. Her widow's pension was $40 a month in 1945. By the early 1940s Anna was living at the Old People's Home (Department) of the Hartford (Conn.) General Hospital, where she died.[16] After Dr. Scott relinquished his practice in the Midwest, he moved to Boston, where, no doubt, he could often reune with his Bay State army buddies. By early 1900, knowing his health to be failing and yielding to nostalgia, he and Anna returned to his native town. In poor health the winter of 1900-01, Dr. Scott died in Johnson, where the Rev. S. E. Packard officiated at his packed funeral held at the Baptist Church.[17]

In late April 1865 incessant rains shut out Julian's intended drawings of Richmond's fortifications in favor of indoor scenes as in Libby Prison, where he had an emotive investment (Lucian), where, too, he picked up relics for studio props. Back in New York City he trained further under Leutze (1816-1868). At twenty, Julian, eager to travel, accompanied Henry Clark to Paris to examine Western art and study under European masters. Julian's first show of paintings before public view at the National Academy's Spring 1870 Exhibition—"General O. B. Wilcox in Libby Prison" and "Rear Guard at White Oak Swamp"—resulted in his being elected an associate member of the National Academy. That year he married a pretty urban girl, Miss Mary E. P. Burns, 21, daughter of the owner-editor of the popular *New York Sunday Dispatch.* He and "Mamie" took a 14th Street apartment. Their only child, Elizabeth or "Bess" was born in 1871. In 1870 his home state commissioned him to do a memorial battle scene of Vermont soldiery.

Then, at a reunion in Rutland ex-Union officers petitioned Governor John W. Stewart that Scott's depiction be a scene from the Battle of Cedar Creek (Union-588 killed, 3516 wounded, 1891 missing; Confederate—3000 k & w, 1200 m.), where the greatest number of Vermont regiments were engaged. Governor Stewart traveled with Scott to the battlefield with a special consultant, Col. Aldace Walker. Scott interviewed many veterans of the battle and executed over 200 preliminary drawings of *them.* He planned a 10' x 20' painting, so large his N.Y.C. studio was inadequate; no American canvas supplier stocked that dimension; hence, a special European linen canvas was required. Up the Hudson at West Point in ampler quarters he embarked on his greatest single endeavor. General Sheridan and G. B. McClellan (Gov.-to-be of N.J.) visited the studio with Secretary of War W. W. Belknap. Sheridan had himself led the critical final charge that snatched victory from imminent defeat. Having expended three years and $8500 on it (Vermont's contract had been for $5000), Scott brought his painting to the August 1874 GAR encampment at Burlington, where it went on display at City Hall. That November Vermont eked out $4000 more, netting Scott a relative pittance, $500.[18]

In his graduate thesis, Robert Titterton affirms that Scott avidly collected military accoutrements, that these redounded to greater accuracy in his portrayals, that he gathered artifacts as links to past cultures, a passion that finally found expression via his 1890 Census work as a special agent among Indians of our Southwest. Not well groomed for matrimony, Scott "frittered away" choice family time, with studio idlers, socializing among creative notables, and belonging to societies and fraternal orders. He sacrificed assured blessings of a home life for the fanfare of public life, all along slipping toward strong drinks. Partly for Bess's sake as well as his own, Mamie won him over to moving out of New York itself in June 1875 to an affluent Plainfield, New Jersey, suburb. But he did not sever the big city or its distractions. His bohemian habits estranged him from family. He did not go to Europe with Mamie, Bess, and his mother-in-law. As Mr. Titterton assesses:

> *The loss of family did not shock Scott into altering his lifestyle...yet he realized they were more important than his vices.... Late in 1878 Mamie, Bessie and Mrs. Burns returned from abroad and settled into a house Scott rented in Plainfield.... He tried to reject his "bachelor*

haunts." Drink became uncontrollable. By spring 1881 his family left Plainfield forever. They booked passage to Stuttgart, Germany, where they lived modestly on Mrs. Burns' income.... Scott continued to paint Civil War scenes.... Though he created some of his most enduring pictures now, he could not lose himself in his work.

By a timely coincidence the W.C.T.U. brought evangelists Mabee and English to Plainfield in winter 1883-84.... At the First Baptist Church Scott joined hundreds of Plainfielders in signing pledges not to touch alcohol. The signers established a temperance society, "The Reform Club," to maintain their promises. Scott, as corresponding secretary, lectured before the group. Abstinence served him much as alcohol had—its psychological power displaced that of liquor. Enlisting his talent, he even created a large allegorical mural at Reform Hall—a public display symbolic of his own effort. Whatever backsliding that occurred was reportedly not chronic.

While many artists tried to hide their reliance on photography, Scott saved *his gelatin dry plates and gleaned details from the same prints over many years.... Technology gave him the means to arrest subtleties of spontaneous gesture and fleeting motion, and to convey that motion on canvas. Scott saw photography as a primary tool enabling the historical artist to provide greater pictorial accuracy.*[19]

Brief as "Colonel" Scott's representative life was, by 1890 he had begun to outlive his chosen school of historical painting, for new European artistic ideas and styles were "coming in."[20] Nonetheless, art historians have ever since appreciated his professional hallmarks—authenticity, precision and nobility of treatment of his subjects.

One last great adventure came to Col. Scott: a presidential commission from Benjamin Harrison to report on the condition of native Americans in our Southwest during the 11th Census Survey, 1890-91. Again, like his famous fellow Vermonter artist-photographer, Wm. H. Jackson, he traveled widely in the West. As artist-writer, Scott studied the Comanche, Navajo, Wichita, Hopi, Kiowa, and Pueblo. Some 80% of the census report (& later bulletin) illustrations were his work. Their genocidal betrayal by Europeans so captured his sympathy that the respective tribes regarded him as their friend. By 1894, Julian Scott was entering his final phase; encumbered with rheumatism and heart trouble, he drew a token $6 monthly Civil War pension on Certificate No. 979 707; ultimately, he'd see it "climb" to $8 a month. He retreated to his 212 West Front Street home in Plainfield. Civil War themes continued to well out of him. Among mature portrayals is his emotive "The Sentinel" (1899), one of his most telling (haunting) achievements—a lone Confederate threadbare of uniform holds vigil over a barren wintery terrain. The closing days of strife are at hand. On his lachrymal countenance is registered a paroxysmal hopelessness for the Lost Cause. Appropriately, Scott's large "Battle of Antietam" hung in Plainfield's Veteran

Zouaves Armory for years. The Drake House Museum in Plainfield has "The Death of General Sedgwick." "Song of the Ancient People" (16 watercolors) remains at the Peabody Museum of Archeology and Ethnohistory at Harvard, Cambridge, Massachusetts. In fine, Julian Scott's creations, transcending the status of collectors' items, have long since attained the canon of celebrated—even sacred—Americana.

Julian, 55, died at Muhlenburg Hospital, Plainfield, on the Fourth of July 1901, leaving a widow, daughter, brother Percy, and two sisters. His funeral was held at the local Grace Protestant Episcopal Church, where Masonic rites were observed. Fellow comrades of Winfield Scott Post 73, G.A.R., fired a triple staccato over his grave—the highest point in Hillside Cemetery. Their bugler sounded the doleful "Taps," a melody the departed soul himself heard (and likely rendered) a number of times.

Today, in Johnson, Vermont, at the Dibden Center of Johnson State College, one may visit the Julian A. Scott Memorial Art Gallery and ponder over permanent showcases of Scott memorabilia—old photographs, his inkwell, gloves, and broad-brimmed western hat. An occasional devotee/aficionado of Scott lore can usually be found who will gladly assist an inquiring visitor. Just such an individual was John E. Lord, Registrar at Johnson State College, who generously donated much of his nooning to guide the writer (8/14/95) to key local interest points in our story. Some of Mr. Lord's Scott enthusiasm resides in the fact of his own great-granddad Daniel R. Gilchrist's service in Company H., *Third* Vermont Infantry. Private Gilchrist (Apr. 3, 1843-Feb. 7, 1933) who grew up in Monroe, New Hampshire, enlisted in March 1862 at Concord, Vermont. An embattled soldier of his regiment, Daniel at length suffered two amputations on his left leg. Returning to his home in August 1865, he eventually served in the New Hampshire Legislature and closed out his many days in Barnet, Vermont, a few miles north of his former home-one of the *very* few then left of the old Third Vermont. One may detect a ghostly presence, a tangible heroic mystique (mythopoeic aura) that lingers quietly over the environs of these brothers' nativity. Long gone the old way down in deference to mortality's behests and even meeting them halfway, the Scotts endure as a legacy, like Vermont granite. One may safely predict a centennial observance with bunting and oratory, with displays and exhibits, in just six more years—July 4, 2001—commemorating the passing of Johnson, Vermont's most celebrated son.

We should observe that in the summer of 1995, a most excellent and permanent tribute to Julian Scott the artist took place, the *largest* printing *ever* (in the millions) of a Scott original. "The Drummer Boy" posted as he is at the reader's top left corner of the already famous block of twenty Civil War Commemorative stamps "printed with finest color and historical text on the back" by the United States Postal Service on the 130th post bellum anniversary...confirms Scott to be a national figure "alive and well."

(William) Martin Purcell

Nov. 11, 1851 – Nov. 8, 1902

Of Beloit, in Wisconsin's very southern Rock County, ever since his July 12, 1865, discharge at age 13 years 8 months, "Marty" Purcell was a native of Rutland County, Vermont. His parents were John and Bridget Purcell, immigrants from Ireland, survivors (likely) of the Potato Famine and an English "coffin" ship. They would have seven children, some of them Wisconsin natives. Like scores of youths that opening war summer of '61, Marty cheerfully drummed for recruiters and got paid accordingly. For the better part of a year he kept it up, all the while "working on" his folks, trying to "soften them up" toward the idea of his own volunteering. Seemed like new regiments were organizing near Madison almost every month. Popular for his dwarf's height, barely four feet, Marty's reputation for percussion preceded him. The 19th Wisconsin well before its organizing in March 1862 wanted him enough to send a delegation to the Purcells' farm home seven miles from Madison. On the strenuous promisings of prudent and forethoughtful protections of their boy by a persuasive delegation of "non-coms," Mother and Father gave in, entrusting Marty to their care. Having initially enrolled February 20, little Purcell enlisted at Racine Mar. 1, 1862, as a musician, for three years.[1] Though set down as age fifteen, he was 10 years 3 months 19 days. Musician Purcell, of Company I, 19th Wisconsin Infantry, too young to carry both his blanket and drum, had volunteers aplenty ready to lighten the burden. They left for Washington on June 2. For nearly a year they performed garrison duty at Norfolk. But, as of Apr. 14, 1863, they were in the Siege of Suffolk until May 4. Private Purcell's battle tour with his comrades of the 19th Badger Staters lasted nearly ten more months:

-Action at Edenton Road (N.C.), 4/24/63
-Operations on Norfolk & Petersburg RR, 5/15-5/28
-Move to Norfolk, 6/17
-Move to Yorktown, 6/18
-Dix's Peninsula Campaign, 6/24-7/7
-Garrison Duty at Yorktown until, 8/16
-At Newport News until, 10/8
-Moved to New Berne, N.C., 10/8-10/11
-Outpost & picket duty at New Berne thru January[2]

After these weary months as a drummer on the Virginia front with the Army of the Potomac, Pvt. Purcell was, sensibly, rotated back to Wisconsin. That his feelings might not be hurt—he had always been a dedicated, able performer—, Marty was assigned detached service to drum for recruiting officers. Shortly after returning to Madison, he requested and got a fifteen-day furlough to visit home with the family in Verona. Some citizens, seeing him in uniform, did actual double takes, incredulous he was in the Union Army. At about this time—late February '64—preparations for a 36th Wisconsin were afoot. Upon organizing in Madison, and, wanting an experienced percussionist, they learned Musician Purcell could become available. Colonel Frank A. Haskell offered to make him Drum Major of the 36th, if he would consent to join.[3] Most willing to accept this honor, Marty was given a timely transfer, so that on Mar. 1, 1864, he was enrolled in Company A, 36th Wisconsin Infantry by W. H. Hamilton.[4] Once in, however, his extreme youth—then 12 years 3 months—worked against him. The regimental drum corps in a body protested against such a mere boy being set in power over them. They succeeded, but Marty replaced a newly deceased drummer boy.

The 36th Wisconsin entrained May 10 to Washington and marched almost directly to Spotsylvania Court House. Few blue-clad units saw heavier battle service those final ten months:

-Totopotomy, 5/28-5/31/64
-Bethesda Church, 6/1
-Cold Harbor, 6/2-6/12 (Col. Haskell killed)
-Before Petersburg, 6/16-6/18
-Weldon RR, 6/22-6/23
-Deep Bottom, 7/27-7/28
-Strawberry Plains, 8/14-8/18
-Ream's Station, 8/25
-Boydton Plank Road, 10/27-10/28
-Battles of Dabney's Mills/Hatcher's Run, 2/5-2/7/65
-Pursuit of Lee, 4/3-4/9
-Surrender—A.N.V., 4/9-4/12
-Grand Review in D.C., 5/23
-Move to Louisville, Ky., 6/17
-Mustered out at Louisville, 7/12/65[5]

The 36th went into battle at Ream's Station with 309 effectives, including musicians, and came out with 43 men, among whom was Martin Purcell! One can only imagine how much was made of this smooth-cheeked lad, 13, by the nigh-traumatized survivors. At Hatcher's Run, Purcell was among 200 taken prisoner and marched off at once to Libby Prison.

A non-com took Marty's hand and told him he must feign exhaustion, fall down, and, for his youth, manage to be left behind. Obeying, he soon fell prostrate in the road. Gruffly a guard brought him to his feet. But Marty went down again, crying he was unable to walk. A Reb's broad foot said otherwise, and he straggled on. A third time Marty dropped, resolved to stay down. A gray corporal stormed, swore, worked his feet—all to no avail. Had Marty been older, he would have felt a bayonet. As it was, an officer learned of the disturbance, detailed a young Johnny to stay with the boy, and fetch him along later. Soon word came for Marty to be abandoned.

He found his way into Petersburg still in Southern hands. After observing, undetected, for 24 hours, he then furtively made his way west five miles to Union lines. He went before Brig. Gen. Egan to share information. Effectually a spy, Purcell conveyed enough news or data to warrant his being taken up to Gen. Gibbon, division commander. Finally, he was introduced to Gen. W. S. Hancock, Corps Commander, who was so impressed with the 13-year-old's intrepidity and *youth that he promised to use his influence to secure a cadetship at West Point after the war. (Hancock kept his word to "the Drummer Boy of the Potomac." A crippled hand—which never hindered his drumming skills—made Purcell ineligible.)*[6]

It is apparent Marty Purcell experienced some of the war's worst scenarios, that he lost many close comrades, that muffled drums were his frequent lot and duty. Then, too, an explosion at Petersburg on Jan. 15, 1865, did enough injury to his eyes to require a surgeon's evaluation. He had been building a fire on which to cook his supper. "In the dark he gathered up combustibles with fuel and threw these on the fire causing an explosion that sent ashes, fire, dirt into his eyes, weakened ever after. Adam Fry was detailed to take care of said Purcell while sick with inflammation of the eyes."[7] Though but one in three who had ever fought in the 36th Wisconsin marched in their Grand Review May 23 down Pennsylvania Avenue, Musician Purcell was among their more than thrice decimated ranks, personifying that nostalgia-invested day those souls who could not be there.

In Parkersburg, headed home, as these remnant veterans marched from the railroad depot to the Ohio River boat landing, they were cheered by thousands awaiting along the way who had heard of the Wisconsin 36th's valorous quality. Marty, 14, provided cadence, got many attentions, and wrung hearts, especially of the womenfolks:

"Oh, look at that little boy! God bless his little heart!" Sometimes tears welled from those who had lost their own. A beautiful young woman, eyes aglow with compassion, rushed down her walk straight for the drummer boy. "My dear little fellow," she exclaimed, "if you will give me the sack you carry

your eatables in, I will fill it." Marty, ablush before his lovely ministrant and amid winks and sly grins from comrades, pulled off his haversack. He had to keep moving and her house soon disappeared. Two hours at the wharf and the girl had not shown up. Marty became the butt of a joke every few moments. "When you get older, you'll know more and won't give yer stuff away to every pretty face." Just as Marty was resigning his haversack as a casualty, a tilbury dashed up to the wharf. Out stepped his benefactress with his sack chock full of dainties and a large basket besides. Suddenly Marty had more friends than he could supply with chicken and angel food cake. It is said to this day that Mr. Purcell never picks meat from a wing of chicken without thinking tenderly of the Parkersburg maiden.

After the war, veterans of the 36th Wisconsin presented Marty with a silver shell drum, which he treasured to his final day. It and his original drumsticks are long since on exhibit at the Wisconsin State Historical Society. By war's end the Purcells were living in Beloit. Here he soon found work at A. A. Green's Shoe Store. In 1873 he formed a partnership with a Mr. Moody in the shoe business. That December 11 Martin Purcell married Mary F. Ackley (12/14/53-12/31/81), daughter of George Ackley, a native of Whitehall, New York, and sister of George F. Ackley of Beloit.[8] Their two sons were Arthur Thornton (b. 12/5/74) and Walter Ackley (b. 12/23/77).[9] Mary, age 28, died of tuberculosis.[10] On Aug. 22, 1883, at St. Paul, Minnesota, Mr. Purcell was married by Rev. N. K. Marshall to Mrs. Harriet Isadore Perkins (July 1860-May 19, 1917) of Cook County, Illinois. Their daughter was Miss Florence I. Purcell (12/30/84-2/3/59).[11]

Martin was a commercial shoe salesman and sold his wares over a wide area. He belonged to the Equitable Fraternal Union at LaCrosse. He was a Gideon and a member of the Methodist Church.[12] The first and third Tuesday evenings usually found him with his local G.A.R. brethren at Beloit's L.H.D. Crane Post 54.

In November 1881, his first wife failing, Marty bought Lot No. 183 SW at Beloit's Oakwood Cemetery, where he was laid to rest Nov. 11, 1902. He suffered a paralytic stroke July 1, 1901, from which there was no hope of recovery. He went to a hospital in May 1902. Transferred to Milwaukee, he died there— "probably the youngest drummer boy who enlisted in the Civil War."[13] [He *may have been* among the twenty-five youngest musicians in the Union Army.]

Albert E. Tisdale

Aug. 12, 1853 – Aug. 17, 1906

Collegial serendipity (Prof. Richard H. Condon, History Department, University of Maine, Farmington) placed in my path about 1982 a July 1, 1906 feature story in Boston *Sunday Post* entitled, "These Are Winners in Contest to Decide Who Is Oldest and Youngest Veteran of the Civil War in New England." *Post's* contest had begun only 44 days earlier, May 18, since which date "hundreds of photographs and records poured in to the G.A.R. editor." Volume was such that but a small fraction of these photos could be published. "Every case was carefully considered; the decision was arrived at only after every doubt had been dispelled." Part of the incentive to enter the contest was the award(s)—two special jeweled G.A.R.-like, 3-part badges on which would be engraved "Oldest (Youngest) Civil War Veteran" and the years "1861-1906." Pictured in the July 1, 1906 Boston *Sunday Post* were the winners: William Welch (Mar. 29, 1800-Feb. 28, 1907) of East Lempster, New Hampshire, and Albert E. Tisdale of South Framingham, Massachusetts. Welch, 106, then twice the age of Tisdale, would live beyond their mutual recognition and distinction five times longer or 242 days vs. 47 days respectively!

Born at St. Andrews, New Brunswick on the St. Croix River across from Calais, Maine, Welch was to serve in the "Aroostook War" of 1836-39. He assisted in building Fort Fairfield. When Gen. Winfield Scott (1786-1866) visited in March 1839, Welch introduced him to his friend, Lt. Gov. John Harvey of New Brunswick. Welch joined Company I, 14th New Hampshire, on Aug. 21, 1862, being set down as age sixty. He shared all battles with the 14th, was wounded in his left arm at Cedar Creek, stood guard over Jefferson Davis, Gov. Zebulon Vance and other C.S.A. notables before they were sent to Ft. Monroe, and was mustered out at Savannah on July 8, 1865.[1] The *Post* touted Welch also as "having the distinction of being the oldest pensioner on the rolls of Uncle Sam." However, that lofty eminence belonged solidly to "Uncle Henry" Dorman (Jan. 10, 1799-Mar. 14, 1914 —Co. F, 7th Mich. Cav.) of Liberal, Missouri.[2]

Less is known of Albert E. Tisdale, a native of Newburyport, where he did *some* of his childhood growing-up. *Some* because his folks moved to Norwich, Connecticut about 1856, *some* because on Sept. 3, 1862, when he was precisely 9 years 22 days old, he enlisted as 3rd Class Boy aboard the frigate USS *Sabine* at New London, Connecticut. The *Sabine* carried 52 guns and a crew of 504. Albert's brightness, alertness and sincerity quickly fetched him a prize billet—messenger boy to Commodore Cadwalader Ringgold (1802-1867), who on Oct. 2, 1861, had rescued Maj. John G. Reynolds and his battalion of U. S. Marines from the sinking U. S. transport *Governor* (of Port Royal Sound Expedition off Georgetown, S. C.),[3] who rescued USS *Vermont* May 29, 1862, and who retired in 1864 from a 45-year naval career. Within a month Albert was getting his sea legs, for *Sabine* straightway sailed under a roving commission to ferret out the dreaded CSS *Alabama.* A popular journalistic story (quite certainly apocryphal) allows that, after cruising far and wide several months, *Sabine,* while lying off Port-O-Pryor in the Azores, encountered her nemesis. In January (?) 1863, presumably[4] the two battlewagons exchanged broadsides, doing some mutual damage. One of *Alabama*'s shells passing over, knocked Tisdale down with a stunning effect, while on his way with a message from the Commodore to the gundeck below. "He fell through a hatchway from one deck to another, striking his head and receiving two cuts—one just over the left eye and one below the eye on the cheek bone."[5] The injury was severe enough to require Surgeon's Steward Edward H. Blake to examine Albert in sick bay right after he fell through the forward hatchway. He complained of pain in his head and eyes. Fear was of a brain concussion, a skull fracture. Blake believed the optic nerve injured but felt that youthful vigor and health would heal these setbacks. Indeed, recovery in the ensuing months appeared to be complete.

However, the writer is inclined to place credence in this following version—a primary source (Certif. #12,348, Docket #52,048 of Feb. 6, 1895, p. 12): "Colonel Charles Heywood, the present Commandant of the U. S. Marine Corps, on 2 April 1898, deposed" and said, in part:

> *I commanded the guard of USS* Sabine *in 1862. I joined in Sept. 1862 and was with that vessel until April 1863. Shortly after I joined, the claimant joined this ship as Apprentice Boy. He was about eleven. (?)*
>
> *When I first knew the claimant and during the first part of his service, he was a sound active boy and I am fully satisfied that he had nothing the matter with his eyes...*
>
> *During one of our cruises off the Cape de Verde Islands, we had occasion to fire a shot across the bow of a merchant vessel, and Tisdale, for some reason, fell through one of the hatchways, and struck the left side of the forehead just above the left eye, injuring him severely, and it took quite a little while to heal up.*
>
> *Lieutenant Kelly picked the claimant up as he was unconscious. I saw this fall and the injury. Sometime after this accident the claimant's eyes commenced to show weakness. The accident occurred in either Dec. 1862 or January 1863 and I noticed this weakness of eyes before I left the ship*

in April 1863. I made a shield for him to wear to protect his eyes.... I told my men not to let him read at night, as it would be injurious.

Messenger Boy Tisdale was furloughed home to Norwich in February 1863, but he returned a few weeks later to serve aboard until his October 1863 discharge. That last fortnight Commodore Ringgold discussed plans several times with Albert, then 10 years 2 months, about the boy's future. Accordingly, they agreed that Albert would immediately return home and begin preparing himself for Annapolis and a naval career—their dream. But this was all shattered within three months, for in late December, after studying diligently, he lost the sight of his right eye. By 1869 he was losing use of his left eye. By 1870 he was blind. Pensionless, sightless and undaunted at seventeen, he set a goal: to become a lecturer on geology and astronomy. He "saw this through" all the way to an enviable reputation for delivering talks, mainly in southern New England. Albert eked out a living this way until Congress, at length, early in the 20th century granted him $100 a month. But this took *years.* Only on Aug. 8, 1890, at age 37, did he first apply, and his claim was allowed in June 1891. He was since rejected (loss of pension) twice on *invalid* judgments, corrected though not deemed reimbursable; even so, in 1899 Albert was still getting a paltry $12 a month, in the full admission that "appellant's blindness is due to traumatism."[6]

Albert seems to have been a bachelor. His brother, James W. of Providence, Rhode Island, and his sister, Mrs. Emma H. Glenn of Taunton, Mass., were supportive and confirming in his case. His brother Edward, who died in Andersonville prison, was spiritually present. Albert lived most of his 20s, 30s, and 40s in Norwich, Conn., where he was a comrade in Sedgewick Post 1, G.A.R, and in New London as a member of Perkins Post.[7]

Late in life he joined the Farragut Naval Association of Boston. To the *Sunday Post* reporter at his "cosey" home on Waushakum Street in South Framingham that June day in 1906, Albert Tisdale, 53, confided, "My observations of life were very short but, as I gave my eyes in the service of my country, I have no bitter feelings. With my thoughts and memories I am happy and content, and the knowledge that my sacrifice was not in vain gives me strength to bear my affliction without a murmur."[8]

Charles Carter Hay

May 26, 1850 – 1908

He would be one of the Confederate South's most gifted in those qualities strategic to "little Rebdom"—respect for elders, commitment to States' Rights, primacy of family, outdoorsmanship, integrity, loyalty, obedience, gentlemanliness. A native of Stewart County, likely, he was the youngest bona fide *soldier* to come out of Georgia. [We say *soldier* with no discredit to Stewart County's other standout, B. F. Williams (1854-1943), of Louvale, who at age 7-1/2 years humbly served as a homeguard commissary wagoner.] Birth *and* death dates fuzzy in all available sources, C. C. Hay is (unjustly) one of the last personalties to get his due place in our report. But an utterance he himself made in a moment of unimpeachable sincerity comes to his rescue: "I afterwards joined the Carter Guards, Company C—color company for the 45th Alabama, Cleburne's Division—with which I surrendered at Greensboro(ugh), N. C., lacking *just one month* of being fifteen years old, and in service from 1861 to 1865."[1] Since the capitulation of "all arms & public property to be deposited by Confederates at Greensborough"[2] took place on April 26 '65, C. C. H. pinpoints his birthdate. This landmark parole date was an event by which he repeatedly affirmed his birth, being ever after among credible contenders for "the youngest C.S.A. soldier."

The boy was named for his mother's father, Charles Carter, of Washington, Georgia, whose success in agriculture originated an old Wilkes County expression— "more than Carter had oats."[3] Reportedly, C. C. Hay (some two years prior to his birth) had an uncle, Thomas Berry, who while mayor of Columbus, Georgia, died there in 1848.[4] The names of C.C.H.'s parents are not presantly available, though a family history form discloses they were both born in 1825, that they married in 1845, and that he had an uncle, Dr. Gilbert Hay. Secondary write-ups on C.C.H.'s Confederate career appear to be a bit confusing. Providentially, we may cite our subject's own summary of his C.S.A. "tours," undated, but deliberately composed in the later 1890s to minimize guesswork and to clarify his contribution:

To The United Daughters of the Confederacy
W.P. Rogers Chapter No. 44, U.D.C., Victoria, Texas—Texas Division

Mrs. J. M. Brownson, Secretary:

Madam—At your earnest request, in order that your Chapter may have the honor of giving to the three youngest Ex-Confederate soldiers—Dr. McNeill, Father Brannan (whose company I helped to raise and drill for the 15th Alabama Regiment), and myself, hereby present this certificate of eligibility for a Southern Cross of Honor.

I entered the service of the Confederacy in the Spring of 1861, as Drill-Master, Glennville Guards, afterwards Co.H, 15th Reg't Alabama Vols., at Fort Mitchell, Ala., where I voted for James Cantey for Colonel; John F. Treutlen, for Lt.-Colonel. I was Drill-Master of the Carter Guards, at Enon, Ala., one year before the organization of the 45th Alabama Reg't at Auburn, where in 1862 it became a member of said Regiment, designated as Co. C, & afterwards the color company of the Regiment which company I joined in November 1863; as Drill-Master of the "Hay Invincibles," at Creek Stand, Ala. That month I joined with a gun, not as an orderly or drummer. I was then a resident of Enon, Macon County, Ala.

Sword in hand in 1861, I helped to organize and drill three companies; was honorably discharged by parole, signed by J. E. Johnston & W. T. Sherman on 26 Apr. 1865, at Greensboro, N. C., at which time [I] was Orderly-Sergt., Co. G, 1st Alabama (consolidated), having previously declined two commissions, and lacked one month of being fifteen.

I never sought a furlough—a Cadet Captain, appointed by Rev. J. B. Cottrell, at Glennville, Ala., at 11 years of age; in service from 1861-1865, and at the surrender walked up to the ambulance and received one Mexican dollar for my entire services. The aforesaid company & regiment was attached to M. P. Lowry's Brigade of Patrick R. Cleburne's Division, Army of Tennessee.

Subsequently, I was private secretary to Hon. Alexander H. Stephens, who sent my uncle, Dr. Gilbert Hay, to school. I am author of the book The Youngest Soldier Boy with Pat Cleburne and His Flag.

My brother, a distinguished U. S. Naval officer, was with Cyrus W. Field laying the first Atlantic cable in 1859, for which service he received a gold medal from the New York Chamber of Commerce. Afterwards he was assigned to U.S. Steamship Hartford *(later the famous flagship of Admiral Farragut). The fleet was ordered to Chinese waters and on its arrival at Hong Kong, learning of the commencement of war between the States, Surgeon William G. Hay refused to serve against his native State [Georgia], tendered his resignation. He was offered and accepted the position of Surgeon-General of the Imperial Army of China during the Pekin Rebellion of 1862.*

Respectfully,
Charles Carter Hay

We endorse the above certificate of eligibility: M. T. Wright, Co. C, 45th Ala. Regt., Tuskegee, Ala. E. Herndon Glenn, Co. C, 45th Ala. Regt., State Treasurer's office, 15 yrs. Probate Judge of Russell County.—"Was roommate, classmate, and in the war, messmate, & surrendered with applicant at Greensboro, N.C."[5]

Should question arise as to C. C. Hay's worthiness to be in *CB&T*, let us cite just his last 24 months with "the Carter Guards" (Co. C.), or color company of the 45th Alabama Infantry of whose 125 men...24 were killed in battle; 53 died in service; 48 came home (of whom 29 were wounded). Some 40 were under 17; a dozen, under 15.[6] The 45th fought under Gen. Cleburne at Chickamauga; they were at Mission Ridge, Ringgold Gap, and wintered at Dalton; they shared liberally in the Dalton-Atlanta resistance (esp. at Resaca) & up at New Hope). On July 22 at Atlanta their casualties were 46% of effectives; losses were large again at Jonesboro. *They* were in the disastrous march into Tennessee. *They* opened the brilliant fight at Spring Hill on the eve of the Battle of Franklin and were in the next day's gory assault by Cleburne's Division. So decimated were they as to require consolidation with the 16th and 33rd Alabama regiments.[7] Reminiscing in 1902, Mr. Hay, 52, had a knack for reviving certain C.S.A. scenarios:

> *...many were the pranks played upon us youngsters, and, as for sickness and hard service, we bore it well as those toughened by maturer years.*
>
> *On inspection in Dalton, Ga., Capt. Buck, of Cleburne's staff, had a way of pitching the gun back which made it look to us little fellows like a piece of artillery coming our way; despite the firm brace of the feet to catch it, we would weaken and the force of the gun would almost carry us out of line, which afforded a little merriment, and, with a smothered laugh from Capt. Buck, he would pass to the next with similar result. On a forced night march in Georgia a very hard rain salted us; mud clung to us with the tenacity of a brother and its fond embrace carried us down. One little fellow, short of stature, could scarcely be seen below his shoulder. Men in an adjoining company sang out to us, "Go back, Company C, an' git your man; when we saw him last only his hat was in sight, and he was still gwine [going] down!"*[8]

Accounting for this ex-C.S.A. Wonder-Boy's nearly 43 *post bellum* years remains a challenge. Data on a marriage, wife, children, domesticity are lacking. Certain truths are harvestable. Veteran Hay, whose peacetime civilian efforts were consistent with those of a prodigy drillmaster, earned his living primarily as an educator. Then, too, he enjoyed a writing career, using "Dried Grass" (a light disguise for his surname) as a byline on some of his articles. He was a dedicated reader of and contributor to *Confederate Veteran*, a beloved monthly that flourished until 1932 when the Depression doomed it. The title "C.C." most wanted to be remembered for was his semi-autobiographical *The Complete Romantic and Dramatic History of Cleburne and His Flag.*

From it we lift this one passage—"Engaged with Pat Cleburne, the hardest fighter of the age and in the hardest arm of the service, we, barefoot and with feet bleeding at every step, waded frozen streams. I had no horse to mount for relief."

A restlessness spurred him to travel frequently. He spent up to a decade with his brother in California. From the early 1890s on, he traveled widely to U.C.V. reunions, being a pioneering energizer for the late-forming brotherhood. Comrade Hay *probably* knew more youngster-Rebs like himself than any other veteran of the war, South or North. At one time living several years in Jacksonville, he knew Frank M. Ironmonger in Frank's "own backyard." We know that most of his senior years "C. C." Hay lived in Alabama; during 1902-04, at Calera, Shelby County; and, finally, 1905-08, at Hurtsboro, Russell County, where he fought his last hard holding action. Among his physical failings was rheumatism, a legacy of his stark C.S.A. years. Here he died, nearly sixty and within forty-five miles of his birthplace. Due homage was paid by many mourners individually and by whole delegations of the U.C.V., U.D.C., and S.C.V. He was laid to rest in Hurtsboro City Cemetery, where, today, his weatherworn military stone can be made out to read:

C. C. Hay
Co. C 45th Ala. Inf.[10]

Though his dates have never been on his little "monument," ex-Sgt. and ex-Capt. C. C. Hay, Army of Tennessee, U.C.V., rests more easily, now that his rightful place in *Callow Brave and True* is assured. As with so many fledgling innocents here, we sense how the four-year, trauma-laden tragidrama was so baptismal . . . so soulfully enthralling upon survivors, like Charles C. Hay, as to overshadow their remaining lives with an emergent nostalgia, undulant in its ongoing convictions . . . of unutterable loyalties . . . loyalties to the idea(l)s of their youth . . . of their having risen . . . once . . . to a supreme and sacred duty. Inwardly, the C. C. Hays never ceased paying homage to the Cause . . . that had been worthy of their lives . . . and deaths.

Thomas L. F. Hubler

Oct. 9, 1851 – Mar. 21, 1913

Thomas L. F. Hubler probably *was* "the youngest soldier in the Union Army" *when*, claiming to be fourteen, he volunteered at Warsaw, Indiana, his hometown. The date was April 19, 1861. Of all the youngest who served during the next four years in the Union Army, it is most probable that Tommy Hubler was the earliest or first of his extraordinary breed. That May 7 at age 9 years 7 months Tommy enlisted for one year and on May 19, 1862, he re-enlisted for three years, thus serving the entire war in this same regiment—the 12th Indiana Infantry, mostly in Company A, though both Companies E and H were fond of claiming him. "It is thought that he beat the first 'long roll' of the great civil war."[1] He was, then, at this early point in the War of the Sixties, quite likely *the* youngest in the blue uniform. (See Appendix G.)

Tommy was born at Fort Wayne, Indiana, the son of Henry Hubler, whose parents were Henry Hubler, Sr., and Barbara Edres, and whose grandparents were Jacob and Margaret Hubler and John Edres—all of Centre County, Pennsylvania.[2] With his brothers John L., David and Reuben, Henry (Jr.) had lived a short time (c. 1848-53) in Ashland County, Ohio. Tommy was but two when his folks moved to Warsaw, where, in the next seven years, he did much of his growing up. His father had been a lumber dealer and a leader in the Pennsylvania Militia prior to the Mexican War, of which he was a veteran. Hence, by the spring of 1861, Henry Hubler's military experience easily recommended him to officer status so that right away he became Captain Hubler. Also, Henry's sister Jemima's husband was Lt. Reub(en) Williams, a promising young newspaperman, who had been among the earliest to answer Lincoln's first call for three-month volunteers. It is conjectured that Tommy's mother, Mary A., knowing her husband (Capt. Henry, later Major) was in poor health, sacrificed her son in the belief his father needed him. Too, she shared a common belief: that a show of strength and three months' time would convince the South to give up its secession.

The Warsaw ladies presented their company with a silken flag inscribed in gold letters Kosciusko Guards upon its departure for Indianapolis. Tommy's military career was that of the 12th Indiana—training at Evansville, then off to Baltimore, to Sandy Hook, Maryland, July 8th; duty at Harpers Ferry, Williamsport and Sharpsburg until March 1862; advance on Winchester, Mar. 1-12; skirmish at Stephenson's Station; operations in the Shenandoah till April; duty at Warrentown Junction; reconnaissance to Rappahannock Rr.

with skirmish at that Crossing, Apr. 18; march to D.C.; muster out May 14, 1862, on expiration of duty.[3] Drummer Boy Tommy Hubler, "one of the most expert drummers in the Army of the Potomac," according to historians of the 12th Indiana, saw much heavy battle action, particularly during his second enlistment while serving in the Army of Kentucky and in the Army of the Tennessee. We can be sure that Tommy personally mourned the loss of his friends among the 12th's 100 men who were killed or the 195 who died of diseases during and after bloody contests at Holly Springs, Miss.; Siege of Vicksburg and of Jackson; he lived the heavy truths of the Chattanooga-Ringgold Campaign, the Battle-siege of Atlanta; Jonesboro, Bentonville, the Bennett House surrender-finale. The little percussionist lent cadence to the 12th Indiana's jubilant, precisioned paces up Pennsylvania Avenue with Sherman's Army on its Grand Review of May 24, 1865,[4]—the day he saw more fellow blue-clads than ever before or since. Early in 1865, Tommy's Uncle Reub Williams received a brevet Brigadier-Generalship at the request of President Lincoln; Tommy, at this time, became Gen. Williams' aide.

Returning home to Warsaw, Indiana, Tommy Hubler easily, willingly came under the tutelage of Reub Williams, now editor/publisher of *The Northern Indianian* (today*The Warsaw Times-Union*). Young Thomas Hubler, by the early fall of 1865 a seasoned veteran not yet fourteen, began to learn the printer's trade. As he advanced in his teens he picked up the finer points of newspapering and acquired a variety of journalistic skills that included writing—a flair for nonfiction. Meanwhile he had lost his father, Major Hubler, who died Nov. 18, 1865, a casualty to the strains and exposures of his Civil War duties.

On Dec. 17, 1869, Tommy married Frederick Aspinall's daughter Sarah F. "Sadie" Aspinall, whose folks lived in Goshen, Indiana. They would have three children; while one died a child, Lena E. grew to young womanhood, and Thomas Jr. survived his father. For several years Tommy was foreman of the composing room at *The Northern Indianian.* About 1885, he moved his family and home to Milwaukee, where he accepted a position in a large printery. Then, about 1890, he relocated in Chicago, where for some twenty years he was employed by Donelly & Company and by Rand, McNally & Company. Tommy originally joined Henry Chipman Post 442, G.A.R., in Warsaw. Wherever he moved to, he kept up an active presence as a Grand Army comrade and always enjoyed popularity, especially beloved for being "so much younger than the rest of us." Tommy died in Chicago at his 5847 Prairie Avenue home, where his funeral service was held. Among his many mourners were his son, his widow, and three sisters—Mrs. Reub Williams, of Warsaw; Mrs. Michael Cline, of Cleveland, Ohio; and Mrs. Sarah Taylor, of Sexton, Missouri. He was conveyed by the Pennsylvania Railroad to Warsaw, where his fellow charter members of Chipman Post met him and took charge of his burial at Oakwood Cemetery that Easter Sunday.[5]

Whatever may be said, few others, if any, among all the youngest patriots in "The Boys' War," served the *entire* war or had so lengthy a tour of wartime service in the war as did this magnificent drummer boy Hubler...the pride of the Twelfth Indiana Infantry. (See Appendix D.)

On Memorial Day 1978, the Kosciusko County Historical Society dedicated a newly installed bronze plaque on Tommy's gravesite in Warsaw's Oakwood Cemetery—the result of a feature story by Ruth Thayer Kain and Virginia Scott Miner, whose poem "For Tommy Hubler" was read followed by a seven-gun salute. Her (Miner's) elegy opens this way:

In battle you would hear such sounds
As surely no boy should hear—the screams
Of desperately wounded men.
The horses' frantic neighing, and the rain of bullets,
Then artillery's great crash and thud.
And there was mud, knee-deep at times, and winter cold
Gnawing at bones. Your treble, though,
Lifted at campfires as the men, longing for home,
Sang out their hearts.
And though the mystery haunts us still—
How in the world your mother let
You go, still off you went, tall, slim,
A ten-year old, beside your father.
Tommy Hubler, you kept the faith
You pledged the Union. There were men—
More than we like to say—deserted:
Not you, Tommy Hubler—no,
You were a boy who was a man—
A man in courage and in soul.
Your drum the company's heartbeat,
You faced death.[6]

Kosciusko County Historical Society

Headstone at Oakwood Cemetery, Warsaw, Indiana.

James Lawrence Scholls, Sr.

Oct. 29, 1852 – May 5, 1919

Youngest and latest born of the 1150+ who served in the Confederate States Marine Corps, James L. Scholls effected the coup of his youth when on Feb. 24, 1864, he enlisted as a drummer boy at Richmond, Virginia, for duty with Company A then stationed at Drewry's Bluff, Virginia. It was the proudest day of his life and he was exactly 11 years 3 months 26 days. Though he could scarcely ever have known it, on that day he earned himself a permanent place several times over in this national report. James places among the pre-twelvers of "The Latest Born" early in this study. How he achieved this feat derives from a peculiar set of circumstances far from foreign (by now) to the reader. To appreciate his family situation that late February day, let us expand upon his birthright and heritage.[1]

The paternal Scholl(s) lineage is traceable to at least the tenth generation here in America and originally to Germany's Rhine Valley. James was descended as follows:[2]

Carl Jacob Scholl

Johan Nicholas Scholl (of Moore Twp, Northampton Co., Pa.)	m.	Anna Barbara
Dr. Philip Nicholas Scholl	m.	Johanna Magdalena Ehro (7/7/1738-2/16/1815)
Dr. Henry Scholl (3/27/1768-6/10/1828)	m.	Margaret Strauss
Jacob L. Scholl (7/10/1798-5/13/1837) b. Lehigh County, Pa.	m.	Regina Steckel (2/6/1803-1860)
Jacob S. Scholls (3/15/1822-8/31/1862)	m.	Bridget Montgomery

Jacob S. and Bridget were married Jan. 31, 1847, at Pensacola, Florida, his duty station during the Mexican War. By that time, at age twenty-five, he was well embarked upon a military career. While still seventeen he had been enlisted at Easton, Pennsylvania, by a Major Graham on Aug. 25, 1839, as a resident of Lehigh, where for some five years he had learned by apprenticeship the coachmaker's trade. Assigned to Company K, Seventh U. S. Infantry, Jacob served five years to the day until discharged as a sergeant at Barrancas, West Florida.[3] Two days later he enlisted in the U. S. Marine Corps, finding the military compatible. He recouped his standing as sergeant by a promotion during this initial (Mexican War) tour and re-enlisted July 14, 1848, and he did so a third time on May 14, 1852, having already reached the highest enlisted rank in the Corps of that era—orderly sergeant. By expiration of his third Marines enlistment, now with a wife and five young ones, Jacob found his limited pay and benefits insufficient to maintain them comfortably. With some reluctance certainly, ex-Sergeant Scholls sought higher pay as a civilian. In the best interests of his family, he did so.

But, with the obvious maelstrom of hostilities fast descending, he knew, as an established Southerner now, what recourse he must take. With a passing (but not surpassing) twinge of conscience, given his Pennsylvania heritage, he cast his lot with his adopted Alabama and went to Montgomery to offer himself. He promptly enlisted in Capt. Rueben T. Thom's Company that March 25th, *the* day of Thom's commission in the C.S.M.C. His service record already extensive, Jacob was immediately made 1st Sergeant of Thom's Company. Sgt. Scholls trained and disciplined scores of raw recruits sent to Warrington, Florida, during April-October 1861. With Sgts. J. Charlesworth and T. Grogan, also former U. S. Marines, this company had to have been the best drilled of the Pensacola Regiment of eventually 25 officers and 350+ men. Grateful for such timely efficiency must Col. Lloyd J. Beall, Commandant of the C.S.M.C., surely have been when shortly he needed and drew upon these schooled trainees "to form guards for the ironclad CSS *Virginia* and her consorts CSS *Jamestown* and *Patrick Henry*."[4] Jacob left home with comrades entrained for Norfolk and his greatest military adventure. As senior non-com of *Virginia*'s 54-man Marine guard, 1st Sgt. Scholls intensified their training to include actual servicing of this historic vessel's heavy guns. Never before or after would the total tension, suspense and terror of battle so completely grip Mariner Scholls as during the ever-after famed Battle of Hampton Roads, where they were instrumental in roundly defeating the ill-fated heroisms of USS *Cumberland* and USS *Congress*. Their acid test—(for all the gunsmoke—acrid test) came with the ensuing climactic duel against USS *Monitor*, for this dreadful inferno evoked in all hands the ultimate enthralling impact, as hour upon hour, amid deafening decibels, they visited violence upon their adversaries...and themselves. So unsavory was this sustained baptism of hellfire that over a third of his severely tried Guard would desert by payday Sept. 30, 1862, but 1st Sgt. Scholls adhered to his Corps.[5] The May 10 abandonment of Norfolk and *Virginia*'s excessive draft for ascending the James River to safety required her dismal destruction, surely a somber event for all who had served in her. Scholls' Marines and those of the James River Squadron were posted to duty at Drewry's Bluff, a strategic site on the James, whose tenability was a must for preserving Richmond. On May 15 a Union Navy squadron attempted its subjugation. Sgt. Scholls with two companies of C. S. Marines helped rebuff the assault by pouring in rifle fire from a line of riverbank trenches, effectively trouncing their foe. His unit of Confederate Marines helped host invaders to another defeat at the Seven Days' Battles. In the well earned lull that followed, Drewry's Bluff became their permanent base. Here it was that battle-weary and on duty, 1st Sgt. Jacob S. Scholls, 40, died of heart disease on Aug. 31, 1862. Fittingly, he was buried with full military honors at Richmond's Hollywood Cemetery, which would become the greatest *campo santo* of Confederate heroes anywhere.

Jacob lived to see his eldest child, William Henry (Jan. 21, 1848-Mar. 30, 1931), a native of New York City (Jacob was then stationed at Brooklyn Navy Yard), enlist as a musician in the C.S.M.C. on Apr. 3, 1862. William was 14 years 2 months 13 days when he was assigned to Capt. Thom's Company C at Camp Beall on Drewry's Bluff. Because Virginia's Marine Guard had a musician, William did not get to serve under his father. Musician duties were needed, however, aboard the station's receiving ship, most likely posted to CSS *Confederate States*.[6] While much of William's tour seems to have been routinely spent at Camp Beall, he may well have been transferred to an ironclad in the James River Squadron prior to the collapse of Richmond. Parole records issued to members of Semmes' Naval Brigade at Greensboro, North Carolina, in late April 1865 bear his name.[7]

To the Widow Scholls had fallen the burden of support for herself and several children; for many mid-war months she eked out a living sewing uniforms for the C.S.M.C. Quartermaster's Department, who probably were as concerned for her as they felt beholden to her. As those heavy months beset with poverty wore on and Bridget's domestic struggles matured, most of the psychological (and actual) pre-conditions for young James' remarkable entry into the Corps (and history) were met and set: *orphanhood, a martyred father, a beleaguered mother, an older brother already "in his dad's footsteps" exemplary and exercising a certain peer pressure, and the lad's being consumed by two passions—patriotism and the hope he would ease his mother's burden.* By February 1864 everything was in place for this practical solution, for now James was well into his twelfth year ready for just such an adventure. Accordingly, he recited his "Good-byes" to a wistful (disconsolate?) Bridget and sister Eliza, age seven, and left for Richmond. James provided cadence at Camp Beall, where he served for over a year or nearly to the cessation of hostilities. His name appears on numerous muster/pay rolls and on clothing receipt rolls, which verify his presence for duty with Company A, C.S.M.C.[8] Reported to have been among the Marine Battalion remnant there, James witnessed the A.N.V.'s Stacking of Arms on Apr. 12, 1865...which emotive drama—far from lost upon his 12 years' conscience—remained indelibly with him unto his dying day.[9]

Returning to his hometown, Pensacola—his nativity had been at Warrington (possibly Woolsey), just seaward of Pensacola—the pre-teenager, let it be hoped, partook of the last of an abbreviated childhood. But it is easily imagined that he shouldered adult tasks early and was a credit to his mother's household. Soon he again patterned himself on William and thereby became a local harbor pilot. As such, he rose to the office of Secretary of the Pensacola Bar Pilots' Association.

On Apr. 1, 1877, James married Rosa Leigh Jones (Mar. 21, 1859-Apr. 1, 1930), a Pensacola native. An August or September 1976 letter whose salutation is "Dear Rebel," written by their granddaughter, Ethel Marthine Scholl, to a grandchild of Ethel Leone Scholl and her husband Charles Walter Forum [See Note 9], discloses the identities of their eight children. [Note the final "s" of the surname was dropped in the children's generation.[10]

Robert Walter (1878—"Grandmother grieved many years, not knowing what happened to him but never found any trace.)

Clara (1879—died in childhood)

Rosaleigh (1881-c. 1916) (Mrs. Wm. H.) Merritt had two children

Charles Jr. and Frances H. (Mrs. James B.) Moore.

James Lawrence Jr. (1885-1941), who married Andrea Christopherson, has a daughter, Ethel M. (Me!)

Wm. Henry (1887-1958), a World War I'er, without progeny, is buried at Fort Barrancas National Cemetery, Pensacola.

Susan Anna (Mrs. Hayward T.) Hall (1888-1953), without progeny, is buried at Bonaventure Cemetery, Savannah, Georgia.

Ralph Edwin (1894-?) married and had a son "Bobbie," who was killed in World War II, the one and only Scholl left to carry on the name.

My Grandmother Rosa Leigh Jones Scholls died at Pensacola Apr. 1, 1930, on her wedding anniversary. They were married at Warrington by Rev. Father Lane at St. John's Catholic Church and are buried in that Church Cemetery as are many among the family since. Rosa Leigh was the daughter of George Lafayette Jones, who fought in Maj. Myers' 15th Florida Battn., Cavalry, C.S.A., and Susan Hall.

Our story ends on a note of irony caused by a scarcity of extant wartime records in the post-C.S.A. South, a scarcity which *may have been* augmented by the handiwork of a few "in higher places" who conceivably harbored just enough ill will. Fittingly, we cite him who is *the* source and reason for James L. Scholls' due place in this study, namely David M. Sullivan, for he has excavated the research entrenchments behind these lines:

> *When Rosa Leigh Scholls applied to the State of Florida in December 1919 for her Confederate Widow's Pension, brother-in-law William's affidavit as a comrade-in-arms of the C. S. Marine Corps swearing to the truth of James' service was instrumental in securing the pension.[11] Years later, when William's widow, Prudence Augusta, attempted to claim a pension based upon his service as a C. S. Marine, Florida authorities denied her application stating that there was no proof of his service. His longevity undid the application. All of his wartime associates had preceded him to the grave. Those who had not were perhaps unwilling to give assistance to the widow of a turncoat who had gone over to the other side. There was simply no one left to swear to his service.*

Commodore Perry Byam

Oct. 22, 1852 – Feb. 7, 1922

"C. Perry" Byam or "Perry" goes into our report as one of those child musicians practically unheard of these past sixty years even though his name and identity were almost universally known during 1889-1920 in Grand Army circles. Garfield Post 8, G.A.R., at St. Paul, Minnesota, Nov. 22, 1888, brain stormed themselves a fundraiser: a portrait of their Comrade C. Perry Byam "from a tintype, taken Oct. 13, 1863, in the eleventh year of his age," on whose verso is:

> *To Our Comrades and Friends:*
>
> *The accompanying photograph of Comrade Byam of this Post, is issued that our comrades and others may have the pleasure of seeing the present and former appearance of a person who was the youngest soldier of the rebellion; we wish to also state that arising from the sale of these photographs is a small margin of profit, which is to be donated to this Post, to be set apart as a relief fund for the benefit of all comrades in distress.*
>
> *The Youngest Soldier of the Rebellion*
>
> *C. Perry Byam was born in Kane County, Illinois, Oct. 22nd 1852; was mustered into the U. S. service June 22nd 1862, at age nine years and eight months and served as a drummer of Company "D" 24th Regiment of Iowa Volunteer Infantry.*

These portraits sold in the thousands during the 1890s. Inevitably, he was a favorite at G.A.R. functions and regimental reunions. He was elected Garfield Post 8 Commander in the late 1880s. But, with the passing on of each comrade, and of his fellow veterans of the 24th Iowa, Perry's humble glory and remembrance faded anew. Nor was his life all wine and roses. We tell what little we *can* share.

Perry was the fourth of five known children of Rev. Eber C. Byam (b. 1825) by his first wife whose identity is unavailable. His second wife Hannah (b. 1833 in Ohio) he would marry in the spring of 1863 when he resettled in Marion, Iowa. In the early 1850s the Byams moved to eastern Iowa from Illinois. Perry had two brothers, approximately six and nine years his senior—William W. Byam and Charles L. Byam.[1] They lived in Mt. Vernon, some twenty miles southeast of Cedar Rapids (notable years later as the hometown of Mancil Root, another lad who served single-digitly). In 1858 Perry acquired a baby sister, Jennie.[2] His childhood? Those rural, local-color reminiscences, so often retold by the children of *his* someday, have scarcely been heard these sixty years. War and his own juvenile ambition to do the manly thing effectually abbreviated that formative season of relative contentment—childhood. A deposition taken from older brother Wm. W. Byam (10/29/08) at Akron, Ohio, on behalf of Perry's quest for a pension proves insightful:

> *I am 62, address 131 Market St., temporary-retired from business. I enlisted about June 1862 as drummer boy [shortly] for Co. G, 24 Iowa Inf. and served as such until discharge about Aug. 1865. My father was Col. of that Regt. We [Perry] had both lived at home with our parents up to our enlistments. His [Perry's] health was always good before enlistment... While claimant was with the Regt. I saw him every day as we were in the drum corps. I do not recall claimant was ever sick in service—that is, nothing serious. He did have diarrhea same as most of us... I remember he was discharged at Vicksburg on account of his youthful age... Our brother, Adjt. Charles L. Byam had been wounded in leg at Shiloh and resigned at Vicksburg and wanted to take claimant home with him. Our father had resigned prior to that time and brother Charles wanted to take Perry home, as the Regt'l Surgeon told Charles it was not right for him to go home and leave that child—Perry—in the service.*
>
> *Claimant was always called Perry in our family. I didn't see him again after his discharge until after mine and I'd returned home to Marion, Iowa, in Aug. 1865. My mother had died while I was in the army and father had married again shortly before I got home, and I found claimant at home with father and his wife. We lived in Marion until about 1867 when we went to Ft. Dodge, Iowa. Claimant lived with Father from army discharge to about 1869.*[3]

In his own able penmanship on Aug. 20, 1914, from Chicago, we have C. Perry Byam's summary of his service. "I was drummer of Co. "D" 24th Regt. of Iowa Vol. Infy. Was born in Kane County, Illinois, Oct. 22nd 1852; enlisted at Mt. Vernon, Iowa, June 22, 1862; mustered in at Ft. Madison, Iowa, Aug. 22, 1862, and was honorably discharged for disability at Vicksburg, Miss., July 26, 1863, having served one year, one month, 4 days." Realities that encouraged Perry's impetuosity to leave home? Let's see. (1) Eber C. Byam was the early Colonel of the 24th Iowa. (2) Brother William W. Byam was already assigned as drummer in Company G. (3) Brother Charles L. Byam also had chosen duty in the 24th. (4) Male peer pressure, possibly? ...with the three oldest family men going into uniform(s), (5) Perry missed his father, *already* in uniform. (6) Hadn't he already learned drumming from a neighbor! (7) The boys would lose to diphteria their mother, whose death foreshortened Rev. Byam's colonelcy.

Perry computed his first duty day as June 22 '62, making him but 9 years 8 months; however, his records concur in Aug. 22, '62, as his initial (official) date from which his service is figured. He was, then, two months shy of ten. Assigned to Company D within the month at Muscatine during the 24th's organizing, Sept, 18-Oct. 20, 1862, Perry became the pet of his regiment. They were attached to the District of Eastern Arkansas, Department of Missouri, until December 1862; then they were in the Department of Tennessee until August 1863.[4] Musician Byam's martial tour consisted of these "adventures":

-Exped. from Helena, Ark. to Arkansas Post, 11/16-11/21/62
-Exped. to Granada, Miss., 11/27-12/5
-Gorman's Exped. up White River, 1/13-19/63
-Exped. up St. Francis & Little Rivers, 3/5-3/12
-Skirmish at Madison, 3/9
-Yazoo Pass Exped. & Operations against Fort Pemberton & Greenwood, 3/13-4/15
-Move to Milliken's Bend, 4/13
-Movement on Bruinsburg & turning Grand Gulf, 4/25-4/30
-Battle of Port Gibson, 5/1
-Bayou Pierre (So. Fork & No.), Miss. Skirmish, 5/2-5/3
-Fourteen Mile Creek, Miss. Skirmish, 5/12-5/13
-Battle of Champion's Hill, 5/16
-Big Black River Bridge Engagement, 5/17
-Siege of Vicksburg, 5/18-7/4
-Assaults, 5/19 & 5/22
-Advance on Jackson, 7/5-7/10
-Siege of Jackson, 7/10-7/17

By mid-July, Byam had gone the limit of his endurance, so demanding were the severities of camp routine, inhospitable climate, and borderline sanitation. Plagued with diarrhea and dampness, he would some forty-five years later request a pension for disability and be refused several times. Yet, he was discharged for both youth *and* disability. A truth: The Army was *not* a fit place for child-soldiery, despite all rhapsodic romanticizations then or now. Of the Byams, Brother William served longest, mustering out with the 24th at Savannah, Georgia, July 17, 1865. As an ex-commissioned officer, Rev. E. C. Byam moved into a position after the war with the Government Land Office at Fort Dodge. Perry, living at home, began clerking in a store when not in school. But Perry's absenteeism was 25% in both, due to sickness. "In the spring of 1869 I was sent to take a course of study at Bailey's Commercial College in Dubuque, but three weeks after my entrance I was taken so seriously ill with my complaint (diarrhea) that I had to give up school, and I never returned."[6]

In a remarkable attempt to account for his many moves and efforts to be gainfully employed, Perry, hoping to expedite eligibility for his Civil War pension, penned these data from Detroit, Dec. 6, 1906:

Date	*Residence*	*Occupation*
1863 to 1869	*Linn County, Iowa*	*Invalid & school boy*
1869 to 1870	*Ft. Dodge, Iowa*	*Invalid & student*
1870 to 1874	*Fort Dodge, Iowa*	*Abstract Maker & Real Estate*
1874 & 1875	*Sioux City, Iowa*	*Deputy County Treasurer*
1876 to 1878	*Ottumwa, Iowa*	*Abstract Maker*
1878 to 1880 incl.	*Ottumwa, Iowa*	*Farm Loans & Insurance*
1881 (1/2)	*St. Paul, Minn.*	*Right of Way Clerk C, St. P., M. & O. Realty*
1882 & 1883 incl.	*Duluth, Minn.*	*Real Estate*
1884 to 1886	*St. Paul, Minn.*	*Real Estate*
1886 to 1889 incl.	*Minneapolis, Minn.*	*Real Estate*
1890 to 1891	*Humboldt Ave., Chicago, Illinois*	*Real Estate*[7]
1891 to 1892	*1st Ave.,Seattle, Washington*	*Real Estate*
1892	*Clay St., Portland, Oregon*	*Real Estate*
1892 to 1894	*Harrison Ave., Seattle, Washington*	*Real Estate*
1894 (9 mos.)	*Mason & Post Streets San Francisco, Calif.*	*Invalid*
1894 to 1902	*#2320 Fifth Avenue Seattle, Washington*	*Real Estate*
1902	*#29 Commonwealth Ave. Boston, Massachusetts*	*Mexican Real Estate*
1902 - 03	*Osborne Street Montreal, Quebec*	*Mexican Real Estate*
1903	*Concord Square Boston, Massachusetts*	*Mexican Real Estate*
1904 & 1905	*W. 89th & W. 92nd Streets New York City, N.Y.*	*Mexican Real Estate*
1905	*William Street Rochester, N.Y.*	*Mexican Real Estate*
1906	*King Street Toronto, Ontario, Canada*	*Mexican Real Estate*
1906	*#22 Montcalm Street E. Detroit, Mich.*	*Mexican Real Estate*

I have also lived, accompanied by my family, for a few months each at Freeport, Ill. —1876, 1 mo.; Red Wing, Minn.—1881, 2 mos.; Superior City, Wis., 3 mos.; Winnipeg, Man.—1883, 5 mos.; Tacoma, Wash.—1897, 3 mos.; San Juan Island, Wash.—1898, 3 mos.; Anacostia, Wash.—3 mos.; and Stanwood, Wash.—1900, 4 mos. I have lost all my early records in Puget Sound by the capsizing of my boat on one of my moving trips.

On May 4, 1871, at Fort Dodge, Iowa's First Methodist Episcopal Church, Rev. Wm. F. Morrison married Perry and Miss Cornelia Cox Marshall, sister of Will Marshall and Mrs. J. B. Williams of Fort Dodge. Their children were Charles W. (b. 3/1/73), Richard P. (9/26/75), and Sadie B. Cooper (11/6/77).[8]

In the summer of 1890 the Perry Byams visited with relatives in Fort Dodge. They then purchased a lot in Section F of the community's Oakland Cemetery, but there exists no record of a burial there! C. Perry Byam made a name for himself several times over during a restless life. At the last he was living with his son Richard at Port Gamble, Washington. He died late his last day at a Tacoma hospital, leaving his two sons and daughter, Mrs. R. C. Colburn of Oakland, California.[9] But where *was* Perry laid to rest?

Again, we turn to Perry for a closure only he can confer:

Toronto, Ontario
Nov. 21st 1906

Col. Jas. R. West
Veteran Post 49, Elgin, Ill.
My dear Comrade:

You ask a statement respecting my service.... Numerous have been the claimants for the distinction of having been "Youngest soldier," ranging from 10 to 14. I've never personally taken the trouble to dispute any of these claims, but have remained passively silent.

My parents were both born near Toronto, Ontario, where my two brothers and a sister were also born. In 1851 Father and family emigrated to Illinois, first locating in Cook County, near Chicago, but soon moved to Kane County, where he taught school and studied law. In Nov. 1852 Father, with stout heart, crossed Illinois to northern Iowa, where he began to practice law. He left Mother and children under her brother Lafayette Baldwin's care. Winter '53 we all went by oxen and wagon to join Father in the Winnesheik County wilderness. July 4, 1857, at West Union, Iowa, I first heard martial music. The sound of the drums entranced me. I was given a drum in 1859 while we were at Mt. Vernon, Iowa. I learned from a neighborhood drummer and soon became proficient. In 1861 I was in great demand at all public gatherings, much to my vanity and the envy of the other boys. From Fort Sumter on, my ambition was to be a soldier. I drummed upon slightest provocation.

My tenacious persistence was rewarded. I was permitted to enlist. Then came a time of harrowing doubt. Would I pass muster? In great seriousness I stood in ranks, getting jocular advice—"Stand out of sight...behind your drum." My name was called. I answered with outward confidence, but with inward misgivings. The officer seeming not *to notice me, checked off my name and went on, to my boundless joy. A real soldier I now was—Aug. 22, 1862.*

C. Perry Byam in mid-1863, Co. D, 24th Iowa Infantry.

In our early Southern Camps I was ever on the alert, seeking chances to drum in all parades, reviews. I was first at funerals, first to beat the "long roll," and last to leave off. Could the Rebellion have been put down by drumming, the call for more troops after my *enrollment would have been entirely superfluous.*

My chief suffering was want of proper clothing. The smallest kepi was the only item that fitted. I wore a 13 shoe (children's). Any G.I. garment had material enough for several of me. I enjoined all foraging parties to look out for wearing apparel for me, esp. shoes. Often I was barefooted, rarely had a shirt, for months but a single pair of trousers and short jacket that buttoned to the neck. I was picturesquely lousy.

I spent much time in a battery enjoying the privilege of "pulling off" heavy siege guns after they had been charged and sighted.... Towards the close of the siege [Vicksburg] so much did I desire to be in the van upon surrender that I spent much time in the rifle-pits. With a borrowed musket and ammunition I loaded and fired with the best of 'em.

My eldest brother [Charles L.], 15, was first in the family to volunteer, early in '61. He was seriously wounded at Shiloh and discharged, but re-entered the service and became a 1st Lieutenant at 17. "Promoted for gallantry upon the field of battle."

Father entered the service in the spring of '62 as a Colonel of Volunteers. In several battles, he personally led in the final charge at Champion's Hill.

My second brother, William, 14, went in as a drummer, serving out the war and in Sherman's Grand Review at Washington.

Our sister, 13, next older than I, died of diphtheria in 1863. Mother followed her to the grave a week later, only in her 37th year...but the mother of three sons, all of whom, besides their father, were serving in the army when she died...bitterly illustrative of the irony of fate: that husband and sons should survive the carnage of war, whilst mother and daughter, who grieved for them, should perish in a haven of supposed safety.

This abridged record is the first and only statement relative thereto ever written by me, being preceded by 43 years of silence. Father died nigh a quarter century ago. My two brothers are still living.

Earlier in this biographic accounting, the query "Where was Perry laid to rest?" was wistfully posed—reflecting the fact that this detail has long been forgotten or lost or unknown. But...seemingly, a 12th-hour miracle!

On April 27, 1998, the writer received from Jerold E. Rowe of Fort Dodge, Iowa, the good news that Byam's gravesite has been found. Mr. Rowe, enlisting the talents of Sarah and Leon Ashlock, of Port Orchard, Washington, has forwarded photographs and date on where our soldierboy is buried: at Retsil Veterans Home Cemetery, which sits on a hill that overlooks a bay and Puget Sound Naval Shipyard across the water in Bremerton, home of the historic battleship, USS *Missouri.* Perry and wife Cornelia rest here in the Home Cemetery, Section 63, Lot 1-30, Graves 2 & 3 (across from WWI gravesites).

C. Perry Byam was admitted to Retsil Veterans Home on November 5, 1921, and spent most of his closing three months here, where his government Civil War stone reads:

Musn.
Commodore P. Byam
Co. D
24 Ia. Inf.

Joseph N. Fissell

Sept. 19, 1852 – Sept. 1, 1922

Unquestionably, he was among *the* youngest drummer boys of the Union Army and the war. Pressing age ten, with the war already sixteen months under way, and concerned it might end too soon, Joseph was exactly 9 years 11 months when on Aug. 19, 1862, he achieved his greatest ambition.

Of Darbyville in Ohio's south-central Pickaway County, Joseph Fissell had been born scarcely a decade earlier some ten miles to the southeast at Circleville, the shire town. He was the second youngest of five sons born to John and Katherine Diffendafer Fissell, Pennsylvania natives.[1] Sometime quite early in 1862 the Fissells moved to more rural Darbyville, where they lived fairly "close in" to town. With the onset of hostilities, patriotic fervor ran high, and, locally, many men and older boys had gone away in the first large wave of excitement. Throughout this initial exuberance John, their father, had successfully curbed most of his sons to a wait-and-see-if-it-lasts mindset; further, he appealed to their growing usefulness at home. By midsummer 1862, "Little Joe," for nigh six months, had been treasuring a not-so-secret aspiration—a decided role among fellow Buckeye volunteers. The particulars of how he sold himself are best recalled in Johnda T. Davis' "Joseph Fissell—Darbyville's Drummer Boy" in *Pickaway Quarterly* (Spring 1981, p. 15), and it is, by all odds, the most retellable vignette of Joseph's rather sparsely recorded life:

> *Several young men in Darbyville were caught up in a surge of patriotism. They marched up and down the village streets and dreamed of going. George, John and Wesley Fissell, John and Katherine's older sons, were ardent members of the group, while little Joseph tagged along and was permitted to play his drum to set the beat for their amateurish parading. Joseph, age nine, wanted to do whatever his big brothers were doing. On Aug. 19, 1862, John Fissell, Sr., finally took his sons to Columbus to Camp Chase to enlist. Little Joe went along, presumably, with his drum. The story passed down in the family was to the effect that the father, having bade his three elder boys farewell, looked around for his youngest, but nowhere was he to be found. Joe had convinced the recruiting officer (1) that he could play a drum well enough to be the company drummer and (2) he could take care of himself anywhere the Army*

went. Mr. Fissell had to return to Darbyville, leaving all four sons behind. Joe's mother behaved exactly as might have been expected. She was nearly frantic when she learned that the "baby" had been permitted to enlist. Katherine insisted that John return to Columbus and bring her boy home.

But it was too late. On the very next day, August 20, the new company set off for Kentucky, where they were immediately sent into battle. It was only small comfort that Joe was placed in Company A, 45th O.V.I., along with brother George, who could look after him. Not only brother George, but all the other men in A Company accepted Joe as their mascot...they almost fought for the privilege of carrying him on long marches.

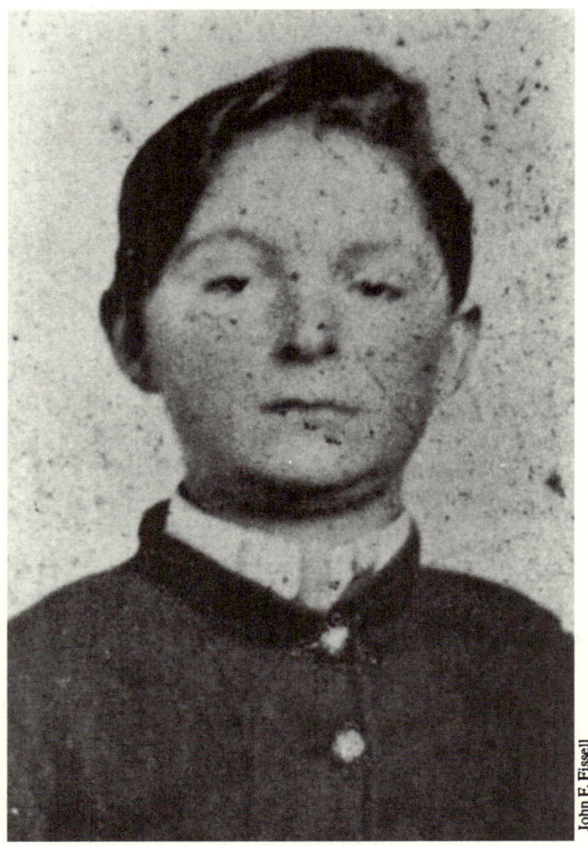

John F. Fissell

Joseph N. Fissell, age 10.

As a human speck in the Army of Kentucky and then in the Army of the Cumberland, drummer boy Fissell provided cadence as the 45th O.V.I. advanced about so:

-To Cynthiana, Ky. & to Covington, 8/20-8/24/62
-Defence of Cincinnati from E. Kirby Smith, 9/62
-Duty at Lexington, 10/62-1/63
-Operations against Cluke's forces in central Ky., 2/18-3/5
-Operations against Pegram, 3/22-4/1
-Action at Dutton's Hill, 3/20
-Expedition to Monticello, 4/26-4/27
-Operations in s.e. Kentucky until 5/12
-Skirmishes against Monticello, 4/28-5/2
-Operations against John Hunt Morgan, 7/2-7/25
-Operations against Scott's forces in E. Ky., 7/26-8/6
-Burnside's Campaign & Siege, 8/16-10/17
-At Cumberland Gap until 2/8/64
-At Mt. Sterling, Ky. until 4/6
-March to Knoxville & to Cleveland, Tenn., 4/6-5/5
-Battle of Resaca, 5/14-5/15
-Battles about Dallas, New Hope Church, Allatoona Hills, 5/25-6/6
-Operations about Marietta & against Kenesaw Mt., 6/10-7/2
-Siege of Atlanta, 7/22-8/25
-Battle of Jonesboro, 8/31-9/1
-Battle of Franklin, 11/30
-Battle of Nashville, 12/15-12/16
-Duty at Huntsville, Ala. until 3/65
-Mustered out, 6/12

Sometime shortly after the 45th had pursued Morgan, Little Joe was given his first and only furlough home. Katherine, heartened to have him home after eleven months' absence, renewed her own campaign to get Joseph "permanently re-assigned" to their home. At her insistence, Mr. Fissell harnessed up their horse and carriage for a third drive to Columbus, where he (& Joseph) were given an appointment with Union Governor David Tod. In Joseph's own words of this meeting (years later), we have:

"Do you want to go back with your Company, Son?"

"Yes, Sir, I do!" I told him.

"Well, we'll let you." (Father had to accept the decision with good grace.)

We do know from the 45th O.V.I.'s heavy itinerary of battles, marchings, skirmishings, sieges and regimen that Little Joe must have hosted a few misgivings in his heart well before it all became "history." Resuming Johnda Davis' account (others apparently do not exist, not even a bona fide obituary!),[3] we learn, for example:

...Joe was lost from his company for three weeks. At Kenesaw he found his captain wounded and helped his commander back to a hospital. There he found his brother John, of Co. C, 45th O.V.I. A few weeks later Joe caught up with Company A and his brother, George. John was seriously wounded and captured at Atlanta and spent the last war months in prison. John got wounded, then, at least twice. I could find no other record of the Fissell brothers undergoing serious misfortune.

Joe had a few stories to tell...of how an old black woman hid him in her hut when he was lost from his Company A and the Confederate Army was scouring the countryside. "In front of Atlanta I visited my brother on the skirmish line one day. 'Be careful!' he told me. 'Keep your head down.' Boylike, I became careless and looked over the trench rim. *Whizz!* A bullet embedded itself in a tree behind the rifle pit."

All in all, Little Joe had three years of hard campaigning. Like his brothers and elders, he foraged through the countryside for food, he slept on the bare ground, often cold and hungry, and saw his friends wounded and killed beside him.

Still a pre-teenager, musician-mascot Fissell had served thirty-four months upon his mustering-out with the regiment and a $75 bounty at Camp Harden, Tennessee, on June 15, 1865—a war record, indeed, that few others could rival. That day he stood 4' 10".[4] Back in Darbyville a few days later Little Joe, his brothers, and several other comrades were accorded their heroes' "welcome home" as the local band and folks from miles around gathered and cheered them down that (old-time) familiar street. But, as admirers applauded with home-grown accolades, a certain twinge of guilt surged up in the heroes' breasts, a tightness in their throats came on at thought of those 63 comrades of the 45th who were killed, at thought of the 276 taken by disease who would never see their homes again.[5]

Of Joseph's adult life—what he did for a living, his matrimonial and family history, rather little is known today. However, one individual has proven helpful: John F. Fissell, operator of a sand and gravel plant, a 30-year Circleville Township Trustee, currently serving as Pickaway County Commissioner, and last of the Fissell name in the county. In his Feb. 11, 1991 letter from Circleville that contains "Notes on the Fissell Family" we discover:

In the 1850 Census, John, 37, was listed as a fence maker, with real estate at $600; Catherine, 36; and six children—Wesley T., 12; John A., 10; Louisa, 8; George H., 6; Sarah A., 4; Adaline S., 2. John had bought Lot #10 Joseph Olds' 2nd Addition for $110 June 4, 1841. He sold "same to Thomas and Elizabeth Shower for $1000 Mar. 19, 1859." By the July 1860 Census the Fissells had a home at #526 Monroe Township and four more children—Joseph N., James S., Mary E., Catharine F. Wesley had *married Sept. 22, 1859, Mary Ridgway, 17, daughter of Lavica and James Ridgway, a Darbyville wagon maker.*

John A.'s Civil War service is recorded as Co. C., 20th O.V.I. Aug. 13, 1861-June 9, 1865—3 yrs. 9 mos. 27 days. Wesley T.'s is Co. H, 30th O.V.I. Aug. 19, 1861-Apr. 5, 1865 & Must. out at Goldsboro, N.C. And George, 18, a merchant, served Aug. 10, 1862-June 9, 1865 in Co. A, 45th O.V.I.

John and Catharine sold their farm of nine acres & 100 poles to Mitchell Timmons for $1000 on Jan. 28th 1862, "the Farm located in 5 points between the Dawson and Darbyville Roads (probably location of Monroe Twp. School). Very likely the family moved to Darbyville at this time and engaged in marketing dry goods and groceries [during & after the war]...After the return of his sons, John Sr. retired from his store to do farming. John Jr. and Joseph continued with it, Joseph clerking and John managing.[6] By the 1880 Census, Joseph N., 27, huckster, was still at home with his mother, then 64 (a widow since John Sr.'s passing Apr 10, 1875), and his brother, James, 24, who worked on their farmstead.

From Joseph's death certificate (sole other source the writer is aware of) a few facts can be gleaned or inferred. He lived in Cincinnati thirty-eight years, the last of these at 2517 Cook Street; he was or had been a bill collector, last employed by one Sara Greenfield; he died of a cerebral hemorrhage at 10:30 p.m. of his last day, leaving a widow, Minnie Curtis Fissell; he was buried at Evergreen Cemetery, Cincinnati. Strangely, he got no obituary but only a printed notice of his funeral "under the auspices of [Cincinnati's] George H. Thomas Post No. 13 at 1:30 p.m. Sept. 5, 1922, from his last residence; at 2:00 p.m. from G.A.R. Memorial Hall," where he had been a longtime comrade—without doubt, the pet of the post for his being the youngest by several years.

Joseph N. Fissell 's place in *Callow Brave and True* is assured, for at or soon after his enlistment he could well have been *the* youngest or next youngest in the Union Army for perhaps some three weeks to some three months. Eddie Black, of Hagerstown, Indiana, born May 30, 1853, was only 9 years 2 months 19 days on Fissell's first day of duty, remaining in uniform through Sept. 11, 1862, as the probable youngest for some 50 days until then. Joseph lived to within eighteen days of being seventy. He knew he was a strong contender for the honor of being the youngest, but he did not personally make that claim or play it up to any real extent.

Albert Corydon White

Nov. 15, 1852 – Feb. 1, 1928

From the first, Albert liked the idea of becoming a drummer boy, of leaving behind his third grade studies, and of going uniformed out into the world to help preserve the United States of America. By springtime 1861, then 8, Albert was seriously into percussion, of his own volition. But that volition may well have been inspired by his overhearing adult war talk and by the yearning hope that he might soon be in a Buckeye regiment. That he succeeded in achieving his enlistment so early—Nov. 14, 1861—appears phenomenal. Could this juvenile dream-come-true have been an unusual ninth birthday concession gift? Two pragmatic truths, at least, came to little Albert's rescue: the 64th O.V.I. was short of drummers and one of the 64th's officers happened to be First Lieutenant Cornelius C. White, the lad's own father. After anxious weeks of waiting and wondering, word came home to Marion, Ohio, one day in a letter to his mother, Frances Electa White, how that the 64th lacked two musicians. Should Albert be given his heart's desire and a chance to earn real federal pay? The mother had supposed that her son's service would lie months, at least, into the future. While we may be sure Frances had reservations (trepidations?) about Albert's becoming a musician for the Army of the Ohio, especially so soon, evidently Cornelius and other officers of the 64th won her over with promises for his protection and assurances about his care. It was arranged that Albert should demonstrate a variety of drumbeats. [Simply to lay eyes upon such a child 4' 6", blue eyes, light hair, doing his stuff with gusto was to plead his cause.] That 14th of November of '61 when Albert took the oath to serve, that final day *before* he turned age nine, he was officially set down as age "18"—a record in itself of at least nine full years of minority, the greatest "underage" recorded, to the best of this writer's knowledge.[1] Just a month later Albert was formally enrolled or mustered-in Dec. 14, 1861, at Camp Buckingham in Mansfield, Ohio, where the 64th O.V.I. had been organizing since early November. Immediately they moved to Louisville, Kentucky, and on Christmas they went to Bardstown. They were in the 20th Brigade and in the 6th Division, Army of the Ohio, at least until September. During February 7-March 13, after duty at Danville & Ball's Gap for a month, the 64th marched to Munfordsville, thence to Nashville. Again, they marched to Savannah, Tennessee, during March 29-April

The Story of Sherman's Brigade

Albert C. White, Co. D, 64th O.V.I., age 9 years 1 month.
December 14, 1861, his first day in uniform.
Standing 4' 6" tall, he poses with his drum and a revolver.

6, moving closer to combat with each step. At such times the pet of the regiment got little piggy-back rides across muddy runs or rivulets. Drummer Boy White's baptism of fire and largest battle experience suddenly engulfed him as he with the 64th O.V.I. tried to make a difference at Shiloh. The acrid smoke of burned black powder, the roar of cannonades, the staccatos of thousands of rattling musketry, the impetuous shoutings, the sighs of so many wounded tore away at the little fellow's feelings. As the ground shook and the sunlight became obscured, thoughts of home began to redeem themselves. But evenings he and his fellow musicians often entertained their troops. Albert was a favorite even within the sphere of musicians alone. With his comrades he advanced on and helped lay siege at Corinth, Mississippi, all during May. Then for the first twelve days of June they pursued the Rebs to Booneville.[2] Musician White drew regimental guard duty along the Memphis and Charleston Railroad until early August, still beating out a variety of drum calls. Admittedly the army life was strenuous for a nine-year-old, even if he did enjoy being catered to by admiring comrades. For them, Albert was an ornament, a morale booster, a reminder of youngsters back home. But the harsh routine and coarse cuisine took their toll on this miniature martinet. With mixed feelings on the part of all concerned and with nine months' service completed, arrangements for Albert White's (the name by which he enlisted) honorable discharge went forward. Saying heartfelt good-byes to scores of comrades, Albert, at 9 years 9 months, left the Army on Aug. 18, 1862, at Washington, D. C. and entrained directly for home.[3] In Marion, he resumed his schooling for a year before the family moved to Columbus, Ohio, in 1863. Here Albert schooled further and matured into his early twenties. In 1876 he moved to College Hill and began training for the ministry in the next three years, living at Amesbury, Massachusetts, during 1880-1.

It is believed Rev. White began his earliest preaching in Augusta, Maine, during 1881-4. Here he fell in love with a local girl, Miss Harriet "Hattie" Ellen Welch (Oct. 25, 1861-May 5, 1933). On Jan. 1, 1883, Albert, 30, and Hattie, 21, were married in Augusta by the Rev. A. J. Patterson of Roxbury, Massachusetts. They were to have eight children: Albert Corydon, Jr., born Nov. 22, 1883; Margaret Frances, b. May 4, 1885; Merritt Oberlin, b. Apr. 26, 1887; Richard Grant, Dec. 11, 1888; Corinne, Jan. 6, 1893; Horace Hudson, Feb. 28, 1895; Walter Cornelius, Dec. 24, 1896, and Helen, Aug. 29, 1898. The Whites did apparently move often, as Albert's church assignments changed. From Augusta, Maine, they moved to Stuart, Iowa, for the period 1884-85; then they returned to live in Waterville, Maine, for three years, 1885-88; they spent the next triennium, 1888-91, at Amesbury, Massachusetts; then they ministered over in Pepperell 1891-95; next, their ministry rotated to Ware, some fifty miles southeast, 1895-1899. Here, he was pastor for the Unitarian Church, while residing at 84 Church Street and later at 29 Pleasant.[4]

Upon leaving Ware, the Whites returned to Pepperell, where he pastored 1899- 1903; for at least two years Rev. White was called to serve at Haverhill, living during this tour 1903-05 at 4 Silver Street. It was early in his pastoral return to Ohio—Oct. 16, 1905—that he first applied for a Civil War pension, complaining of rheumatism, lumbago, bronchitis and heart disease. His physical profile was then reported as 5' 1/2", 162 lbs., gray eyes, light brown hair, and a tattoo on his right arm—Star, Co. D., Sword, A. W., 1852, drum & sticks, spray of flowers.[5] Rev. White's ministry took his family to Hamilton, Ohio during 1905-09. Located so close to scenes of his youth, Marion and Columbus, he surely revisited these points. In fact, Columbus proved to be their next home and ministry for 1909-13. Then, late in 1913, he, Hattie, and their youngest—Corinne, Horace, Walter and Helen—moved to Orono, Maine, where they lived for at least four years. Their son, Walter C. White, entered the Military Academy at West Point in 1918, graduated, pursued a U. S. Army career.

The Whites apparently enjoyed Maine's four seasons—weatherwise, a veritable smorgasbord. As late as 1927 they were living in Denmark, Maine, with the George L. Wentworths (believed husband of their daughter, Margaret.) Now retired, Albert, 75, in failing health, chose New Port Richey, Florida, for his retirement. Having lived here but a few months, he succumbed to "Mitral insufficiency" and artereosclorosis just before sunrise of his last day earthside. He was buried the next day afternoon in Orlando.[6] Within two months Hattie moved to RR #10, Cincinnati, where she began receiving her widow's pension on Certificate 160 4459. Surviving Albert some five years, Hattie made her last home at 4929 Wallingford Street, Pittsburgh, Pennsylvania.

We remember Albert C. White as one of the most mobile (on the move) of his generation; also, he confirms that Ohio was rather wealthy in pre-ten-year-olds who rendered Civil War service.

At one point in his life Albert did get national attention in an item of interest to Youngstown, Ohio, readers that appeared in the September 1904 issue of *The Ladies Home Journal.* A letter had been sent to the *Journal* asking the identity of the youngest soldier enlisted in the Civil War. Replying to that inquiry, Franklin B. Wiley wrote in to the *Journal:*

> *The long controversy over the question was at last settled in favor of the Reverend Albert C. White, born in Newark, Ohio, on Nov. 15, 1853 [sic], and enlisted as a drummer boy in Co. D, 64th Ohio Volunteer Infantry...when he was only eight years old. The next youngest soldier appears to have been Eli Wright of Youngstown, Ohio, who enlisted when he was only twelve. [Co. K, 82nd O.V.I.]*[7]

William Orlanda Neubold Lea

Sept. 17, 1855 – May 6, 1928

It is well that this biographical review depends as much as it does upon genealogical data, family records, a census report, and epistolary testimonials from next of kin. History herself, scarcely aware of little Lea and his tiny role in the War for Constitutional Liberty could hardly be expected to have taken note of *this* veteran. Somebody should.[1]

W.O.N. Lea personifies the essence of our youngest study for his exceptional youth; by his serendipitous sheer presence he rewards us, conferring bonuses;[2] he occasions a refulgence of twilight truths probably long obscured. Although there *well* could have been a *few* other Civil War veterans (homeguardsmen) born in 1855, Lea remains the only one to surface in the past quarter century. His immediate ancestry allows us to notice a family who devoted three generations to the Confederate forces—outstanding and exceptional!

William's birth at Thunder Bolt, Georgia, is affirmed in the 1900 census of Pender County, North Carolina. His father, William Pell Lea, Jr., (Aug. 1824 at Smithville, N.C.—Dec. 1, 1876, at Charleston, S.C.) had married Miss Sophronia Carter (Nov. 19, 1836, at Charleston, S.C.—Aug.. 24, 1872, at Charleston) in January 1855 at Charleston. William's paternal grandparents, William Pell Lea, Sr. (1789 at London, England—July 24, 1861, at Charleston, S.C.) and Sarah Louise Conyers (1794, Smithville, N.C.-Dec. 18, 1858, at Charleston), were married in 1811 at Smithville (today Southport, N.C.). Sarah was the daughter of John Conyers (1750-1812) and Sarah Bernard Conyers (b. 1759), who married in 1788.[3]

In his June 24, 1992 letter from Hampstead, North Carolina, Lowell S. Avery, Sr., 60, heightens credibility with his extensive knowledge of family and local history:

> *I'm a grandson of W.O.N. Lea and 1932 native of Hampstead. My folks are Elizabeth Sephronia Lea Avery (b. 1904) and John Paul Avery (1902-65). Capt. John Conyers was somewhat of a local hero, since he was an officer in the Revolution, Captain of the port of Smithville and its first Port Master. He was Constable, Secretary at Smithville Academy, Collector of Revenues (Import Duties—22nd Distr.), and Clerk of the Brunswick County Court.*
>
> *Granddad (W.O.N.L.'s father), Wm. Pell Lea, Jr., was a Captain with the Fourth South Carolina Infy., C.S.A. while his Grandfather Wm. Pell*

Lea, Sr., at 72, was in the C.S.N. In fact, he was pilot of the Savannah Steamer Isabel that carried Major Anderson and his U. S. troops from Fort Sumter to U. S. vessels off shore (verified in Charleston Daily Courier of that date—Apr. 15, 1861.[4] W.O.N. Lea's Uncle John Conyers Lea, a Confederate Balloon pilot, C.S.A., was captured in January 1862, and imprisoned at Fort Delaware. He was exchanged April 1863 and died May 10. Buried in Petersburg, Va., he has a headstone memorial in Magnolia Cemetery, Charleston, S.C. Age 48, he died of diarrhea.[5] Then—more importantly—there was another uncle, a Captain Carter (Sophronia's brother), who was skipper of the Georgia-owned CSS Greyhound (out of Savannah), on which he (W.O.N.L.) went to sea as Cabin Boy in 1862. Thus did he serve in the Georgia Navy, sometimes referred to as "the Mosquito Fleet."[6]

"Willie," as he was known earlier in life (& according to his Confederate pension application), was wounded May 7, 1862, while not yet age seven. My mother and aunts told us that he sustained a serious injury to his head, a shell fragment that required him to wear a silver plate

William Lea at age 45 in 1900, with his son Hampton, age 12.

attached to his skull, that they could feel the screws holding it in place under his skin—apparently part of his cranium missing. At age 57, Grandfather drew a Confederate pension from 1912 until his death. (The 1860 census at Lynchburg, S.C., verifies him as age 5 with his mother and father and a brother, James, age 2.[7]

Yes, he belonged to a veterans' society (U.C.V.). Pictures show him wearing several ribbons as a delegate to reunions, I assume, at Wilmington 17 miles away. He has a daughter living, Eva Mae Lea Riggs.

Willie Lea's C.S.A. service, while not formalized with the customary (required?) paperwork—(One questions if his Uncle Skipper Carter's*Greyhound* ever kept a log, which, had they been captured, could have been instrumental to the crew's undoing), is of real insightful value to our study. Would *anyone deny* this youngster his C.S.A. status? What can be conceded is that it was brief. Since Willie became a Cabin Boy in 1862—likely in March, as earliest—and, since his wound was critical enough to require skilled attentions promptly (which evidently he got), we can safely assume this injury terminated his service aboard *Greyhound.* Worth noticing is his age on that injurious day—6 years 7 months 20 days—, categorically (?), the war's youngest to sustain a wound from the enemy. We calculate W.O.N.L.'s entire tour of duty to be approximately three months.

It would be Dec. 17, 1883, when Willie O. N. Lea, 28, took for wife Miss Eva Elizabeth Gaskill (July 25, 1866-Mar. 5, 1917), a native of coastal New Hanover County, just to the south of Hampstead. Their eight children were/are Bessie Lea (May 7, 1886), who died an infant and was buried on Zeke's Island; William Henry Lea, born Aug. 22, 1888; (Joseph) Hampton Lea, born Jan. 18, 1891; Beulah Isabel Lea, born July 6, 1894; James Ferni Lea, Born Sept. 17, 1897 (?); Elizabeth Sefronia Lea Avery, born Oct. 27, 1904; Mamie Idell Lea, born Nov. 18, 1906; and Eva Mae Lea Riggs, born Nov. 21, 1910.

"Willie" or "Bill" Lea lived for about ten years on Zekes' Island and was a river pilot on the Cape Fear River. About 1890 he moved his wife and two children to Hampstead, where he earned his living as a fisherman. Here, too, in the 20th century he drew his Confederate pension from North Carolina. Perhaps our best closing thought might well be a unifying experience that has fine-tuned the Lea Family for many generations to the present, the Masonic Order. W. Pell Lea, Sr., a member of Solomon's Lodge #1, Charleston; W. Pell Lea, Jr., of this same lodge (oldest in U.S.); W.O.N.L. of St. John's Lodge #1, Wilmington (oldest in N. C.); all his sons were Masons; some 15 grand- and great-grandsons *are* Masons today.[8] He was laid to rest at Topsail Presbyterian Church Cemetery at Hampstead, North Carolina.

We acknowledge this Cabin Boy of the old "Mosquito Fleet" off the Carolinas and Georgia as one of *the very youngest ever* to have had a vital though tiny role in the war.

James Edwin Powell II

June 30, 1850 – June 29, 1929

James E. Powell II was "hands down" the youngest of all Pine Tree Staters to have done service or become embroiled in Our Tragic War of the Sixties, being at the time age ten. He remains a quintessential example of at least three truths to emerge from this nationwide investigation of those *tender* "soldierlings" who performed a tangible service, however humble, in The Boys' War: (1) that sometimes *the* youngest boys served without any formal enlistment papers or kept records *because of their extreme youth and their unit's solemn commitment that they should not be caught as underagers;* (2) that, having no tangible or official paperwork, these underlings have not achieved the canon of acceptance by professional historians or by military authorities generally, *even though they surely did with their comrades;* (3) that those lads who were of the very youngest echelon were *primarily* valets or servants to their commissioned officer fathers and, *secondarily,* mascots and/or musicians. A salient example and parallel case to Maine's "Jimmy" Powell is Washington's (& Indiana's) "Corporal" Willie H. Bush (b. Sept. 21, 1857!), valet to his father, Capt. Asahel K. Bush, a veteran of the Fourth Indiana Light Artillery Battery, when they were stationed at Elmira, New York.

Enough ancestral data and eventual legendary fragments have survived via family tradition, oral and written, to sketch in a fairly credible background for our Jimmy Powell. Today, some three or four generations *since* are in basic agreement about the James E. Powells I and II. James Senior, a native of England, came of a wealthy English family. Allegedly, a sort of black sheep, he was given a dowry and sent to America that he might settle here. By tradition, he had a trunk of papers believed to contain records on the family in England, which, according to James II (Junior), a preacher/minister absconded with when his father died. The younger James, consequently, distrusted clergymen all the rest of his life, feeling they robbed him of his birthright.[1] Born in 1806, James E. Powell was first married in 1833 to Fannie Nickerson, 20, who was born in 1813 in England. Where they lived we have only a clue, for tragedy befell this couple: Fannie and their several children were killed by Indians and their log cabin burned. Returning home from a scouting mission, James found his family slaughtered.

Perhaps to attempt to refocus his life and thus somewhat assuage his grief, James enlisted Aug. 4, 1847, to be a private in Company A, Ninth U. S. Infantry, during the Mexican War. So well did he adapt to the discipline and strictures of combat, with instances of exemplary bravery noted, that within a year or by Aug. 28, 1848, he was made a sergeant. Although the relative contentment of this military regimen appealed to him, James returned to a civilian life and chose to try himself once more as a family man, *if* the opportunity presented itself. He settled in the hinterlands of Somerset County, Maine, on the upper reaches of the Kennebec River near its confluence with the Dead River, some fifty miles north of Skowhegan. As a war veteran he acquired acreage mainly just by living there at "Hangtown," a section of the remote hamlet known as The Forks Plantation. Here he met and courted a Canadian lady, Mary Ann Hunter (1832-1900), daughter of Frank and Fannie Nicholson Hunter. They were married at The Forks Sept. 9, 1849, by William Hanson, J.P. Their children were James Edwin II, Winfield Scott (Oct. 3, 1853-Sept. 20, 1917), and Albert Tracy (Oct. 3, 1855-Nov. 29, 1869), all born at home in The Forks Plantation, where they prospered as a family nearly six years.[2] *Prospered* may be somewhat an overstatement, for it was not an easy life—wresting a tolerable living from the land and animals. Money was scarce; luxuries, few. The only visible indulgence James permitted himself was joining the Masonic Order, but this did not occur until after the fourth year of his marriage. Records of Keystone Lodge at Solon indicate Brother Powell had begun in the work and participated in a few of the rites. But on June 7, 1855, word came of his appointment as 2nd lieutenant in the Regular Army. Given that the home life was proving a struggle, that the domesticity fell short of ideal, within seven weeks he left his fireside—left it "for good," although *at the time,* this probably was not his intention. Additionally, fate decreed he should never return. That July, Lt. Powell—taking little James, *just 5,* and leaving Winfield (18 mos.) with Mary Ann and their yet unborn Albert—reported for duty. While this "move" guaranteed steady income, it effectually broke them up (physically and emotionally) as a family.

The precise itinerary of the James E. Powells, upon their departure from Maine, though unknown today, rather soon took them west to duty stations in Tennessee, Arkansas, Texas and Indian Territory. Father Powell *may have* made provision in two particulars—a small allotment (partial support) for his estranged family and hiring a Negress or "mammy" that Junior might have a mother figure. The boy's daily routine, not always predictable, was overshadowed by his father's career moves from time to time—temporary camps, scouting missions, living at frontier forts. James made 1st lieutenant on Dec. 8, 1856. Jimmy, nearly 10, and his father, 53, were in Texas when on Sept. 3, 1860, Mary Ann was granted her divorce in the fall term of the Supreme Judicial Court at Norridgewock, Maine, her plea being that her husband had left without making *any* provision for her and the two younger children.[3] At about this time Lt. Powell was rotated to Fort Arbuckle on the Washita River in southern Indian Territory. Probably it was here that the second most harrowing incident of Jimmy's military childhood took place. Passed down by

Powell descendants, this account is found in "A Boy Goes to War" by Donna B. McAllister of Caratunk, Maine, an educator and historian in Somerset County:[4]

> *During a scouting mission Powell's regiment, along with Jimmy, stopped by a small stream to eat lunch. A band of Indians attacked the resting soldiers. Jimmy's pinto pony was tied to a nearby tree. His father shouted for him to cut the reins, as there was no time for him to untie it. In his haste, Jimmy mistakenly cut upwards toward his face with a knife and struck his left eye. He was badly injured, but managed to get astride the pony. Father Powell saw his son's plight, but, with no time to stop, he grabbed the boy's bridle and kept the pony beside him as whooping Indians followed in hot pursuit. The weary soldiers somehow escaped and made it back to their camp. Jimmy's eye was cared for and eventually it healed, though it would be weaker and give him trouble the rest of his life.*

It is believed that Jimmy got tutorial instruction while in the West, but how much and from whom is not known. The classroom of the Great Outdoors, the U. S. Army, and his enduring role as valet to his commissioned officer father combined to teach him tougher lessons in life: foresight, planning, survival, bravery, and interdependability. Since Jimmy had already been in service as valet-waiter to his father for over two years when Fort Sumter's bombardment greeted the dawn of Apr. 12, 1861, he is entitled in *this* study to the distinction of being *the first of the youngest Civil War soldiers to be on duty*—10 years, 9 months, 13 days. And he held the distinction for one week until April 19 when he was displaced by Thomas L. F. Hubler, of Warsaw, Indiana, a drummer boy of the 12th Indiana Infantry, who that day was 9 years, 7 months. But, of course, *no one knew this* or gave much thought to it—certainly not Jimmy Powell. *His youngest age during the Civil War* is the single most alluring fact for purposes of Jimmy's key place in *Callow Brave and True;* yet we note in passing that his earliest military valet status reached back to when he was barely eight.

On June 11, 1861, Lt. Powell was promoted to Captain, Company F, 1st U. S. Infantry Regiment. With this promotion there came inevitably many "Good-byes" to those with whom Powell had served since summer 1855, for Capt. Powell was, within a month or so, transferred to the 13th Missouri Infantry, then newly organized.[5] In September it was designated the 25th Missouri and attached to the Department of Missouri until March 1862. The 25th were in the 1st Brigade, 6th Division, Army of the Tennessee, until July 1862.[6] Therefore, the Powells were in Missouri until mid-March 1862, much of their effort given to training recruits, instilling discipline, guarding railroads. The 25th Missouri were ordered to Pittsburg Landing, Tennessee. Later that week Capt. Powell got word that he had just (3/24/62) been promoted to Major.

We are fortunate to have his entirely probable last letter to his family, long since an heirloom, for certain:

Army of West Tennessee
March 31, 1862

Mary,

By the merest accident in the world, I received your letter. I am very glad to hear that Win and Tracy are well, and good little fellows. I should very much like to see them. Give my love to them and tell them that I don't forget them.

It is very easy to find fault—I have no money. I have not for some time.

We are now in front of the enemy near the Alabama line, and, provided I live through the coming fight, I will send you money as soon as I get it. That may be two months yet!

Jimmy is with me. He sends his love to you and Win and Tracy. I cannot tell you when I shall write again. The difficulties of sending letters is very great at present. When I get pay, then I shall write—I congratulate you! Jim sends his love to the baby.

Yours,
James E. Powell

It is evident Powell had real premonitions he might not survive what promised to be a major killing-field. On the eve of the battle, hours before its name became known for sure, he entrusted to his friend, Capt. E. W. Dimmock, Jr., of Newark, New Jersey, the immediate care of his son, his papers, and personal effects, in the event of his own demise. It was well he did so. For what happened, we go to Lt. Col. Robert F. Van Horn, Hdqtrs. 25th Missouri Inf'y—his account written near Pittsburg Landing, Apr. 9, 1862, as reported in Series I Vol. X Part I *Official Records*:

> *...The regiment occupied the right of the 1st Brigade under Col. Peabody, acting as Brig. General, and had the honor to open the fight on the 6th, the attack being made on its front at 3:00 a.m. By Peabody's order 3 companies—Capt. Schmitz's Co. B, Evans' Co. E, and Dill's Co. H—under Maj. Powell were dispatched to engage the enemy's advance, which was successfully done until re-enforced by the 21st Mo. under Col. Moore. The fighting now became general and heavy, and I was ordered to support with the whole regiment. The enemy were now within half a mile of the encampment, where they were checked and held till near 7:00 a.m., when we fell back to our encampment line. We made another stand. The fighting was very severe until 8:00 a.m., when we were compelled to fall back...on the Division, which had formed a battle line on an elevation in our rear. By this time our 25th had become badly cut up, but we rallied and took position on the R of the 12th Michigan, but with loss of several of my most valuable officers. The fighting became most determined...for three hours. The enemy, thrice repulsed, finally moved to our left.*

It was in this part of the action that Major James E. Powell, a most valuable officer and brave soldier, fell mortally wounded, and Sgt. Matthew Euler, color-bearer, was killed, clinging to the staff until it had to be disengaged from his grasp by Sgt. Simmons. My command was then detached to Col. Hildebrand, acting brigadier-general, where it remained...I must be permitted to bear testimony to the distinguished bravery of Major Powell, who fell in the hottest of the battle, cheering on his men.[7]

The massive slaughter and mayhem that so shocked our nation the ensuing fortnight is captured in the Apr. 6, 1968 words of Lena B. Merrill, of Caratunk, Maine, great-granddaughter of Major Powell:

This battle brought home to the entire country the full horror of the great war.... After evacuating Nashville Gen. Albert Johnston withdrew his Confederate Army to Corinth, Miss., a key point on the Memphis-Chattanooga RR, that carried western produce to Southerners in the East. Grant's hopes of striking a decisive blow were dimmed when Gen. Halleck diverted part of his army to Mississippi River fighting...Grant's forces camped by Shiloh Church near Pittsburg Landing on the Tennessee border across from Corinth. Johnston struck the Union Army at dawn Apr. 6, 1862. In a day-long battle Grant's forces came perilously close to defeat. A. S. Johnston bled to death and the fields were strewn with dead and dying. Grant, reinforced all night by fresh troops under Generals Buell and Lew Wallace, resumed the fighting at dawn the 7th, rallying Union troops and forcing the Confederates back to Corinth. Too battered and exhausted to pursue, the Union had 13,000 casualties, with 1754 killed outright, while Confederate losses were 11,000, with 1728 killed. Many wounded would die in the ensuing week(s).[8]

History and records indicate Maj. Powell was killed close by Shiloh Church between 8:00 and 11:00 a.m. The night of the 6th was made more miserable with heavy rains, for many of the severely injured lay where they had fallen...victims of a protracted hell only they could know and screech to.

Jimmy, 11, alone, homeless, grief-stricken, suddenly found his military career ended. Now came the challenge of getting him united with the rest of his family. Capt. E. W. Dimmock sent him to Newark, New Jersey, to live at the Dimmocks pending efforts to locate the Powells and get word to them. The Captain's father sent an open letter to the Governor of Maine, Israel Washburn, published in *The Bangor Whig:*

Newark, N.J., Aug. 5, 1862

To His Excellency, Governor of Maine:
Dear Sir:

While my son, Capt. E. W. Dimmock, was at Pittsburg Land, Capt. James E. Powell, Co. F, 1st Infantry, U.S.A., acting Major of the 25th

Missouri Volunteers, placed his son, a lad of some 14 [sic] *years, in my son's charge in case he was killed.*

The Major was killed and the lad says he is from Forks, Maine, on the Dead River [sic]. *He says he left with his father at the age of 7, and only remembers the name of "Burnham," who "kept a hotel at Forks, Maine." I find no post office of the name in the books of the P.O. The young lad is very intelligent, and if he has friends they should know his condition. Without doubt, he is entitled to back pay from the Government.*[9]

I have the lad with me and am doing for him all I can. His father's commission &c, are in charge of my son, Capt. D.

Any information or advice you may give me will be duly acknowledged, and very much oblige your obedient servant.

E. W. Dimmock

It can only be theorized how Mary Ann (Powell) Stafford at length got this news, but likely it was relayed to her by an old friend and family associate, Abner Coburn.[10] It was late fall, perhaps early winter 1862, when Jimmy journeyed home by stagecoach. His arrival home—one of the three or four most indelible memories of his life—he was to vividly recall ever after:

I remember the stage driver stopping in the yard and a woman come rushing out of the house. The driver asked me—"Jimmy, do you know where you are? Do you know this lady?" I looked at her for quite some time and, finally, I noticed a small mole on the side of her neck that looked familiar, "Yes," says I, "I know *her . . .* She's my mother!"

By September 1860 James' mother, Mary Ann, had married Obadiah Stafford, whom she named guardian of her three boys. It was Obadiah who arranged with E. W. Dimmock to have Jimmy sent home. With Obadiah's own early demise (11/30/63), Mary applied for and obtained legal guardianship of her three sons. Her Civil War orphans' (not widow's) pension commenced May 9, 1864, retroactive to Major Powell's date of death and to be terminated Oct. 3, 1871, on son Albert's 16th birthday. Rather tragically, by her brief second marriage, James' mother became ineligible for a widow's pension for all her thirty-seven remaining years. She married a third time, July 1, 1866, at the Forks, to William Adams, son of Thomas and Ann Jane Neill (spelling?) Adams. Their four children were Ardelia B. (Mrs. C. C.) Stewart; William T.; Olive (Mrs. Oscar) Clark; Eliza J. (Mrs. Charles) Foss. We trust she did a "parcel" of grandmothering. Mary Ann H.P.S. Adams died July 2, 1900, at age 67 years 11 months.

The rest of the Jimmy Powell story follows a normal course of events. On Oct. 25, 1870, after wooing and winning her, he married Miss Lizzie Turner Bates (July 7, 1854-Apr. 8, 1919), the daughter of David (Jr.) and Jane Potter Adams Bates, in her native Bingham, Maine. Their twelve children were Tracy Franklin (1871-1934), who married Cora Adams; Mary Elizabeth (1873-1890), who married Benjamin Russell; Eugene David (1875-1961), who married (1) Minnie McGivern & (2) Addie Kelley; James Edwin III (1876-?) who married Florence Williams; Evelyn Stewart (1879-1971), who married John Redmond; William Henry (1881-1903), who married Mary Kelley; Agnes Annie (1884-1905), who married John Durgin; Alfred Allen (1888-1962), who married (1) Lois, (2) Ada E. Martin, (3) Elizabeth; Winfield Scott (1893 - ?), twice married; infant who died; Alta Mildred (1896- ?), who married Guy Beane, and Avis Althea (Alta's twin), who married Morris Martin.[11]

As for "Jimmy" Powell, he lived out his 79 years on his "Hangtown" acreage, often given to hunting (gunning) and fishing when not tending or working with his favorite horse "Ned." While it is true that descendants, especially Mrs. Lena Beane Merrill (6/2/1914 - 6/12/1986) of Caratunk, have preserved this father-son story—reflective of many others [the last such duo being the Jellisons of Clifton, Maine—John, 47, of Co. D, 18th Maine 1815-1905 and Melvin S., 16, of Co. B, 6th Maine 1846-1947], there is no evidence to indicate that Maine's James E. Powell II ever played up or "traded on" his actual Civil War veteran status. He and Lizzie are buried near his brother, Albert T., in a small secluded cemetery in the Forks. (We trust, however, that a diminutive Old Glory flutters over his gravesite in the Forks Cemetery nearby other family resting-places.) Convinced Jimmy is entitled to recognition as Maine's youngest to go to the Great Cruel War, we are pleased today, Apr. 6, 1997 (135th anniversary of the largest battle ever fought to that time in the Americas) to recognize him in his rightful place among these elite ranks.

James Edwin Powell II, Maine's youngest.

Donna B. McAllister

Mancil V. Root

June 18, 1854 – July 6, 1929

It was one of those fortunate flukes of happenstance that he should have been named Mancil or *"little man."* How prophetic! Incredibly late in his arrival—he was still just six at the time of Fort Sumter—Mancil was born at Cleveland, Ohio, the son of Augustus (1821-1863) and Marcia A. Hanchett Root (1826-?), native Buckeyes. For many years until his passing, Mancil enjoyed quite widely, and certainly in the G.A.R, the distinction of being known as "the youngest veteran of the Civil War," a title he was worthy of, arguably and actually. He does appear to have been the latest born soldierboy to have served in the Union Army or in an actual regiment (on either side) above and beyond homeguardsmanships. How did this extraordinary service arise?

Feb. 1, 1864, went down as a remembrance-worthy date in the history of Sheboygan, Wisconsin, for this was the time and place where "Manny" Root first volunteered himself and became somebody. Callow though he surely was, conscience-wise, the lad was fully aware of the considerable services already rendered by his father and older brother. Augustus, a cooper by trade, had enlisted Sept. 7, 1861, at Plymouth (his hometown), Wisconsin, for three years, had served the 8th Wisconsin Infantry as a soldier in Company B and Head Musician, had contracted typhoid fever and died July 29, 1863, of congestive chills at Camp Sherman, near Black River, Mississippi, and been buried at the Messengers Ford Cemetery nearby—a veteran of major actions at Frederickstown, Missouri; New Madrid; Island No. Ten; Siege of Corinth; Iuka; Jackson; Assault and Siege of Vicksburg; and Richmond, Louisiana.[1] Brother Wilber M. Root, 17 (though set down as 18), of Plymouth, had lost no time getting into Company C, 4th Wisconsin Cavalry, on Apr. 23rd, 1861, at Sheboygan, a three-year obligator. Mustered-in July 2 by Captain McIntyre at Camp Utley in Racine, Wilber —gray eyes, dark hair, 5' 7"—had already learned to be a cooper from Augustus. Though furloughed frequently for sickness and several times erroneously charged with desertion, Pvt. W. M. Root did take part in engagements at Camp Brisland (Apr. 12-13, '63); at Olive Branch (May 3, '64); and at Brashear City, Louisiana, where he became a prisoner until paroled. But his parole was declared null and he was ordered to his unit, ultimately being discharged July 16, 1864, on expiration of service at Morganza by order of General Canby.[2]

When on Feb. 1, 1864, a general call for volunteers came to Sheboygan County, orders were issued that unless fifty more men were obtained from the county, a draft would be ordered. Men signed up rapidly at the rally, but they totaled only forty-eight. "Manny" Root, not quite 9 years 7 months, that moment took in the situation, became inspired, and bounded to the platform, his face flushed and a hand held high. "*I'll* go!" he yelled, as cheers drowned out his high soprano. Captain Jerome Greeley, in charge, protested initially, as did perhaps a few others. But Manny, intuiting destiny, waged a hard holding action and prevailed, for he was a robust lad who had thumped a drum from early childhood and had already joined the Plymouth Town Band. However, there remained the delicate matter of winning approval from his mother, Marcia, then newly widowed, struggling to keep her family—Jane A., 17; Mancil and Caselon (twins?); Ashley, 5 (a daughter)—together under the burden of a $400 mortgage. With Captain Greeley's intercession, it was pointed out to the distracted mother that the 36th Wisconsin might well never leave her state [of course, they did!] and that she would receive Manny's $500 bounty money—a veritable godsend to her financial woes. Late that day amid promises aplenty, Manny Root was allowed to join Company B as a drummer boy. His actual enlistment took place that February 29 at Fond du Lac, where one J. F. Brooks signed him up for three years. Mancil's description on that day? Hazel eyes, brown hair, light complexion, a farmer, age 17 and 5' 0".[3] A farmer! 17! 5' O"!—perhaps "on paper." That particular day he was 9 years 8 months 11 days old and of commensurate height. Truth got some stretching several times over that day in Fond du Lac. Let us bear in mind that Mancil was 75 years 18 days on July 6, 1929, his last day of life.

Scarcely more than two months later Mancil found himself in the Battle of the Wilderness, his first bitter trauma, where some 5600 of his comrades were killed outright and 21,463 more were wounded. Detailed to carry supplies to the front line, he got into the thick of action. Wounded in the shoulder, he was able to get to a Federal ambulance. At Deep Bottom, Virginia, in August, Pvt. Root was captured by the Confederates. At sight of such a boy about to be sent to Libby Prison, the Reb officer broke down and wept. Though Manny protested that he should *not* be given special privileges, he was allowed partial liberty in Richmond and shortly exchanged with other prisoners.[4] Mancil got back to his regiment in time to provide percussional services in all their varied renditions for the 36th Wisconsin well before their efforts at Boydton Plank Road (Hatcher's Run) in late October. Sometimes the drummers from sundry regiments would all meet for a general practice or to rehearse for some ceremony. Root helped provide cadence for the 36th at Dabney's Mills in early February. His weary feet felt the Virginia terrain, for day by day he lived the entire Appomattox Campaign. He had witnessed the collapse of Petersburg. He played his humble role/roll all along the retreating path/pathos of Lee's valorous A.N.V. vestiges—so far decimated had they by this time become. Certain place names—Sailor's Creek, High Bridge,

Wilber M. Root, 19, and Mancil, 10.

Mancil V. Root, age 11.

Both photos courtesy of Wisconsin State Historical Society

Farmville, Appomattox Court House—would endure with a lifelong indelibility all their own in his consciousness. The desperation and courage of Lee's men were far from lost upon this impressionable youngster's conscience. He, too, "took in" the emotive impact of their surrender and stacking of arms. The sense of its epic sweep he would carry in his heart to his dying day. With his 36th Wisconsin and hundreds of other regiments, Mancil Root marched into Washington, D. C., during early May 1865. Absent on sick furlough from May 17 for twenty-five days or more, Manny missed being in the Grand Review of the Army of the Potomac on May 23. He had survived—narrowly enough—where 342 of his fellows of the 36th twice and thrice his age had not.[5]

Completing nearly seventeen months, the heft of them in heavy battle service, Manny Root was discharged that July 12 at Jeffersonville, Indiana, "by reason of General Order #26 from the Headquarters of the Army of the Tennessee,"[6] rather than being mustered out that very same day with his regiment at Louisville, Kentucky, which, after all, lay only a mile south across the Ohio River!

Back in Plymouth, Wisconsin, Mancil, now eleven, got some schooling and became a vital credit to his embattled mother. He liked horses. For perhaps nearly a score of years he ran a livery stable business at Ripon. For longer yet he was a commercial traveling salesman. On Apr. 30, 1896, he married Ida C. Barnhart (June 3, 1868-1939), the fourth daughter of Henry A. (July 18, 1815-Apr. 12, 1880) and Martha Hoover Barnhart of Harrison County, Iowa. For the last thirty-five years of his life Mancil increasingly became a Hawkeye Stater; for his third and final twenty-five years he and Ida were citizens of Cedar Rapids. Here he became a member of St. James Methodist Church and a comrade of T. Z. Cook Post 235, G.A.R. More than ever before, the word gradually spread of Comrade Root's youthful military endeavors until he reached near celebrity status, becoming nationally known at the 60th National Encampment at Des Moines during Sept. 19-25, 1926, as the youngest Civil War veteran alive—an incredibly fair assessment, especially when given that he had been repeatedly a candidate for injury near the front for months.

Fortunately, we have a most helpful Feb. 12, 1993, letter from Cedar Rapids' Richard D. Harman, 59, a former art teacher, a Christmas card designer, a harpsichord and pipe organ builder and organist, a vocalist in the First Presbyterian choir and at the Jewish Temple Friday evening services, a furniture maker and stained-glass window craftsman, who often does painting, papering and carpentry, and a confirmed bachelor. Richard, being a grandnephew by his great-Aunt Ida's marriage to Mancil, brings us gratifyingly closer to our drummer boy, his life, and the saga of his drum:

> *I owe much of what I learned about "Uncle" Mancil to my father, A. Ray Harman (1889 - 1955), whose mother, Annice Elizabeth Barnhart (Mrs. Spear Tipton) Harman (1858-1911) had six sisters—Emma Bucklin, Mary Lehman, Annice, Ida, Millie Griffin (1871-1947), Genevra Sutleff (1873-1943), Effie (1875-1879). I'm the youngest of A. Ray and Helen M. Collingwood (1896-1971) Harman's seven children. As a small boy I listened to Dad tell the story of Uncle Mancil, the little drummer boy relinquished by his mother (near poverty), thinking Manny would be fed and clothed better than she could have done. We think he* was *captured and briefly imprisoned. I'm sure Dad told Mancil's story to scout troops, P.T.A., the Legion & whoever. He'd finish off with a demonstration on* the *drum, using Mother's granddad's (Mr. Collingwood's) drumsticks. Dad visited Uncle Mancil on more than one occasion. Here is part of the story my dad told:*
>
> > *President Lincoln was reviewing the troops and asked the Secretary of State Seward which regiment was coming along. Mr. Lincoln went out to see the regiment of Wisconsin men up closer and spotted small Manny. Mr. Lincoln reached out and took ahold of both of Manny's hands, and, as he gazed upon the small boy's face, tears rolled*

down his cheeks and he said, "I never thought it would come to this." *Mancil's first impression of Lincoln was that he was the homeliest man that he had ever seen. Then, after Lincoln had spoken to him in his soft voice, he thought, "Here is a beautiful man."*

You will be pleased to learn that Ida and Mancil have a daughter, Eleanor G. Root Furnace, who lives in Murrieta, California. Cousin Eleanor gave Mancil's drum to my brother George (b. July 4, 1929, two days before Mancil died). George tells me that once when Dad was sharing the story at a church function (likely a dinner), one elderly woman, still very sharp, stood up and said how they used to be neighbors to the Roots and she remembered Mancil's going out on the porch roof and playing his drum each 4th of July along about 1910-1920. Eleanor [we talked on the phone] says Mancil's ebony drumsticks (valuable) were given to her cousin, Carlton Suttliff, who died a few years ago in New Jersey. Eleanor says that a long time ago she sent some tintypes of Mancil to a museum in Madison, Wisconsin. Pictures of Mancil may be possible here in Cedar Rapids because, whenever there was a patriotic parade, Uncle Mancil was invited to play with the Fife, Drum & Bugle Corps. The drum stays at my house for safe keeping away from children and curious adults who might try thumping on it.

When George, born with spina bifida (often fatal within a year or two), turned 60 in 1989, my sister, Phyllis Brooks, gave a surprise birthday party for him, inviting classmates, friends, former neighbors, besides family. It was held at a school air-conditioned and ground level for wheelchairs. One of George's classmates owns two antique fire engines and brought one along. George had a great ride. A patriotic day, we all (Nieces & Nephews) wore a costume made by Phyllis for the local parade. One of my nephews, Joshua Moore, carried the *drum but did not play it. The heads may be original skins, as they are quite yellow and tough—not much tension on them anymore. Eleanor says that her father had the ropes and leathers replaced, which tightened the heads. The former gut snares on the nether side have been gone for quite some time. The wooden barrel of the drum was made from a half bushel measure.*

One last thing—when I woke up this morning, I recall that when I was 12 or 13 Dad used to go to the upstairs bedroom, close the door, and practice various drum rhythms and rolls on Uncle Mancil's drum. I remember asking Mother—in an adolescent and semi-sarcastic tone—why he was doing that. She said not to let it bother me, that he just wanted to be alone and this gave him a certain amount of satisfaction. I realize now that the drum was his friend. Many of my musician friends have a bond with their instruments.

Here are pictures of Mancil's drum taken this 128th winter since Manny brought it home to his anxious mother and family, pictures taken by photographer George J. Naxera, Jr., of Cedar Rapids.

In her Feb. 25, 1993 letter from Murrieta, California, Eleanor Garden Root Furnace, 88, "deeply touched" by our present renewal of her parents' memory, reaches back over eight decades for her thoughts:

I was born in Chicago Dec. 1, 1904, with a twin sister Margaret G. Griffin (Mrs. Laurence) Rohrbacher (1904-1987). Our father, John Garden, was born in Scotland. Mother died soon after Margaret's birth. We had three older sisters. He (John) came to Cedar Rapids when we were six, and his sisters insisted we be adopted out, so Ida and Mancil took me, and Ida's sister Mildred "Aunt Millie" Griffin and her husband took Margaret. We were raised close together. Margaret has a daughter, Virginia Rohrbacher, who is a retired art professor living in Centralia, Illinois. Margaret, never sick, died of a massive heart attack. I have a daughter, Susan Dezarov, Librarian at Lake Elsinore Elemmentary School; Susan has two daughters—Elizabeth, at California State University at Northridge; and Melissa in high school, who is now excited about your letter and wants to study about the war Mancil was in. We went to our large library, made copies of your letter, and sent them to these two great-granddaughters. We got books and a tape about the war too. Dick Harman sent me the Gazette *clipping. We are so thrilled and excited to hear from you, Professor Hoar.*

Mancil was given a pair of black ebony drumsticks by another prisoner while in Libby Prison. They are valuable family heirlooms today. Father was adoring toward me—never drank or smoked. He never raised his voice in anger and never spanked me. We had a black Allertun horse named Kiever. Sundays we rode in our buggy. It was a sad day when Kiever died.

Father did not talk much about his early life or the war. I (c.1942) gave his War drum to George Harman, Dick's brother. Mother sent all tintype pictures of my father (Mancil) to the Wisconsin Capital—Madison, for their Museum, so I am sorry I have none to lend you. My father's father was killed in the war—Augustus Root; also Father's brother Wilber M. Root and baby sister Ashley died of TB, so his mother signed him over for a sum of money when he was nine. He told me this. And often he was carried on the shoulders of his regiment, as he was too little to walk far.

Father played his drum for parades, church, and school, and I often played the piano for him; he had double rolls and played for many neighborhood children...a wonderful Christian father. About that July 7, 1929 C. R. Sunday Gazette & Republican.... *What an unusual story—a car door handle striking his mouth, spinning Father around, etc. This boy driver didn't stop for my father crossing. My Uncle (Court Reporter for Judge Ring of C. R.) checked at the time and found no witnesses. But the insurance company awarded Mother $1000. Judge Ring said we could sue but Mother said, "No."*

In April 1969 I moved to California to be near my daughter Susan Dezarov, who wishes to "chime in" here with a fond boast: "I have a breakfront built of black walnut and handmade by my great-grandfather Augustus Root, who used it for holding tack and harness. Grandfather Mancil changed it into a china cabinet by adding dipped glass windows and changing the knobs."

I have traveled to Cedar Rapids for the past three years, usually in June, and may go again this summer. It is fulfilling to renew friendships, to meet Virginia Rohrbacher from Illinois, to have breakfast with Dick Harman at The Village Inn, and to call at Dick's home to see his latest projects, for he's a busy young man. He always brings me fresh raspberries from his back yard. Could I be the only living daughter of a Civil War soldier? [Ans. No, not yet by a few hundred, but you are definitely a member of a sparse sorority.]

In a 1993 letter from Marion, Iowa, Evelyn Harman Beadle, 71, offers:

"Uncle Mancil" was my father's mother's brother-in-law. Mancil married Grandmother Annice Elizabeth Barnhart Harman's sister, Ida Barnhart. I remember Ida vaguely but don't recall Uncle Mancil, though I was nine years old when he died—just his *age when he was a drummer boy in 1864. I notice the* Gazette & Republican *of July 7, 1929, listed his age as eleven when he volunteered—an incorrect age, since he died at 75 in 1929. I live about three miles north from my cousin, Richard D. Harman. After the snow melts, we will walk over to Oak Shade Cemetery here, a matter of three blocks, and take a picture of Mancil's tombstone.*[7]

Tragically, within three years of that September Sixtieth National G.A.R. Encampment in Des Moines, when Comrade M. V. Root's fame reached its zenith, his noble life was accidentally abbreviated in his own hometown. While walking across First Street (West) at Fourth Avenue and almost to the east curb, he [reportedly] turned back, changing his mind and direction; at that instant a car door handle struck his mouth, spinning him around and causing his head to strike on the back of Herbert Selby's car, thus throwing Mr. Root to the pavement. Suffering a fractured skull and cerebral hemorrhage, he succumbed hours later at St. Luke's Hospital.

Popular and widely beloved locally, he was, understandably widely mourned among his Grand Army brethren far beyond Iowa's borders. But we may all now rest more easily knowing that Manny Root—himself the essence of this national study—has at length caught the cadence in *this* parade, they who were the youngest soldierboys of America's Saddest War. Here, he will once again and forever more be an exemplary standout, a star of the first magnitude—for he *was* the latest born of all Grand Army brethren, a distinction worthy of mention.

Abram Furman Springsteen

July 5, 1850 – Jan. 20, 1930

While Johnny Clem's name and personality categorically eclipsed mention of all other child soldiery from the very midst of the war itself even unto the end of his long life (1851-1937), there were a few other Union Army youths who later (1875-1930) began to enjoy a measure of recognition nationally, *this* fame arising more among their fellow G.A.R. comrades or regimental brethren than among our civilian or non-veteran populace. So largely loomed Clem for his youthful heroisms and nearly 45-year, Regular Army officer career that today it can only be guesstimated as to who else among the eligible scores were celebrated as symbolic names or by-words for their Civil War "youthdom." One such eligible name, proverbial for the drummer boy image, did attain appreciable visibility—Abram F. Spring(s)teen (misspelled by journalists who did not always supply the second s). Springsteen, after all, had in common with Clem certain obvious pluses: an early and lengthy Union Army service tour (38 months to Clem's 37); a longtime post bellum employment by the federal government (clerkship in the Bureau of Pensions, Dept. of the Interior, 1882-1920); an expansive geographical identity-orientation. Springsteen's story embraced no less than the all-American trend westward—a Brooklyn, New York, nativity; an Indianapolis boyhood and youth; a Washington, D. C., work-life; a Los Angeles retirement and final retreat.

"Abe" was born in Brooklyn, New York City, to Jefferson (1820-1909) and Ann O'Connor Springsteen. Jefferson was a native of Harrison, Ohio, while Ann's people, as indeed his own, were from New Jersey. The infant Abram F. Springsteen, having a Dutch-German-Irish ancestry, was baptized at St. Paul's (Roman Catholic) Church in Brooklyn by the Reverend Father J. H. Schueller on July 28, 1850 according to the Baptismal Register. In 1852, when he was two, the family journeyed mainly by water from Brooklyn to Indianapolis. During their eventful trip the Springsteens were shipwrecked in a storm on Lake Erie. But they were put ashore safely at Erie, Pennsylvania. From there they were soon again afloat on the less turbulent Ohio River. They drifted downstream to Madison (s.e.) Indiana, and overland to Indianapolis. Here, they first put up at Little's Tavern, a stagecoach inn at New Jersey and Washington Streets. Little Abe's father had already lived in this growing town twice before.

Looking back now on their long adventuresome lives, we are struck with elements of similarity that defined "Jeff" and "Abe" as a pair whose father-sonship only confirmed their relative status. Before age ten Jeff had run away from home to follow a circus to Indiana. Ever appreciative of a good show, he was said to have never missed a circus.[1] Jeff was no less than a pioneer of early-day Indianapolis, for in 1835, as a fifteen-year-old, he had induced *his* father to settle here when only a few houses stood on what became South Illinois Street. While still but fifteen Jeff had become a government mail carrier, his route running (e.n.e.) sixty-five miles through Strawtown to Winchester. On horseback, he often encountered winter snows and spring freshets. At Strawtown (near Noblesville) he early on made fast friendships with many redskins. He would tell of these adventures to three generations of Springsteens.[2] In 1837 Jeff, with his father, backtrailed all the way to Brooklyn and New Jersey to visit Jeff's Grandfather Springsteen.

Eventually Jeff settled in Brooklyn, where for several years he operated a restaurant at the then famous Fulton Market. Meanwhile, he had married Ann O'Connor and they had a son John J., who became a 20-year-old private Aug. 31, 1861, in Company I, 1st Regiment of New York Engineers. John died of typhoid fever at Hilton Head, South Carolina, July 4, 1862.

But Jefferson's father returned to Indianapolis and bought property on New Jersey Street between New York and Ohio Streets. Citizens ridiculed him at the time, predicting the city would never grow that far from its center—then on South Street by the Madison Railroad Depot and Illinois and West Washington Streets. By 1854, his son Jefferson, having sold out his restaurant in Brooklyn, joined his folks in the Hoosier Hub, and was appointed "captain of the peace," for he was robust of physique. Jefferson served four terms as town marshal between 1855 and 1861. In 1856 he won election when the Democrats swept the whole ticket except for prosecuting attorney, won by Benjamin Harrison, the future general and U. S. president. Though a fine physical specimen from his mail delivery years, at age forty-one Jefferson felt too senior for soldiering in 1861. Easing his mind, however, was the satisfaction of contributing two of his three sons to the Union Army. His youngest son, Robert E. Springsteen, born in 1858, became Indianapolis postmaster 1912-22, city councilman, and vice president of the Federal Finance Company. Prior to his postmastership, he had founded and operated The R. E. Springsteen Merchant Tailors at 9 North Pennsylvania Street.[3]

On Oct. 15, 1861, at 11 years 3 months 10 days, Abram was enlisted in his hometown by a Captain Conklin, who set him down as age fourteen to be a drummer boy for three years. Accordingly, he was mustered into the 35th Indiana Infantry by a Capt. Morris (Norris?) on October 27 as a musician with Company A, being, in fact, among the regiment's earliest enlistees, their full muster completed only by Dec. 11, 1861. Jefferson and Ann gave in to Abram's pleadings, for he had already long demonstrated his talents in per-

Abram F. Springsteen, age 11. Photo attached to his pension papers at National Archives.

cussion at age ten by drumming for local recruiters who "made it worth his while." Because these parents readily understood that the 35th Indiana was to be permanently stationed locally in a home guard capacity and could expect their son home frequently, they had few qualms about granting consent. However, dire misgivings consumed them when on December 13 the 35th was ordered to Bardstown, Kentucky, and, presumably, to the front. Within hours of his regiment's entraining at the old Madison Depot on South Street, Abram's parents "kidnapped" their son by hiding him on a farm owned by relatives near Noblesville. Missing his drummer boy at Cincinnati, the captain of Company A wired back to Indianapolis, threatening arrests. Straightway on December 14 the boy was charged with desertion. How many thousands of such charges were made (& stood) on far less than complete knowledge of the circumstances? But, upon discovery a few days later of his being three years younger than what certain officers had understood he was and, further, that his parents had absconded with him, this charge *was* dropped upon their demand, though the incident is preserved in his records.[4] Abram was honorably discharged on Dec. 23, 1861.[5] Glad enough for the Christmas holiday, ambivalent Abram returned to his schooling and to the tough pre-teen assignment of growing up fast. He bore with these chores, practiced his percussion, and added another birthday—his twelfth. In the spring of '62 he beat his drum about the streets in a recruiting effort for the 63rd Indiana.

On July 29, 1862, at 12 years 24 days, Abram was reenlisted, again at Indianapolis, by Henry Tindall, who would be commissioned captain on August 9 and become the first of Abram's five captains in Company I, 63rd Indiana.[6] This time the boy's age was correctly recorded as twelve. Again, he had parental consent. Blue of eyes, hair dark brown, Abram again signed for three years, this time very nearly completing the triennium as Company I's musician in the 63rd Indiana. Just a passing thought: Few, indeed, the number of *re*enlistees, either side, who could have been *this* youthful! But a few there surely were! This record may already have been set seventy-one days earlier on May 19, 1862, when Tommy L. F. Hubler, of Warsaw, Indiana, reenlisted in his same 12th Indiana Infantry at age 10 years 7 months 10 days.

Under a succession of three colonels—John S. Williams, of Lafayette; James McManomy, of Covington; Israel N. Stiles, of Lafayette—the 63rd rendered extensive service. They did remain at Indianapolis on provost (guard) duty until Dec. 25, 1863, which certainly must have pleased Jefferson and Ann. That last night—the eve of departure (Christmas Day)—when his regiment was all set to entrain next morning for service farther afield, these two were given permission to take their son home for that night. Mistrustful of a repeat attempt to keep him out of fighting, Abram slipped out of his upstairs bedroom window and scurried back to camp. From mid-January to February 25 several of the companies, including I Company, were at Camp Nelson, Kentucky, under Colonel Stiles. They marched over mountains that winter of '64 to Knoxville. That spring and summer they advanced toward Georgia, destroying the Tennessee railroads and joining in on the Atlanta Campaign. They occupied a position on the left of the line during the action at Rocky Face Ridge, losing two killed and four wounded. They then moved through Snake Creek Gap to Resaca. As a unit of the 23rd Corps., Army of the Ohio, drummer boy Springsteen's 63rd Indiana participated in these events:

-Battle of Resaca, 5/14-5/15/64
-Operations on line of Pumpkin Vine Creek
-Battles about Dallas, New Hope Church, Allatoona Hills till 6/5
-Operations about Marietta & against Kennesaw Mt., 6/10-7/2
-Assault on Kennesaw, 6/27
-Nickajack Creek, 7/2-7/5
-Chattahoochee River, 7/5-7/17
-Siege of Atlanta, 7/22-8/25
-Battle of Jonesboro, 8/31-9/1
-Lovejoy Station, 9/2-6
-Pursuit of Gen. Hood in Alabama, 10/3-10/26
-Battle of Franklin, 11/30
-Battle of Nashville, 12/15-12/16
-Pursuit of Hood to Tennessee Rr., 12/17-12/28
-At Clifton, Tenn. till 1/16/65
-The Carolinas Campaign, 3/1-4/26

-Advance on Goldsboro, 3/6-3/21
-Occupation of Goldsboro, 3/24-3/31
-Advance on Raleigh, 4/10-4/14
-Bennett House & Johnston's Surrender, 4/26
-At Raleigh till 5/5
-At Greensboro till 6/21
-Mustered out at Greensboro, N. C., 6/21/65. [7]

As the phrase goes, 188 of Abram's comrades in the 63rd "never came home." Just prior to the Battle of Franklin (or in its early phase), Abram was captured with a wagon train at the Battle of Spring Hill, Tennessee, Nov. 29, 1864. But he escaped after dark, small enough to hide under a wagon and thus elude his captors.[8] At Resaca, Abram had been stunned by an exploding shell the previous May 14. Further, he had contracted bronchitis on the march from Marietta to Atlanta about July 9-12, exposed as he was to heavy cold rains and having to sleep on chilly wet ground. Considerable of his military life comes through in A. F. Springsteen's own words:

Washington, D. C., November 23, 1894

Hon. John G. Carlysle
Secretary of Treasury

Sir:

I have the honor to make application for a clerkship in your department. I was discharged from the Records & Pension Office July 25 /94 on account of reduction of force. My efficiency record to Dec. 31, 1893 (the last issued prior to my discharge) is 79.6.

The Secretary of War has kindly promised to re-instate in the War Department & then transfer me to any place which may be found. I have endeavored diligently since my discharge from the R. & P. Office to find employment to enable me to provide for my family, consisting of a wife & two children, with the necessaries of life but have been unable to find work.

My physical condition is such owing to a disease contracted during the late Rebellion, that it is almost impossible for me to endure manual labor, but, having had several years experience in department work, I am confident I shall be able to give satisfaction in whatever place assigned.

A place as messenger or watchman would be preferable to walking the streets in idleness.

I have a military record which should entitle me to a position of some kind under this great and magnanimous government. When the call was made for troops in the Spring of 1861, being an expert with the drumsticks, I buckled on my drum & offered my services to a recruiting officer at Indianapolis (my home) & continued beating the drum for various recruiting officers at that place until Oct. 15 /61, when at age eleven years I enlisted in Co. A, 35th Regt. Ind. Vols. & served until Dec. 23,

1861—I again enlisted July 29, 1862 at twelve years in Co. I, 63rd Regt. Ind. Vols. & served until June 21, 1865.

When honorably discharged with my Company at Greensboro, N. C., I returned to my home at Indianapolis on the 3rd day of July 1865, just two days prior to my 15th birthday, having served 39 months.

During my service the music of my drum was heard on the marches & in the camps from Camp Nelson, Ky., to Burnsides Point, Tenn & thence over the Cumberland Mountains to Knoxville, thence to Burnt Hickory, Buzzard Roost & Resaca, Ga., thence on to Atlanta, thence to Nashville, Franklin, Columbia & Pulaski, Tenn, thence to Washington, Alexandria, Fort Fisher, Smithville, Ft. Anderson, Wilmington, Raleigh &Greensborough, where finally discharged.

I was not a soldier for money nor for glory, but because I loved my country & the dear old flag. I love them still & only ask to be given a chance to live & to properly provide for my wife & little ones.

I am willing to perform any kind of work that my physical condition can endure & if you will kindly provide me with a place in your department, you will forever receive the thanks and blessings of

Your obedient Servant
s/ Abram F. Springsteen[9]

Abram, to round out his interrupted academics, attended a private school in Indianapolis He finished out his second decade first by learning the bricklayer's trade from his Uncle Abram [father of Harry Springsteen, who during the 1920s & early '30s would be the City Market Master] and pursuing it during 1866-69, and, second, by clerking in a clothing house during 1869-1881. He had come home from the war with bronchitis, and, because of this, he found himself unfit for outdoor labor. Abram grew up close to his nearest relatives, including another brother, (besides Robert E.), who would later live in Champaign, Illinois; and two sisters who became Mrs. Joseph Beckwith and Mrs. E. P. Beerbower, both of North Delaware Street, Indianapolis. Then there was his father's sister —Aunt Eliza Springsteen Hanna.

Abram, 21, was first married to Laura May Longfellow Jan. 11, 1872, at Huntington, Indiana, but Laura died from childbirth complications on Apr. 13, 1873. Their daughter, Laura A. Longfellow Springsteen, died later that year. Not until some twelve years later, July 22, 1885, did Abram take his second wife, Emma Isola Combs [sic] at St. Patrick's Church, Washington, D. C., where they were married by Rev. J. Walter. Their children were Ruby Marie, born July 4, 1887, and Perry Harrison, born June 6, 1891. Emma and Abram were divorced on June 28, 1912, at Indianapolis. Finally Abram, a veteran several times over, did take a third wife on Oct. 29, 1912, in a ceremony conducted by Rev. Clarence W. Eddy—Mrs. Birdie Crosier (the former Mrs Charles) Rosengarten of West Los Angeles, a Zanesville, Ohio, native who was living in Indianapolis.

Mr. Springsteen began his nearly thirty-eight years of Federal employment on Sept. 22, 1882, when he held a clerkship in the Surgeon General's Office until 1885, having passed a Civil Service examination in 1884. He worked conscientiously in a variety of clerkships:

Ordnance Department, 1885-87
Office of the Surgeon General, 1889-91
Pension Office, Dept. of the Interior, 1891-93; 1903-09 & 1910
Main Post Office, Washington, D. C., 1897-99
Quartermaster Dept. ($75 per month), 1899-7/1901
Jeffersonville, Indiana, 9/1901-03
AWM Office at Fort McHenry, Maryland
Pension Office, Indianapolis ($1200), 1911-13
Pension Office, Washington, D. C. ($1400), 10/1913-5/31/1920
Pay raised to $1000 per annum, 4/1/1902
Pay raised to $1200 per annum, 3/22/1907
Pay raised to $1400 per annum, 10/17/1913 [10]

In an effort to prolong his work life, he volunteered for employment at the Land Office at Visalia, California, where he had but a brief tour until mid-summer, thus concluding his days as a wage earner.[11] Ex-drummer boy Springsteen over the years managed in August to be present for a fair number of fondly anticipated reunions when survivors of his old 63rd Indiana Volunteers counted on seeing one another. At Covington, Indiana, on Aug. 24, 1911, it was noticed that many familiar faces were missing, but the rainy day might have been a factor. "The oldest and the youngest members attended—Bob Briggs, 89, and Abe Springsteen, 61. The dinner, usually served by the ladies at the fairground, was given by them at the Grand Army Hall."[12] Their Thirty-First assembly, again at Covington, on Aug. 20, 1912, was especially well attended. "A fife and drum corps enlivened things in the courthouse yard—interesting to the rising generation, but with a touch of pathos to others. Miss Lottie Jones of Danville the speaker, was escorted to Grand Army Hall, where a bountiful repast was served by the W.R.C. of John C. Femont Post No 246. The speaker had two brothers in the 63rd, George W. Jones, quartermaster, and Jas. Jones, a surgeon. Uncle Bobby Briggs, of Silverwood, was too feeble to leave home, though he sent word he was present in spirit. Letters were read from many comrades. Among them was a message from Abe Springsteen, for a press of business in the Pension Bureau prevented his presence.[13]

To his great credit, A. F. Springsteen did not apply for his own Civil War pension until July 15, 1927, when he had turned seventy-seven. His regular Federal retirement allowance was but a modest $600 annually to start with. Within a month he would be diagnosed as having prostate cancer, his final battle. During his last years at the Sawtelle Soldiers Home the aging veteran had time to reminisce, to recall how he had laid his childhood life on the line (and on the bare muddy Georgia ground night after damp night). Wistfully, he pursued a long-thought ambition—conferral upon himself of the nation's highest military award. Perhaps in his career and Federal station he had known of a few such efforts that bore fruit, as in the application of Wm. H. Horsfall. Thus, from out of his final retreat and moribund condition came this swan-song mission, reflected in a Dec. 10, 1928 letter from Samuel M. Shortridge, Chairman, United State Senate Committee on Privileges and Elections, who on that date did as he was requested:

To the Commissioner of Pensions
Washington, D. C.

My dear Mr. Commissioner:

I beg to submit to you herewith for your consideration a letter addressed to me by Abram F. Springsteen, Ward 14, Main Hospital, soldiers Home, Sawtelle, California. You will note his desire to secure a Congressional Medal of Honor in award for the services rendered by him in the Civil War.

I shall greatly appreciate any information which you may give me as to the eligibility of Mr. Springsteen for the honor which he seeks.

Sincerely yours,
Samuel M. Shortridge[14]

Though unsuccessful in this dying endeavor, Springsteen will forever place high in our memorial to the child-soldiery of America's Saddest War; his thirty-seven plus months in uniform nearly qualify him for "Those Youngest Who Served Longest." Because his final late move to California was/is not generally known, a protracted nondiscovery of the time and place of his demise has held up his joining the ranks of those who march across these pages. "Pushing eighty years," Abram Springsteen became in his own right an old-soldier personality before his passing on in January 1930 at Sawtelle Soldiers' Home Hospital. He left a widow, Birdie; a daughter, Ruby Springsteen, a son Perry; his sister, Anna Beerbower (St. Louis, Mo.); and two brothers, Robert (Indianapolis) and Charles (St. Joseph, Mo.).

Patterned on Jefferson before him, Abe F. Springsteen fulfilled the promise of his surname again and again evincing a resiliency, a capacity for rebounding, a buoyancy that kept him moving upward in his daily living as in the hearts and minds of those who personally knew him. To this day, there hangs a framed portrait of Abram F. Springsteen in the north basement of Soldiers' and Sailors' Monument (Room) at Sawtelle Military Hospital at West Los Angeles, where he died and at whose Los Angeles National Cemetery he is buried.[15] On the frame endures this forgivable slight overstatement—"The Youngest Soldier in the Union Army."

George William McDonald

Aug. 17, 1851 – Feb. 6, 1930

Henry and Agnes McGregor McDonald were living in St. Louis, Missouri, when their son, George William arrived. Both Henry and Agnes were natives of Scotland. St. Louis would be their hometown for eight more years until moving to Chicago in 1859. Little is known today of Henry's precise work life, but he settled his family somewhere along Illinois Street. One sentence does survive in George William McDonald's Civil War pension folder which reflects upon what his father did for work, a statement that also hints of a possible motivating factor (the assumption of a man-size responsibility) behind the son's insatiable passion for military service: "His father [Henry] was shot and killed on the *City Of Alton*, whereon he was a pilot, in April, 1861."[1] Thus, four months before reaching age ten, this "laddie" fulfilled the condition known as orphanhood (loss of one *or* both parents). A few strategic knowns attaching to George's pre-military boyhood have "come down"; the first, found in his pension record and of a decided mythopoeic dimension (because difficult to verify), is certainly worth passing along, namely: "As a boy prior to his becoming attached to the Sixty-Fifth Illinois, he discovered and, through information furnished by him, foiled a conspiracy to release military prisoners and to burn and sack Chicago."[2] Again, also in H. R. 820-Mar. 3, 1921, is this statement: "Soldier when a boy received his instructions in drumming from 'Billy' Nevins, of national fame" [presumably, during 1860-61]. In both instances, young McDonald appears to have prepared himself as a ready patriot for service in the Union Cause. How could a recruiter deny so compelling a record and reputation as this one? Set upon overcoming all obstacles, Little George—he was "about four feet, blue-eyed, of light complexion[3]—as of the summer and fall of 1861 had an occupation: drummer for a Chicago recruiting office. He was still earning an income with his percussion talent in February 1862. On the twelfth of that month George, 10 years 5 months 26 days, ran away from his Illinois Street home and "sold" himself as a musician. He did so under an assumed name, "*Hirom* King" (his folk version of *Hiram*), hoping to escape his mother's clutches. By March 28, 1862, he had mustered in with Company C, 65th Illinois, "the Scotch Regiment," then organizing at Chicago's Camp Douglas.[4] "He became Company C's mascot and was a great favorite of the officers and their wives, who furnished him with his uniform and drum and all the spending money he required. He participated with the regiment in all its movements."[5]

The 65th Illinois left Chicago in early June for Martinsburg (future West Virginia). Here they had duty all summer guarding railroads and supplies. On September 7 they were caught up in a skirmish at Darkesville while helping to besiege Harpers Ferry. While in camp near the Ferry at Bolivar Heights (W. Va.) during September 12-14, the entire regiment was caught off guard, surrounded and captured by C.S.A. troops under Gen. T. J. Jackson. They had to surrender. However, instead of being marched off to prison through a "no man's land," they were paroled the next day (Sept. 16) and sent to Annapolis, Maryland, whence they entrained back to Chicago. [The 65th Illinois remained at Chicago till April 1863 when they were declared officially exchanged and ordered to Kentucky,[6] thus instancing Winston Churchill's *The Last War Between Gentlemen*]. Once drummer boy "King" and his comrades arrived home (late Sept. '62), Agnes found her son and took him away from his command [under at least a mild barrage of protests!]; she could do this, owing to George's extreme youth, then all of eleven years one month. Undaunted, George ran away again, returning to Camp Douglas. Agnes then had her son arrested and taken to court, where she secured his release on a writ of habeas corpus. That was mid-October when George was but one more month older. While records of this court action were consumed in the Great Chicago Fire, the essential facts are corroborated (1) by reports from the War Department records and (2) by testimony of several of George's 65th Illinois comrades. George's unorthodox separation from the Army seems to have precluded his receiving a formal discharge, which he quite certainly did deserve, a document whose troubling absence caused problems sixty years later when he sought a Civil War pension for disability. Mascot-musician McDonald's Union Army tour was a matter of some 170+ days if we begin counting service upon his actual mustering-in. We know that pension authorities, efforting to deny him, tried to assert how that his actual service time was under ninety days! Clearly untrue. His long-enough baptism of battle was sufficient to diminish preconceived ideas of military glory.

In 1874 he married Miss Elizabeth Bloxom (Sept. 1, 1850-Sept. 18, 1886) and they lived in Evanston. A victim to "chronic purulent bronchitis,"[7] she was interred at Rosehill Cemetery, Chicago.

On Dec. 6, 1886, George married Miss Ida Charlotte Soderstrom, a June 17, 1864, native of Moheda, Sweden; they were married in Chicago by Rev. David R. Breed. They named their daughter, born May 23, 1889,

Ethel Elizabeth.[8] George made his living as a painter and interior decorator until his late 60s. By 1920 he was considering the virtues of a Civil War pension. He was then employed at light janitor work, was 5' 4", weighed 164, and lived at 5452 Race Avenue. For quite a few years until about 1925 he was a comrade of Chicago's first, largest (and last) G.A.R. post—George H. Thomas No. 5. Eventually he transferred his membership to the fourth of Chicago's twenty other posts—U.S. Grant Post 28, where he remained, ever in good standing. It is all of interesting to note that the former colonel of the 65th Illinois Infantry "vouched for him and had him join the Grand Army of the Republic."[9] With his earning capacity reduced two-thirds from chronic lumbago, leg and thigh muscle pains, impaired hearing and age, George was on March 3, 1921, by a Special Act of Congress awarded a $50 per month pension and placed on the pension roll by the Secretary of the Interior.[10] At the time, he had no property except household goods valued at $100; his weekly janitorial income was $8. While Comrade McDonald was undoubtedly well acquainted with dozens of G.A.R. members, we know of at least three of them who place in this study: Stephen Mauer (1847-1913) of Post 5, who lived his last forty-two years in Chicago, who had served as a bugler when only thirteen; Charles O. Brown (1848-1941), who was Commander of U. S. Grant Post 28 in 1930; and James Crugom (1850-1948), last survivor of their Post 28, who had served in the First Wisconsin Infantry at age eleven.

Ex-mascot-drummer boy McDonald—[His surname, frequently misspelled M(a)cDonald, was a confusion that followed him all the way to his grave[11]]—was "very probably" one of the twenty-five unnamed boys age ten or under referred to early in Cora E. Gillis' *Final Journal of the National Grand Army of the Republic* (1957), who had officially performed duty in the Union Army. Though he was surely touted in Chicago G.A.R. posts as the youngest to have served, he did not actively trade on this claim or personally go out of his way to encourage it. The myth-truth [essentially, NOT the oxymoron that scholars might be prone to croon over] mix of it afforded him a not unjust, pleasant distinction for some sixty-eight years. Having lived seventy years in Chicago or its suburbs, George W. McDonald died at his 1416 N. Mason Avenue home of heart failure in a uremic coma at 9:20 p.m. of his last day. He was laid to rest at Memorial Park, Chicago, two days later, having been given daughter and wife's best care.

We conclude McDonald's story on a positive note—namely, that a covey of comrades or survivors of the 65th Illinois were swift to write letters during March-October 1930 on behalf of his widow Ida that her pension might be assured (and it was). From these we extract a couple of statements. The first, by Cmdr. Charles O. Brown of Post 28, written to Mr. Earl D. Church, U. S. Pension Commissioner, Washington, D. C., Apr. 23, 1930:

I have known Comrade McDonald for 25 years and am intimately acquainted with his family. He was a member of this post at his death, and I, as Commander, with post comrades, conducted his funeral. Mrs. McDonald and her daughter Ethel, who is a public school teacher, are people of absolute integrity.... He was with his regiment when it was captured by the enemy on Bolivar Heights near Harpers Ferry...near the close of his service.

As he was a mere boy, only 10 years old, same age as a drummer boy as Maj. Gen. John Clem[m] of your city, his parents prevented his returning with his regiment by legal proceedings...I knew him to be the same person who served in Co. C., 65th Ill. Vols. And that he received a pension by Act of Congress under Pension Certificate No. 1,187,491.[12]

The second, written from Los Angeles and sworn to (before Notary Public John B. McDonald) by Selden M. French, deposes and says:

That he has known the McDonald family for 21 years. That George W. McDonald was a comrade of his in the Grand Army, that they played in the same fife and drum corps for many years, and that he was the husband of Ida C. McDonald.[13]

In the sizeable constellation of our youngest drummer boys, "Little George" W. McDonald is here observed to be no less than a star of the first magnitude—in a word—stellar.

Walter Xonpher Broome

Feb. 18, 1851 – Apr. 30, 1933

Of Utica in Hinds County, Mississippi, virtually his entire life, Walter X. Broome, who would exceed age eighty-two, traced his immediate ancestry to the Carolinas. His paternal grandparents, William and Naomi Amy Bell Broome had been colonials in the Palmetto Colony well before her statehood and our Constitution were thought of. The Broomes were of an energetic and thrifty Scots-Irish stock. One of their sons, Mathew Broome (Jan. 3, 1795-July 28, 1874), in 1827 first married Nancy Robinson (1796-1835), they both being of Fairfield County, South Carolina.[1] At age 76, Mathew, a planter, reminiscing, noted, "From April 1833 to June 1865 I resided constantly on my own place—500 acres. During the past 15 years 380 acres of it have been under cultivation, the balance under pasture and woodland, all under fence situated on the edge of Utica."[2] On June 15, 1837, at Utica, Mathew, having lost his first wife over two years earlier and with four youngsters, married Martha Elizabeth "Betsy" Brown (1817-1883), originally of North Carolina, daughter of William and Martha Brown of Utica. They had at least ten children: John Matthew, 1838-1895; Mary Evalyn "Eva," 1839-1863; Infant, 1840-1840; Charles A., 1841-1843; Cyrus Lafayette, 1842-1917; Alonzo R. "Lon," 1844-1872; Elley Harris, 1846-1915; Martha Cora "Mattie" (Ford), 1848 -?; Walter X; Seymore B., 1853?-1885. Mathew and Betsy's farm home (& acreage) was near Main and Carpenter Streets in Utica, equidistant between Vicksburg and Jackson, Mississippi.[3]

The Broomes went down as "Confederates of the First Degree." John, 23, and Cyrus, 19, enlisted in May 1861. "Lon," 19, joined about May 1863. All three were to be in Capt. J. C. Davis' Company C, 16th Mississippi Infantry.[4] The 16th's original organization was for twelve months; in May '62 they re-organized for the war. Private John M. Broome joined at Corinth under Col. Garnet Posey. John gave constant and faithful service; even while sick at CSA General Hospital (Charlottesville, Va.) in March '62, he re-enlisted that April 14th. He was on a detail of men acting as nurses at General Hospital. John was listed wounded on Posey's Brigade Casualty Report from battles around Chancellorsville. He was hospitalized in Richmond (5/8-6/3/63). Pay records show his service until at least Feb. 15, 1865.

Cyrus joined Company C at Crystal Springs, Mississippi, and went with the 16th to Virginia as a support unit for the First Manassas—Trimble's Brigade, Ewell's Division, Jackson's Corps. A. R. "Lon" Broome was wounded at Sharpsburg 9/17/62, for it was there that the 16th lost 65% of their men in killed and wounded. Elley or Ellie enlisted in 1863 in Company K, 36th Mississippi Infantry. He served with Capt. Cobb's scouts in his home county and in Warren County along its western border. Consequently, Elley became a prisoner upon the fall of Vicksburg.

As if the contributions of these brothers Broome were not quite enough, what did Walter X, age twelve, do but wangle himself into the Montgomery Scouts. They were composed prevailingly of young boys whose primary duty was to act as advance scouts (yes, even spies) for Stubbs Battalion of state cavalry. Led by Captain W. A. Montgomery of Edwards, these boys, so young they were largely (& unwisely) ignored by the Yankees, time and again proved themselves a distressing annoyance in their surprising capacity as "eternal gadflies" for "stinging" the Federal troops.

Although *physically* more boys than men, Montgomery's Scouts were fully as serious and duty-conscious a cadre as any element of effectives in the C.S.A. Eloquent of this fact was a near-tragic episode Walter suddenly found himself hosting. At length, Walter, then thirteen, was captured and identified as one of the vexing "Scouts," and was condemned to death as a spy. Will Lloyd, S.C.V., of Cody, Wyoming, has preserved this tense drama this way:

> *Walter was strung up by rope in a wooded area that is now in the city limits of Utica. His courage and defiance in the face of death, his refusal to expose secrets soon won the respect and admiration of the enemy. A soldier cut the rope and let him down shortly after the noose tightened. Walter and his brothers never took the "Oath of Allegiance" and several brothers moved to Texas to escape the new government.*

Walter chose to stay in Hinds County, where he matured to manhood. He went west—but only slightly, to Warren County—to find a bride in the Folkes Family. This he did Nov. 10, 1870. Anna A. Folkes (May 5, 1849-Feb. 17, 1908) became his wife and gave him Grace (1871-1925), Benjamin M. (1874-1934), and Elizabeth Ann "Bessie" (1877-1962). About 1909 Walter took his second wife, Cammie Clifford McCoy (1890-1980).[5] Their six children were Walter X., Jr., 1910-1937, who married Cyril Cobb; John Clifton, 1911-1991, who married Mary E. Ford; (Eula) Katherine (Mrs. Marion) Laudumiey, 1915- 1974; Lamar Green, b. 1919, who married Elizabeth Ford; Robert Eugene, b. 1927, who married Pearl Serpas; and Dorothy Nell (Mrs. Renfro) Pittman, b. 1930. Perhaps the best news to share is that here in 1996, the Walter X. Broome, Srs., have two Real sons and a Real daughter.[6] In fact, Lamar, of Bolton, nearby, offers on Oct. 10, 1996:

> *He liked all foods. Custards were his favorite. Father and I loved to ride horses. He bought a horse just for me and we rode all over. We were always together riding when I was not in school. He really was my best friend. As a younger man he started a construction company and hired crews to build roads throughout many counties in Mississippi. He retired in 1925 at 74. He returned to his land and brought some of his workers to work in his cotton fields. Others rented acreage and lived on the field they worked. He belonged to the Utica Methodist Church. Everyone came to ask his advice. Riding horses and having fellowship with friends was what he liked most. I last saw him at home the day he passed away...the last survivor of a large family. His service was held from his local Methodist Church.*

We conclude with the sweeping realization that the "X" in Walter's name was preeminently appropriate, that he derived considerable contentment from its symbolism—the Saint Andrew's Cross of the Confederate battle flag. Further, *it's on for* [Xonpher] Walter, 82, to go down as having attained the essence of "Old Rebdom."[7]

Franklin D. Peck

Aug. 22, 1850 – Oct. 4, 1936

"Little Franklin" Peck has proven to be an elusive standout and, "researchwise," a truly late arrival among these elite ranks of Blue and Gray, elusive because the writer cannot claim laurels for his discovery; such go to Jerome Orton of Syracuse, New York, who phoned his discovery on January 7, 1999. And this reality smacks of poetic justice, for Orton and Peck have been upstate New Yorkers. Anyway, Peck has surfaced in his own good time—a key phrase, for his credentials are quite in order. By good time, we mean that musician Peck served some fifty months from May 1861 into July 1865. This fact does, indeed, place him high among "Those Youngest Who served Longest" (Appendix D). He must surely have had a prevailingly good time to have completed an initial two-year enlistment and within three weeks have reenlisted for another two years or the duration of hostilities. Franklin makes the twelfth youngster is this study who is known to have been age ten upon assuming Civil War duty.

Franklin D. Peck, according to his death certificate,[1] was born in New York City. If so, he has this in common with three other youngster musicians among the Union Army's youngest volunteers: Abe Springsteen (1850-1930) of Los Angeles, who was 11 years 3 months 10 days at enlistment; Andrew H. Burke (1850-1918) of Roswell, new Mexico, who was 12 years 2 months 2 days at enlistment for the 75th Indiana and who would become governor of North Dakota from 1891-3; Gustave A. Schurmann (1849-1905) of Manhattan, who was 12 years 1 month 7 days on his enlistment for the 40th New York Volunteers. However, Peck's obituary states that he was born in Onondaga County, near Syracuse. This contradiction remains unsolved (as of late February 1999). Franklin's father was Isaac Peck. The absence of his mother's identity on his death certificate may indicate that he had already lost his mother by the spring of 1861, given that somber norm in this present report.

Franklin was among the Empire State's earliest volunteers, and enlisted as a drummer boy on or about May 13, 1861, at Elmira, for a two-year tour in Company I, 12th New York Infantry. By late May the 12th moved to Washington and was attached to Richardson's Brigade, Tyler's Division,

McDowell's Army of Northeast Virginia, during young Peck's first war summer. They trained in the D. C. defense perimeter, where he practiced some dozen drum calls. What indelible memories Peck would have from duty with his regiment, the "Independence Guard!" Among them were these, surely:

-Advance on Manassas. Battle of Bull Run
-Defenses of D.C. till 3/10/62
-Move to Virginia Peninsula 3/22-3/24
-Warwick Road 4/6/62
-Siege of Yorktown 4/5-5/4
-Battle of Hanover Court House 5/27
-Seven Days before Richmond,
Gaines's Mill, White Oak Swamp, Malvern Hill
-Duty at Harrison's Landing till 8/16
-Pope's Campaign in Northern Virginia,
2nd Battle of Bull Run 8/30/62
-Maryland Campaign, Battle of Antietam
-At Sharpsburg till 10/30
-Battle of Fredericksburg 12/12-12/15
-"Mud March" 1/20-1/24/63
-Chancellorsville Campaign & Battle 5/1-5/5
-Mustered out 5/17/63

Of those comrades who never came home, Franklin knew his share of the 64 killed and the 60 taken by disease, for playing a muffled drum was an inevitable duty that made few allowances for tender years.[2]

In June 1863, after a brief furlough home, Pvt. Peck reenlisted for two more years, this time to be with the 12th New York Cavalry or, "the 3rd Ira Harris Guard." During May-December 1863 they left their state by detachments for duty in the Department of North Carolina. While cavalry duty proved less sanguinary, Franklin, now twelve, found himself often "on the go" and "brushes" with their foe more frequent but much smaller. Scoutings, raids, operations and expeditions were to take place near White Oak River, Smith's Mill Bridge, Swift Creek, Tarboro, Hookerstown, Williamston, Foster's Mills, Sparta, Chowan, Rocky Run, Janesville, Greenville, Kinston, Chincapin Creek, Young's Cross Roads, Swansboro, New Berne, Whiting, Brice's Creek, Beach Grove, Tom Mack's Fork, Batchelor's Creek, Kinston, Best's Station, and the Bennett House Surrender of Johnston.[3] Protected by any number of adoptive, doting cavalrymen comrades, Franklin, nearly fifteen, mustered out with his regiment at Raleigh July 19, 1865, providentially not among their 34 battle deaths nor the 175 taken by disease.[4] Somehow he avoided Secretary of War Stanton's early release order that sent most of our Union Army's underage volunteers (including Johnny Clem) home forthwith.

Ex-drummer Peck returned to school. He studied and practiced as an attorney in Syracuse until 1877, having passed the New York Bar. That year he moved to Three Rivers in southwestern Michigan and a little later to Grand Rapids, his home for nearly 50 years.[5] Here he was active in the furniture manufacturing industry. Of an inventive mind, Franklin Peck is credited with the first paper pail, the first automatic carving machine (lathe) for furniture decoration, and the first screen gravel machine. Toward the end of his work life during 1927-32, he was employed by the John S. Nole Electrical Company of Grand Rapids. He married three times, surviving each wife.

Mr. Peck lived his last three years in the Pierson, Michigan, home of his daughter, Mrs. Susan A. Merrifield. Here, in his 85th year, he suffered several strokes. Toward the last, he was at the Holland Home in nearby Cutlerville, where he was ill for three weeks. He was buried at Fairplains Cemetery, Grand Rapids, Michigan, leaving descendants in generations of 3 - 10 - 16.

An almost entire lack of official paperwork for this underager made possible his lengthy soldiering tours, while purposely deferred official paperwork on Johnny Clem finally caused his premature release from duty.

John Lincoln Clem

Aug. 13, 1851 – May 13, 1937

"Johnny Clem"—the most captivating, enthralling, disarming, romance-charged name and personality in all child-soldierdom—single-handedly proceeded to win himself first-place standing among hundreds of extreme youth who did de facto service in "The Boys War." And, for all practical purposes or by available assessing data, he emerges as worthy of retaining *some* of his great distinction(s). "Johnny Clem" became an enduring byword for youth in uniform, and he achieved this status within his first year away from home! Hero material, Johnny rapidly became their symbol, their embodiment, their epitome, their quintessence, their *ne plus ultra.* He won hearts wherever he performed in the war. And afterward when peace settled down once again upon our land and for the rest of his own natural days—[he would enjoy some 72 post bellum years of them]—he savored,if not with *complete* justice, then with *poetic* justice, the universal *reputation* for having been the war's youngest soldierboy. Remarkably, he personifies today both a mythopoeic dimension and historical truth, a confusing, confounding mix which continues to nurture the Clem mystique.

Of prevailingly German ancestry, John Joseph Klem was born at his family's small dwelling on the outskirts of Newark in Ohio's central Licking County. John was one of nine children born to Roman and Magdalene Weber Klem, only three of whom would reach adulthood. The Klems came originally from Alsace-Lorraine.[1] Though his acreage was rich with fertile soil and most families were farmers, Roman worked for the railroad locally as an engineer. The Klems kept a vegetable garden, most of the credit going to Magdalene. Their oldest surviving child was baptized John Joseph Klem at Saint Frances de Sales Church. The lad became inseparable from his sister, Mary Elizabeth "Lizzie," and brother Louis. Though they attended parochial school, Johnny found book learning downright distasteful and church going most uncongenial. But he was never a disciplinary problem. This could well have been a consoling thought for him in 1860 when at barely age nine he lost his mother. While crossing a railroad yard, Magdalene was fatally injured by a train.[2] Thus Johnny, as so many of his Lilliputian brethren, took on orphanhood, one of the more consistent commonplaces behind a phenomenal syndrome, children as martial musicians-mascots.[3]

Already, Johnny was focused on daily rumors of the South's wish to separate from the Federal union. As 1861 "rolled in," and states kept seceding, his excitement escalated. Current events easily eclipsed ciphering, spelling or conning a reader. Upon the fall of Fort Sumter, Newark began hosting enlistment rallies. Its railroad line was soon transporting recruits to Columbus, some forty-six miles westward. Parades, drum rolls, flags, volunteers—all enraptured him; however, Roman Klem was not awed. In fact, anticipating enthusiasm from his senior son, Roman shortly read the boy's mind and expressly forbade him from attempting to enlist. Once the traumatic crossroads of civil war became reality, his zeal for wanting to offer himself proved unquenchable; the spirit of adventure, patriotism, the wish to serve, and local boredom gripped him.

Sundry accounts affirm that Johnny ran away from home. He figured to join up with any unit that would have him, trying repeatedly. He presented himself before a Captain McDougal, recruiter for the Third Ohio Infantry, but McDougal did not believe the offer serious and only laughed, "I'm not enlisting infants."[4] Humiliated, the lad returned home. Johnny plotted strategies. With Lizzie and Louis he was sent to Mass that May 24th, but just before entering church, he told them he was going to swim in the canal. He raced to the railroad depot and to a northbound train to Mount Vernon, where the next day he called at the home of Mrs. Dennis Cochrane, a former neighbor. Surmising Johnny had run away, she escorted him to the depot and charged a conductor with returning him to his home. So home he went. But not for long! He had been thinking to leave to go with the Ohio Third Infantry, a three-year outfit, to their mobilization center at Camp Dennison, near Cincinnati. Within hours, Klem learned that the 24th Ohio, still recruiting, was scheduled to pass through Newark (ca. May 27) on its way to Camp Chase, Columbus. Furtively he returned to the depot area to board the train by one of its remotest coaches while Newark's festive welcome and excitement were culminating. His 40" stature and 52 lbs. allowed him to hide beneath a seat. He stayed hidden probably all the way to Columbus, a physical feat in itself.

Whether Johnny had *any* inkling that an uncle was then among (or soon to join) the recruits of this very regiment seems elusive of determining today. Providence sometimes rescues those of little faith, whether they be children or well educated mature adults. Somewhat of a mystery has apparently endured as to precisely when, where, how and with whom Johnny served during much of his pre-enlistment military time—a matter of no less than 23 months or up to May 1, 1863, when he was formally enlisted as a private (still a musician) for three years with Company C, 22nd Michigan. Also, on this particular day (5/1/63), he first went on paper with his new name—John Lincoln Clem, in honor of the president. This writer believes he understands an important detail or two that led to his qualified (at the time—5/30/61) acceptance in the 24th Ohio: the presence in its ranks of an uncle, a key factor in this nine-year-old's coup. Nearly all accounts (mostly cryptic or nonexistent) of his earlier service neglect all mention of a specific unit, neglect to cite the 24th O.V.I. as the regiment he got into shortly after the 3rd O.V.I. rejected him. Some chroniclers who do advert to his uncle's presence *assume* this to have been bad news for the lad's cause.[5] Not so! Johnny's mother's brother, Christian Weber, 26, enlisted May 30, 1861, in the 24th Ohio for three years. What an exemplary uncle—to do *this* for his dead sister's oldest boy! And to do it on the very day of his absconding nephew's new adventure— May 30, 1861.[6] He would be a living family presence, able to report on the boy to his father, Roman, both an uncle and a stay for this nephew. Plausibly, he proved to be so during those crucial first ten weeks (this writer suspects). Uncle Christian, unforeseen, got discharged at Cheat Mountain on a surgeon's certificate of disability in mid-August 1861.[7] He could no longer keep Roman, Lizzie, Louis and the new stepmother, Elizabeth, informed of the boy's whereabouts which long term assumption accounts for no frenzied repeat effort to drag the youngster back home again. Newark relatives lost their "hot line" liaison when Uncle Christian left ranks, an understatement IF we may place any credence in Johnny's sister Lizzie Klem Adams' sentiment that the family had *no idea* of his whereabouts *for over two years,* believing Johnny to be dead. (Truly a radical statement to be making if, all the while of June '61-Aug. '62, her brother had been at home or in Newark!)

Syndromically, the presence of a relative was the crucial key or social reality that made a child-soldier's military service possible. Parallel examples abound. Lewis H. Easterly, "the Baby of the Civil War," but 8 years 9 months, went along with his Uncle David Jones in the 9th Illinois; James Crugom, age 11 years 4 months 5 days on enlistment, had his father and older brother with him; James M. Lurvey, at 14, had his father with him, as Captain (a dentist) James T. Lurvey of Company A, 40th Massachusetts; Willie Johnston, 11, served with his father in the 3rd Vermont.

Surely, too, several Newark recruits joined the 24th Ohio at the Newark depot, other men whose voices were "music" to Klem's ears. Even so, he kept out of view. Yes, a few tense hours, days at Camp Chase, where he made bold to win friendships and converts to his mission. Yet his elfin size and youth elicited only laughter from many. But Klem adhered with minimal encouragement. It was the end of May 1861. He was then 9 years 9 months 17 days and blondish. That ensuing two weeks (May 31-June 17) the 24th organized at Camps Chase and Jackson. Unenlisted, without uniform or pay, he held his ground as a camp follower. Perhaps his fellow Buckeyes would accept him, at least unofficially, if he acted soldierly and wore down their resistance. He performed mundane camp duties—ran errands, watered horses, delivered messages, saluted; he practiced his penchant for percussion—drum-taps or rolls (paradiddles, daddy-mammies, flams-and-ruffs, flamdiddles and ratamacues). Regimented resistance toward

Klem's youthful blandishments eroded, melted amid these demonstrative loyalties until he took them by storm, ultimately disarming them officer and man. Thus Johnny, as a volunteer, began building up his legendary service record from approximately mid-June 1861. By Aug. 1, 1861, though not enlisted, "Pvt." Klem, at 9 years 11 months, had so far succeeded as to begin receiving a monthly $13—the pay of a beginning private. Whence his pay? A free-will offering, donation by his officers. Because too little is said of Klem's 1861 and 1862 service in *any* regiment other than the 22nd Michigan, commentary on this dearth of data is justified. Our mandate resides in certain ineluctable facts: the 22nd Michigan Infantry did not *begin* to organize (at Pontiac) and muster in *until* Aug. 29, 1862, nor did it leave Michigan for Kentucky until six days later;[8] The 22nd could not have been at Shiloh (4/6 - 7/62); Klem was at the Battle of Perryville (Ky. 10/8/62); the 24th Ohio was in battle at both Shiloh and Perryville; Klem was at Stones River with the 24th, but the 22nd Michigan were not in that five-day fracas. By tracing the steps of the 24th O.V.I. from its inception up through its march to Nashville during Oct. 22-Nov. 7, 1862, where they had duty until December 26, we can report what Klem's Civil War consisted of for those eighteen months:

-Depart Columbus 7/26/61, arrive Cheat Mountain, 8/14—Clem turns ten.
-Action at Cheat Mountain, 9/12—Christian W. goes home.
-Greenbrier River, 10/3-10/4 & 10/31
-Move to Louisville, Ky., 11/18
-To Camp Wickliffe till 2/62
-Advance on Nashville, 2/14-2/25
-Occupation of Nashville, 2/25-3/18
-March to Savannah, Tenn., 3/18-4/6
-Battle of Shiloh, 4/6-4/7
-Advance & Siege of Corinth, Miss., 4/29-5/30
-Pursuit to Booneville, 5/30-6/12
-Buell's Campaign in N. Ala. & Mid Tenn., June to August '62
-At Athens, Ala. till 7/17
-March to Louisville in pursuit of Bragg, 8/17-9/26
-Pursuit of Bragg to Loudon, Ky., 10/1-10/22
-Battle of Perryville, Ky., 10/8
-Nelson's Cross Roads, 10/18
-March to Nashville, 10/22-11/7 and duty there till 12/26
-Advance on Murfreesboro , 12/26-12/30
-Battle of Stone's River, 12/30-12/31 & 1/ 1-1/3/63
-Action at Woodbury, 1/24
-Duty at Readyville, Tenn. till June '63
-Tullahoma Campaign, 6/23-7/7 [9]

It was sometime during the 22nd Michigan's guard duty of the railroad at Nashville (4/149/5/63) while the 24th Ohio was in Mid-Tennessee (6/23-7/7 most likely) that "Johnny Shiloh" plausibly transferred to the 22nd Michigan. Why? History has never said nor has (auto)biography. It was also sometime during his protracted service with the 24th Ohio that Johnny, age ten, learned he had acquired a stepmother, Elizabeth,[10] probably from his Uncle Christian's letters.

After but a few weeks or sometime in July 1861 our Johnny, at length, gained the accolade of a uniform. None small enough existed. Efforts to find one his fit proved futile. But the regimental tailor cut down and shortened a small-sized one to almost his fit. It is believed this authentic garb bore a private's stripe, thus affording the boy boundless pride and contentment. There was little pampering, for he, too, marched in heat, rain, mud, sleet, snow. Broad shoulders often carried him across a stream or run. His rations were no less crude than the fare laid before his comrades—the Federal cuisine of hardtack, beans, coffee. His stride shorter, he stepped faster. Insect bites, humidity, sleeping close to or on the ground, 5:00 a.m. reveilles and 6:00 am. breakfasts (or none) surely diminished the anticipated glory of soldiering. Disciplining, regulations, drills, keeping uniforms presentable curtailed personal liberty. But Johnny found his fun times too—handball, townball, cards. Poker he learned as a rite of passage, as also imbibing strong drinks—another premature rite that intoxicated him to early slumbers, to the amusement of some.[11] But the boy capitalized on his assets—a pleasant disposition, quick-wittedness, seeing the humor(ous) potentials.

Klem first achieved fame from his drumming in the midst of the mammoth maw of death that was Shiloh, where 24,000 (Rebs & Yanks) were killed, wounded, or missing. The Union commander, U.S. Grant, within earshot of the battle din, ordered Gens. Buell and Wallace to prepare for action. Grant hastened to Pittsburg Landing to stem the initial Confederate assaults. Johnny Klem, reportedly (Clem) was with Grant near Shiloh Church, a key position that overlooked roadway from Pittsburg Landing to Corinth. By late afternoon (4/6/62) the Rebs had forced Gen. W.H.L. Wallace's surrender. Though Gen. Albert S. Johnston, C.S.A., was fatally wounded [he would be buried at Austin, Texas] and *his* forces, too, were in disarray by dusk, the Southerners held all the battlefield except the Landing sector. Gen. Grant's forces were demoralized amid severe losses; however, in the next eleven hours they reorganized and consolidated their positions. Grant boldly did the unlikely—an attack all along his front at 5:00 a.m. The colonel of the 24th Ohio was ordered to have a drummer ready to "beat the long roll." Johnny, at 4:15 a.m. was roused abruptly from sleeping and told to report to Gen. Grant's tent and to remain there. Moments later, equipped, and having dashed cold water several times over his face, the ten year-old stood at attention before the general and saluted. Grant, taken aback by the diminutive musician, questioned him. Could he stand up to it? Beat the long roll (call to battle), sustain it amid distractions without losing his concentration? Still at attention, Johnny vowed he could.

Moments later he began to beat his drum incessantly as hundreds of Union troops poured past to the front against Gen. Beauregard's concentrated battalions. Near Shiloh Church, where the fighting became fiercest, Johnny "took it out" on his drum as he was told. Amid the roar and smoke of musketry, not a few Henry Fleming types (raw recruits) fled headlong in fear and shame while the boy, preoccupied with his drumming, held his ground. He might even have wished *he* could have retreated, but he never gave the older ones a chance to laugh at him. Obedience to U. S. Grant in keeping up the cadence was his sole thought. Only when an exploding shell fragment smashed his drum and rendered it useless did he attempt to rejoin the relative safety of his own ranks. His arms and hands seemed ready to fall off.[12]

Word of the boy's bravery spread swiftly and within hours he acquired his first epithet: "Johnny Shiloh." President Grant, impressed by the little Buckeye, would remember this "incident" and appoint him (12/18/71) 2nd Lieutenant, 24th U.S. Infantry. And, yes, Gen. Grant himself praised his little percussionist. Having proven himself in battle, he was, within a month (5/1/62), *first* extended the *amenity* (unofficial) of enlisting; his Shiloh exploit earned him recognized soldier status (just short of official), his mascot days essentially gone. Johnny Shiloh, outfitted with a new drum and tailored uniform, improved his repertoire of routine drum calls. A story Clem liked to tell on himself, according to his nieces—Anita Sanderson and Elizabeth Birmingham—was that once when told to beat the call for retreat, not knowing that rhythm, he drummed *the charge.* Soldiery heeded the *unmistakable* beat, remained on the field, and defeated their foe!—(Rodriguez 39, n. 95).

"Little Shiloh," now nearly 44" in his stocking feet, soldiered on with his Buckeye comrades at Perryville (Ky. 10/8/62), where 843 fellow blue-clads were killed or mortally wounded; at Stone's River (12/31-1/3/63-1730 k. or m.w.) . Largely because his Uncle Christian Weber had been in Company H (of intensely German nationality) during his short tour with the 24th O.V.I. are we led to believe this was Klem's immediate unit. Yet, during the lad's tenure with this regiment, it would not have been extraordinary for him to have been considered a member of a few other companies. His name is *not* in the *official* list of thirteen who made up their Regimental Band.[13]

Because *no* government records exist on Klem prior to his service with the 22nd Michigan Infantry, some historians posit that he did not leave home until the early winter (Dec. '62) or spring of 1863.[14] Many revered standard, authoritarian chronicles would have us believe he went directly into the 22nd Michigan just hours, days or weeks after his rejection by the 3rd Ohio—a stellar flaw of the first magnitude reprinted a zillion-fold these past 130 years.[15] Mercedes Rodriguez's master's thesis, *The Drummer Boy John Lincoln Clem: The Civil War Years* (San Jose State Univ., June 1974, 19) has "John" offering himself to the 22nd Michigan just after his Third Ohio rejection. The illustration of Clem with sergeant's strips holding his kepi, presumably how he looked at Shiloh, and captioned "Unofficial drummer of the 22nd Michigan, he was probably, at 10, the youngest in the battle" is deceptive in *Civil War Times Illustrated* (May 1978, 19). In B. A. Botkin's *A Civil War Treasury of Tales, Legends and Folklore* (337) we are told, "the *first* we *know* of him, though small enough to live in a drum, was beating the long roll for the 22nd Michigan."[16] The deceptive accounts have perpetuated into the present, with *Echoes of Battle* (Baumgartner & Strayer, 88), allowing that Clem was with the 22nd Michigan impossibly too soon. "Scholars," regrettably, are currently *adding* to the Clem confusion. We now have popular accounts like Kenneth C. Davis' in *Don't Know Much About the Civil War* (1996, 334) that promote a blatant untruth that little Clem in the spring of 1861 got into the 22nd Massachusetts Infantry! The "Silver Cannonball" an extensive Civil War Card Series of the 1990's (Atlas Editions) has a card (D3 602 03-12 by Stephen T. Foster) also declaring that Clem was in the 22nd Massachusetts—one of *the* most stultifying "mythstakes" of all. John Clem went *on record officially* only upon his formal enlistment, which is recorded in *Michigan Volunteers, 1861-1865 - 22nd Infantry,* 42 - 43: "Enlisted in Company C, Twenty-Second Infantry, as Musician, May 1, 1863, at Nashville, Tenn. for 3 years, age 13. *[sic]* Mustered May 1, 1863. Missing in action at Chattanooga, Tenn., Oct. 10, 1863. Discharged Sept. 19, 1864."

Greg Pavelka, in his Apr. 20, 1996 generous response letter from Yankton, South Dakota, offers a plausible solution to the mystery of *where Johnny was* during June '61-June '62. He reasons that if Johnny was, in fact, in Newark, he undoubtedly would have been enrolled at his parish school at St. Francis de Sales Church. That school's attendance records *may still exist.* Possibly, too, Johnny attended public school in Newark, for which also his attendance *may* yet exist. *If* such could be found showing him present, this would be proof positive he was home until getting into the 22nd Michigan, whose recruits did on Sept. 5, 1862, he avers, pass through Newark by rail from Cleveland to Cincinnati, where they arrived at midnight. One would suppose that with such steady schooling during 1861-1862 and 1864-65, he would have been eligible for graduation from Newark High School a bit earlier than 1870 when he was approaching age nineteen, given the graduation requirements of that day. An argument for Clem's earlier military exploits is the vast array of photographs taken of him from his earliest army weeks on all across the time span from June '61 to his mandatory discharge Sept. 19, 1864. This multifarious photographic record—as a subject for the camera he apparently was irresistible material—evinces unto itself Johnny's transparently perceptible gains in maturation.[17] Could the immensely popular hit song "The Drummer Boy of Shiloh" (words & music by Will S. Hays) that summer of 1862 have been occasioned by some *unknown* worthy youngster; could it have had nothing to do with Clem?

On Shiloh's dark and bloody ground
The Dead and wounded lay
Amongst them was a drummer boy
who beat the drums that day.
A wounded soldier held him up
His drum was by his side.
He clasped his hands, then raised his eyes,
and prayed before he died—
He clasped his hands, then raised his eyes,
and prayed before he died.

By Chickamauga time (9/19/63), Clem had already been with the 22nd Michigan, Company C, several months up to a possible year, if, as Greg Pavelka suggests, he joined them on their troop train passing through Newark. However this adoption or transfer by Clem came about, a fundamental question arises, one which nearly all Clem authorities neglect and/or eschew. What precipitated Clem's transfer or termination of duty with the Buckeyes? A possible explanation could have been that, after long months of sturdy performance and loyalty, and, at Shiloh, heroic behavior, he never felt fully accepted on an official basis as an enlisted soldier. The *not being qualified for his own service record,* the *preservation of his unofficial status,* the entire want of credentials finally "got" to him. Was he capable of such rebellion? We believe so. Sensitive to the condescensions, to what he felt was shabby treatment, his patience ran out. Could he have been offended? Just a theory of the writer, who, unable to report on Clem's "doings" for June '61-Aug. '62, any authentic record these 130 years lacking, must ask the reader to decide where and how this lad was accounted for all this long time. If everything before September '62 is a fraud or heresay only, then Clem's standing with scores of other "soldierlings" on *these* pages is much reduced indeed! But his *known* 24 service months were to permit him ample time to earn much of his fame...*whatever* preceded!

As a speck in Gen. Rosecrans' Army of the Cumberland and in Gen. Gordon Granger's Reserve Corps, at McAfee's Church near Rossville, Clem was on the northern edge of the lengthy Chickamauga battleground on opening day and saw little action beyond great sound effects. But, on Day Two (9/20/63) Gen. Thomas' regiments were severely struck by Gen. Leonidas Polk's troops. Longstreet's veterans were soon able to drive the Union right from the field, leaving just Thomas, who, anon, formed a new battle line on Snodgrass Hill, where their defensive perimeter took the shape of a horseshoe, close to where the Union right had given way. Here Thomas' hard-pressed infantry on the Union left withstood murderous onslaughts from Longstreet's battalions. Granger intuitively hastened to Thomas' support with his 1st Division under Brig. Gen. James Steedman, under whom Brig. Gen.

Walter Whitaker's Brigade(s) were newly composed—22nd Michigan, 89th Ohio, 18th Ohio Battery. A certain pictorial seems always to have been universally endorsed: Johnny rapidly covers the five miles southward riding, bouncing on a caisson with an artillery man. Arrived at their key position, Whitaker's six regiments form two lines, the 22nd Wolverines at left in the forward line; at 3:30 p.m. he orders them to charge. For the 22nd's 455 effectives (one company is posted guard at Thomas' Hdqtrs.) this is their baptism of fire. Clem, legging it, advances as a regimental marker or guidon for comrades to align themselves on to keep their ranks even and organized. This six-regiment assault dislodges the CSA divisions under Bushrod Johnson and Thomas Hindman, who retreat, rally, and counterattack, forcing Whitaker's forward line to fall back. "Pvt. Clem sees his fellow companions, Cpl. Jonathan Vincent, 1st Sgt. Wm. F. Atkinson, and Sgt. Oscar Kendall by turns catch their Company C flag and hold it aloft in the face of the enemy."[18] In the same hour three bullets pierce Clem's kepi, testimonials to his lack of physical stature, to his bravery. Whitaker's men hold their terrain on Horseshoe Ridge, but the foes see-saw for this ground *several* exceedingly slow hours. They were "at it" till dusk when ordered by Thomas to retire to their hilltop. With the 89th Ohio on their right and the 21st Ohio to their left, the 22nd fought fresh divisions led by Gen. Hood. Reportedly four Rebel assaults went forward, the final one carrying this key position. They bought the godsend of time with a lavish blood flow, both Gray and Blue. Clem's unit were encompassed, as he straggled to stay with his retreating comrades. At this moment transpired perhaps *the* most telling of all Clem vignettes and anecdotes— whether authentic or mythopoeic seems long since consigned to the maw of ambivalence (favored by time's passage?). Pavelka passes it along in Johnny's own recounted rendition: "At the close of the day our Union forces were retiring toward Chattanooga and my brigade was sore beset by the enemy. In fact, we were in a tight place. A Confederate colonel rode up and yelled at me. 'Surrender, you damned little Yankee!' Raising my musket without aiming, I pulled the trigger and he fell from his horse, badly wounded."[19] Apocryphal versions end with "and I killed him" or "and he died." Third person narratives often go..."By way of answer the boy halted, brought his piece to 'OrderArms,' (thus throwing the colonel off guard). In a moment the piece was cocked, brought to aim, fired, and the officer toppled dead from his horse." We are to understand that it was for this gallantry more than for anything else that he was promoted to lance sergeant, presumably in that same battle month—September, the boast ever after being that Clem was the youngest "noncom" in the Union Army, age 12 years 2 months, which does endure as true.

Outnumbered, surprised from behind, Clem's 22nd Wolverines suffered 32 killed, 96 wounded, 262 (including himself) captured.[20] But, quick-witted (when among prisoners being led away a guard ordered them to lie prone)

Johnny played dead, as a few others did, simply not resuming the march. With him was 2nd Lt. Albertson,19 and furtively they crept back into friendly held Chattanooga. Alive, tearful, excited, mournful, defiant, Clem unburdening, verbalized an enfilade of emotive thoughts, eager to share his long afternoon and evening. Albertson, fortunately, could and did readily affirm much of the boy's news—an essentially articulate mix of reporting under simultaneous ebullience of satisfactions and trauma over loss of his friends. Clem's own deeds of courage spread like prairie fire in late summer. Within hours Gen. Thomas knew all and gave the battlefield promotion. The media caught wind of it, and Clem's life from that week would never again be quite the same. *Harper's Weekly* pictured him and extolled his exploits, as dozens of newspapers caught the story. A Miss Babcock of the Sanitary Commission suggested to a Chicago ladies sewing circle that they tailor him a suitable uniform with sergeant's chevrons and a cut-down sword.[22] This they did with dispatch, getting Johnny's measurements from his immediate officers. Before long he was presented a silver medal by a daughter of Secretary of the Treasury Salmon P. Chase, inscribed:

Sgt. Johnny Clem
22nd Mich. Vol. Inf'y
from N.M.C.[23]

Augmenting Clem's expanding image came shortly (10/6/63) another major escapade. That day as part of a railway guard assigned to a supply train, they came under attack by CSA cavalry between Chattanooga and Bridgeport, Alabama. Sergeant Clem was taken a prisoner and whisked away, perhaps as far as Tallahassee, for a few weeks that he would remember as humilitating for the wealth of insulting remarks crooned by his captors. Most offensive of all was Gen. Joe Wheeler himself, who delighted in announcing the boy's presence, widely quoted in Clemiana: "See what sore straits the Yankees are driven to when they have to send their babies to fight us." What upset Clem most was the theft of his jacket, shoes and kepi—which latter he had set his heart upon as a keepsake, being proud of its three bullet holes.[24] Happily, his detention was abridged (barely 3 wks.) by early parole; accordingly, he was shunted to Camp Chase, Ohio, close to home.

He enjoyed a furlough home for November-December; whether officially sanctioned or self-awarded, it was well timed and logical. His AWOL status on the 22nd Michigan's Muster Rolls for these two months became "academic," for on Jan. 4, 1864, by Special Order Gen. Thomas had Sgt. Clem assigned to his own staff as a mounted orderly. Meanwhile, the little hero was celebrated and photographed considerably in Newark. The local paper carried a story (reprinted 10/9/1915) picturing him with four members of the W.A.R. Women's Club, organized to assist Licking County sick and wounded.[25]

Sergeant Clem carried dispatches from Headquarters, Army of the Cumberland, to Gen. Thomas' subordinate C.O's. Such duty was not without peril during the sanguinary Atlanta Campaign. In fact, while hustling with a message to Maj. Gen. John A. Logan, Johnny, nearly thirteen, sustained a slight wound of the right ear from a bullet that then burrowed into his pony beneath. Johnny soon "picked up" another wound, a shell fragment to his hip.[26] These nine months close to Gen. Thomas were some of the most memorable he would ever have. The General took a paternal interest in his little sergeant. He had his aide and nephew, Col. Sanford C. Kellogg, tutor Johnny in geography, history, math, and spelling.[27]

Secretary of War Edwin M. Stanton, while visiting Sherman's headquarters in fallen Atlanta, learned of Clem's risky missions. Contemplating the boy's possible fatality and the negative criticism and blow to Northern morale it would have, Stanton issued an order rather abruptly—Clem must be discharged, as all such boys must be. Doubtlessly disappointed, he was discharged then and there, Sept. 19, 1864, at 13 years 1 month 6 days. Depending on which school the reader belongs to, Clem closed out 39 Union Army months or 24 1/2.

Once home, Johnny resumed local schooling. He studied two years at a private academy in Indianapolis to help prepare for admission to West Point. Upon graduating in 1870 from Newark High School, he was appointed a cadet at large to West Point by President Grant. Unable to pass the entrance exams, academically *or* physically (he was barely 5' tall), he was denied. Briefly he worked in the Washington, D.C., Census Bureau. He gained audience with President Grant, who—(remembering Shiloh?)—personally appointed him a second lieutenant on Dec. 19, 1871. This turning-point inaugurated a 43-year Regular Army career, the highlights of which were:

-Trains for infantry officer
-Graduates from Fort Monroe Artillery School, 1875
-Patrols the Texas-Mexico Border[28]
-Helps control American Indians
-Serves as a signal officer
-Teaches as Prof. of Military Science & Tactics, Galesville Univ., 2 yrs
-Convenes with fellow members, National Cemetery Board.
-Serves Army Quartermaster Corps until 1915 as its ranking Colonel.
-Retires on his 64th birthday, a brigadier general (By Act of Congress for all Civil War veterans who attained a colonelcy by their legal retirement age)
-A 1916 Act of Congress awards him rank of major general. (Conferred on 65th birthday)

Although Gen. Clem was the last Civil War veteran to retire from the Regular Active Army Rolls, ranking all other officers on that list, he was not

Lt. John L. Clem, 1871.

the last Civil War veteran to retire as a commissioned officer. Admiral George Dewey, a lieutenant in the Civil War, who died Jan. 16, 1917, by Act of Congress was *never* allowed to retire until his death. (See also Reginald F. Nicholson.)

In May 1875, Lt. Clem married Anita Rosetta French, daughter of Maj. Gen. William H. French. Of their four children, only John Jr., born June 8, 1885, at Fort McHenry, Baltimore, survived to adulthood. In 1879 the Clems would live in Galesville, Wisconsin, for two years. In their 24th matrimonial year Anita died Aug. 5, 1899, at New Castle, Delaware, just as John Jr. began schooling at West Texas Military Academy in San Antonio. Major Clem eventually met and wooed Elizabeth Sullivan, a Southern belle and daughter of financier Daniel Sullivan. Of Indianola, Texas, Elizabeth, still 24, married John, newly 52, Sept. 23, 1903. [We note in passing one of this groom's attainments scarcely noticed—an aggregate of nearly 58 years of matrimony.] His career required them to live in the northern states and territories at first and then to travel to wider duty stations—the Philippines, Puerto Rico, Japan and China during the Spanish American War era. Their only child, Anne Elizabeth, born June 24, 1906, in San Francisco two months after the catastrophic earthquake, brought much happiness to the family.[29] As Chief Quartermaster, Department of California, Col. Clem had organized a 34-car relief squadron kept busy around the clock for weeks. Despite loss of his own office and records, he brought this exigency off with relative pizzazz. Major Gen. Clem was immensely popular in the G.A.R. He was elected Senior Vice Commander-in-Chief at the 51st Nat'l Encampment in Boston, Aug. 20- 25, 1917. He seldom missed a reunion. He was a 32nd Degree Mason, a Shriner, a comrade of the Loyal Legion and of the United Spanish War Veterans. He was several terms president of the Society of the Army of the Cumberland.[28] He voluntarily spent generous time in D. C. fighting for and securing pension legislation (benefits) for veterans—another reason he was their idol. He never forgot family. Yearly he returned to his hometown, Newark. In his own right, he grew into an old soldier personality. Becoming frail in retreat at his 404 Braodway Street home in San Antonio, he died there in the old manner...in his own bed. He went to his final honored glory-rest in Arlington National Cemetery just below the Lee Mansion under the staccato of a thirteen gun salute. On his impressive, though simple, stone is engraved:

THE DRUMMER BOY OF CHICKAMAUGA

Commemorative Envelope.

The aging Clem was an instrumental pioneer in what has become, via Jerry Russell and his battalion, a sacred mission to save the battlefields. In 1959, Newark, Ohio, named a new school in honor of their favorite son: the John Lincoln Clem Elementary School. Souvenir plates abound. Medallions have proliferated. Fort Sam Houston Museum devotes a room to Clem memorabilia. His primal place among our youngster "soldierlings" appears assured, *all contingencies considered*, despite the fact that some other youths on these pages eclipse Clem's verifiable attainments. Among enduring valedictory truths are:

Absolute Myths about John L. Clem:

1. That he was the Union Army's youngest hero.
2. That he was the Union Army's youngest enlistee.
3. That he was the latest-born Union soldier.
4. That he was the last Civil War veteran to retire as a commissioned officer.
5. That he served with the 22nd Michigan Infantry anytime during June 1861-Aug. 31, 1862.
6. That he was the youngest (latest born) of the 55,000+ veterans at the joint 50th Battle Reunion at Gettysburg in July 1913. (He might have been one of the five youngest on enlistment there, but he surely wouldn't have been among the 125 latest born.)
7. That he served in the 22nd Massachusetts Infantry.
8. That he was the youngest Civil War vet when he died.

Absolute Truths about John L. Clem:

1. He was a hero.
2. He was one of the shortest and lightest.
3. He was/is the war's most celebrated youth.
4. He was beloved widely by fellow veterans.
5. He lived up to demanding expectations of the American Public.
6. It is necessary to report both the legendary and the historical Clem, to admit there is a Clem mystique.
7. When Clem died, our nation was still wealthy in ex-child-soldiery from "The Boys' War," though we could scarcely have known it.
8. So thoroughly has he served all during 1862-1996 as a venerable/veritable "smoke screen" for the *entire* topic, or writing field on youngest Civil War veterans, as to render said field seemingly nonviable, unrewarding, unworthy of exploration!
9. How ironic that this best known soldierboy should remain controversial for puzzling questions as to the extent of his service!

Casper Androus Ricks

Feb. 28, 1851 – June 16, 1937

Of Angelina County in East Texas from 1872 on, "Captain" Ricks lived nearby or in Lufkin for sixty-five years. Rightly, he went down as one of its original pioneers. But his paternal ancestry were Virginians, going back to his great-great-grandsire Christopher Ricks (& beyond), a veteran of the American Revolution. While a few accounts, including one of his own, assert Rome, Indiana, as his birthplace, family genealogists believe Louisville, Kentucky, is indicated. An August 15, 1850, Census Record for Louisville lists his future parents as John W. Ricks (1829 - ?), 21, a teacher, and Louisa Elizabeth Androus [later Mrs. Llewellyn Dean] Ricks (1815-1892), 35, an Ohio native. When Casper came along, he already had three half-sisters—Eliza A., b. 1833; Josephine, b. 1838; Harriet F., b. 1842—and a half-brother, James Eugene E. Rich (b. 1845), who would enlist in Allen's 4th Louisiana Infantry at Clinton, East Feliciana Parish. One day in 1858 this family—Casper, his mother Louisa Elizabeth (Ricks *then),* and his half-brother James Eugene Rich—took passage on a riverboat and floated down the Ohio and Mississippi. The father evidently had already departed to parts unknown, while the three half-sisters seem to have stayed in Kentucky or Indiana. Casper, then all of seven, could seventy and eighty years later dimly remember this adventure and how they at length arrived at Jefferson, Texas. His clearest memory was of his schooling at Clarksville (Red River County), at Rusk (Cherokee County), at Scottsville and Elysian Fields (Harrison County), and in Natchitoches, Louisiana, where, early in 1863, he was expelled from Catholic College because he would not tell at early mass who was guilty of a phosphorous prank by some of his classmates in chemistry. Lifelong friendships sprung from days at Natchitoches, among whom was John P. Hartman, later of Lufkin, who, until he died in January 1930, belonged to C. A. Ricks' same U.C.V. Camp 1683. Always an avid learner and highly literate from his youth up, C. A. Ricks, as he often signed himself, was given to writing retrospects. Citing one of these incorporated in *History and Genealogy of the Ricks Family of America* [Revised Ed. 1957, Sect. V, pp. 598-603],[1] we may enjoy directly his gift for narrative:

After my expulsion I went to Shreveport and enlisted in Co. C of a Courier Battalion in which none of the privates were over age 15. I was the youngest, enlisting on Aug. 15, 1863, when 12 years 5 months 15 days. Later our battalion was divided, and formed the 1st and 2nd Trans-Mississippi Cavalry, C.S.A. We were sent on military routes, and the men were sent to the front. Reuben J. Estes, later, long a traveling representative of The Shreveport, La. Times, *was a member of my company, both in the battalion and in the 2nd Regiment of Courier Cavalry; Hawkes was captain; Carlisle, Lt. At the National Reunion at Washington, D. C., 1917, I met my comrade F. R. Chandler of Plain Dealing, La., and at the Little Rock, Arkansas, Reunion in May 1928 I met a Mr. Smith (of my Company C) of Camden, Ark.*[2]

My official tour of C.S.A. duty ran from Sept. 1st 1863, until about mid-Feb. 1864 when I was discharged after a severe spell of meningitis. Early in March having recuperated (& without re-enlisting), I was promised by Gen. Kirby Smith, my mount and accoutrements, whereupon I reported to Gen. Dick Taylor for volunteer service on his staff in lower La. At the Battle of Mansfield, La., I was made a prisoner. The mount I happened to be on had no Confederate brand, and I claimed him. It was a beautiful roan that the governing yardmaster at old Muggensville, near Shreveport, permitted me to smuggle on the steamer after dark for two Mexican silver dollars, without branding him. The colonel of the regiment gave me $75 in greenbacks for him, because he was private property.

Mother had come down with me from Shreveport on the steamer, and she and I got off at Cotile Landing, above Alexandria. I went by horseback to join Gen. Taylor's forces below while she remained at home on a visit and business matters at the home of State Senator Lewis De Hatter. As I came back a prisoner, we passed within a mile of the DeHatter plantation; I gave the sergeant in charge of us a Mexican silver half dollar to stop at Col Hunter's plantation, and let me send word to my mother. By next morning daylight, she arrived at the prison in an old hack pulled by two decrepit mules, driven by an old trusty darkey. A native Buckeye, she got me paroled and secured us passage on the same steamer that carried us prisoners and many wounded officers, to New Orleans. Mother acted as a nurse, and through the offices of a Col. Lee of Maine who'd lost an arm, made my life as a prisoner easy on the vessel. In New Orleans, she at once went to the office of the Provost Marshal, with letters from Col. Lee and other officers and secured my parole for the city. Major Harry Porter, the Provost Marshal, had been her schoolmate in Ohio.... When, after another spell of meningitis, I got well enough to go north,

Mother and I were sent to N. Y. on a U. S. transport, via Key West; I was on parole a few weeks in Baltimore and in Washington, D. C., until ordered to Camp Werton, a prison near Indianapolis.[3]

While at D. C. I saw many noted northern political and military leaders. After a few months I was told I need not report myself any more. I rambled over much of Indiana, Ohio & Kentucky as I had many kinfolks there. After the war, I returned to Washington, D. C., where I remained until Feb. 17, 1867, when with my brother Eugene Rich and a Dr. Bishop I started back to Texas with a lot of blacks for plantations of the father of T. W. House of Houston, the Sessions of Galveston, and others. That August I had malaria. I went back over to Fort Bend County in 1870. In July 1872 at a protracted meeting at Sulphur Springs in Angelina County, I joined the Missionary Baptist Church. In August I started to go east to D. C. to visit Mother. I'd come in to old Homer, then Angelina's county seat. I spent the night with old Brother Stephen Treadwell, now of Lufkin, whom I'd met at the Sulphur Springs revival. Uncle Stephen persuaded me to go back to Shawnee Prairie to teach. On Sept. 9th I first met my wife as a student in the highest (8th) grade, and on Jan. 21, 1873, we were married by Elder Joe Lambert, who had baptized us both in 1872.[4] *In the fall of '73, I taught another term at Lambert's Chapel. From then on, I farmed and drove logging teams.*

Yes, it was while teaching school in Shawnee Prairie that Casper met Miss Sarah Jane Weaver (Mar. 29, 1856-Jan. 21, 1928), age sixteen, of Angelina County, Texas, daughter of Larkin Chivers Weaver and Caroline Grimes Weaver, Georgia natives. Their children were Larkin Eugene, 1874-1960, who married Etta A. Squyres; Louisa Elizabeth, 1876-1940, who married King D. Gann; Frances Caroline, 1878-1961, who married Wm. Thos. Page; Llyellian Dean, 1881-2; Edward B., 1884-1946, who married Etta E. Young; Nixon, 1896-1976, who married Hollye Youngblood; and Mayon, 1899-1967, who married Orrin Lucille Brown Lynch.

Casper's and Sarah Jane's first home was in Homer, then eight miles southeast of Lufkin (now, three miles southeast). Toward the last of their living at Homer, Casper was appointed its postmaster, but on Dec. 17, 1881, he resigned and moved his wife and four children into a "rough edge" camp in old Lufkin—its first settlers but for farmers living outside the townsite. For a while they lived in a tent. As Casper himself later (c. 1912) wrote:

About July-August 1882 the Houston, East & West Texas Railroad laid out Lufkin and sold lots. W. H. Bonner, Capt. J. H. Kerr and Uncle Jim Denton had commenced work on their houses. I contracted with W. J. and George Townsend to build them a business building, and in Sep-

tember I also built the first house in New Lufkin on what is now the northwest corner of Fire Station Park. Until 1887 I worked as a barber also, then I moved to a farm 2 miles east. In 1889 W. H. Bonner built Lufkin's first two-story brick building. In 1894 I lost everything I had in a sawmill venture. In September 1911, I bought on credit The Huntington Herald, *which I published for ten years until I sold out in 1921. That May I started publishing* The Courier *at Lufkin. On Dec. 1, 1928, I sold my plant to Collins Hadiburg and on Apr. 25, 1929, I sold my home at 310 Lufkin Avenue.*

In her May 1, 1991, letter from Port Neches, Texas, DeLois Harris (Mrs. Mahlan) Broussard, great-granddaughter, amplifies welcome details:

My great-Grandfather Casper A. Ricks while he owned the Lufkin Courier *wrote trying to get his father-in-law a Confederate pension.... "Does any veteran or person remember Larkin Chivers Weaver, now 89, who enlisted in Captain Laird's Co. G, Walker's Division, at Rusk, Cherokee County, Texas? He was detailed as a cooper in the government shops at Minden, on the Arkansas River. While Larkin was there, a Captain Vines or Bryans was shot by order of General Magruder (Court Martial) and Larkin saw those guns smoke. Mr. Weaver and his wife, helpless and blind, live with me. They came here in 1849 when it was a wilderness." From what I've heard—and it was family knowledge for years before me—Great-Grandpa {quite a character} and only a few other men knew that Wm. Clarke Quantrell during his last days went by another name. Family tradition held that C.A.R. once met Mr. Q. , who requested of his confidants strict silence (a virtue C.A.R. was proverbial for) because of a wife and children.*

About 1910 Mamie Yeary visited Captain Ricks, one of 2100 Texas Rebs she interviewed for her 1912 *Reminiscences of the Boys in Gray 1861-1865.* Her interviewee, whose middle name *Androus* got folk-etymologized to *Andrews* (p. 639), reflected briefly these thoughts on that occasion: "I enlisted in the Confederate Army at Shreveport, as private in Company B, Battalion of Couriers, E. Kirby Smith's Brigade. My first Captain was Hawks, and the first Lieutenant was Carlisle. I do not remember much about the war, as I was discharged on account of sickness, spinal meningitis, and my memory has been somewhat impaired. I remember the works for the defense of the city (Shreveport) and the outer route of Bank's Army as it got into Alexandria, La., as we were captured and taken there just before he got in."

Orrin M. Ricks (Mrs. "Bill") Felice, 72, daughter of Casper's youngest (Mayon Ricks), of Huntington, Texas, lends us a few more insights from her April 29, 1991 letter:

Grandpa ran for Congress in this the 2nd District in 1916 and in 1918 but did not get elected. He was outspoken. It was said that you might not agree with him, but you knew where he stood, for he told you plain and straight. Some folks liked that, some didn't. Although he had enlisted as C. or Casper Ricks, he did at age 17 upon his mother's request, add Androus to his signed name, or "C. A." He had a stroke 3 years before he died and spent his last two years at the Confederate Soldiers Home in Austin. A son, Llyellian, that died in infancy is marked in the same plot with Grandpa and Grandma.

Some three and a half years after the death of his beloved on their 55th wedding day and in a somber lonely mood on Aug. 9, 1931, "C.A." wrote:

The only way we can serve God is by serving our fellows. Unless we willingly love our neighbors as ourselves (God's Commandment), we fail to fulfill the will of God. As I stand half way of my 81st year, I feel that I've fallen short of my duty to both God and man, that such failure has cost me much sorrow. Personal injury to me, I forgive, as I have hope to be forgiven. **Even if Christianity proves to be a myth, it makes people better parents, neighbors, citizens.** *Soon I will pass over, to realize that, if I dwell in a Beaulah Land of Love, with loved ones, that this will be by the atoning blood of the Savior.*

In her Mar. 31, 1991 letter from Lufkin [Fairview], Opal L. Whitehead, daughter of Larkin Rick's son Carson Allen, authoress of the "Free Press" column for *Fairview News,* supplies these somewhat elusive yet worthy thoughts:

I was five when Great-Granddad died. I am trying to get a large tombstone on his gravesite here from the Army V.F.W. He sure deserves one. Casper's mother, "Granny Dean," was a lady of society in Washington, D. C. , Mississippi, and Indiana, for her second husband was Senator Llewllyn Dean. She was buried in Kensington, Md. My baby brother was killed in Vietnam December 1968, Larry E. Ricks. His name is on the Wall.

Latest born of the 2100 Texas Rebs visited during 1907-1912 by Mamie Yeary for her *Reminiscences* and *the* youngest Confederate veteran of Angelina County, Captain Ricks' funeral service was held at 4:00 p.m. Friday June 18, 1937, from Lufkin's Gipson Funeral Home, Rev. W. S. Moody officiating. Some eighty Ricks family descendants were among the huge press of mourners that day. Lufkin seemed to know this was their last opportunity to pay homage to one of their colorful pioneers, and they "made the most of it." A vivid detail about the Ricks procession that day came to the writer March 31, 1991, via telephone—the voice of Elwyn M. Gipson, then 69, current President-Director of the Gipson Home, a family commitment of over 100 years. ..."I was just fifteen at his funeral, impressed by the Confederate flag that covered his casket. Our Lufkin High School Band marching along behind him played "Dixie" as loud as they could. It was a parade fit for our hometown hero." Casper A. Ricks was laid to rest at White House Cemetery, four miles south of Lufkin. Pallbearers were great-grandsons Milton, Robert, Philip, Curtis, and Jack Ricks and William Crain. His descendants were then in generations of 6 – 29 – 48 – 2.

Casper A. Ricks with his Southern Cross of Honor.

Thomas W. Daniel

Mar. 22, 1849 – June 10, 1938

This biography has been donated and largely written by John Rix Seibert, II, of Akron, Ohio, a great-great-grandson of William Thomas Daniel, 1813-1889, whose last vital link with the Daniel saga was Thomas W. Daniel's youngest sister, Arminta.

On a quiet hill in Old Union Cemetery in the town of Young Harris, Georgia, are the graves of four Confederate soldiers—a father and three sons. The youngest of these sons and last to go to his rest was Thomas W. Daniel.

Grandmother Julia Mary Dooley (Mar. 22, 1885-Jan. 9, 1979) related to me this story of her Grandfather William Thomas Daniel and his four sons, all of whom gave personal service to "the Lost Cause." I am descended from William's youngest daughter, Arminta Adeline Daniel Erwin (Apr. 27, 1859-Jan. 7, 1952); thus, I am Thomas W. Daniel's great-grandnephew. Grandmother Erwin referred to him as "Uncle Tom." I recall as a small boy going into Granny Erwin's bedroom to "fix Granny's eyes" by putting eye drops into her eyes at bedside. Her last seventeen years Arminta Erwin spent bedridden and blind. She used to feel my face when I came to her bedside. During 1864-65 she had (at age five) assisted her mother, Mary, in darning socks for Confederate soldiers. Their "sock darnings" would be sent to the Army of Tennessee, C.S.A.... You could say she was one of the last living links to all the women who assisted the Confederacy through their humble work at home. With pale blue-green eyes, Arminta stood at 6' 2" and in the admiration of those who knew her. She passed away, at nearly 93, on Miller Avenue in Akron, Ohio, and was buried at our Lakewood Cemetery.

Both William T. Daniel and his wife, the former Mary Rutherford, had grown up in Buncomb County, North Carolina. They settled off to their southwest in Towns County of very northern Georgia. Among their children were Reuben P. "Uncle Rube" Daniel (Dec. 12, 1833-Aug. 17, 1922); Asa Lafayette "Uncle Ace" Daniel (Nov. 1839-Jan. 17, 1922); James "Uncle Jim" Daniel (1845-Nov. 23, 1870), and Thomas W. "Uncle Tom."

For the Daniel family the approaching war became "a family affair," all recruitable males to be inducted into Confederate service. Thomas lost little time before achieving his enlistment as a private for Company E, "the Talbot Guards" (of Talbot County), Ninth Georgia Infantry. He did this on July 11, 1861, in Geneva, Georgia, at 12 years 3 months 19 days! Captain E. R.

Cpl. William Thomas Daniel, 6th Georgia Cavalry, 1864. Father of Thomas William Daniel, 9th Georgia Infantry.

Goulding was in charge of Thomas' unit, at this time assigned to duty in the Army of the Shenandoah. After a few months the Ninth Georgia was rotated to the Department of Northern Virginia. It was assigned to Gen. George Thomas Anderson, whose command was already in the thick of the fighting from the Seven Days Campaign (June 26-July 1, '62) to Cold Harbor and Appomattox, or, in all, some forty-five contests in arms. Young Thomas would be admitted to two of wartime Richmond's hospitals during his C.S.A. service. Records show he was admitted to Chimborazo Hospital on Apr. 17, 1862, and released that May 1st; he was admitted to Wayside Hospital on Feb. 18, 1863, though his release date from there is not specified. A record confirms that Thomas was issued his second uniform on Sept. 6, 1864. Their Brigade was transported with Longstreet to Georgia, the better to support Bragg's Army of Tennessee then besieging Chattanooga. (My Grandmother Dooley would recall her Grampa William Thos. Daniel telling of how at one point he and his son had a joyful reunion upon her Uncle Thomas' arrival with the Georgia Ninth from Virginia.) "Uncle Tom" was to serve with the Ninth Infantry back in that great "Siege City" of Petersburg, as in the ensuing Appomattox Campaign, those strenuous last C.S.A. and A.N.V. months, indeed, conferring upon this new sixteen-year-old the status of a heavily embattled, diehard Reb. An examination of the paroles granted at Appomattox Court House reveals that not quite 200 of the Ninth Georgia's officers and men surrendered there. Of its staff there was but one major, one adjutant, one surgeon, one assistant surgeon, and one chaplain; of Company E who surrendered, but one captain, one 1st lieutenant, two sergeants, three corporals, and nineteen privates (among whom was Thos. W. Daniel).[1] In a study of those youngest soldiery who serve the longest this lad, Thomas Daniel, places high (See Appendix D). Thomas W. is cited in Appomattox paroles.

Tom's brother Reuben enlisted Aug. 31, 1861, at Big Shanty, for service with Company K, 23rd Georgia. After one of his tense moments, Reuben "returned thanks" for the providential lodging of a bullet in his pocket Bible. Perhaps this poignant experience was what caused him to request a twenty-day leave from his regiment on Feb. 8, 1865. Arriving home, Reuben wrote a letter back to the 23rd expressing his desire to remain at home. Nevertheless, Reuben had laid his life on the line for over forty months when he left the C.S.A. that late February.[2] He lived to be nearly ninety when he died at the home of his daughter, Mrs. Mary "Mollie" Burkett, in Highland Park, Tennessee. He was buried in an unmarked grave at a country courtyard near Rossville, Walker County, Georgia.

Tom's father, William T. or "J. D." (as youngest daughter Arminta often called him), meanwhile had enlisted at Blairsville, Georgia, on Feb. 14, 1863, through a Capt. B. M. Ledford. Frustration and worry over what was happening to his boys may have prompted him to join Company I, Sixth Georgia Cavalry. The regiment served in the opening phases of Chickamauga at Reed's Bridge and Jay's Mills. The Sixth was also to give conspicuous service in the Atlanta Campaign and at Knoxville. "J. D." sustained a serious shoulder wound at Averasboro and finished his service a corporal; he ultimately surrendered with the Army of the Tennessee. Young Thomas Daniel had surrendered with the A.N.V. and received his modest portion of the 25,000 rations handed out to Lee's veterans, and had begun his long trek home to the Southern Blue Ridge Mountains of northern Georgia. Grandmother Dooley told me, "Upon the Daniel Boys' return, their lice-infested uniforms were burned out behind their parents' home. James Daniel's health was never the same afterward, and this came from sleeping on the ground many a night without so much as a blanket." This "Uncle Jim" would be the first of the boys to join "the Great Army in the Sky" when he died of a heart attack while touring the site at Lookout Mountain, where he fought seven years before.

William returned to his simple two-story home to live an inconspicuous life of toil as did so many of his fellow Rebs. "J. D." never took care of his shoulder wound properly; this, combined with tuberculosis, caused him to breathe his last on March 15, 1899. The only known photograph of him confirms a satisfying fact—that he was among the U.D.C.s early awardees of the Southern Cross of Honor.

As for the youngest Daniel, he too opted for a quiet private life on his farmland with family and neighborliness, the values uppermost in his heart. As his granddaughter, Mrs. Gladys Twiggs, of Young Harris, Georgia, relates, "Uncle Tom generally sat on his porch viewing his dooryard scenery." Although a religious man, he did not attend church...was a kind of "retiree" until finally joining his father and brothers Asa and James in unbroken ranks on their hill in Old Union Cemetery.

William Henry Bush

Sept. 21, 1857 – Oct. 25, 1938

A Hoosier by birth, a "soldierling" for his earliest serious role, a paragon of filial pride, a pioneer settler and townsman, and a kindly human spirit by nature, Willie H. Bush turned in an exemplary American life preeminently representative of his generation. Of all the childlike martinets who were to "perform duty" in the Union forces—musicians, powder monkeys, messengers, orderlies, guidon markers, mascots, valets or waiters—"very probably" the latest born and youngest of all was Willie H. Bush. His birth date was so late that one would assume he could not have fulfilled any meaningful role in the Civil War. So late was Willie in "arriving" that upon the opening salvo at Fort Sumter (4/12/61), he was only 3 years 6 months 22 days. In fact, he was the only "man" born in 1857 to wear the Union attire and wear it *during* hostilities *while occupying a specific billet.* True, he was never issued formal enlistment papers, never had pay records, never drew a Civil War pension, and practically never mentioned himself as ever having done anything in or for the war effort. Truthfully, outside of his father, a few kin, and a score or two of his older comrades (staff & guards at Elmira, New York), Willie, for all his 73 post bellum years, was assumed to have had nothing to do with the war. Indeed, no mention of his low profile veteran status is found in any write-ups about him, including his obituary. These truths rest primarily upon two facts: (1) he was a non-enlistee without written records, (2) he did not proclaim himself a veteran.

One salient instance of awareness of Willie's humble Civil War "contribution" to his father, surfaced about 1874 when "Gen. Philip Sheridan tendered to Dr. Bush's son, W. H. Bush, of this city {*Montesamo* (Wash.) *Vidette,* 11/21/02}, a cadetship at West Point on account of his father's record."[1]

Willie Bush's candidacy for recognition as the youngest wearer of Union Army attire does not in any respect jeopardize St. James, Missouri's Charles Knecht (Nov. 1, 1853-Jan. 18, 1948), for *his* solid first place as the youngest *enlisted* soldier (Fife-boy, Benton Barracks Cadets Band)—7 years 10 months 14 days—has held since the writer's discovery of him in late 1971. But Bush's scarce credentials, while not quite in neat order [unarchived], are, for all their humble nature, unmistakable, credible, reportable.

William, an only child his first seven years, was born on a farm just outside Porter, Porter County, in very northern Indiana, within four miles of Lake Michigan. His parents were Dr. Asahel K. and Eliza A. Congdon Bush (Dec. 16, 1835-Aug. 29, 1890), who had married on June 16, 1855. Asahel (Sept. 9, 1830-Nov. 19, 1902) was a native of Yates County in west-central New York. The Bushes moved to southern Michigan in July 1839 and from there to southern Wisconsin in 1846. Within another year Asahel, 17, began reading medicine under a Rufus Howard, M.D., and he did so for several years. On Dr. Howard's recommendation, Asahel was admitted to Rock Island Medical College, where he graduated in the early 1850's.[2] Some two years after Willie's birth, the Bushes moved a few miles northeast to the outskirts of Michigan City, Indiana, where they lived on their quiet small-time farmstead. This larger town's citizenry benefited from Asahel's medical studies.

Mark Weldon

"Corporal" Willie H. Bush, 1st Bn., 11th Regt., V.R.C., Elmira.

Rightly, our interest in Willie depends greatly upon his father's illustrious Civil War career, for Dr. A. K. Bush would be of strategic value as a surgeon with any unit he joined. His service had at least four distinct phases and even outlasted the war. Almost at opening gun, A.K.B. volunteered himself and enlisted on Apr. 16, 1861, for duty mustering in as 1st lieutenant in Company B, Ninth Indiana Infantry. A three-month regiment, they organized at Indianapolis until April 27 and drilled until mid-May. Ordered to Grafton, Virginia (today's W. Va.) May 29, they were attached to Kelly's Command and fought an action at Phillipi on June 3rd. The Ninth was then attached to Morris' Indiana Brigade for July. They fought in the West Virginia Campaign, skirmishes at Laurel Hill, July 7-8; at Bealton, July 10; an action at Carrick's Ford, July 12-14; pursuit of Garnett's forces, July 14-17. They were mustered out Aug. 2, 1861, with but 3 killed and 2 taken by disease.[3] Ex-Lt. A. K. Bush returned in a blessed homecoming and life with Eliza and Willie (crowding age 4) for little more than a month while he set about personally organizing what became the Fourth Independent Battery of Indiana (Mounted) Light Artillery, his favorite branch of the Army. As captain (9/5/61), Asahel K. Bush mustered-in and organized them at Indianapolis (9/27-10/3). [Willie put up a big fuss about this father leaving him. He was prescribed stern medicine: learning to read, helping mother, building with homemade wooden construction blocks, maneuvering toy soldiers.] Captain Bush with his Fourth Battery was ordered to Louisville, Kentucky, on October 4. Their duty station until early February 1862 was at New Haven and Munfordsville, Ky. They served, unattached, with the Army of the Ohio till June 1862 then with the Army of the Cumberland. They functioned as part of that Army's Artillery Reserve. This portion of A.K.B.'s Civil War service was as follows:

-Advance on Nashville, 2/10-3/3/62
-March to Savannah, Tenn., 3/17-4/7
-Advance on & Siege of Corinth, Miss., 4/29-5/30
-Pursuit to Booneville 5/31-6/6
-Buell's Campaign in No. Ala. & Mid-Tenn.
-March to Louisville, Ky. & pursuit of Bragg, 8/21-9/26
-Pursuit of Bragg, 10/1-10/15
-Battle of Perryville, Ky., 10/8
-March to Nashville, 10/20-11/9/62 [4]

Early in 1862 Capt. Bush was offered an official regimental surgeon position, which he declined; and also, a colonelcy of a new infantry regiment in 1862, which he likewise declined, having promised his men that he would not leave them, even if offered promotions.[5] A letter of witness among A.K.B.'s pension papers (Certif. #60056) reveals that he sustained some physical setbacks from the daily demanding strictures of camp and field:

Washington, D. C., March 9, 1866

Joseph H. Barett

Commission of Pensions

Sir:

I hereby certify on honor that I served in the same Division of the Army of the Cumberland with Asahel K. Bush, late Captain, 4th Battery, Ind. Vols.; that at the Battle of Chaplin Hills, Perryville, Kentucky, Oct. 8, 1862, said Captain Bush, while in his line of duty, contracted a cold which settled on his lungs, and terminated in Hemoptysis, in consequence of which disease he was left in hospital sick.

I further certify that I have been personally acquainted with said Captain Bush at intervals since the date above mentioned and know he has continued to suffer from the aforementioned disease.

James G. Bernam

Capt., Co. B, 214th Pa.

Between being Captain of his 4th Indiana Light Artillery and inevitable demands upon his medical expertise, A.K.B. rendered a fatiguing service to his unit until Oct. 31, 1862, when he was put in a hospital for several months, a place where (not surprisingly to himself) he performed a dual role as a patient *and* doctor to many in need around him. A factor in saving lives wherever duty called him, it is believed he returned to his beloved 4th Indiana Battery comrades. After hard service that included the Battle of Chickamauga, Capt. Bush was transferred on Sept. 30, 1863, by Maj. Gen. George Thomas' Order No. 22 to the Veteran Reserve Corps. By mid-October, after farewells to surviving artillerists of his 4th Indiana Battery, most of whom he would never see again (In all, they would lose 13 in killed and 15 by disease), Asahel was permitted a furlough home for about six weeks of "R&R" or home cooking and comforts. We know he was with Eliza and Willie late in 1863 because nine months later, Willie acquired a baby sister, Hattie C. Bush, born at Michigan City, Aug. 17, 1864. However, Willie was not on hand for the birthing nor for a fair bit of the pregnancy. Christmas 1863 for this six-year-old was an ambivalent season: he was joyous to be near this father and show off his learning; he was depressed at interdictive thoughts of Asahel's soon-approaching departure for goodness-only-knew how long. Something about the Vee Arr Cee was where Dad was slated to go. Word arrived from Washington that Asahel was to be stationed at Elmira, New York, that he was to report to Washington, D. C. for tentative planning sessions for a possible Confederate prison complex fronting the Chemung River near Elmira. Meanwhile news of an address by President Lincoln to dedicate a Military Cemetery at the Gettysburg Battlefield was carried in the newspapers, stirring public comment. Eliza read it aloud to her husband and son. Willie, already fascinated by the giant figure and prints of Abe Lincoln, now inaugurated a kind of fixation. When, at length, he learned that his father's next destination was to be where Lincoln lived, he abruptly plotted out his life ambition—to meet the President. By early January, with Asahel's furlough nearly expired, Willie became upset, pleading, eloquent, and fractious. He tried every argument, stressing that the captain, already strained by extensive service, needed an orderly-aide-messenger-waiter. Father Bush for his part missed the boy, but still felt he should be a man at home for Eliza. Upon due deliberation, the little family apparently came to a compromise: Willie could go with Asahel to visit the Capital City (& perhaps the White House), then maybe he would be lonesome for home and return with a family acquaintance in early March. Willie was ecstatic and on best behavior. The train rides east were thrilling. Could he be a locomotive engineer?

Wide-eyed Willie Bush, 6, was amazed by the size of everything and quantities of soldiers. Following a meeting called by Secretary of War Stanton on the topic of the V.R.C.[6] and plans for Confederate prisons, a meeting Asahel attended, the father and son in a party of White House visitors were scheduled for a brief walk-by and greeting from the president. The affair came off almost magically. "Uncle Abe" beamed way down to the boy, each extending a hand, and inquired, "Your name, Son?" "Willie!" exclaimed the six-year-old, not realizing that this giant "Commander-in-Chief" (a title Asahel had been teaching Willie), had and lost a son named Willie, whose tragic death at about this lad's tender age, had plunged the First Family into deep grief. The Great One swallowed hard, and, stooping, conferred upon the surprised youth a huge hug. W. H. Bush was to treasure these moments for life.[7]

Willie Bush, with parental consent (Eliza is believed to have lived with relatives while carrying her second child, Hattie), achieved the rest of his "dream" in being allowed to stay by his father's side. Shortly after their arrival at Elmira (approx. late March '64), where Asahel joined the 11th Regiment8 (& later, the 12th) as Captain, I.C. (or V.R.C.), at this juncture, the younger Bush, now 6 years 6 months, acquired the accouterments of a corporal's uniform—chevron, McClellan Cap, brass belt buckle, buttoned tunic, overcoat, a weapon sized down to his Lilliputian 4' stature, and bayonet. We are, indeed, fortunate to have a portrait for Corporal Willie Bush, printed from a carte-de-visite taken of him. On the verso of this c.d.v. is an "Elmira" back-mark. Whether there was ever more than one such pose made of Willie is problematic, but we presume the earliest destination of this one was to be Michigan City, Indiana, for Eliza Bush. Our gratitude goes out to Mick Kissick, of Albany, Indiana, down-state just northeast of Muncie, who is *the* supportive source of both our photographs.[9] While Corp'l Willie performed as valet-orderly for Capt. Bush, the latter assumed a variety of equally serious duties, the most valued being medical. Working under far less than ideal conditions, he doctored for unfortunate Confederate prisoners and for ailing Union Army comrades alike. It is pleasant to realize he saved lives and reduced some of the severities the Southerners were exposed to. Corporal Bush may well have done some small guard duty at the stockade, but his primary commitment was more personal for his father's benefit. Surely, too, his sheer presence was a morale boosting phenomenon for the men of both sides, so long absent from their families. Whether Willie remained with Asahel *after* his sister's birth (8/17/64) or for Asahel's whole tour at Elmira or returned home shortly after Hattie's arrival, it appears reasonable that this lad served contentedly up through his seventh birthday. Claims for his Civil War tour extending later than the last six months of his seventh year are long since beyond our ken. Stoutly he served six months. But could he have served until his father's discharge "on the return of the 12th Regiment V.R.C. for Nov. 1865 [when] he is reported a Captain 'Mustered Out Nov. 29, 1865, in compliance with G.O. No. 155, A.G.O, Oct. 26, 1865,'"[10] a matter of twenty months? Far *less likely,* for Willie's early patriotic enthusiasm would *surely have worn exceedingly thin by then.*

Asahel, upon discharge, went home to Michigan City and resumed family values and a local medical practice for 15 months until Mar. 14, 1867, when he returned as a 2nd lieutenant for a final two service years in the Army—his preference, the 2nd U. S. Artillery.[11] He would "recapture," in a less intense setting, the glory days of when he was thirty-one and with the 4th Indiana boys. But family soon again called him and he came home for good exactly two weeks after the birth of a daughter, Dora E. (Feb. 14, 1869- Sept. 24, 1878).[12]

It was in 1870 that the A. K. Bushes began their new adventure in the Far West, even to the Pacific Coast. Selling their Indiana farm and closing out a modest medical practice, these pioneers trekked to Fort Stevens, Oregon, where they lived two years until Asahel was appointed lighthouse-keeper at (Toke Point) Shoalwater Bay. He held this position two years, whereupon they moved to Willapa, just east of South Bend, Pacific County, Washington. Here, still together, they farmed some eight years. Here, Willie's baby sister Dora, 9, died. Asahel and Will, now 21, ran a successful lumber business near Willapa Harbor until 1883. That year the Bushes made their final move—to Montesano, Chehalis County (until 1915), where they liked the spot enough to cheerfully die there. Straightway, on arrival Asahel revived his physician's practice; he conducted an apothecary shop several years, Will being especially helpful with operating the shop while Dr. Bush was out visiting the sick or called away as coroner of the county and health officer. He was an ardent Republican Party leader and vital comrade of James A. Garfield Post 13, G.A.R. "Captain" Bush gave the 1895 Memorial Day address, two of his thoughts that day being, "Our lives should be such that we may encourage all efforts to instill a greater degree of patriotism in all classes of American citizens, especially the young.... Let our lives be so ordered that dear ones left behind may dwell with pleasure upon their remembrance."[13] From the start, Will took to "Monte" (Montesano "mountain of health"). Early on he was printer's devil at the old *Vidette* office helping to run off *the* first issue; he was a founder and early-day chief of Monte's Fire Department; he was postmaster from 1883 to Jan. 1, 1886. In 1885-6 he was made deputy sheriff by Sheriff Jas. A. Perkins in Old Chehalis County. Will did so well that he was elected Sheriff in 1886.[14] While postmaster, Will, on May 20, 1885, was married by Rev. W. T. Cosper to a local girl, Miss Annie Phelon, oldest daughter of the A. K. Phelons. They were then serenaded by the *Vidette* Cornet Band. Fifty years later, upon their Golden Wedding, they would go to Tacoma with their son Kenneth and his wife to spend a quiet weekend with their other son Lyle and his wife.[15] For his efficiency and popularity as Monte's fourth sheriff, re-elected in 1888, he was presented "a magnificent gold watch and chain."[16] W. H. Bush was an early mayor of Monte twice and a councilman.

Will's mother, Eliza, died in August 1890, leaving a void in the family. But on May 13, 1892, Asahel married Miss Julia A. Carlile (Dec. 7, 1873-May 6, 1933), a native of Eureka, Kansas, and a daughter of the R. G. Carliles, who had settled in Monte in 1877. The ceremony was performed by Rev. E. V. Claypool. Will acquired a half-brother, Silas C. Bush, July 5, 1893, who some nine years later qualified as a Civil War orphan (#571686) at $14 a month until sixteen. Julia belonged to the Eastern Star and American Legion Auxiliary and lived her closing years at her sister Ora L. Watson's home.[17]

Will led a happy full life in Monte—a longtime member of its Chamber of Commerce; he belonged to Silvia Lodge #38, I.O.O.F., holding all offices in the gift of that brotherhood. Along toward 1911-1913, W. H. Bush ran a Monte dealership for Rambler Motor Cars, which he advertised in the *Vidette* thusly: "Every car carries a 10,000-mile guarantee with 3 years of driving in it, the greatest guarantee ever given an auto."[18] He was one of extremely few Civil War men who ever sold automobiles. Still later Will Bush was a partner in manufacturing at the old Montesano Sash and Door Factory.[19] His father, who suffered a lung condition, died late in 1902 at seventy-two, leaving among survivors a brother, Hon. A. S. Bush of Pacific County.

Perhaps W. H. Bush's grandest moment or swan-song in senior life came on the evening of Feb. 3, 1933, at a 50th Anniversary dinner celebration of the first issue of*The Vidette,* attended by over 100 guests. The affair climaxed in a reenactment of the printing of the first *Vidette* on their original $400 old Army press by two members of the earliest staff—Mr. Bush, inker, and J. E. Calder, co-founder and first editor. They are pictured with Chaplin Collins, then current editor.[20] Will was a co-publisher with James Divilbiss some dozen years, 1884-1896. He died at home. All businesses in Monte closed during the 2:00-3:00 p.m. hour of the funeral at Whiteside Chapel. William Henry Bush, laid to rest in the Wynooche Cemetery lot purchased by his father, went down as a pioneer, businessman, and town-father widely mourned.

Nimshi Nuzum

Dec. 30, 1853 – May 4, 1939

Nimshi was a son of Abraham and Martha Franklin Nuzum, and he was born near Boothsville, where he grew up. Thus, was he a Virginian by birth before his northern and western county (Marion) became part of West Virginia. At age eleven Nimshi went into camp near Boothsville as a drummer boy with the West Virginia Home Guards. He served under Captain Napoleon Altop during and after the Civil War. Too young for service at the time of the Confederate attack upon Fairmont (Apr. 29, 1863—1 killed, 6 wounded),[1] Nimshi heard the cannonade that day.

With his son Audrie A. Nuzum, Nimshi attended the last great conclave of the Blue and Gray, some 155 miles east to Gettysburg, where, for his youthful eighty-four years, he was the marvel of many a near centenarian. The last of ten children, he left behind his wife, Della Powell Nuzum, and four children—Audrie, Donovan, Mrs. Emma DeBolt, and Mrs. Maggie Robinson with her son, Samuel.

Reginald Fairfax Nicholson

Dec. 15, 1852 – Dec. 19, 1939

Reginald F. Nicholson served in the Union Navy aboard USS *State Of Georgia* in the blockade off Wilmington, North Carolina, a vessel captained by none other than his own father, Somerville Nicholson (Jan. 1, 1822-May 1, 1905), who would attain the rank of commodore.[1] Both father and son were to be career navy men. In point of fact, few American families have laid down a stronger military tradition than the Nicholsons. Major Augustus Nicholson, Reginald's grandfather, was our first quartermaster of the U. S. Marine Corps. Reginald's mother Hannah was a daughter of Dr. William Jones, a surgeon who took part in the Battle of Bladensburg, of War of 1812 note. Reginald's brother, William Jones Nicholson (Jan. 16, 1856-Dec. 20, 1931), was appointed by President Grant as 2nd Lieutenant (1876) in the 7th U. S. Cavalry, that regiment having just been depleted at the Little Big Horn massacre. William put in thirty-seven years with the Seventh Cavalry, sharing all frontier hardships in campaigns against the Apaches, Nez Perces, and Sioux that climaxed in the battle (inglorious misfortune) known as Wounded Knee in 1890.[2] Somerville had already rendered considerable Union Navy service aboard USS *Marblehead*, then holding the rank of lieutenant. As such, on May 1, 1862, he was in charge of *Marblehead* at the shelling of the Confederate positions at Yorktown, Virginia. Again, "Lieutenant S. Nicholson, of USS *Marblehead,* and Lieutenant Thomas H. Patterson, of USS *Chocura*, in the Pamunkey River, supported Army withdrawal from White House, Virginia, with gunfire and support. Other Union gunboats escorted transports and moved up the James and Chickahominy Rivers in close support of General McClellan's army, June 28 - 29, 1862."[3]

As for "Reggie" himself, his naval career spanned three wars—the Civil War, Spanish American War, World War I—and six decades. At approximately age eleven years and four months in early 1864 this lad came under Confederate fire during the blockade of Wilmington. Reginald, like his brother and father, was a native of Washington, D. C. He would retire there in 1920. He was one of two in our history who wore four stars *after duty in the lower naval ranks,* the other—John Paul Jones. Little Reggie was an orderly, a messenger, a waiter aboard *State Of Georgia* for at least the length of his father's service as captain of the vessel, which was for a year or more.

Naturally, Reginald was destined for schooling at Annapolis. He did, indeed, graduate from the U. S. Naval Academy in 1873. As a Lieutenant Commander at the outbreak of the Spanish American War, he was Chief Navigation Officer in USS *Oregon* during her historic voyage Mar. 19-May 24, 1898, around Cape Horn from San Francisco to Florida to join the Atlantic Fleet. Commander Nicholson was aboard the *Oregon* that July 3rd at Santiago de Cuba when Admiral Cervera's fleet was destroyed or incapacitated. Robley D. Evans (Aug. 18, 1846-Jan. 3, 1912) commanded USS *Iowa* in that battle, Evans who was an Annapolis cadet and ensign in the Civil War.[4] In 1907, Captain Nicholson took command of the battleship *Nebraska.* By 1909, he was chief of the Bureau of Navigation, with the rank of rear-admiral. During 1912-14, he was in the Orient as Commander of our Asiatic Fleet. On reaching age sixty-two in December 1914, Rear-Admiral Nicholson was transferred to the retired list. However, with the onset of our participation in World War I, he was recalled to active duty to head up American Naval Missions in Chile, Peru, and Equador.

In Rear-Adm. Reginald Fairfax Nicholson we do indeed have a Civil War youngster whose career was closely comparable to that of the more widely popularized John L. Clem. Nicholson was the Navy's answer to the Army's General Clem. Yes, at the time—Aug. 13, 1914—of Clem's retirement and status as the last Civil War veteran on the Army's Active List of Commissioned Officers, Clem was senior in longevity of service. But Nicholson remained on the Navy's Active List until that December. Further, he returned to the Naval service for his World War I tour of duty well after General Clem was retired. Though both men's careers reached into their sixth decade, it appears that Admiral Nicholson finally became entitled to the distinction of being the last Civil War veteran to retire from active duty as a commissioned officer.[5]

We note that Nicholson was born sixteen months later than Clem, that he survived Clem by thirty-one months and outlived him by fifteen. But let us not forget Lt. George Dewey, Union Navy, who never did retire![6]

Finally, we observe a truth that goes with the territory of this national report: that the Nicholsons were one of at least a few dozen families who had three Civil War generations—Major Augustus (father/grandfather), Somerville (son/father), Reginald (son/grandson). (See Lea).

Dr. Robert Blake Tyler

Mar. 12, 1854 – Apr. 2, 1941

"Little Robby" Blake Tyler was "quite probably" the latest born of all naval veterans of the war—certainly no inconsiderable distinction. It is likely that he was both latest born and the youngest on enlistment of all who served in the Union Navy. It is well that a Navy man appear among the five latest-born youngest, for youthful lads of Tyler's era were proverbial for filling out the ranks in shipboard complements; they were known for cheerfully performing the more humble duties on a man-of-war. Even though holding the less-than-awesome grades of Apprentice Boy, Third Class Boy, Second Class Boy, or First Class Boy, these fellows, too, could accurately call themselves man-of-wars-men. By birth, Tyler does appear to have been our youngest bluejacket, being seven months junior to the mythopoeic Tisdale of South Framingham—Tisdale, who himself was eight months junior to young Nicholson from the District of Columbia area. (See Latest Born).

Born at Hague, Westmoreland County, Virginia, to Walter Hannibal Tyler—a nephew of another Virginia native, John Tyler (Mar. 29, 1790-Jan. 18, 1862), tenth president of the United States—and Julia Grimshaw, also a Virginia native, Robert was but an infant when she died. Julia's family had lived in Kentucky for many generations and were kinfolk to John C. Breckinridge, James Buchanan's vice president.[1] Robert's father, Walter (1801-1863) grew up on a large cotton plantation worked by several hundred slaves. Though he was wealthy and inherited the 2000 acres, Walter was a physician-surgeon. Because he was not comfortable with some of the unfortunates in slavery and, possibly, wanting improved prospects as a doctor, when the war broke out, he sided with the North. Consequently, he lost everything when he moved the family to Washington, D.C. However, we can be reasonably sure that the good doctor in his final years and months was a life saver and life extender for scores (perhaps hundreds) of unfortunate wounded. Few citizens led busier lives than surgeons during the war. Such demands may likely have shortened this humanitarian's own years, for he died while his son was afloat with the Union Navy.

During 1861, Robert, large for all his extreme youth, was brimming with excitement over every little piece of war news. He longed for adventure. He wanted to help free the slaves—to do something heroic. Time and again his father refused him the needed permission to join up. After two years of longing, Robert, now 4' 7" and one month beyond his ninth birthday, ran away from home and, giving his age as fourteen, enlisted on Apr. 10, 1863, at Piney

Point, Maryland. He signed aboard the USS *Racer* for one year as Second Class Boy. But his duty aboard the 252-ton, 105 foot long, 18' 10" beam, 9' 6" draft, mortar schooner lasted until Oct. 30, 1864. Purchased by the U. S. Government in August 1861 and sold in 1865, *Racer* carried two 32-pound guns and a 13" mortar. One action little tar Tyler witnessed occurred July 18, 1863, when the USS *Jacob Bell* (Acting Master, Schulze) with USS *Resolute* and USS *Racer* in company drove off Confederate troops firing on the ship *George Peabody*, aground at Mathias Point, Virginia.[2] Because of Robert's mature appearance and conduct, his officers believed him older.

From Oct. 30, 1864, to Jan. 31, 1865, Robert, now a First Class Boy, served aboard USS *Lodona*, an iron ship and screw steamer whose maximum speed was seven knots. *Lodona*, carrying one 100-pounder Parrott rifle, one 30-pounder Parrott rifle, one 9-pounder Dahlgren gun, and four 24-pounder howitzers, drew duty with the South Atlantic Blockading Squadron at Sapelo Sound, Georgia.[3] Sold by the U. S. Government in 1865, *Lodona* was 750 tons, 210 feet long, 27' 6" in her beam, and required 16' 5.5" of water.

Robert, still only ten years old, was now assigned to his third ship, the USS *John Adams*, on which he continued duties as powder boy Feb. 1-June 30, 1865, and finally as Cabin Steward July 1-Sept. 22, 1865. One of the oldest craft in the Union Navy, the 700-ton, 127' *Adams* was launched at Charleston, South Carolina, on June 5, 1799, and finally decommissioned and sold Oct. 5, 1867, at Boston, Massachusetts.[4] During Robert's tour aboard *Adams* she was stationed at Morris Island inside Charleston Bar, near Fort Sumter, having for her armament one 30-pounder Dahlgren, one 30-pounder Parrott, two 8" guns, four 32-pounders, and two 20-pounder Dahlgrens. During his thirty months in the Union Navy Robert saw his full share of adventure. At age eleven years and six months, he was paid off in full on Sept. 22, 1865, and discharged at Boston. A Civil War veteran destitute of family, lacking book knowledge, the lad was very much alone. He knew he must acquire an education, must grow up to be a man worthy of his Virginia/Kentucky ancestry. His folks might have already been proud of him had they lived.

Robert went to Binghamton, New York, where he studied in the public schools. With a quick mind he got through the curriculum when no older than his classmates. For seven years young Tyler performed effectively as a schoolmaster at various points across New York state. While teaching, he read medical books, wishing to follow in his father's profession. One day he entered the employ of Dr. H. H. Nye in Wellsville, New York, and studied for two years under him. Because he realized he could never be more than an assistant unless he earned a medical degree, he entered the Medical College at Buffalo, entered with Dr. Nye's hearty approval, and graduated in 1879. Dr. Tyler immediately became a partner with Dr. Nye, and their joint practice flourished until the young doctor chose to go west. He went directly to Joplin, Missouri, a mining camp without qualified physicians, arriving Oct.

8, 1881. In time, Dr. Tyler, by spending a few months each year in New York, Chicago, or St. Louis hospitals, specialized in gynecology and obstetrics.

A detailed account of Dr. Tyler's achievements may be found in Joel T. Livingston's 1911 *History of Jasper County, Missouri*:

> *He is progressive in his methods of treatment...no new theory or discovery...that does not receive his immediate scrutiny. He is a member of the city, state and American Medical Associations. For several years he was president of the Jasper County Medical Society and for thirteen he was local surgeon for the Kansas City, Fort Scott and Memphis Railroad (now the Frisco System) and also for the Missouri Pacific Railroad.... He is an ardent Republican and was mayor of Joplin in 1890-91, the first mayor under the present charter, converting the town from a mining camp to a city.... He owns valuable farmlands and has been active in mining. He is recognized as the first man in this section to raise thoroughbred horses. He has raised, trained and raced some of the best thoroughbreds on the turf, both trotters and pacers.*

On Apr. 18, 1882, Dr. Tyler married Miss Sarah Maggie Heathwood, daughter of Thomas Heathwood of Massachusetts. Their four children were Walter H., 1884; Robert M., 1887; Dorothy F., 1893; and Harry B., 1898. Sometime prior to 1915 this marriage was ended by divorce. On Mar. 31, 1917, he married Rosa Olson of Joplin, who would survive him. At the time of his initial application for a Civil War pension, Mar. 24, 1904, he was 5' 8", weighed 137, had brown eyes and gray hair.

In his Mar. 10, 1976 letter from Joplin, Winfield L. Post, M.D, .F.A.C.S. (Fellow of the American College of Surgeons), explains:

> *Your recent letter to our city clerk was referred to the Joplin Historical Society's Dorothea B. Hoover Museum. It happens that Dr. Tyler attended my wife's birth and that of the late Dorothea Hoover. Dr. Tyler was a prominent physician and civic leader—dapper, small, energetic, a man with a flair. He was a member of the Odd Fellows, The Modern Woodmen of America, the Elks, the First Presbyterian Church, and, incredibly, the G.A.R.—O. P. Morton Post 14.*

In a March 13, 1976 letter, Victor J. Hinton shares further details:

> *Dr. Post is a near neighbor and, like myself, a member of the Joplin Historical Society. Dr. Tyler presided at my birth in 1894, and at the birth of Dr. Post's wife, Elizabeth, as well as at hundreds of other new Joplin citizens shortly after Joplin became a new lead and zinc mining town in 1873. He practiced medicine here until his death. We have no detailed record of him from 1911 on, but he was a busy doctor. At one time he was a partner with my Uncle Robert Lisch in the Tyler & Lisch Drug Store, where he had*

his office in the back. This store later became Miners' Drug. Dr. Tyler was mayor of Joplin four different terms, two before 1911 and two after. He was buried in Joplin's Fairview Cemetery, laid out and surveyed in 1873.

Dr. Robert Tyler was apparently *the* youngest comrade of the G.A.R. from the time of Mancil V. Root's accidental death on July 6, 1929, until his own passing on Apr. 2, 1941, a period of nearly twelve years. Charles E. Merrick, of Los Angeles, eight days older than Robert, then held that distinction for the next two and a half years. These two G.A.R. comrades were the youngest and third youngest of the 1,845 Civil War veterans who regaled at their week-long 75th Battle Reunion at Gettysburg in 1938. And they did at that time meet each other for the first and last time of their lives. The fourth youngest present at the Diamond Reunion of the Blue and Gray was Nimshi Nuzum of Fairmont, West Virginia, some two months senior to Merrick. (The Reb home guard wagoner, Benj. F. Williams, born between Tyler and Merrick, was at Gettysburg in 1938.)

Comrade Tyler was a vital spark and standout among his G.A.R. brethren. He stood high with the Missouri Department, who elected him their state commander for not only 1933-34 but for 1940-41. Supernally appropriate is the fact that he who never really retired from medicine, he who was widely known as "the Poor Man's Friend" should, as Missouri state commander, have died "in office."[5] Underscoring Tyler's impressive youth was the fact that Joplin's last G.A.R. comrade and personal friend, William Henry Osborn (May 7, 1843-Oct. 28, 1948) was born some eleven years earlier than he but would die over seven and a half years later at age 105 years. Those qualities that made Dr. Tyler a success in his chosen fields have won him a primal place of honor here among our youngest Civil War personalities who lived long enough to be among the last survivors.

Dr. Robert B. Tyler, age 82.

Joplin Historical Museum

William Lee Owens

Mar. 26, 1854 – Dec. 18, 1942

Of Niceville, Okaloosa County, well west in Florida's Panhandle, William L. Owens was a native of Tifton, Tift County in south central Georgia. Surely he was one of the latest born defenders of the late C.S.A. It may truly be said that he did what he could. At the time, he was nine and ten. Billy Lee served in Captain William Jones' Home Guard Company along with Hutto's and McKinnon's Companies. On Dec. 9, 1922, in an effort to procure a Confederate pension, he signed a statement before G. B. Anchors, Notary Public, that included this passage:

> *I enlisted in Marianna, Jackson County, and rendered faithful service for the State of Florida in Capt. William Jones' Company. We went forward with Captain Jones to meet the Federal soldiers. Some of our Company was captured and some killed. Captain Jones was captured by the enemy. The rest of us got away as best we could. We did not desert his service or the State of Florida. After this battle we were not called on for further service, as the war was soon over.*[1]

The fact that Confederate pensions were not so easily won by former homeguardsmen may safely be inferred by Owens' further efforts of seven and a half years later when he signed an affidavit at DeFuniak Springs, Florida, on June 20, 1930:

> *It is impossible for me to remember the names of all the Boys who were with us and rendered service. I recall Bill Taylor, the two Pender Boys, Dickson, Lee, Johnson, Swan, three McCormicks, two Parkers, some Stephens, John Wright, Chas. Howell, Geo. Stanley, Geo. and Bart Nichols, Abner Bishop, Jas. Sconniers, Geo. Reddick, Robt. Hatcher, Elder Gomillion, Math. Clark, some McCaskills, Crawfords, McQuaggs, and Lassiters. A Home Guard was organized at Eucheeana. Part of our Company crossed the River at Douglass Ferry and went to Vernon for some time, and then went with Capt. Jones on to Marianna, where we were in service at the end of the war, or rather, when the Town was taken, every one of us that could made our getaway and returned to Vernon to be informed our part of the War was over, and that we could go home....*

We helped each other keep up a force of men and boys, to try to protect what was not taken by the Deserters or raiders, and to try to defend our places against enemies when they came.

I trust that I have made this statement as full as could be expected of any man of my age [75], and the age that I was when rendering this service [10 yrs. 15 days].[2]

Quite certainly, this last "battle" Owens mentions was the Sept. 27, 1864, action at Marianna, when they engaged greatly superior numbers—a detachment of the 1st Florida Cavalry, a detachment of the 2nd Maine Cavalry, and detachments from the 82nd and 86th United States Colored Troops. While the old men and young boys of Jones' Home Guard and a few other C.S.A. fragments resisted, inflicting casualties amounting to thirty-two wounded, no precise figures on their own losses are readily available.[3] From Owens' testimony, an opportune insight would rightly have the reader infer that perhaps several dozen homeguardsmen in Jones' outfit ranged in age from nine to thirteen. Indeed, the identities of many of those worthies—once locally known and honored—have long since faded to oblivion...in particular, those who died before early old age, those who chose not the boon of a pensionary pittance.

In his Apr. 24, 1981 letter from Niceville, George Reddick, 64, offers: "My mother, Rose Lee Owens Reddick, 90, and Aunt Annabell, 86, are all who live of his eight children (the others—Lelia (b. Aug. 1893), Nettie (Sept. 1897), Jessie Mae (d. Mar. 16, 1976), Dock Owens (d. 1936), Parker D. (d. Apr. 8, 1964, John Dowd (d. June 1980). Grandfather Owens was a homeguard in 1864-65. He homesteaded about fifty acres on Choctawhatchee Bay in Walton County."[4]

Owens and Gomillion, of Redbay, Florida, last survivors of William Jones' West Florida Home Guards, who operated in their tri-county area, were then buddies of the same unit and died within fifty days of each other the same winter seventy-eight years later![5]

Elder Gomillion

Aug. 5, 1852 – Feb. 4, 1943

Of Redbay off Choctawhatchee River, in Walton County, Florida, Elder Gomillion (Apt enough name for any aged veteran!) was the last survivor of all the boys enrolled in Capt. William Jones' Home Guard Company that sometimes operated in concert with Hutto's and McKinnon's Companies. Much of Gomillion's Civil War service was identical to that of Wm. Lee Owens, of nearby Niceville, for they were in the same unit. Even at just age eleven, Elder was elder to at least half of Jones' effectives. Once again, we must not pass up this opportune moment to announce a truth: enough of some 300 original eastern West Florida homeguardsmen (several cited in the Owens story), taking in Gilchrist and Columbia Counties, survived into the late 1930's and beyond—at least ten!—to call our attention to a certain *little* publicized truth that the eastern region of the Florida Panhandle, indeed, had the greatest single concentration of extremest youth to render tangible and creditable service to the Cause of 1861-65. *Perhaps* 40% of them lived long enough to apply for a Confederate pension and *perhaps* half of these succeeded in obtaining it, but not without delays, red tape, and patient effort, in many cases.

The discovery of Elder is partially attributable to his attendance in July 1938 at the Diamond Blue-Gray Gettysburg Reunion. There he was thrilled to meet some 600 fellow Rebs, himself one of the dozen youngest attending. Though few reportable details are available on his Christian life, the greater Florida Panhandle was his favorite part of the world. He was an outdoorsy soul whose hobby was neighborliness. For these distinctions, he appears here today with several comrades whom he knew longest and best.

James W. Harper

Oct. 12, 1853 – Apr. 29, 1943

Jimmy's abbreviated childhood took place in rural Gilchrist County, Florida, where homeguardsmenships were "serious business," were vital to law and order, especially across Florida's Panhandle. While these Confederate units were staffed largely by pre-twelvers, they were officered by a cadre of aging men, usually over fifty and unquestioned authority figures (Nathaniel Jackson Williams, for example, of Mexican War vintage). Diminutive Jimmy Harper, of bantam weight and under four feet at inception of his Confederate duties, was accepted for service on or about Apr. 22, 1864 as a member of Captain Oscar Underwood's Florida Home Guard Company.[1] He was 10 years 6 months 10 days. He was one of an estimated 200 to 300 youths ages nine through twelve who during 1862-65 served faithfully in home guard companies all across West Florida east to his own Gilchrist County. Enough of their original numbers survived into the 1930's and beyond, just enough of them drew C.S.A. (state) pensions to afford us this conclusion or finding: categorically, veterans like Harper, Owens, Gomillion, Reddick, the three Keith Brothers, the Osteens, W. C. Ward , and Jos. P. Morgan, Sr., represent(ed) nationally the greatest concentration of extreme youth who "played" a serious, recognized, and pensioned role in the war.

Remarkable as Harper himself was, his late-life marriage and family were even more so. In 1942, at Bell, Florida (surely, one of *the* last five Civil War weddings), he took Minnie Lee for his last wife. He was 88, she was 28. Their first child, a daughter, may very well be the youngest living offspring of a Civil War veteran! But their second child, Jimmie Lee Harper (Oct. 16, 1943-June 20, 1987) was all during his lifetime *the* youngest Real Son or offspring of a veteran, Yank or Reb. This writer treasures his "Jimmie Lee Harper" autograph from Bell, Florida, dated Mar. 22, 1982, among an utterly unique 13-page specialty feature garnered during 1971-1992 and entitled "Autographs of Sons, Daughters & Widows of Our Last Living Civil War Soldiers." By 1971 Minnie Lee Harper (Oct. 8, 1914-Nov. 29, 1981) enjoyed her reputation as the youngest Civil War widow, being then 56-57. At that time, by coincidence, the eldest such widow was Loudie M. Harper, 104, of Perry, Georgia, who had married a Confederate veteran twenty-one years her senior in 1889.[2]

On a tragic note, the writer was shocked in April 1988 to learn of Jimmie Lee's death in an automobile accident of almost a year earlier—a real sense of loss. There is little evidence that Jimmie ever "traded on" his distinction, perhaps partly because, half-orphaned, he never knew his father. Too, while old James hoped to live to see and hold the baby, he could scarcely have been expected to go forth during March-April 1943 and announce *his* distinction as the war's very last prospective daddy. The widow, Minnie, gave us our last Civil War orphan. As one of the eight youngest Civil War veterans "in the world," Mr. Harper, on his final day, did an extremely rare thing—died in the mid-1940s as an octogenarian Civil War veteran.

Lewis Henry Easterly

Nov. 17, 1852 – July 18, 1943

"The Baby of the Civil War"

Of Gunnison, Colorado, his last sixty-three years, Lewis was born on a farm near Murphysboro, Illinois, to Philip and Sarah Jones Easterly. Lewis' surviving son, David, 85, of Englewood, Colorado, informs us (Dec. 1976), "Father was born on Gen. John A. Logan's father's farm, but he was raised on his father Philip's farm twenty miles to the north just outside Ava, Illinois."[1] As an infant Lewis was baptized in the Methodist Church. Little else is known of Lewis' childhood. On the Illinois farm he did chores, knew how to care for animals, and learned about the workings of the land. When the war "came on," Lewis was eight years and five months. Like thousands of youngsters, he itched to get off the farm, to go adventuring. Written off in neighbors' minds as altogether too young, few dreamed the war would last long enough for little Lewis to be old enough. That seemingly remote possibility, however, suddenly opportuned and sooner than could ever have been supposed.

Several understandings of Easterly's Civil War service have come down. We have the traditional generalized view—what the world believed it knew. This version recognized Easterly as "the Baby of the Civil War," or youngest in uniform, the lad who "ran away" at age nine with his uncle to be a drummer boy or fifer in the Ninth Illinois Infantry. Rather strangely, this view, as nearly all printed accounts, gives his age as more than he actually was. The truth is that Lewis had his ninth birthday three months *after* he joined up in late August 1861 at Cairo. Lewis performed as a fife-boy with the Ninth Illinois until about mid-April 1862. Thus, we can summarize his military career with the following events:

-Expedition to Paducah, 9/5-9/6/61
-Occupation of Paducah until February '62
-Skirmish at Saratoga and Eddyville, Ky., 10/26/61
-Demonstration on Columbus, Ky., 11/7-11/9
-Reconnaissance to Fort Henry, Tenn., 1/15-1/25/62
-Operations against Forts Henry and Heiman, 2/5-2/6
-Investment and capture of Fort Donelson, Tenn., 2/12-2/16
-Expedition to Clarksville and Nashville, Tenn., 2/22-3/1
-Battle at Shiloh, 4/6-4/7
-Advance on Corinth, Miss., 4/9-4/14 [2]

In her Sept. 27, 1976 letter from Gunnison, Colorado, Helen Easterly (Mrs. Roy) Winslow assures us, "Grandfather had no official papers, so it took an Act of Congress to declare his eligibility for a Civil War pension. He trained with his Uncle David W. Jones in the Illinois Ninth Infantry. His Uncle David was killed at Shiloh. Grandfather had a fantastic memory. He was alert and active until his last illness. He wanted to live to be 100 and likely would have, except he insisted on traveling all over to various G.A.R. functions and caught pneumonia. I have an uncle who until recently lived in Denver—Grandfather's son, David, who knows more. You'll be hearing from him, for his mind is still sharp."

In his Dec. 17, 1976, nine-page letter from Englewood, Colorado, David H. Easterly, 85, bequeaths us these choice details:

> *Father's Uncle (his mother's youngest brother) David W. Jones joined the Ninth Illinois and they trained at Anna, half way between Carbondale and Cairo. August Mercy, a German trained in Germany, was elected Colonel. Father visited his Uncle David and Warren Jenkins, a 24-year-old Peoria schoolmaster, who led the regimental band and got Father to play a fife in the band. When the Ninth moved south, my father went with them. I think they were in Gen. John A. Logan's Division, but this was before Logan became a corps commander.*
>
> *The 9th fought at Ft. Henry and Ft. Donelson. (One of my father's uncles—Caleb Easterly's—wife's brothers, Benjamin Jacobs, was killed in the 9th at Ft. Donelson. He was cut in two with a cannonball.) David Jones was 21 in March 1862 and was killed on Easter Sunday Apr. 6, 1862, at the Peach Orchard. Conrad (Warren?) Jenkins, whom my father met later in 1898 at Gunnison and who later lived at Canon City and died at age 91, said that the troops on either side of the 9th fell back and Col. Mercy ordered them to fall back also. The 9th had been lying on their stomachs firing over a ridge. Jones failed to move. Jenkins crawled up to see what was the matter and he had a bullet hole in the middle of his forehead. After Shiloh, Col. Mercy said, "I sent that danged kid home. I had verbally discharged 'im as early as February for bein' under size. He'd already overrun his supposed six-month enlistment by at least two months."*
>
> *In March 1970 my wife and I visited the Shiloh National Park and the ranger could find no record of David Jones of Company G and told me what I already knew: that the 9th Illinois lost more men than any other regiment in the battle and that probably 60% were buried without identification!*
>
> *Father was written up in Ripley's "Believe It or Not" when he attended the 64th Nat'l G.A.R. Reunion at Cincinnati in August 1930. I can name two Civil War veterans younger than my father, though older*

at the time of their service—Frank M. Ironmonger, Jr., of Jacksonville, Fla; and the cabinboy, Robert Blake Tyler, of Joplin, Mo. Father corresponded with them, and, when they held the Blue & Gray Reunion at Gettysburg in 1938, I went with him as his attendant. He, Ironmonger and Blake Tyler had a great time visiting. And there was Dave Wood, who was a year older than Father. My father knew him from the 1880s, as he was the biggest freighter in Colorado and likely in the West. I read that in 1883 he had 500 head of horses, mules and oxen. He went broke in the 1893 panic, but he recovered. My sister-in-law Nellie Clamp (who was raised a Carey) taught some of his children in school before she married my oldest brother, Philip. Another veteran from a Missouri regiment we met on the train to Gettysburg in '38 was Solomon Baughman of Farmington, New Mexico, with his daughter. He had been released from a Confederate prison and was steaming home from Vicksburg on one of two steamboats racing each other up the Mississippi when the boiler exploded on his boat, killing nearly all the crew and released prisoners who were drowned. A colored man fished him out almost a mile down from where the explosion took place and revived him.[3]

I'm sending you a picture of my father at the 73rd Nat'l Encampment Parade in Pittsburgh, Pa., riding the Mayor of Pittsburgh David Lawrence's $4,000 white Arabian stallion Sept. 1, 1939.[4]

The battle death of his Uncle David surely was a large reason why little fife-boy Easterly was sent (encouraged to go) home. That sad return to Jackson County in southern Illinois had to have held some of his life's darkest hours. Ex-bandsman and veteran though he now was, Lewis resumed his schooling as the war progressed and wound down. He went on to study at what is now Southern Illinois University at Carbondale, where he prepared to teach. He taught about seven years in Illinois. In 1878, he first tried Colorado, settling on the Divide, near Sedalia. Here, too, he taught school. Boom times in nearby Gunnison County eventually drew him. It was in May 1880 that Lewis arrived in Gunnison with the Allen G. Teachout family, driving a freighting outfit for Mr. Teachout. Family tradition says Lewis arrived *the* same day as his longtime friend, Joseph Blackstock, who was born eight days earlier than Lewis in Murphysboro, Illinois. Within six months, upon due study, Lewis filed on a homestead along the Ohio Creek (what for years had been the Buffington Hereford Ranch) north of town. In the meantime he was courting Miss Cynthia Husband of Salina, Kansas. Preventing any possible jumping of his Ohio Creek claim, Lewis went back to Salina and on Sept. 15, 1881, married Miss Husband. They first lived at Colorado Springs, but in 1883 they moved to their ranch for good. Lewis and Cynthia had almost fifty years together until her passing in February 1921 and five children: Philip, LeVan, David, Sara E. Forsyth, and Alma E. Van Voorhis. Lewis developed his land and made it one of the most productive ranches. He joined the Gunnison County Stockgrowers Association, serving many years as its secretary and historian. He was also Secretary of the School Board in the Fairview School District for over fifty years. As a skilled surveyor, Lewis often answered requests to lay out plots, survey ditches, and adjudicate water and range. In 1922 he joined the Odd Fellows. In 1930 he helped organize the Gunnison County Pioneer and Historical Society, being himself a charter member, its historian from inception, and two years its president.[5]

Besides all these interests there was still another—his deepest commitment, what became increasingly important to him personally his last eighteen years: The Grand Army of the Republic, which he joined Dec. 31, 1893, at just about the moment of peak enrollment, 3400 comrades, for "the Department of the Mountains" or Colorado-Wyoming. In 1936, he was elected

Lewis H. Easterly, age 84, in 1936.

vice-commander of the Colorado-Wyoming Department, and in 1938, commander. He was five times re-elected, becoming, in effect, a life commander much esteemed. He attended very nearly *all* national encampments during 1920-1942; hence, he knew well many of the comrades nationwide. The most telling evidence of support from his G.A.R. brethren in Colorado occurred when on Apr. 13, 1928, Greenwood Post 10 came to comrade Easterly's rescue in his effort to qualify for a modest Civil War pension. In the neighborhood of seventy-five, Lewis lacked papers or any formal record of his eight months service and thereby had little prospect of winning a pension. The following verbatim statement drafted by Post 10 Quartermaster W. Y. Jenkins speaks for itself and made believers of the federal congressman:

> *For the use of Senator Tyson, Chairman, Military Committee U. S. Senate, 70th Congress. A bill for the relief of Lewis H. Easterly.*
>
> *Canon City, Colorado, April 13th 1928*
>
> *The original Roster of Company G, 9th Ill. Vol. Infty, was 177 Officers and men. Co. G's total loss was 99, leaving only 18 to be discharged at Springfield, Ill. Aug. 30th 1864, as follows:*

Commissioned Officers:	*Captain Isaac Clements*	*1*
	1st Lieut. Nimrod G. Perrin	*2*
	2nd Lieut. Benj. T. Brown	*1*
Non Comm. Officers	*Sergt. William Hampton*	*1*
	" Ben K. Mulkey	*2*
	Corpl. G. M. Wise	*1*
Privates:	*Columus C. Aken*	*1*
	John Beggs	*2*
	Wade Hampton	*3*
	Patric Leary	*4*
	Robert Marshall	*5*
	Charles W. Miller	*6*
	John F. Quinlan	*7*
	Ben H. Stotler	*8*
	Ben E. Slavens	*9*
	John J. Tippy	*10*
	Richard J. Worthing	*11*
	Louis Wise	*12*

The remaining 99 were either killed in action, died of wounds or sickness, or were discharged on account of wounds or other disabilities. This 99 includes Lewis H. Easterly, who was verbally discharged at Paducah, Kentucky, on account of being under 18 and under size. His name had been dropped from Company G Roll. [Copied from Illinois Adjutant General's

Report, Vol. I, pp. 447-450 by W. Y. Jenkins, late Fifer Co. H., 9th Ill. Vol. Infty. Address 624 Pike Avenue, Canon City, Colo.]

Commander Easterly was one of the Centennial State's twenty-six Civil War veterans who took the trains east late in June 1938 for their week-long Diamond Battle Reunion at Gettysburg. We already know from his son David's testimonial how profoundly satisfying, glorious, and emotive that whole affair became for anyone privileged to be there. When, a year later, G.A.R. Chief Robert M. Rownd was officially invited by the U.C.V. to attend their 49th National Reunion at Trinidad, Colorado for Aug. 22-25, 1939, he appointed comrade Easterly, the Colorado-Wyoming Department Commander, to represent him at the only Reb National conclave held in the West.[6] This, Easterly did with pizzazz. Just a few days later came one of his greatest honors ever—his leading the 73rd National Encampment Parade on the beautiful white Arabian stallion through downtown Pittsburgh in late August 1939. Perhaps at that moment not many spectators realized a certain fact: that the Civil War veteran riding out front in equestrian splendor was one of the Union Army's and G.A.R.'s (then 1700 strong) three youngest survivors. Considering that a full third of his military service was rendered *before* his ninth birthday and that a good half of it was in *1861,* it is this writer's judgment that Easterly need never have apologized to anyone for falling short of having earned his memorable epithet (not that he ever did!)—"the Baby of the Civil War."

Lewis attended the 74th National Encampment in Springfield, Illinois, in 1940; he was one of ninety-three comrades who went to their 75th in Columbus, Ohio, in 1941; he was one of fifty-two at their 76th in Indianapolis in 1942. Easily, he and Joshua C. Pearce were the last Coloradoans to attend the Nationals. Lewis was Gunnison Post 17's sole survivor. He had become an institution. Even now—55 years after—a few senior locals recall how he enjoyed daily visits with friends at Mr. Blackstock's Store. As much westerly as he was Easterly, he goes down in this book as an All-American. Gunnison's Community Church overflowed with his mourners. Legionnaires were honorary pallbearers. A quartet sang Civil War melodies and "Oh Love, That Will Not Let Me Go," and "There's a Wilderness in God's Mercy." He died in the line of duty, as he saw it. In obedience to Governor John C. Vivian's request, he went to Denver to attend a called meeting of the Board of Control of the Soldiers Home in Monte Vista. This trip in frigid winter brought on pneumonia from which he did not recover. Five months later he succumbed at his ranch home and was laid to rest at Gunnison's Masons & Odd Fellows Cemetery, leaving a posterity of 5 – 6 – 1.[7]

Benjamin Franklin Williams

Mar. 7, 1854 – Aug. 26, 1943

This story has proven slow in the composing. Of some 900 aged personalties, South and North, among our nation's last surviving veterans of the War Between the States whom the writer has researched during 1971-1995, this C.S.A. wagoner-patriot-youngster proved to be the second toughest (most challenging) of all to verify and authenticate—second only to Willie Johnston, a drummer boy of the Third Vermont Infantry and early (and youngest ever) recipient of the Congressional Medal of Honor. Because the Williams story has resurrected its own memorable odyssey-in-the-unraveling, I would like to pass along precisely *how* its tarrying truths suspensefully came to light. Hence, this present departure from an ordinary narrative mode.

I believe that I first learned of Williams' identity when in 1972 I noticed on page 279 of *Pennsylvania at Gettysburg,* "C -WILLIAMS, BENJAMIN FRANKLIN, 1800 Wade Ave., N.E., Atlanta." I did not think much about this name for quite some time, noting only that I had far fewer Ben Franklins among my 900 oldsters than I had George Washington Somebodies. The following is from a one-page featurette entitled "A Lingering Mystery Shrouds Benjamin Franklin Williams (185? - 194?)—An Active C.S.A. Patriot at Age Nine"...the death year pure guesswork...and it appeared in *Confederate Veteran* (Mar.-Apr. '92) with this opening confession of failure:

> *After some nine years of fruitless research, this featurette is my ultimate effort on behalf of an apparently all-but-forgotten Confederate personality. My ambition remains the same: to discover Benjamin Franklin Williams' date and place of birth that I might more fittingly honor him among the last [and youngest] grand old Boys in Gray. The one encouraging piece of evidence I have learned in recent years is in an* Atlanta Constitution *story (10/14/41) on the 51st National Reunion of the U.C.V. {& 46th Reunion, S.C.V.} in Atlanta. Pictured among twenty aged veterans of the Gray is "B. F. Williams, 87, of Columbus (Ga.), fingering a golden sword that was his father's, a memento of the Mexican War; he recalls how, as just a little shaver, he drove supplies to Columbus to feed the troops there." Of Georgia's then 56 known Old Rebs, he was one of ten attending. This confirming evidence that he was indeed alive then was sent to me on April 10, 1991, by Charles Kelly Barrow, Georgia Division Historian, S.C.V. and Historian M.O.S.B., whom I wish to thank heartily.*

Had it not been for an enterprising and prescient writer, Martha N. McLeod, who interviewed Cmdr. Williams, U.C.V., around 1938 for her forthcoming Brother Warriors *(1940), we today would most likely be unaware of Williams' humble role in the "War Between the Yankees and the Americans." What Ms. McLeod learned in 1938 directly from him we are privileged to share from her collective biography and from mine found in* The South's Last Boys in Gray.[1]

> *At the age of nine I was engaged in the War. My older brothers and father carried gun powder and shots. I carried supplies. I was too young to enlist as a soldier and carry a gun, but I did duty at the Quartermaster Supply Department throughout the four years of the War.*
>
> *My father served as an enrolling officer at the beginning of the War. He got up a company of young boys and drilled them. When the last call for volunteers came, Father went to the War. The company of young boys he had prepared, gave their services by hauling supplies to the camp depots. These provisions were gathered around the country from the farmers, who gave a certain portion of their foodstuff to the quartermaster at the camp commissary. I carried lots of supplies to Wheeler's Cavalry.*
>
> *One exciting come-off was when I ran a bunch of Yankees about two miles by myself. You bet, I was leading them—they tried to catch me, but I outrun 'em. They shot once in a while, just to see how fast I could run, but if they meant to hit me, I outrun the bullets.*
>
> *You've heard us folks down here in Georgia referred to as 'Georgia Crackers;' Well, that label dates back to the ox-cart days. A long time ago traveling was mighty slow. People drove oxen hitched to little covered wagons. In order to get to town to do a little trading, a fellow had to start out in the middle of the night. Now, oxen are slow animals and sometimes they like to just stop and stand still in the middle of the road. The drivers carried rawhide whips which they twirled in the air and snapped with a loud crack. The noise drove the oxen on. Lots of times the crack of the whip awakened people living along the roads to town and they would remark, 'There goes a cracker.'*

This, then, exhausts my knowledge on Cmdr. Williams. His C.S.A. service was good enough for his fellow comrades, quite obviously, and it is good enough for me...that I want to honor him in a forthcoming national study, Callow, Brave and True, *where he surely is worthy of careful mention. It* would appear *he left no descendants. Possibly his attendant, Mrs. Langley (of Atlanta?) might have children yet who knew Cmdr. Williams? What ever happened to him remains the haunting question. Can any loyal Southron rise to this (admittedly awesome) challenge? I will confer a signed hard-*

cover on whoever is first to disclose further details on Cmdr. Williams, softbound copies upon the next two who can expand my knowledge of him and signed original tabulations from my latest unpublished study for any helpful contributor who can remove this stubborn enigma.

Among fruitless ploys had been an October 1982 search by the Georgia Department of Human Services to verify Williams' death during 1938-42. But their report stated "No record on file."[2] A later search extending up through 1946 yielded the same result. In late 1983 I consulted two Atlanta U.D.C. Chapters—Alfred H. Colquitt No. 2018 and Atlanta No. 18—hopeful they could offer the precise where and when of Cmdr. Williams' passing from their midst. Perhaps one of *their* historians or secretaries had noted his demise in chapter records or minutes as noteworthy...since he must surely have been the youngest Georgia Reb alive and been so possibly for a lifetime...since he had starred as a luminary in Atlanta's own late-surviving U .C. V. Camp Howell #1825. But—no. Nobody knew of his identity and nobody was stirred to *want to know.* Forty years had obscured him beyond rescue or deliverance from oblivion. By late 1985 at manuscript deadline for *The South's Last Boys in Gray,* a report that Williams quite frankly deserved a detailed visibility in, I still lacked his vital data—date and place of death. Embarrassing! Ashamedly, I "guesstimated" him to have reached age ninety and to have lived into May 1943 (rather than leave that information a complete blank).[3]

My featurette in *Confederate Veteran* provided the means for Williams' fuller discovery that had been so elusive. Though reader response was light (two letters), these proved strategic to the cause. Immediately, an Apr. 2, 1992 letter from David L. Bridges (S.C.V. Camp 1347), of South Daytona, Florida, conveyed data from his copy of *History of Stewart County, Georgia,* identifying Williams' hometown, Louvale, and his parentage, family, and burial site. This was a breakthrough! A Sept. 17, 1992, letter from Linda M. Hallman of Thomaston, Georgia [husband & son, S.C.V.—John B. Gordon Camp 1449], confirmed everything and added some to Bridges' disclosure. The accuracy of Bridges' swift data enabled me within hours to fire off a querying letter to the editor of the nearest newspaper to Louvale. That letter went to Rena Cobb, Editor, *The Stewart-Webster Journal* of Richland, Georgia, circulation 1,517. Yes, to Rena (Mrs. Eugene) Cobb, of Richland, whom I had little appreciation of, at this juncture, but who would achieve near-sainthood upon the eventual culmination of our cause. [I had no inkling of Editor Cobb's redemptive powers as an experienced officer in Clement A. Evans Chapter #783, U.D.C.] Among the *Journal's* readership Williams would have, conservatively, a score of descendants and kinfolks. The first letter—from Joseph F. "Joe" Carter—arrived from Omaha, Georgia, in my May 17, 1992, mail. Joe, a great-grandnephew to Williams, and, like him, an outdoorsman, happiest when catfish, bass and bream tauten his lines, does philosophically, remarkably recapture (as best one can in the 1990s) his C.S.A. ancestor's rustic flair for wholesome rural values. During our year-long letter-swaps Joe sent photos of the Nathaniel Jackson Williams Family Cemetery and some Georgia products, including pecan syrup for griddle cakes. Paraphrasing, we summarize his offerings:

> *We have at least 13 who served in the Cause, whose C.S.A. careers run the gamut from killed in battle, to wounded, to being prisoners, to being at Appomattox and returning home, to homeguardsmenships. "Uncle Tobe" (rhymes with* robe) *everyone knew him as. Some confusion arose here, as he went by "Uncle Buddy" also, causing some of the family not to recognize his identity as B.F.W. I definitely have his grave located. Like many older family burial grounds, our small Williams Family Cemetery was overgrown. Several of us, including my cousin, "J. D." Richardson, have gotten together and done a clean-up there. This plot lies on property they owned off west of Louvale village and fronts along the west side of a dirt road, not far from B.F.W.'s birthplace, Louvale-Holloman Creek Church Road. The graves n. to s. are B.F.W. (no d.o.d.), Nathaniel (his father,), Louisa A. Cleveland (his mother), and Ida (his sister). They face west. Flat rectangular slabs cover each.*
>
> *Uncle Tobe did marry Lucy Harriet Lightner. Their children were Eloise, Lucile (her twin), Robena "Bena" M. Wilson, Cleve (Brendle b. 9/12/84), Bass Eli, and Tigner F. These latter two—"real characters." Many, back then, in our family, could well have inspired Erskine Caldwell's personalities for* God's Little Acre *and* Tobacco Road. *B.F.W. made a living partly by his bootlegging talents.... We are restoring Fort McCreary, an Indian War era (1836) outpost prominent in local history—a challenge that puts me "in hog heaven."*
>
> *Absolutely nothing exists here in the Stewart County Courthouse relating to B.F.W.'s death. I've researched all the records as has my cousin, who, indeed, is Probate Judge in charge of them.... I'm not going to allow all your hard work on a family member to "go down the tubes" without "walking the last mile" and crawling the last few feet, if need be. Uncle Tobe is hiding out somewhere (in time). I'm rather enjoying all this, to be honest, but it is frustrating...you definitely have a dragnet going down here.*
>
> *Our local S.U.V. Camp #1607 had a dedication last weekend for an Old Reb who, elderly, fathered a son, now in his 80's. A mounted Rebel cavalry officer charged out of the woods at a gallop with the Stars and Bars flying on a staff to present to him, amid Rebel Yells, goose-bumps and chills. In our courthouse is an authentic Confederate Stars & Bars that the 17th Georgia took north with them. Uncle Will Shierling refused to burn or surrender it at Appomattox and brought it home under his*

jacket. The U.D.C. and County Commissioner are giving it to the S.C.V. and we are going to encase it in a gas-tight vacuum in an effort to preserve it from harm, for it is a sacred banner redolent of our heritage (bloodstained).

In her June 23, 1992 letter from Louvale, Thelma Anna Richardson (Mrs. Thomas Lee) Wilder, known widely in Stewart County as "Sambo," we are offered a direct harvest of thoughts on her kin and great-granduncle:

Uncle Tobe is certainly not forgotten. Many of us children remember him. I was born here in Louvale in May 1926 to John B. (1897-1966) and Sybil Ross Shierling Richardson (1894-1073), Stewart County natives. Sybil's parents were Richard Thos. (1872-1959) and Bernice Peed Shierling (1874-1937), also Stewart Countians. Richard Thomas' father was John Anderson Shierling (1842-1930) of adjoining Webster County, who married Martha "Mattie" Salima Williams (1852-1933) in 1868. Our great-Grandmother Martha Salima was Uncle Tobe's older sister. I have five sisters and a brother related to him like me—Billie Jacque (Ross) Gordy, 1912; Emmie Bernice, 1923; Martha Sybil, 1924; Amelia Beth, 1928; Johnnie, 1930; James Richard, 1935.

Uncle Tobe lived near Link, "a wide place in the road," and would come in to Louvale on a sled 5' long x 3' wide drawn by a mule. With a solid wood floor and low center of gravity, it had a removable straight-back chair mounted mid-way. He loved children. We knew him at a distance by his big brown felt hat. He could speak in a local Indian vernacular, his favorite phrase "Ark-a-tooma Von de booma." (Indecipherable today.) We have no idea how he came by this ability. Uncle Tobe lived some 70 years at or near his birthplace but in the early 1930's he moved from his old home place to a small cabin he and his son Tigner had built in a hollow off the highway north of town 2.3 miles. They had a dug spring large enough to bathe in. We were baptized in it. Hear tell Tigner may've had a still for his own private stock.

Uncle Tobe's father was Nathaniel Jackson Williams (Jan. 8, 1816-Sept. 23, 1874), a native of Covington, Georgia, whose wife was Louisa A. Cleveland (Mar. 3, 1827-June 24, 1913), daughter of Col. Benjamin (2/12/1792 - 1/26/1879) and Amelia M. Hooper (4/1/1798 - 11/9/1870), the youngest of eight children born to Elizabeth Adams Word, who in 1783 in Halifax County, Va., had married Richard B. Hooper (May 1756- Feb. ? 1864). I (Sambo) applied in October 1986 for membership in the D.A.R. certifying my eligibility as a descendant of Sgt. Richard B. Hooper, who in March 1776 enlisted at Lunenburg Court House, Va., with Capt. James Johnson to serve in J. T. McAllister's 6th Virginia Militia.[4]

Uncle Tobe had 8 siblings—

Martha Salima (Mrs. John A.) Shierling (7/22/52-1/26/33)
Benj. Fr. Williams, b. 3/7/54
Fannie B. (Mrs. J. J.) Burks, 3/30/1857
Ida Williams (12/10/58-2/10/1944)
John W. Williams (1/20/60 -
Thomas S. Williams (9/1/63-
Josephine M. Corledge Bowe (2/14/65-
Nathaniel Hooper Williams (9/17/67-
Minnie M. Rinker (9/8/70-

This data is from my mother's Family Record {Hist. of Stewart Cty, p. 554}

Aug. 8, 1992

I still can't find Uncle Tobe's death date. Have searched records in Lumpkin & Columbus. The Stewart-Webster Journal *for the 1940's has been at Athens (Univ. of Georgia) well over a year for microfilming. Will keep trying. Tobe married Lucy Lightner (July 28, 1858-Apr. 31, 1912) about 1877. Lucy was buried at Old Jamestown Cemetery, Shiloh Methodist Church, near Cusseta, Ga., to our north. Oldest to youngest, they had:*

Bass Eli, who married, went to Texas, and had a daughter Grace (Mrs. Herman) Gips in Houston

Eloise M. Foster, whose daughter Clemmie married and died in Savannah; whose son Clinton died in Atlanta c. 1987

Lucile, Eloise's twin, married W. E. Dalton and raised Clemmie & Clinton, last descendant known to have had Tobe's father's Mexican War sword & Tobe's's portrait that he was going to bring to me, but he died of a heart attack

Robena, who married Isaac E. Wilson of Savannah Beach. Their children were Lucille Elizabeth W. Jackson, Joanne W. Boop, and Harry Franklin W. of Pompano Beach, Fla.

Tigner, unmarried, lived in Atlanta many years but finally moved back to Louvale to live with his father in their cabin. Today, Uncle Tobe has descendants enough still in our area & the older ones remember him.

We should note, at this point, a remarkable revelation—namely, that Williams' mystery occasioned, via Sambo Wilder, the discovery of one of the South's centenarian "Dixie Doodle Dandies" (Southern Revolutionary War veterans yet alive during/after the War Between the States—a glorious tabulation largely unharvested even now, mid-1990's) in the person of ex-Sgt. Richard B. Hooper, 107 years when he died in 1864. Inaugurated in *Confederate Veteran (*May- June '93, p. 5), the search "In the Name of Justice" for this elite Old Soldiery, who were grandfathers of C.S.A. veterans, became a world premiere upon its appearance as "The Rest of the Story" in the May-June '94 issue.

Late that same August '92 as some of Sambo Wilder's thoughts were flowing into my Williams file folder, a correspondence arose between me and James Gaston, Jr., of Fair Oaks Plantation, Friendship Road, Americus. Initially, Jim was after copies of my Southern study to give to Southwest Georgia Academy (Damascus) and to the Southland Academy Library, Americus. He was inquiring also about Wm. Jordan "Daddy" Bush of Fitzgerald, who had been Georgia's ultimate Old Reb, who closed out some 107 years late in 1952. Jim himself is a graduate of nearby (to Fitzgerald) Plains High School two years ahead of Jimmy Carter's oldest son. By Feb. 8, '93 Jim Gaston, a consistent, prize-winning peanut farmer who grows considerable corn "on the side," was urging me to accept an invitation to speak at an accommodatingly delayed May meeting of Alexander H. Stephens Camp #78, S.C.V., at Americus. By mid-April, promising plans for a productive trip into Georgia had fully matured. To Patsy and Ben Thornton, of Cordele, goes much credit for making my itinerary a workable and successful trip. [Patsy is the daughter of my friends James B. & Elsie Pilcher, of Cordele, who hosted me on research/speaking jaunts in 1980, '84, '88. "Jay-Byrd," 96, is a grandson of Pvt. Lucius M. Bailey (Co. D., 63rd Ala.), who lived to be 99 in 1947. See *Confederate Veteran* Nov-Dec '93, 8-10].

The Wilders had wished that I could come to Louvale and meet "the crew." Providentially, everything fell into place, and on a sunny afternoon I arrived at their large, white ancestral home. At once Sambo answered her north door, most cordially admitting me into a central high-ceilinged hallway of heirlooms, pointing out a portrait of Uncle Tobe's father and mother. Which bed chamber would I like? [I had planned on a single night's lodging but soon was weaned from that folly.] I was given a spacious, 1st-floor room and antique bed with an imposing headboard. [It crossed my mind, "Somewhere in his 89 years Uncle Tobe has slept in this very bed," reminiscent of the three nights I slept in Robert W. Pickens' Easley, S. C., bed—(1847-1948), Co. G., 2nd Bttln., S. C., State Res.] I was made right to home and introduced forthwith to "Muscadine Wine grown, processed and bottled by Sambo and Tom Wilder—NOT FOR SALE." They steered me to the *Stewart County History* and its April 1916 portrait of Uncle Tobe and 31 other C.S.A. veterans taken in front of the Methodist Church of Richland, Georgia (a site I would visit and photograph on my return Sunday a.m. to the Gastons and to Cordele).

Louvale—unincorporated, a tiny post office, a folksy restaurant, a small grocery-variety, a quiet, peaceful retreat—is a delightful, half-forgotten little paradise. Its quite famous Church Row of four historic rural churches lends a quaint, friendly atmosphere. Historic Antioch Institute (c. 1853) is used today as the Louvale Community House, home, too, for the Sybil and John B. Richardson School of Sacred Harp Singing.

That Saturday morning Sambo, Tom, Jimmy-Dick (her brother) and I leisurely toured (with bouquets) three cemeteries, the first one the Nathaniel Jackson Williams, near the old site of Williams' birthplace on the Louvale-Holloman Creek Church Road. We visited resting spots of four, five and six generations of Hoopers, Shierlings, Williamses, Clevelands, especially at Holloman Creek Cemetery.

As I talked with Williams' descendants and relatives during a two-day-fantasy-come-true, there crept over me an ampler approximation and appreciation of the character of Little Tobe's C.S.A. service than I had ever understood before. He seems to have been the youngest male in his clan remotely within service age, yet he was the eldest son in his own family line. One glimpse of this 1861 seven-year-old's little world allows us to sense the lad's growing need, his self-conceived ambition and compulsion to render his individual share of support. To review the givens:

> *- Some 13 males among his kin were soon performing duty. The Shierlings alone gave five to the Cause—Isham (1819-1862), Co. D., 46th Ga.; Robert Franklin (1828?-1897), Ga. Inf.; William B., Co. I, 17th Ga.; John Anderson, Jr., (Son of Wm. B.), Co. I, 17th Ga. (Prisoner, Rock Island, Ill.)*[6]
>
> *-Within a few weeks after Ft. Sumter, his father, a Mexican War veteran, began organizing and training a local Stewart County Home Guard of boys 9 to 13 years, some Tobe's friends or neighbors.*

Although formal papers and records of Williams' humble C.S.A. career are entirely lacking and nothing on him is researchable at the State and National Archives [why I feel called upon to do him justice], we have the consolation that his acceptance among fellow Gray as *legitimately one of them* was a blessing he could count on *all* during his last eighty years. Given that his father was commanding officer of the local homeguard, that Tobe was a shade younger than the youngest members, that he later asserted service in all four war years, mildly put, could there have been a wee bit of peer pressure from his slightly older youngster comrades? There he was—aching to be exemplary by joining, looking on as an outsider disconsolate for his lack of "manhood," watching his "Napa" (father), with foresight, transforming an assortment of youngsters (and a few older men) into a creditable cadre of effectives. Napa's ability to instill discipline and preparedness upon his paramilitaries prompted stirrings of *amor patriae* in the little fellow, worked a powerful yearning of heart in the would-be soldierling.

Most of their specialty assignments Little Tobe increasingly felt himself well capable of executing—mail carrier, forager, messenger, hostler, water boy, spy, lookout, produce gatherer, wagoner. "Nat" Williams, supportive of his wife Louisa, "a fond mother, a friend to all," in keeping Tobe occupied with domestic chores and favored pastimes, withstood barrage after barrage of pleadings, reasonings, arguments from the unhappy outsider. At length, that first war summer over half gone, father (& mother) and son reached a compromise; Tobe won himself a mascot status. Tobe *probably* gained the privilege of attending training sessions by mid-August. Knowing the terrain, roads, trails, waterholes and natives encouraged him toward becoming a commissary supplier in northern Stewart County and western Chattahoochee. After learning which farmers could supply what foodstuffs and familiarizing himself with a penciled map (eventually memorized), Tobe bethought himself of a duty Napa could entrust to him. Acquiring a mule and wagon-cart, Tobe made bold to offer himself as a gatherer and purveyor of fresh farm produce (his main item), home comforts (soap, towels, clothing, knits), and letters to the Confederate depot and outpost at the southern edge of present-day Fort Benning, near the Alabama line. The proposed status of produce-gatherer and wagoner implied a promotion psychologically and strategically. Needs for such billets first arose that autumn of '61. After Tobe's parents duly weighed the matter over, the lad, all smiles, won this major concession.

We note, in passing, that it being by then mid-September, Tobe was all of 7 years 6 months 10 days on assumption of his cherished billet in Georgia's 780th Militia District. However, concerned to want to preserve the benign myth of greater maturity, as indeed hundreds of others most youthful, North and South, eagerly chose to do, Tobe agreeably was set down as nine—some seventeen months in his favor. Fellow guardsmen inevitably knew the tender truth, while pride in the fact and a low-profile "What-of-it?"-ness prevailed. We suspect that among the 32 veterans pictured in 1916 a couple of others assumed their earliest C.S.A. duties at age twelve or less.

In warmer months he gathered staples on his route every ten or twelve days, faithfully fulfilling his commissary mission to an element of Gen. Joe Wheeler's forces. It took a day to collect his load, another to haul it to the Quartermaster's Depot, and a third to return home, a matter of at least sixteen miles one way. In colder months he delivered about every three weeks or as weather and grammar schooling permitted. Folks along the way gladly gave shelter, sustenance for boy and beast, encouragements, sometimes adding to his wares.

Nathaniel "Napa" J. Williams, with mixed feelings, relinquished his S.C.H.G. Command (Co. I, 3rd Georgia State Troops) in mid-June 1862 to enlist that July 1 for service with Company F, 62nd Georgia Infantry. Since, for two years until July 16, 1864, much of Cpl. N. J. Williams' duty was near Columbus, Georgia, Tobe could occasionally visit and even lodge overnight with his father. That final July of the war Cpl. Williams was transferred to Company F., 8th Georgia Cavalry, A.N.V., whereupon he was sent to Virginia for the defense of Petersburg.[7] He served *in uniform* some 27 months. For all but his last nine service months he had been relatively available to his family and a kind of aegis under whose sponsorship Tobe the Child Reb could perform with a measure of confidence. By July '64 (N.J.W.'s rotation to A.N.V.), Tobe , being 10 years 4 months, was an experienced wagoner able to bring independence, self-reliance, resourcefulness [Remember his fleetness on being chased by federal bullets?] to carrying out his express duties. His pay? Mainly it was the satisfaction, fulfillment of self, what he felt to be his destined privilege. Not to be overlooked was Tobe's mule—the issue of a mare horse and a jack donkey—a remarkable creature easier to manage than a horse, more even-tempered, less susceptible to heat, less erratic, more efficient on food. As nearly as can be calculated (allowing for sickness), Tobe, for his part, accrued "in the neighborhood of" 40 C.S.A. months—surely a lonesome tenure for one so young. At war's end Williams truly was one of *the* youngest bona fide veterans—11 years 1 month. This distinction was his for life, but exceeding few were ever aware of it. Nationally, only eight other veterans were later born than Tobe: Willie H. Bush, John H. Osteen, Franklin L. Wall, Wm. Thomas Keith, Wm. N.O. Lea, Mancil V. Root, Wm. Lee Owens, and Robert B. Tyler. Only three others have surfaced who were under age eight at inception of their duty: John H. Osteen, Charles Knecht, and Wm. O. Neubold Lea. (See Appendix B.)

Of these youngest, only Robert B. Tyler and Williams were among the 1,845 veterans at the 75th Battle Reunion of the Blue and Gray at Gettysburg in July 1938. [Had Tobe stayed home, this account would never have been written.] Tyler, rightfully, believed himself the youngest there. During the six reunion days, Williams and Tyler "quite inevitably" shook hands. However, the Georgian did not "trade on" or boast of his martial youthdom. He was that week, categorically, second only to Tyler in lateness of birth, a mere five days difference. But as to tenderness of age upon inception of duty, Tobe Williams apparently ranked #1 at the Diamond Reunion, this record unacknowledged until now. These youngest, while curious for the topic, were barely aware of one another or of their relative standings. Tyler; Charles E. Merrick (3/4/54-10/11/43, of the 147th Illinois and Los Angeles); Nimshi Nuzum (1/30/53-5/4/39, of W. Virginia Home Guard and Fairmont, W. Va.); and Frank M. Ironmonger (3/4/53-12/10/39, Courier, 17th Virginia Infy., and of So. Jacksonville, Fla.) knew one another. Tobe knew Ironmonger from a few U.C.V. reunions.

Midday Saturday, May 22, 1993, I strolled through Louvale, entered a couple of rustic churches, basked in the sun, inquired of older folks if they recalled Tobe Williams. (They usually did, but were unsure of his last living there.) About 4:15 p.m. Tom Wilder, Lt. Col., U.S.A.F. Ret., drove me out north of town on Route 27 to see a few landmarks. Returning, he pulled up to the left embankment 1 mile from town and let me disappear down below, where, by Tom's guidance I found *the* hollow. Within minutes I saw ruins of a small structure—a few beams, boards, a door case, a window frame. Nothing standing. Exploring, I spy bed springs and pry one loose; I salvage a door hinge; these rusted trophies become instant keepsakes—[Tom knows all along what I am "up to."]—a tiny part of Williams' nearly forgotten microcosm. This, *fifty* years after, was as close as I could get to him on whom I'd decided sainthood was overdue.

That evening the Wilders hosted a major family time, a reunion of kin, an opportune grand moment in my life, for they enabled me to meet some three dozen affable, warm-hearted folks, perhaps eight of whom had attended Tobe's funeral! While everyone agreed his closing rites had been in 1943 and that summer midway of World War II, none could say for sure its precise date [Sun. Aug. 29th].[8]

Our evening climaxed in a sumptuous banquet of delectables, many of the scrumptious dishes directly from Sambo's kitchen, laden with her cuisine and with yet more treats brought in as parties arrived—hors d'oeuvres, biscuits, fricasseed chicken, meatloaves, sweet potato pie, black-eyed peas, hushpuppies, pies, you-name-it! Classic Southern hospitality and a red-letter day. "We all" sat down to great tables in a dining room that would have done credit to Scarlett O'Hara's Tara...largely in the name of Uncle Tobe!

In her June 4, 1993 letter from Richland, Georgia, Rena (Mrs. Eugene B.) Cobb, President, Clement A. Evans Chapter #783, U.D.C.—[I had spoken by phone with Rena Sunday a.m. in my last hour with the Wilders, and she promised me Tobe's obituary soon.]—sent to my home *the* long-awaited key piece to a trying (so many had tried so hard for so long) puzzle:

> *Dear Professor Hoar: Thank you for your letter and enclosures of May 30. Luck and the Almighty were with me today. Here is B. F. Williams' obituary. He died in Decatur, near Atlanta, in DeKalb County, Aug. 26, 1943. My youngest son Glynn, is Commander of the Stewart-Webster Camp 1607, S.C.V., and he heard you talk in Americus and brought me one of your handouts. It was real enjoyable to talk with you and reminisce.*

[N. B. Only upon receipt of Pres. Cobb's letter on June 9th 1993, did I learn where and when Williams saw his last sunset.] He had been living about a year in the Decatur home of his daughter Lucile, Mrs. W. E. Dalton. It is interesting to note that one other Confederate veteran was living in Decatur at the time and he had the same middle name, James Franklin Webb, 96, of Company K, 10th Georgia Cavalry, who died Dec. 28, 1943.

In my 1975 survey at the Georgia Archives Williams' name never surfaced among some 43 Confederate pensioners who were living in Georgia during the 1940's. Either (A) Tobe never applied (most probable), or (B) he applied too late for supportive testimonials from those he'd served with (2nd most probable), or (C) he applied and was rejected. Though this form of recognition was denied him or unsought those closing years, we have the con-

Lucile Wilson (Mrs. Ralph A.) Jackson

Benjamin Franklin "Uncle Tobe" Williams.

solation that Tobe's identity and just place among Georgia's last Old Rebs is finally known and confirmed. Upon his death Georgia had but twenty-five Confederate veterans.

Uncle Tobe Williams' services were held Sunday afternoon, Aug. 29, 1943, at Louvale's Methodist Church, Rev. W.W. Whaley officiating. No mention was made in the brief obituary of Tobe's Confederate status. Was there perhaps a passing comment or two made on that front by a few that afternoon? Though admirable standards of official documentation have been and remain confessedly impossible for those unsung heroes like Tobe Williams, we trust that on some not too distant day a fluttering banner, even the sacred Confederate Tricolor, may yet grace his humble grave.

On Saturday, May 25, 1996, at the Williams Cemetery 2.8 miles outside Louvale along a dirt road into the woodsy countryside, the long anticipated memorial service for Benjamin F. and Nathaniel J. Williams "came off" beautifully. Fearing dusty terrain and roadways as the appointed day and hour drew closer, we (Johnny, Amelia & Gladys Ann Pate, the J. R. Richardsons, the Wilders, Joe Carter, the Cobbs, some 40 descendants, SCV Camps #1607

& #165—some 2/3rds of Louvale and myself) all prayed for rain. Perhaps too many of us petitioned for a saving moisture, for in May 24th's gloaming amid much rumbling and increase of wind, a veritable cloudburst let go. The downpour came steadily until after dark when a heavy drizzle set in during the banquet at the Wilders' home and lasted into the night. Hopes dimmed for our holding the ceremony out at the cemetery. Preparations went forward for the service in town at Church Row. But high winds blew steadily, hastening the drying-off. Joe Carter, on assignment, at length (almost literally the 11th hour), reported the dirt road to be passable after all.

With last-minute scurrying, a procession of vehicles and toted cannon duly arrive at the wilderness site. For our ceremony.... Not a speck of dust amid perfect temperatures! At 11:25 a.m. Commander Glynn Cobb gives the "Welcome." David Orr voices the invocation. Gordon Smith introduces Professor Hoar, who speaks ten minutes, commenting on B. F. and N. J. Williams as typical of two CSA components—those ages 8-14 years, those over 45 years. Hoar says, "We are also honoring unknown scores of Uncle Tobe's age group, identities now lost to time, who 'did' for, even died for, the celestial Cause(s) sacred to their Southern homeland." Commander Cobb presents a Camp #1607 Certificate of Appreciation to Prof. Hoar and Cmdr. Charlie Lott, of McDaniel-Curtis Camp #165 (Carrollton, Ga.) , gives the professor a Camp #165 SCV cap, a Georgia CSA heritage auto plate, and a large R (a reminder to rhotacise that letter as in "park the car"). Mrs. Thelma "Sambo" Wilder places roses upon the two graves decked over with the Confederate flag. President Rena Cobb, of C. A. Evans Chapter, U.D.C., places her wreath of magnolia leaves. Commander Lott and comrades fold the two flags and present them. They then fire cannons in a Colorguard Salute. Bernard "Bubba" Cobb's guitar "Dixie" penetrates the audience and wilderness. Camp #165 fire five muzzleloaders thrice by cadenced count. The Benediction. All of us admire the informative granite Confederate markers. Everyone returns to town for dedication of a new flagpole at Church Row. The day climaxes with a gala Southern-style community picnic beneath an old water oak as a talented lady belts out popular Country and Western hits with an amplifier and electric guitar. Consensus is.... "It's been about the grandest day Louvale's ever seen."

Charles Eugene Merrick

Mar. 4, 1854 – Oct. 11, 1943

One of the youngest to have served in the Union Army, Charles, with every good right, believed himself one of the three or four youngest ever to have worn the Northern blue. Until he met Robert Blake Tyler at Gettysburg in early July 1938, Charles could not remember of ever knowing another who had served so youthfully as himself. Even then, Charles was but eight days senior to Robert.

At 10 years 11 months 9 days he joined up on Feb. 13, 1865, at Chicago to serve one year in Companies M and C, 147th Illinois Infantry. In so doing, he added *just eight years* to his age—the largest claim made by any youngster that the writer is aware of. Twenty-one days shy of eleven, Charles straight-facedly allowed he was eighteen.[1] [Until studying Merrick's papers, the writer supposed that five years were the greatest number added to reality, as in the case of George Ney Lockwood (Oct. 15, 1851-Sept. 28, 1945) of Co. K, 9th Mich. Cav., and Los Angeles.] Although he performed military (guard) duties for nearly a year, Charles was still only eleven when he was mustered out Jan. 20, 1866, at Savannah, Georgia. He had duty chiefly at Dalton, Albany, Americus and Smithville and, finally, at Savannah.[2] A son of Charles E. And Lorinda Olive Helmer Merrick, he was born in Kendall County, Illinois, his folks being New York natives. He was a retired insurance agent and lived his last forty years in California, much of it at 717 N. Wilton Place, Los Angeles. As the youngest comrade of Stanton Post 55, G.A.R.—destined to become the last extant post in the nation—he was well acquainted with the famed Lincoln Room in Patriotic Hall. Almost a second home to him, it was here that he was often referred to as "Captain" by his Civil War brethren, invariably four to twenty years his senior. Mystery still shrouds how he managed to get himself into the Union Army, yet the late-datedness of his success tells us that this lad had been wanting for months "to get in."

He was one of California's twenty-nine Grand Army men to attend their 70th National Encampment in Washington, D. C., during September 20-26, 1936. He was one of California's dozen marchers afoot in that grand parade. It was on that occasion that he discussed a key factor about his own compulsive desire to serve in uniform early in 1865...peer pride]...."I wanted to fight because I had two older brothers at the front, ages thirteen and fourteen."[3]

Charles E. Merrick died at Sawtelle Military Hospital, leaving his Elizabeth, 58, a widow. His services were conducted at the Jones and Hamrock Chapel on W. Washington Boulevard, with G.A.R. rites, and he was interred October 16 at the Rosedale Cemetery Grand Army plot, Stanton Post 55 officiating.

David Wood

Aug. 25, 1851 – Mar. 9, 1944

Most of America who viewed the 1989-91 repeated programmings of Ken Burns' TV miniseries *The Civil War* got their first actual glimpse of the uniformed David Wood, age ten (Navy Colt pistol in hand) for nearly three seconds as the camera focused upon the still portrait that accompanies this tribute...although they scarcely knew it, for David was/is not identified.

David's entry into the Union Army followed a likely pattern the reader, by now, has become well familiar with—namely, the youth having a father or older brother who was already an officer in the unit. David's father, Samuel Wood, had only recently been elected to the First Kansas Legislature, with whom he sat for their initial session on Mar. 26, 1861. Kansas had then been a state less than two months. Legislator Wood scarcely a month later began preparations for responding to President Lincoln's first call for volunteers. Wood raised a company of Kansas men and went with them as their captain. So swift were developments, he forewent a return home when the legislature adjourned. He distinguished himself leading Wood's Mounted Company at the Battle of Wilson's Creek on Aug. 10, 1861, where his good friend, Gen. Nathaniel Lyon got killed.[1]

Shortly after, Capt. Wood raised a battalion in Missouri, making his own Kansas Company a part of this new unit—the Sixth Missouri Cavalry. He then became a major and, before the end of 1861, he was a lieutenant colonel.[2] For some eight months the Sixth was stationed at Rolla, Missouri, from which point it executed many scouting expeditions into southern Missouri and Arkansas. While at Rolla—being now in one place long enough—his wife Margaret and son David were able to join him.

It was at about this time (November 1861) that David began laying down importunate barrages on his father, pleading to be included on these frequent scouting missions. But the sapling's salvos were firmly answered time and time again. How David at age 10 years 4 months 7 days managed to join Company A, Sixth Missouri Cavalry, on Jan. 1, 1862, and some of his own verbatim reminiscences of his service tour are best captured by Frances and Dorothy Wood in a 1977 biography of their father, *I Hauled These Mountains in Here*— [3]

But one day, when Wood was leading his men on a long expedition and they were many miles from headquarters, he sensed that something was going on behind him. He turned his white stallion and rode back, in spite of various efforts along the way to distract his attention. In the rear he found a piece of excess baggage—his young son riding along on a pony, the center of an admiring group of hardened soldiers. David takes up the story:

He didn't say much to me. I guess he realized he might as well yield to the inevitable. From then on he kept me with him, and on Jan. 1, 1862, at Rolla, I was regularly enlisted. My duties were principally those of an orderly, carrying dispatches here and there and sometimes going where grown men could not go.

We were stationed for a while at Houston, Texas County, Missouri, and did scouting from there, under direction from Rolla headquarters. One day word came that some Southern sympathizers were organizing and drilling at a town sixty miles away. Father took a company and started that afternoon. At daybreak we sent a shell from a mountain howitzer screaming through the upper story of the frame courthouse where

David Wood, age 10.

the rebels were quartered. They needed no further coaxing but came crowding out as fast as they could. When we returned to Houston, each of our men had a prisoner riding by his side.

Another time five or six of our men were out for a ride on their own account. They rounded a corner where a company of rebels was drilling...Our men had ridden squarely into it! They knew that if they ran, it would be a run for life. So two or three of the men turned in their saddles, waved their hats, and began yelling to an imaginary force following them. Then they all began shooting and charged. The rebels scattered in every direction, going to cover in the surrounding timber as fast as they could, leaving our men to rejoice in a bloodless victory.

At Houston we were quartered in a brick courthouse, and the rebels sent word they were coming to get us. We barricaded the windows and sent word to come and see us any time—we would be there to greet them. But they never came. The Missouri troops, as I remember it, were not very hard after each other. It was too much like shooting at one's own family.

Colonel Coleman, with his command, was recruiting men for the Confederates. One day we learned that he was leaving for Arkansas with about 300 men. We didn't think Col. Coleman and his Missouri men were needed in Arkansas—we felt he shouldn't leave us alone in Missouri. We decided to see if we couldn't induce him to stay and were soon on our way, with fully 300 men, to hold a conference with him.

Some of our advance guard came to a mill where there were twelve or fifteen men with their grist, getting it ground. The men, thinking we were after them, tried to run. We were anxious that no one should go ahead of us to announce our coming to Col. Coleman, so the advance guard used every possible means to stop the fleeing men, even firing shots. Father found one of the men on his knees with his arms around a wounded rebel, crying over him.

"Oh, Colonel, I never expected it to come to this!" the man said.

"What's the trouble?" Father asked.

"This is my brother!" the man replied. "I shot him off his horse."

Well, put him in the wagon and take care of him," Father directed. The wounded man recovered, much to everyone's relief.

In early morning, after a day and night of hard riding, we came upon the place where the Coleman Company had camped overnight. Their campfires were still burning, and their tin plates sat with breakfast on them untouched. We were that close to Coleman! As our main command neared the camp, we found our advance guard with a strong sapling bent over, holding a rope tied around a man's neck. They were all ready to let go and hoist him into the world to come. The man was so scared he was almost speechless. He was one of the men at the mill who had promised not to give us away and who had sped on as soon as he could to warn the Coleman forces. The boys wanted to hang him then and there, but Father said, "No, he has done us all the harm he can. Let him go."

According to his daughters, Frances and Dorothy, a noted writing team, who, with Scott Foresman & Company, edited the famous (ubiquitous?) Dick-Jane-Spot-Puff school reader series, David's father had been raised a Quaker, while the neighboring Lyon Family kept a station on the Underground Railroad. The son of Samuel N. and Margaret Lyon Wood, David was born at Mount Gilead, Morrow County, Ohio. In 1854, they traveled to Kansas Territory, where Samuel became a Free Stater.

Well before David's nine army months were concluded by a desperate bout with malaria and pneumonia and after he was taken home to Council Grove, Kansas, he displayed a virtual talent for high finance that prefigured by some twenty years his stellar career as owner-operator of an historic freighting service strategic to the opening up of the western slope of the Great Divide. David's fleet of huge freight wagons hauled out ore and hauled in food, machinery, dynamite, coal—everything needed by the silver and copper mines. He followed the Denver & Rio Grande Railroad into the Rockies; his passenger and freight lines, headquartered at Montrose, Colorado, were the most expansive ever to operate in the Centennial State.

But, to return to David's Civil War service. It seems the entrepreneurial spirit kindled early, for his role clearly exceeded that of an orderly. Returning to David's own words, which, by volume, account for a full two-thirds of *I Hauled These Mountains in Here,* we learn how he blossomed into a sutler:

I secured a cask of fresh water and some lemon extract and started making lemonade and selling it to the soldiers. This venture was so profitable that I made enough to buy some real lemons for a second batch. From this beginning I developed a sutler's outfit that made me in the neighborhood of $2000 while I was in the army. Finding that there was a great demand for small delicacies, I loaded up with everything I could think of that men would buy. One of the generals from the main army loaned me an ambulance for the outfit, and soon I was handling quite a business. Among other things, I changed bills for the men, who allowed me 25¢ for changing a five-or ten-dollar bill. This was robbery, of course, but was allowed throughout the army until Lincoln printed small bills, called "shin plasters," for change.... We were the advance guard for Gen. Curtis's army from Batesville to Helena, Arkansas, where Father was appointed Provost Marshall. He protected the merchants and Southern ladies (though their men were in the C.S.A.) from pillaging and murder.[4]

When peace came, the Woods returned to their farmstead near Cottonwood Falls, Kansas, which Col. Wood had acquired in 1859. Although in poor shape by springtime 1865 from neglect, this was *the* spot on earth closest to Dave Wood's heart—"our old home," as he fondly called it. With his brother, William L., he finished growing to manhood here, hunting in nearby timber, and swimming and fishing in the Cottonwood River that flowed below their home. Today the property is a National Historic Site, largely to commemorate the revered Kansan, Col. Sam Wood. Usually joining in on his father's cattle drives, Dave Wood lived here until 1876 when he located in Montrose, Colorado, where he earned just fame as one of the West's great freighters.

As mining camps became towns—Sapinero, Ouray, Ironton, Silverton, Teluride, Lake City, Horsefly, Portland, Red Mountain, Dallas—he extended his transport lines from his base (Montrose), hauling sewing machines, pianos, lard, flour, whiskey, cigars, chinaware, syrup, canned goods, brooms for storekeepers' shelves.

David married Miss Mary Dill on Christmas Day 1884 at her father's Topeka home. The piano was one of her talents. Tragically, Mary died from childbirth fever shortly after their Baby Marguerite's birth Oct. 4, 1886, and, less than a month later, she too died. David took them back to Cottonwood Falls for burial. Grief-stricken and hardly himself for months, this was not his first loss, for a fourteen-year-old sister had died in Kansas. But business kept him hopping. "One month," he noted in 1886, "I made better than $8000."[5] We know that he was often written up in Colorado newspapers. This was especially true of the Ouray *Solid Muldoon,* whose editor, Dave F. Day, 1847-1914, had also been a youthful soldier at ages 14 to 18 years while with Co. D., 57th Ohio, had even earned a Congressional Medal of Honor. These two did know each other rather well, as evidenced by Day's account of Wood's marriage, which indicates the wedding plans were unknown in Colorado. Wrote Day:

> *Dave Wood, the rascal, a few days prior to his departure for the East, informed us that he was going to Kansas and Missouri on a brief trip, the object being to secure "mules." And now comes the Emporia (Kans.)* News *with anything but a mule item:*
>
> *"Of very many friends the few who happened to hear about it dropped in this morning to congratulate Miss Mary Dill, wish her much joy and happiness, and sorrowfully bid her good-bye. The happy event takes place tomorrow morning at Topeka. The fortunate young man who is to lead Miss Dill to the altar is Mr. David wood, son of Hon. S. N. Wood, editor of* The State Journal.[6]

Dave Wood did marry again, in Denver at "The Little Church Around the Corner," and Governor of Colorado Alva Adams and his wife attended on July 18, 1888. Dave's bride was Fannie B. Parker (1869-1958), originally of Providence, Kentucky. Of their eleven children, seven grew to adulthood.

Before taking their vows he had bought a house in Montrose and furnished it. Not long after, he had Studebaker Brothers build a special phaeton—dark blue, canopy top with heavy silk fringe, and soft blue satin interior.[7]

Dave Wood was also great friends with William Henry Jackson (Apr. 4, 1843-June 29, 1942), the famous photographer (& artist) of the West, who himself had soldiered in Company K, 12th Vermont Infantry. A treasured token of their friendship was a large, tinted panoramic photo by Jackson of the Wood Ranch overlooking the Uncompahgre River near Dallas, Colorado, that this artist presented to Fannie and Dave.

Albert, Dave and Fannie's youngest, was an equestrian at age three, but it was David Wood, Jr. (1890-1982), who became the family raconteur. Often he would recall these episodes from 1902 and 1918:

> *I like telling of the time Dad and I went to Montrose on a train that carried Arthur Ridgway in his private coach. Dad, of course, rode with Mr. Ridgway, but I rode in the engineer's cab. I was twelve. The engineer, a big fellow, let me hold the throttle—pulling it back and e-e-easing it forward—his big gruntleted hand on top of mine. We got safely into Montrose, and the engineer told Dad, "Your Dave is the best damn hogshead on the road." I didn't know what it meant, but I sure was proud. I told Dad the engineer said there was a lot of brass back in the private car and asked if I could go back and see it. The engineer coughed, and Ridgway laughed.*
>
> *Another time I delivered a horse to a man in Placerville and took the train home. I was riding the back end of the passenger car, my saddle lying just inside the door. Somewhere up there we saw three coyotes. I had a .22 Savage rifle on my saddle, and I picked it up and started shooting at them from the back of the train. Billy Jay, the conductor, stood there watching me. Somehow one of the coyotes got in the way of a bullet and got hit. Billy pulled the whistle cord three times for an emergency stop and said in a resigned tone, "Go get it, Dave. It's worth $12 or $14." When Dad met the train I swung off carrying my saddle with one hand the coyote with the other. He said, "Where in the consarned nation did you get that?" Bill told him.*[8]

The Depression of 1893 and the competition of railroads impacted against his once lucrative freighting service. Dave Wood retreated into successful ranching and farming until after World War I when he realized none of his sons would carry it on. By the 1930s the children were out on their own; Ruth was a teacher at Grand Junction, Frances and Dorothy were Chicago editors, the boys had families.

In 1937 Dave Wood was one of 12,500 pensioned Civil War veterans who were invited to the 75th Battle Reunion of the Blue and Gray at

Gettysburg. Again, early in 1938, their ranks reduced to only about 8400, the Civil War men were re-invited, and 2610 of them pledged they'd attend.[9] Dave did, though he spurned the offer of two free train fares; rather, he chose Albert to drive him and Fannie. Along about June 23, 1938, in two cars, most of his family motored to Gettysburg, where they saw F.D.R. light the Eternal Peace Flame. In his Feb. 5, 1977 letter from Montrose, David Wood, Jr., 87, offers:

> *Father's biggest thrill was having so many there mistake him for an attendant because he looked so young. Father, who was discharged Aug. 12, 1862—13 days before his eleventh birthday, well remembered talking with Mr. Ironmonger and Mr. Easterly at Gettysburg in July 1938. It takes little imagination to guess one of the key topics on their minds—their being noticeably younger-looking than most of the 1845 veterans present, their ascertainments of who among them was the latest born, who was youngest while in uniform.*
>
> *Thanks for remembering Father in your national study.*[10]

On their return west Dave and Fannie visited in Indiana with Frances and Dorothy, who hosted their golden wedding anniversary celebration on July 18. Frailty eventually caught up with this grand couple, who spent most of their sunset years at Grand Junction with their daughter Ruth, who gave them excellent care. One of Colorado's last fifteen known Civil War veterans, David Wood, 92, was given a military funeral in Montrose and buried there. His name will forever belong with those of certain other great standouts of America's Saddest War, those who were barely ten years of age, yet were performing martial duties single digitly during the *first* third of the conflict (April 1861-August 1862)—names like Tommy Hubler, Charles Knecht, Susan Haines (Clayton), Lewis Easterly, Johnny Clem (?), Gilbert VanZandt, whose incredible profiles are amply examined elsewhere across these pages.

Gilbert Vanzandt

Dec. 20, 1851 – Oct. 4, 1944

"Youngest volunteers of the Civil War have put forth their claims by the dozen since the close of the great conflict, but it has remained for Gilbert VanZandt, now a citizen of Kansas City, Missouri, to demonstrate that the honor rightfully belongs to him."

The San Francisco Chronicle, *Oct. 20, 1901*

The above "preamble," itself typical of scores of such assertions, was undoubtedly written with conviction, even though VanZandt himself made no such claim. He may even have believed it, at least for a while, but, fairly early on in his eight postbellum decades, he quite surely came across half a dozen {conservatively} born later than himself, though he plausibly might never have met a veteran who was younger on enlistment than himself. One of the most likely such candidates would have been Dr. Robert B. Tyler, of Joplin, some 150 miles south of Kansas City. Another would have been Charles Knecht, of St. James, Missouri, at least as far off, to the southeast. However, Gilbert did not travel in Grand Army circles. More likely, he would have read a newspaper story about one or both of these two or about Mancil V. Root (b. June 18, 1854), whose youthful status customarily generated several articles annually up through his death in mid-1929. What Gilbert believed (to himself—in his heart) *was* very close to the unobtainable truth: that he had been one of the five or six youngest to have served in the Union Army. For interviewers, Gilbert merely "told it like it was," a straight-forward parading (if you will) of the unalloyed facts. Most of the following details, for example, derive from the 1901 *Chronicle* story.

Gilbert was born in the hamlet of Port William, in Ohio's southwestern Clinton County. His infancy and early childhood passed here where he first went to school. All during his ninth and tenth years, rumors of impending war were spreading like a prairie fire. Indeed, the onset of hostilities came when Gilbert was age nine and four months. Some fifteen long months trooped by while he impetuously watched for his chance. In Gilbert's words we have:

On the 6th day of August 1862, I enlisted as a Drummer Boy for Company D, 79th Ohio Volunteers. My father was a sergeant in this same Company D. You must understand I also had six uncles and a grandfather in the Union Army. Of a patriotic family, I was, of course, highly wrought up over the war, little dreaming that I would ever be permitted to take a hand in it. After a call for troops was issued, there came to our village a recruiter with two or three privates and a Government wagon. Notices were posted that a war meeting would be held in the schoolhouse. Port William was alive with excitement, and the building was packed. I had hammered around on tin pans with sticks since I could walk. As I had quite a reputation in town as a snare drummer, I was engaged to handle my sticks, while a fellow-townsman blew the fife. We furnished the music for this occasion. For my services that night I received a silver 50-cent piece from Lt. Ellwood. I carried it all through the war until it was stolen...this first money I'd earned as a soldier.

My father, my uncles, and nearly every other man and boy in town enlisted. I was wild to join. Lt. Ellwood needed a drummer to pep up his recruiting meetings. He gave me a chance on an old drum he found. He was going from town to town in our neighborhood and let me go along. Father had already enlisted. He knew how crazy to go I was. I believe both he and Mother thought that, if they gave me a chance to try it out with Lt. Ellwood, I would come back home cured. But the longer I was at it the better I liked it. I filled the drummer's job all over that section, and, on August 6, when the enlistees were brought together, I was enlisted as a regular drummer. And from then on, I was in the thick of it. I was 10 years 7 months and 16 days. I remained with the 79th O.V.I., sometimes doing duty as an orderly at regimental headquarters, until I was detailed as a dispatch carrier at division headquarters, 3rd Division, 20th Army Corps, serving in that capacity to the close of war. Thus I served through the Atlanta Campaign and to the Sea. I was in all engagements our division fought in.

Described on Oct. 31st 1862, at New Haven, Kentucky, by Lt. A. H. Bolkin and H. A. Langdon (Examining Surgeon), as having blue eyes, dark hair, a fair complexion, and 4 feet in height,[1] Gilbert became a favorite of the 79th. At Nashville his regiment presented him a silver and blue mounted drum as an expression of their appreciation of his bravery under fire. During the "March to the Sea" an adjutant saw Gilbert struggling along in the mud with his drum, trying to keep up with the men, and called him. He named him his orderly and told the men to get Gilbert a horse. But Gilbert was too small to mount the horse they found. His services as orderly had to await the finding of a pony.

When the pony was finally found (confiscated) for me at Milledgeville, this was a high point of joy in my young life, for I was lonesome in Georgia. Truthfully, too small a boy to be so far from home and in such surroundings. In one village three small girls were standing in a gate as we marched by. I was so lonesome I rode up and talked with them. One girl, about my age, asked my pony's name. Up to then I'd never thought of it. The pony had no name. "Why don't you name it for me—Fanny?" she asked. Then and there Fanny became the pony's name and the whole regiment so designated it.

Gilbert was in the Grand Review at Washington, D. C., where about sixteen days later— June 9, 1865—he was mustered out, being then 13 years 5 months 20 days of age and a veteran of over thirty-four months of service. And this tally gives him *no Civil War credit* for those weeks he drummed for Recruiter Ellwood. Arguably, Gilbert performed highly valued military duties (just like Abram Springsteen was doing in Indianapolis in the early summer of 1861 while still ten, and just like John L. Clem, too, who performed duties well prior to his official enlistment date) as, evidently, quite a few aspiring miniature martinets managed to execute before formal paperwork for them was done. Unknown numbers of these Lilliputians performed probationally, ultimately victorious in their official acceptance or defeated dismally by a variety of imposing odds.

Having become much attached to "Fanny" during those plodding (whether on two legs or four) months of stress, strife, and strong-minded struggles, Gilbert, concluding his military tour, found himself facing a doleful prospect: since all captured property belonged to Uncle Sam and had to be turned over to him (including ponies appropriated by diminutive dispatch carriers), how could Gil ever hope to keep Fanny? Through his superior officers, "Little Girl," as soldiers of the 3rd Division were often wont to nickname him, was granted an interview with President Andrew Johnson, who had become interested in VanZandt's extreme youth. Recalls our subject:[2]

With my feet well off the floor when I sat in his White House chair, I told the President of my plight, how I wanted to keep Fanny.

"Well, Gilbert, he says, "This is rather unusual, but I think your country owes you something." He asked me quite a few questions. At length, he made me an offer and asked which would I prefer: to keep the pony or to be given training for a regular army commission?

"The pony," I shot back.

He allowed me to keep her and had the Government ship Fanny to my home in Port William. Fanny was my constant companion until she died in 1872.[3]

VanZandt's military record from the National Archives prompts at least a few comments—

(1) The silent d in his surname is consistently absent,
(2) He replaced, apparently on enlistment, one John L. Holloway, whose time was then expired,
(3) Company Muster rolls show him nearly always present for duty until "detached as orderly to 3rd Div. Hdqtrs."
(4) He was last set down as age 14—a year beyond actuality, despite his true age being common knowledge.

Although no record exists that Gilbert was ever awarded any kind of decoration for his model behavior at the battlefronts, he did prize among his late-life possessions copies of certain letters, two of which were these:

Wellington, Kas.[4]
Jan. 16, 1898

Gen. Russell A. Alger
Secretary of War
Washington, D. C.

Dear Sir:

In behalf of Gilbert VanZandt, the youngest "old" soldier of the late Civil War and a member of Co. D., 79th Ohio Volunteers, I beg of you to award him a "badge of Honor" for his display of bravery on the 19th of March 1865. During a severe engagement at Bentonville, S. (sic} C., the 14th Army Corps was summoned to the front.

With our division (the 3rd, commanded by W. T. Ward) on the left, I was ordered to bring all available pioneers to the front to cut and cause a defile through the timber to effect an enfilading fire, with Captain Gray's artillery to support our infantry. This noble little trusty and brave soldier took the order and in less than 30 minutes returned with my pioneers and reported to me during the thickest of shot and shell. Just as he rode up to me, my horse was wounded by a piece of shell from the rebel guns, and the little soldier took the animal through the fire to the rear. Throughout the engagement he displayed the noblest of bravery, for which I beg at your hands a "badge of honor." Other members of the staff will cite you deeds of bravery done by him. Though but a child soldier, he knew no fear.

Most respectfully,
William Ardenbrook
Lieutenant and Captain
Co. H, 70th Ind. Vol. Infy.
Chief of Pioneers & Provost Marshal
Third Division, 20th A. C.

Taylorsville, Kentucky [5]
Jan. 22, 1898

Gen. R. A. Alger
Secretary of War
Washington, D. C.

Dear Sir:

At request of Captain Hardenbrook, I address you in behalf of Gilbert VanZandt, late of Co. D, 79th, O.V.I. If being an excellent soldier at a very tender age entitled a man to a "medal of honor," VanZandt certainly deserves one. He enlisted in 1862 as a drummer boy or musician at the age of 10 years. In 1864 his regiment was in the 1st Brigade, 3rd Division, 20th Army Corps. I was Assistant Adjutant-General of the division. On the Atlanta Campaign, sometime near Resaca (May 15th, I think) my attention was called to the little fellow struggling along with the regiment, and I detailed him as my orderly at division headquarters. He was so small that he could not mount his horse, so we had to "find" him a pony. VanZandt continued with us as an orderly to Atlanta, stayed with the Corps cut off when the balance of the Army followed Hood, and finally went with us to the sea, also through the Carolinas to Goldsboro and then to Washington, where he was in the Grand Review of the Army. We tried to be easy on the boy, but he always insisted on doing full duty, and he did it. At the investment of Savannah, Ga., our division was on the left of the Army on the Savannah River. Part of the command was over on the Ogeechee River, 12 or 15 miles away. It was to be recalled. I wrote the order and called for an orderly. It was, it seems, Gilbert's turn. The little fellow came at the summons. I told him to send one of the men. He said he could go anywhere any man could go. I gave him the envelope, and along in the night he brought back the receipt. At Peach Tree Creek July 20, 1864, between the assaults I saw General Newton of the Fourth Corps sitting on a log with Gilbert on his knee, caressing him. This gives an idea of how small and childish he was. He writes me that his discharge (1865) called for "a soldier 13 years old and 4 feet high." On the Atlanta Campaign, which lasted just four months, the 3rd Division lost in killed and wounded over 40% of its effective strength, and VanZandt only 12 years and small for his age, did full duty all through. I think he deserves it and respectfully ask that a medal be awarded him.

I am, General, your obedient servant,
John Speed
Late Captain & A.A.G., U. S. Vols.
Third Division, 20th A. C.

Of all the late surviving Civil War veterans of the 1940s and after, little Gil VanZandt *may indeed* have been the shortest, never quite reaching five feet, even as an adult. The official minimum stature to get into the Union Army was supposedly 5' 3". Thus, "Little Gil" contrasts with Weiser, Idaho's Edward Anson Paddock (Mar. 29, 1843-Jan. 20, 1940), of Co. E, 40th Wisconsin, who was 6' 7" while in his twenties.[6] "I've been asked many times why I am not larger," often observed VanZandt during his last eighty years. "My only answer is that probably I was scared out of three years' growth early."[7]

While his father, John, 34 in 1862, and a shoemaker,[8] did not survive the 1870s, Gilbert was privileged to have his mother, Nancy J. VanZandt (1833-1925) until he was nearly seventy-five himself. With no family of his own and being one of the bare one percent of lifelong bachelors among our last living Civil War veterans of the 1940s and after, he devoted his life to his mother, for she was his closest companion. When he worked in Chicago twelve years at the great department store of Marshall Field & Company, he took Nancy with him there, after his father's death. After this employment they lived in Washington and in Paola, Kansas (40 miles s. of Kansas City), where she became blind for her last fifteen years. Upon her demise in Paola in 1925, Nancy was *reputedly* the last (?) of the Civil War mothers. [*Perhaps* in her Miami County.] Now fairly much alone in Paola, the son, 74, lost little time in executing his final maneuver—rejoining family folks at 3702 Benton Boulevard in Kansas City, Mo. Here he made his final retreat to live with his sister, Mrs. Martha Edeburn, and a niece (Martha's daughter) Mrs. Carrie Spaulding.[9]

Eased by a modest Civil War pension, he made all their waning years lighter (perhaps even buoyant).

Among his mementos was an abbreviated sword and scabbard presented to him by his colonel while the 79th Ohio were on parade near their Nashville camp; he had carried it all through the March to the Sea and in the unique 32-abreast Grand Review of Sherman's Army nigh eighty years before. In many a 1940s gloaming the wizened gent was wont to study the grim loveliness of its every fret and line from out of his dimming eyes—now a-glisten from melancholy or a-twinkle from a bit of drollery, now with a lachrymal dampness at thoughts trooping to the fore. Those sunset hours were most susceptible for him, when entranced in reverie, he relived the boy's emotive episodes and escapades—the mother who had sewn by hand her son's first uniform when he refused to quit the Army, the somber ceremonial muffled percussion yet reverberant within, as ever it would be, for many a comrade who never came home, the varied drum rolls and calls that heralded each day's functions. Memorial Days, still slim, he would strap it on, the leathern girth just a fit! At such rare times Gilbert would renew his fond acquaintanceships with the few other nonagenarian "K. C.-Mo." comrades he had grown to admire—Jonathan Hollingsworth (Apr. 2, 1846-Aug. 3, 1943) of Co. C, 33rd Ill.; Newton Gallagher (1846-1942) of the 140th Ohio; Charles W. Burrill (1846-1943) of Co. E., 134th Ill.; James Wetherton (18471944) [Parkville]; James A. Best (?-?) of Co. C., 50th Ill.; and George Washington Johnson (July 4, 1847-Aug. 1, 1945) of Co. D, 1st U. S. Col. Trps.[10] Predictably within earshot of VanZandt, they, quite out of an insuperable badinage and bonhomie, would choose to question one another incredulously whether "the youngster" could really be one of themselves.

In thoughtful moments, Gilbert pondered wistfully over being the last living male VanZandt in his line; he thought often of his younger brother William, 3 in 1860, who had served in the Spanish American War and then gone to the Philippines and given up his life there in November 1900 and been buried with honors at Arlington; sometimes he thought of their ancestor who had fought in the American Revolution.[11]

His own funeral was quietly held at 4:00 p.m. Saturday, December 9th 1944, at 1800 E. Linwood Boulevard. Among the mourners at Eylar Chapel were delegates from the Daughters of Union Veterans and from the Sons.[12] Somewhere in metropolitan Kansas City, Missouri, there rest today the earthly remains of a mother and son who had always been close. Faded these many years their memory from *our* American consciousness!

But here is the enduring consolation: *here* among his fellow drummer boys where he surely belongs, Little Gilbert remains a standout, one who measures up in stature, for he scores 22 points against a debatable 24 points for the highest scorer, John L. Clem, whose lengthy Civil War tour was within days of being the same as Gilbert's...some 34 months. Each marked time and marked it well; however, we note that VanZandt exceeded Clem in longevity by exactly seven years.

The Wall Brothers

of Surry County, North Carolina

Richard Japeth "Jafy" Wall (b. 1846)
Thomas Henry "Hen" Wall (b. 1848)
Elihu Millard "Lihu" Wall (b. 1850)
Wm. Hastings "Keet" Wall (b. 1853)
Franklin Lafayette "Melly" Wall (b. 1856)

In October 1995 the writer, suspecting inadequacies and inaccuracies in his brief treatment of Wm. "Harting" [*sic*] Wall (*SLBG,* 1986) inaugurated a renewed effort to give this youthful little Reb his rightful place in our present study. Little did he realize the "boynanza" awaiting, for it transpires that this Wall Family—living at the time in State Road Township, Wilkes County—gave three extremely youthful sons to the Cause. Imagine the surprise in discovering that Wm. Hastings was the middle brother of the three youngest of five Walls, who all, in varying capacities, *served!*

About 1000 Surry County men were combatants in the war, while some 240 *young* men (ages 9-14) were cadres in local (1) militias, (2) reserves, (2) home guards.[1] [The writer commends Hester B. Jackson and the Surry County Historical Society in their mentions of some of this latter group whom professional historians, lacking *official* documentation, are not wont to accept as C.S.A. veterans. It arose not infrequently that a young man like, say, Wm. B. Reynolds, scarcely 14 (Hopkins County, Texas), "because he knew the mountains of Arkansas 'like the back of his hand,' would serve as a guide, scout and forager without pay for the troops." (In *his* case, Co. G, 27th Ark.) As with some of Surry's little paramilitaries, Reynolds did not enlist, got no pay, nor discharge in the regular way. Yet they often performed real and vital duties. Sampling striplings of this category are Wm. Thos. Keith; Wm. O. N. Lea; Wm. H. Bush; and Jas. Edwin Powell II. Their lack of records commonly thwarted best efforts for a late-life military pension. This deficit need no longer promote their further (punitive?) estrangement, for *here* we (whoever are of a heart) recognize them wherever/whenever discovered by serendipity or distant kin.]

The Wall ancestry in the Mitchell River country of northwestern North Carolina? There was Capt. John Wall, who had served in the colonial cause of the Revolution. His son, William, who goes down as the earliest (1778) Wall in Surry County, possessed 190 acres. His son Michael, born in 1784 on Ararat River, had married Nancy Johnson, a neighbor's daughter, in 1810, had 100 acres he lived on, a part of the Mining Ridge Community of Wilkes County in the late 1830s. As early as the 1660s pioneering Walls had settled in the northern reaches of Prince George County, Virginia, along the inner-most tidal basin of the James River, near Hopewell. They were among founding families and earliest members of Merchants' Hope Church, erected in 1657. Michael and Nancy's family (using deeds and census records) included seven sons—Crawford, 1813; Burrel T., 1815; Robert, 1817; Newell J., 1826; Minze, 1828; Wesley, 1832; Miles, 1839; and three younger daughters. Indeed, their four younger sons were "eligible for inductance" into the C.S.A.[2] Newell became a private in Company B, 2nd Battalion, North Carolina Troops, Sept. 1, 1862; wounded in the heel in March '65, he was in a Richmond hospital, where he was captured April 3rd. On his Oath of Allegiance he was released June 30th. (Minze's Wesley's and Miles' records are not readily available). We are most interested in Burrel T. Wall, who grew up on his folks' farm near Ararat River. He is earliest recorded in Surry County records in July 1839, then 24 and single, a bondsman for William H. and Elvina Davis Harris' wedding. Soon after witnessing (3/1/1840) a deed to his father from Levi Johnson for "100 acres lying on s.w. side of juncture of Bull Run Creek with Ararat Rr.," Burrel moved to Wilkes County (just s.w.). Here, west of Elkin and near State Road, he met and courted Elizabeth Carter. Ages 27 and 20, they married Dec. 23, 1842. Their children were Martha Jane (Mrs. John W.) Lassiter (11/16/43); Richard Japeth (3/25/46), who married Rebecca Williams in 1869 and died at the Zephyr Community in 1906; Thomas Henry (1848), of Company K, 56th N. C. Infantry, who married Victoria Shepard and died at State Road in 1923; Elihu M. (7/25/50), of Company C, 21st N.C. Troops, who married Laura Stanley (and later, Martha Steele) and died Dec. 21, 1921. William H. "Keet" (1/8/53-3/16/1945) and Franklin L. "Melly" (9/22/1856-12/28/1938) enlisted *the* same day—May 1, 1864—with "Lihu" M. Wall for service in Company C, 21st N. C. Troops.[3] That day Lihu's age was 13 years 9 months 6 days, Keet's was 11 years 3 months 23 days, Melly's was 7 years 7 months 9 days. "Even a Confederacy without hope was not so desperate as to push these boys into battle." Though noble, their enlistment was, as far as front line service, futile. Their duties were confined essentially to in-state errands and usually to paramilitary assignments within Surry or Wilkes Counties. Credited to the 21st N. C. Troops, these three effectually performed as part of a junior reserve. Indeed, family tradition has held that "Lihu" and "Keet" had done some home guard type services *before* their ultimate simultaneous triumviral enlistment. But what precipitated so dramatic a move on May 1st '64 that these youngest males would be allowed to "do their thing?" A haunting question that has come down the years! One can only study the recorded tragedies Wall cousins sustained—in *Surry County Soldiers:*

Andrew J. Wall, of Co. H, 21st N.C., was a POW at Old Capital Prison, Washington, D. C., but came home in '65.

Azariah Wall, 27, of Co. I, 21st N. C., died two months after entering service, Sept.'62, "time and place unknown." (Sharpsburg?)

Dred Ira Wall, 26, a forge hammerman, of Co. C, 21st N.C., was a wounded POW at Gettysburg, did time at Fort Delaware and Point Lookout, but died before 1880.

Hiram G. Wall, 29, of Co. C, 21st N.C., died 1/30/63 of mumps at Guinea Station, leaving $20.65.

Newell J. Wall, 27, already reported.

Sgt. Samuel W. Wall, 32, of Co. E, 53rd N.C., a wounded POW at Gettysburg, went to Fort Delaware.

Stanley Wall, 24, of Co. H, 21st N.C., died of pneumonia 2/2/62 near Manassas.[4]

It is altogether probable that all five of Burrel's and Nancy's sons shared roles in the war. Richard "Jafe", 18 in 1863, was the first brother (before that birthday) to render C.S.A. service; Thomas "Hen", 16 in 1864, is believed to have contributed as a leader in an Old North group of Junior Reserves. However, we focus upon the three youngest.

Lihu Millard Wall, not 14, officially enlisted in Company C, 21st North Carolina Troops, but *may* well *have* served the final war year in a Junior Reserves element. Afterward, he schooled at Traphill Institute, known for its educators. By his first wife, Laura Stanley, he had two children—William Harrison "Dickie" and Emma. By his second wife, Martha L. Steele (sister to his brother Keet's wife), he had five children—Crozier (who died at 99, eldest Wall on record in Surry), Guthrie B. "Buck," Mildred, Mrytle and Callie. Lihu and Martha owned a large tract in the Mulberry Community near their Mulberry Primitive Baptist Church, where they rest in peace.[5]

William Hastings "Keet" and his siblings were natives of the Carter Mill Section of Wilkes County. But well before the on-set of war he moved to Surry County to live in Bryan Township with his older sister Martha and her husband, John W. Lassiter, Co. H, 21st Old North Regt. (Burrel and Elizabeth did not move to Surry until 1874 when they bought 303 acres along Mitchell River in the Zephyr Community. They were buried here on their farm.)[6] Keet, who was credited to "the 21st North Carolina Troops," volunteered for service on the home front. His interview at Gettysburg in July 1938 with Martha N. McLeod, recorded in her *Brother Warriors* (1940) does permit us a clearer perception of his homeguardsman-like duties, which also lend insight into Lihu's and Melly's service(s):

> *The way I was enlisted was like this. Back in 1864, there was a heap of people who ran away from the army and hid in the woods to keep from fighting. Of course, they were a cowardly gang, bad about stealing, and in general a terror to the neighborhoods. We called them bushwhackers. Well, I enlisted to protect citizens and property against the freebooters. Our home guard in Wilkes County made a raid on the bushwhackers, but they were too strong for us. They fired on us from ambush. Doke Sparks was killed, and Buck Colkerhan and Jack Baugus were wounded. The next day the captain of the bushwhackers, with 80 men, went over to Tennessee and joined the Yankee Army because they thought they would be safer. That is one reason for a lot of the atrocities committed in the name of the Union Army, so many of their forces were carrying these skunks. When word came of the surrender, I was at Old Fort, N.C., on my way to join the fight at Knoxville.*
>
> *I'm having a big time at Gettysburg. Florence Wall is my attendant. One of the finest things about this reunion is having someone to see that our every wish is granted.*[7]

William H. Wall (right) with his daughter Florence and other friends including "Abe Lincoln" at Gettysburg in July 1938.

The war concluded, Keet returned to live with his sister's family. In December 1875 he married Miss Phoebe Steele (May 12, 1856-May 6, 1940), a daughter of Doctor *(actual name)* Franklin, (Co. B, 2nd Batt' in N.C.) and Prudence Nickolson Steele and granddaughter of Micajah and Betsy Woodruff Nickolson. Their children were Carey (Mrs. Troy) Melton (1876-1951); Sarah "Bett" (Mrs. Walter C.) Williamson (1878-1960); Martha L. (Mrs. Wm. Henry) Nance (1882); Cyrus Bayard (1884-1973), who married Ethel Boone; Rachel J. Kidd Welborn (1890-1976); Florence V. (1895-1939), single, a teacher; and (Wm.) McKinley (1897-1977), who married Dulcie J. Scott (1900-1993).[8] Keet was a farmer, schoolteacher and Justice of the Peace. He and Phoebe were together 63 years and went to their final rest at Zephyr Community's Gum Orchard Baptist Church Cemetery (Poplar Spring Rd., Elkin). During his last five years Keet lived with his daughter Rachel. Old Reb Keet Wall went to many a reunion of Soldiers of the Old South with his daughter Florence, whether in Raleigh, Richmond, Atlanta, Gettysburg, or Columbia...even up into his high 80s. And each time it was the same story—cameras clicking. People noticed his sensational resemblance to the late-life Robert E. Lee. It became his trademark. At Gettysburg's Joint 75th Battle Reunion in 1938 he met up with a lanky Yankee who was the very image of Abe Lincoln. Inevitably, scores of times "Surry's Own General Lee" was prevailed upon for photographs with "the Rail-splitter."

Deeper insights on the C.S.A. duties of Lihu, Keet and Melly surfaced during November 1995-February 1996 in letters from McKinley's son Royce Dale Wall of Dobson and his wife (Ada) Eloise Edmonds Wall, who live on the Zephyr Road, just outside, where they farm a botanical nursery and grow everything from poinsettias to strawberries. Their thoughts?

> *Father was the baby in his family and so was I in mine. Grampa Keet's Uncle Bernard Franklin Carter, 37, an attorney, and his maternal Granddad, Littleton Carter, were organizers, leaders in the Wilkes County Home Guards. Thus it was entirely possible for the three youngest sons of Burrel and Betty Carter Wall to execute their duties in this Stokes County H. G. and still be near family. Dale remembers Keet well as he knew his grandpa rather closely at ages 5 thru 11. "He gave me his old Elgin railroad watch in 1943, which I cherish. At about that time during World War II I asked him if he fought in the Civil War. His reply was that he drove wagons hauling supplies up into Virginia sometimes. He got a Confederate pension.*

Franklin Lafayette "Melly" Wall, of State Road (just n. of Elkin in Surry County), a second-effort discovery in the 25th year of the writer's trilogy, is a phenomenon unto himself. Given his birthdate of 9/22/56 and his enlistment of 5/1/64, his age on inception of duty was 7 years 7 months 9 days.

At this writing (late 1996) but one other Civil War soldierling-veteran is known to have been later born—John Hance Osteen, of High Springs, Florida: Dec. 22, 1856!

Only one other personality is *known* to have been younger upon assumption of duty— William Orlanda Neubold Lea, of Hampstead, North Carolina: 6 years 5 months *approximately!* Invested with superlatives, Melly Wall is somewhere beyond interesting, even arresting. Yet, relatively little is preserved of his life. Because he does have *a* place in the boys' war, he deserves whatever mention can at this late hour be resurrected. His duties in Wilkes County H.G.—courier, currier, mail carrier, messenger, orderly, servant—naturally, were light...but momentous (for him).

Responses to two questionnaires are the closest we can get to him. In her Feb. 7, 1996 letter from State Road, Emogene Booth (Mrs. Edd) Moody, 76, offers:

> *Grampa Melly married Miss Amanda Shepherd on Nov. 27, 1877 in Surry County and they lived here in State Road, N.C. Their children were John, Jake, Sarah, Martha Ann (my mother), Florence Harper, and Mont. He was a farmer. The family all belonged to the Old State Road Primitive Baptist Church and most of them are buried in the Church Cemetery. Some other grandchildren besides me are Nettie W. Couch, Nellie W. Murray, Pansey W. Martin, all of Elkin; May W. Pruett of Kissimmee, Fla.; Betty W. Cornillous of Camden, Ind.; Tamsy Booth Myers of Bristol, Tenn. Because I grew up in West Virignia, I wasn't near Grampa much.*

In her Mar. 13, 1995 letter from Bristol, Tennessee, Mrs. Tamsy Booth Myers, 79, writes:

> *I'm a granddaughter of Mellie and Amanda Shepherd Wall (Dec. 20, 1856-Nov. 17, 1928) by their daughter Martha Ann (Aug. 10, 1887-May 1982) and Hampton Booth. Grampa Mellie was a blacksmith and shoed horses. He was nice to children. We lived with him some after his wife died and my dad (Hampton) was killed in a car accident. He drew a Confederate pension. He and some of his family are buried at Old State Road Primitive Baptist Church, north about three miles or so from the foot of the Blue Ridge Mts.*

Conclusion: The Walls of Surry County are a must-include in any study of the youngest in the War Between the States.

Charles Knecht

Nov. 1, 1853 – Jan. 18, 1948

A monolithic truth surfaced and slowly confirmed itself during 1972-87: Charles Knecht, of St. James, Missouri, was apparently *the* youngest "man" to serve in the Union Army during The Great Trouble, as Mark Twain called it.[1] Granted, there were at least six other Civil War veterans living after April 1939 who were born later than Knecht, *but we are talking age at time of first service* or enlistment. (See Youngest Who Served).

Page two of Cora Gillis' *Final Journal of the G.A.R.*, Feb. 27, 1957, asserts that there had been in the Union forces twenty-five "men" who enlisted at age ten years or under. Surely, one of these was Charles Knecht, for his Sept. 13, 1861 description upon enlistment as a musician at Benton Barracks, Missouri, was given as follows: "Age—8 years; Height—3 feet, 6 inches; Father's Occupation, jeweler." Some fifty years later he presented proofs of his date of birth with his pension application. His enlistment papers bear the proud legend "By special order of Gen. Henry W. Halleck" (who, for his administrative abilities, in July 1862 would be made General-in-Chief of Union Armies by Lincoln, wistfully ever looking for leadership). As a member of Company A, Benton Cadets, Missouri Infantry[2] (Not for nothing were they called *infantry!),* Charles served three months and twenty-four days entirely within Missouri until discharged at Rolla Jan. 8, 1862—a veteran who had just turned eight (He had actually been seven!) *before* the war was one third over—a record in itself, no doubt.[3] His legs not being long enough to keep up with the men and his tender years must have contributed to his release from duty. But not so.

After re-revising Knecht over an 18-year stretch, while researching at the National Archives our late, aged, pensioned Union Army nurses, the writer stole just enough time in June 1989 to discover data on Charles' father, Ferdinand Gottfried Knecht (1819-Feb. 24, 1894), a native of Wittenberg, Germany. This limited record and Ferdinand's Certificates of Service from the Office of the Adjutant General, Jefferson City, Missouri, lend insights into his son's tour or the Knecht connection.] Ferdinand first enrolled as a drum major on Apr. 26, 1861, at St. Louis, for service in the 2nd Regiment of Missouri Volunteers, a three-month outfit, whose duty expired that July 31. He next enlisted Aug. 4, 1861, at St. Louis, with the rank of musician, and mustered in there on the 24th with the Benton (Barracks) Cadets under a Capt. Hazelton. Father and son both belonged to Company A. As "Principal Musician," Ferdinand enjoyed a close supervision of his son Charles, fife-boy and snare drummer. Both mustered out at Benton Barracks Jan. 8, 1862. Father Knecht, presumably placing Charles with a near relative (the mother never named), reenlisted July 22, 1862, as drummer for Company B, 8th Regiment E.M.M. (Enrolled Mo. Militia). He was promoted to "Non-Commissioned-Staff July 1, 1864." He was drum major all during his final enlistment 8/29/64-8/8/65, 40th Missouri Infantry. In 1864 Ferdinand was age 44, 5' 6", of blue eyes, a brunette, a citizen of St. Louis. Ferdinand Knecht, a musician and silversmith, married Katharina Scheibel May 7, 1867, in St. Louis. Some twenty-six years later when he died at his 1723 So. Third Street home in St. Louis, Missouri, Katharina, 50, would draw her Civil War widow's pension (half of his monthly $12) as of Mar. 5, 1894. Ferdinand went to his final rest at St. Marcus Cemetery, St. Louis.

Knecht's story today is but a scant record and one which, in all likelihood, shall remain so.[4] A bachelor until well into his 70th year [lacking any evidence to the contrary], he left no children. According to his Mar. 13, 1913 registration for admission to the State Federal Soldiers' Home of Missouri at St. James, he was a native of Louisville, Kentucky, his occupation had been that of cook, and he was getting a monthly Civil War pension of $13 for a certified disability—namely, "Rheumatism, with valvular heart disease." His pension jumped to $15 in 1919, to $18 in 1923, and to $21 in 1928. A confirming Aug. 25, 1982 letter from Robert R. Buckner, Activities Director at the Missouri Veterans' Home (the new name) in St. James, states: "Our records show Mr. Knecht, born Nov. 1, 1853, to have been first admitted to our institution on Mar. 13, 1913...apparently a drummer boy. On Jan. 5 , 1922, he was dropped from our rolls after taking a 90-day furlough and not returning. He was re-admitted on July 9, 1925, *as a widower.* We have no information on his wife. On Aug. 3, 1926, he was discharged at his request. On Mar. 11, 1929, Mr. Knecht was re-admitted and took his discharge on the 25th of the same month. This is all we have on our records."

Fortunately, a kind-hearted gentleman, William H. Roster (Dec. 17, 1880-Dec. 30, 1974), 92, of Ozarks Methodist Manor in Marionville, Missouri, volunteered Nov. 29, 1972, what he remembers:

> *I knew Charles Knecht when I was Adjutant of the Missouri State Federal Soldiers Home during two periods, 1912-1917 and 1941-48. Sometime during these first years Mr. Knecht and three other veterans organized a little drum corps. I myself lettered the name of the corps on the bass drum. Knecht played the snare drum, for he told me he had enlisted as a drummer. There was also a bugle and fife. My hobby being*

photography, I took a picture in 1915 of this group who performed in patriotic programs and parades. Here is my original image and I am delighted that you should have it, *though I cannot name the other three veterans today.*

During the thirties, Mr. Knecht requested a discharge from the institution and was married to Mrs. Mary Puschmann Zuver, a much respected and long-time resident of this originally German community. They set up housekeeping in a small cottage in the 100 block of Bowman Street (now E. James Blvd.). While living with her here he died.[5]

Helpful thoughts of Nov. 11, 1972, came from Washington, Missouri, to the northeast of St. James:

I am John O. Hall, son of O. D. Hall, Supt. of the State Federal Soldiers Home during 1920-32. I was ten years old in 1920 when we moved into a cottage at the entrance of the Home. During this time I knew very closely hundreds of old soldiers, one of whom was Charles Knecht. He and I played pool together almost daily and were close friends as only a boy and an old man can be. He was a fine old German and I can say my dad, "The Cap'n," approved of our companionship. As I remember his saying, Knecht joined up with his father just after his mother had died. Once he gave me a wooden fife which he had wrapped with copper wire to repair the cracks. He was a brisk old gentleman with a spry step. His folks had come from Germany as did many others to escape one year of military duty in the old country. They came here to become involved in the saddest and most terrible war. My Grandmother Hall lost three brothers and Grandfather Hall lost his right arm at Gettysburg. He was an immigrant Irish boy paid $1000 to take another's place.

In a Dec. 2, 1982 letter from Mrs. Elizabeth Bailey, Reference Specialist at the State Historical Society of Missouri in Columbia, we learn that Charles Knecht was listed in the 1900 Census as living in Ward 11 in St. Louis at 7618 Broadway; that in 1909 he was in the city directory as a clerk living at 7618 Broadway; that he was still listed in the 1913 directories. In another letter from John O. Hall, ten and a half years later, May 28, 1983, some of the missing pieces (a few carved in granite) help our story:

I took this photo of Knecht's gravesite on a recent trip to St. James. I presume Anna Katherine was his first wife. Mary Puschmann Zuver was of a well known German family here for many years in St. James. There is today a son of a Union veteran, Earl Spurgeon, 70, here in St. James. His father was James Spurgeon. My grandfather was his brother in East Tennessee and all that family were Confederates but for James.

In his Aug. 26 and Sept. 9, 1982 letters, Earl Spurgeon, 70, of St. James, volunteers some late facts:

> *My father, James Spurgeon, 1842-1926, who served in Co. A, 24th Iowa Infy., nine months until Aug. 15, 1865, was in the Soldiers' Home and a friend of Uncle Charlie Knecht, as I always called him. I cut grass and worked for Charlie at his home on East James, as it is now known. It still stands. I can name the men in Mr. Roster's 1915 photo— Steve Dellacella (bass), Mr. Knecht (snare), Mr. Shirley (deeper snare), and George Wright (fife).*

The little drum corps in 1915. Charles Knecht is second from left.

Another mystery is cleared up in an Oct. 29, 1987 note from Ms. Ozella Murray, 88, of St. James, who states that the Anna Katherine mentioned on the Knecht monument, was Charles' sister. Most helpful has been Wanda Webb, of the St. James Cemetery Corporation, for she offers copies of two marriage licenses. The first attests that Charles Knecht was married to Annie Catherine (the former Mrs. Henry) Dopheide, a Civil War widow of St. James, by Paul W. Strenfort at Rolla, Missouri, on July 5, 1929. Annie died Mar. 23, 1934, at eighty-three and was buried at St. James' Masonic Cemetery.[6] The second attests that Charles was married at his St. James residence to Mary Schober Puschmann Zuver (of St. James) on Apr. 8, 1937, by Andrew Szegedin, pastor of St. John's Evangelical Lutheran Church. Mary's background is made clear in a Sept. 11, 1987 letter from Emile C. Hattier, 63, of Rydal, Pennsylvania:

> *My maternal grandfather, John Charles Puschmann, Jr., was Mary's oldest brother. Their parents were John Charles "Carl" Puschmann (1827-1913) and Maria Eva Schober (1842-1912), who had married Jan. 5, 1861, at Natchez, Miss. My research has revealed (1) that Maria was recorded in the 1860 Federal Census of Natchez, Miss., as Mary E. Schoeber, native of Baden, Bavaria, and (2) that John C. Bushman* {sic} *(1870 Federal Census of Loutre Township, Montgomery County, Mo.) was a native of Prussia. Maria E. S. Puschmann's death certificate attests that her mother, Maria Magdalena Schwarz, had married John George Schober on Sept. 11, 1834.*
>
> *Charles Knecht's second wife, Mary, had married George H. Zuver sometime between 1904 and 1910. Mary was born in Loutre township (just across the Missouri R. from Hermann, Mo.) in November 1868. After her wedding she lived in St. Louis. I think that after her husband, George, died in the early '30's, she returned to St. James. The Puschmanns had moved from Loutre Township to St. James in 1875. Mary's father, "Carl" became the gardener at "Dunmoor", the mansion home for William James (1823-1912) founder of St. James. Mary P. Z. Knecht had a sister, Clara (Mrs. Wm. R.) Kendall, a longtime beloved telephone operator in St. James, who died Jan. 1, 1963 at 80. Mary died in 1956 at 87, but there was no obituary!*

Though Knecht's last rites were more civilian than military, all those present knew him to be an old Union Army survivor.[7] His resting place may be found at the St. James Cemetery—Section A, Row 23, Plot 389, Grave No. 6—between his sister, Anna's (No. 7) and Mary's (No. 5). In a *very few* places (the St. James Cemetery Corporation records salient among them), for whatever reason, Knecht's birth year was/is erroneously given as 1854.

One of Missouri's final ten Civil War veterans, he was the last of hundreds who had found a congenial retreat during their sunset years at the State Federal Soldier's Home. Who besides Charles Knecht could have laid so strong a claim to the distinction of being the youngest to render military duty in the Ordeal of the Union? Yet, there is neither rumor nor record to indicate he ever "made a big deal over it." With the Oct. 11, 1943 passing of comrade Charles E. Merrick in Los Angeles, Mr. Knecht became for nearly five years *one of the three youngest (latest born) Civil War veterans in the world.* The other two (See Youngest Who Served) were Confederate homeguardsmen—Wm. T. Keith (Feb. 3, 1856-Oct. 27, 1949) of Caryville,

Florida, and John H. Osteen (Dec. 22, 1856-Sept. 24, 1948) of Bell, Florida. This study has, so far, found five others who gave service in the war—essentially homeguardsmanships—at a younger age than Mr. Knecht; however, *he* was a full-fledged enlistee. We correctly remember "Uncle Charlie" Knecht as *the* youngest of all enlistees verified to have single-digitly worn the uniform— blue, gray, khaki, green, whatever—in America's Tragic War or in any other of our conflicts. We close out this account (the fullest likely ever to be written) with this final observation: the touch of irony that goes with his surname, KNECHT—a medieval word, with a paramilitary connotation for "one who serves, an underling."

John O. Hall

Headstone of Charles Knecht.

Susan Haines Clayton

Sept. 13, 1851 – Mar. 7, 1948

Often hailed by the D.U.V. in the mid-1940's as the nation's eldest and last living Civil War nurse, Mrs. Clayton was then residing in Talent, Oregon, just south of Medford. It *is* highly probable that she was one of the last two Union Army nurses and one of the last four or five ladies alive to have nursed the sick and wounded in the Civil War (See Lavinia Minton, *NLBB,* and Sarah Rockwell, *SLBG*). Although apparently overlooked as being among Oregon's last remnant of Civil War survivors, Mrs. Clayton during her final four years—April 1944-March 1948—was one of her state's last three.

Born in Bethlehem, Indiana, to Quakers, Susan was the eldest of Mr. and Mrs. Enos Haines' three children. When she was two, the Haines moved to Fort Des Moines and later to Vandalia and to Ashton, Iowa. Yet again during Susan's brief childhood, her folks moved, this time to Missouri, where slave traffic and incidents made deep impressions on her. Before Susan was ten, Enos, her father, enlisted for the three months it was believed it would require to win the war. Upon his enlistment in the First Illinois Infantry, the wife and three children returned to Indiana. After Enos reenlisted, this time for three years service with the 125th Indiana, Mrs. Haines and the children kept the farm going as best they could. Susan's girlhood was not without its trials. They were in an area where Southern sympathizers or "Copperheads" were prevalent. The local schoolmistress in her Quaker school, where the needed tuition was raised by subscriptions, was a Copperhead. In after years Mrs. Clayton often recounted young Susan's impatient disgust for her teacher's pro-Southern sentiments, how she marched herself out of the log schoolhouse and down the pike for home, and how her mother had her march right back with the admonition, "Tend to thine own knitting and she will let thee alone."[1]

Most families had no money but much serious illness. Susan's mother, known for her nursing abilities, brought her own children through sickness while attending to many families in their neighborhood. Thus, at age nine Susan began her earliest nursing experiences—at home and with her neighbors She got many months of careful training from her mother. At length, after pleading with her mother to allow her to help in the war, Susan, at age ten, won her way. Assisted by Gen. Benjamin Harrison, a personal acquaintance, who escorted her to Camp Carrington at Indianapolis, Susan soon found herself nursing boys from the 100-day enlistments, numerous of whom were her former schoolmates. "The camp was like a village, with little houses in rows, each with eight bunks in tiers. A door was at each end. The soldiers lay on straw with blankets. Many of them died of smallpox. I had to stand on the lower bunks to reach the upper ones. It had been but a short time since we had bid these young lads goodbye."[2]

After the war the Haines family settled in Leavenworth, Kansas, and then in Oscaloosa and again in Springdale. While in Kansas Susan became a seamstress and worked as a milliner, fabricating women's hats with buckram frames, satins, silks, feathers, flowers. One day an ex-soldier of the 101st Indiana Infantry, one Tom Clayton, ventured into her shop and asked her to make him a shirt. They shortly fell in love. In September 1869, while Miss Haines was still eighteen, their wedding took place in Springdale. "I made him many shirts after that. At the time I had about the only known sewing machine in Kansas, a Wheeler and Wilson."[3] For the next four years they lived on a homestead claim in southern Kansas. While wresting a hard living from the land, they endured floods, tornadoes, prairie fires, and the great grasshopper blight of 1874. They went back to Susan's folks where she took care of her mother. At about this time—1875—she organized the first W.R.C. in Kansas.[4] Many years later the Claytons journeyed to Montana and settled near Columbia Falls, where again she organized a W.R.C. Here in Columbia Falls Susan had a "Millinery Shop" in one room of her home where she displayed some of her beautiful hats. Women would come from all around to have a hat special made from a picture or to buy one that she had already made. Here, too, she helped lay the cornerstone of the Montana Soldiers Home. The first flag ever raised over the Home was one she had purchased the silk for and sewn herself. The Home years later presented this historic Stars and Stripes to her. Even in her mid-90s she occasionally displayed it, "aired" it, and was photographed holding it.

In her Nov. 14, 1977 letter from Canby, California, Alice E. Waterman, 81, writes, "I don't know much about Grandmother's early life before they moved to Montana in the early '90s. Eva Wedge, my mother, had four children. I am the oldest. Ray and Mary are deceased. Bessie (Beck) lives in Medford, Oregon."

Providentially, in her strategic Jan. 6, 1979 letter from Medford, Carolyn A. Beck writes for herself and her mother-in-law, Bessie Wedge Beck, who offers vital details:

> *Bessie suffers from rheumatoid arthritis all through her body. She thanks you for your interest in her grandmother, Susan Clayton. (When Bessie's husband, Gus, died, he left her with six small children. My husband, Freeman, is the youngest.) Family tradition has it that Susan's mother was at least*

half Flathead Indian. Little is known of her today. Thomas Clayton (Dec. 11, 1841-Jan. 17, 1926) was born in Indiana to Thomas (Oct. 27, 1803-Sept. 28, 1842) and Emma Moody Clayton (Apr. 2, 1811-Feb. 24, 1897) of Northern California. They had married Jan. 31, 1832. In his senior years he was a retired carpenter doing some small ranching. The Claytons had three children, though one died early. Bessie remembers her grandmother had brown hair, was happy all the time, and "dearly loved" picnics which they were always going on, but to no places special. What Bessie remembers most is that "Grandmother Clayton" came out to Columbia Falls, Montana, to take care of her at age six in 1909. Bessie had come down with polio, and both her parents had to work, not leaving them the needed time to care for Bessie. Susan promptly went to her little granddaughter's aid. There was a polio epidemic and Bessie's own little friend had just died from it. Bessie's legs and arms were badly swollen and enflamed, needing constant attention. Susan packed her legs and arms with "Denver Mud" poultices—barrels of it to get the pain and swelling out. This helped her. Bessie's feet today are badly deformed from the polio.

Susan stayed in Columbia Falls with Bessie for a year until she was better. About 1921 Bessie went to live with her grandparents for several months while her parents moved to Talent, Oregon, and settled, to be near the Claytons. In later years Bessie would visit her mother, Eva, and grandmother, who were both living at the Parkview Convalescent Home (no longer in business) in Ashland. Susan and Eva, a few months later, both died in 1948. Bessie's husband, Gus, died in 1948 also—a year of much grief for her. Both Thomas and Susan are entombed in the I.O.O.F. Cemetery mausoleum, Section D—off Siskyou Blvd. in Medford, Oregon.

The Claytons went to live in Portland, Oregon, in 1905 and finally settled in 1921 in the town of Talent. During her years in Portland Mrs. Clayton made regular visits to the Veterans Hospital, paying great attention to the needs and morale of its aging inmates. Often, too, she reminisced with them her younger days, commenting upon her seeing President Lincoln's body when he was at Indianapolis and shortly to arrive in Springfield, Illinois, to take up his last resting place; commenting on how she once presented Theodore Roosevelt a bouquet of Oregon grape and on her having shaken hands with President Wilson. Doubtless, the disastrous years on the Kansas prairie bore retelling as did "Uncle Ben" Gen. Harrison and his role in her early nursing pursuits. Among such stories too must often have been mention of how she and Tom, camping on the prairie, had the chief of the Arapahoes and his squaw as supper guests and how they hoped a city would grow there.

After Tom's death, Mrs. Clayton and their son, Fay, ran the ranch nearly twenty years together, with daughter Eva living nearby. Mrs. Clayton was a member of Ashland's Mother Bickerdyke Tent, D.U.V.[5]

Invariably described as a slender, graceful lady who always sat so erectly, beautifully attired in full dresses of her own imaginative design and stitchery, Susan Clayton, one of *the* youngest Clara Bartons in the Civil War, has earned her rightful place here. She was one of Oregon's last three veterans of the Civil War. During her last seven weeks she was one of the eight youngest surviving Civil War veterans in the world.

However one may choose to evaluate the life of Susan Clayton, hers were the garments of a model citizen who always "measured up." She was every stitch an American lady.[6]

Tom & Susan Clayton.

Carolyn A. Beck

Carolyn A. Beck

Susan with one of her flags.

Carolyn A. Beck

Susan in her 90s.

James Crugom, Jr.

June 3, 1850 – May 30, 1948

We have read of it before and we will read of it again: Europeans emigrating from their Old World homes and heritage in the faith that life in the new American democracy will be kinder and gentler. So came the Crugoms from Germany via France—James, Sr., a medical student and practitioner; son Joseph; son James, Jr.; and Mother Crugom, whose beloved identity is obscured. These four made their epic voyage in the "early 1850s while Little James was an infant." Though he never knew it for fact, but may well have often thought on the general topic, young James ultimately became one of the final eight surviving foreign-born Civil War soldiers his whole last year from the Apr. 22, 1947 passing of Henry M. Mingay of Filby, England, of Co. D, 69th New York, and Glendale, California. (See *NLBB,* Foreign-Born).

A native of Paris, France, James by age five was a resident of Milwaukee, hometown to him all during his growing-up years and beyond. But along came "America's Misfortune" or "The American War." Little enough time for their new adventure as Wisconsin citizens had elapsed before James, 39, enlisted on May 1, 1861, at Milwaukee as a "2nd Assistant Surgeon in Field and Staff for the 1st Regiment of Wisconsin Infantry Volunteers, by Governor of Wisconsin, for the term of three months, and was mustered into United States military service on May 21st 1861, by Captain McIntyre at Milwaukee."[1] Further, Surgeon Crugom would reenlist that August 28 for three more years; accordingly, on October 8 he was mustered in by Captain Trowbridge at Milwaukee's Camp Scott for service in the new three-year First Wisconsin Infantry.[2]

A noncom staffer in this same regiment was his son Joseph Crugom, who enlisted to become their "principal musician" or drum major. As if this were not enough, Little James, at 4' 2" and 11 years 4 months 5 days, mustered in on Oct. 8, 1861 (*the* very day his father's second tour began), as drummer/musician.[3] Though both brother and father Crugom were in full knowledge of this lad's precise age, it was apparently "low profiled," the sparse records implying he was twelvish. He had blue eyes, light hair, and a light complexion. During his eighteen months service in Company D (also Joseph's company), young Crugom performed as a percussionist under his brother's lead in the 1st Wisconsin Regimental Band. Like many another drummer boy—e. g. James M. Lurvey (1847-1950) of Co. A, 40th Massachusetts, at ages 14-16—Crugom got to spend many hours toting medical supplies and assisting surgeons. What did musician Crugom's Civil War consist of? At least this much:

-To West Point, Ky., 11/14/61
-To Elizabethtown, Ky., 12/3 & to Munfordsville, Ky., 12/17
-Duty at Camp Wood till Feb. '62
-Advance on Bowling Green & Nashville, 2/14-3/3
-At Nashville till 3/29 including action at Granny White Pike, 3/8
-To Columbia, 3/29-4/2
-To Bigley's Creek & Guarding RR bridges till 5/3
-Rogersville, 5/13 Chattanooga, 6/7-6/8
-To Huntsville, Ala., & duty here till August
-Tto Nashville & Louisville, Ky., pursuing Gen. Bragg, 8/18-9/26
-Pursuit of Bragg to Crab Orchard, Ky., 10/1-10/16
-Battle of Perryville, 10/8
-Guard Duty at Mitchellsville till 12/7
-Advance on Murfreesboro, 12/26-12/30
-Battle of Stone's River, 12/30-12/31 & 1/1-1/3/63
-Duty at Murfreesboro till late March [4]

On his anniversary day in uniform, while carrying bandages at the Battle of Perryville, James, now all of 12 years, thought himself a goner when a shell burst over his head. Again, at the Battle of Murfreesboro (Stone's River), he became a medical aide; as such, he was "kept hopping" by carrying supplies to field hospitals, where dreadful smells nearly overcame him, and by performing inglorious assignments from his father or other surgeons whose grim tasks were suddenly at hand. Finally, Surgeon Crugom resigned from the rugged duty effective Mar. 25, 1863, because of disability.[5] Within three days Pvt. Crugom too, was discharged from the Army of the Cumberland at Murfreesboro, Tennessee, by order of Maj. Gen. Wm. Starke Rosecrans, who at that juncture chose to reduce the role of drummers and musicians, summarily sending many of them home.

Upon returning to civilian life, James Crugom, Jr., went back to school; he took up music as a career and studied it in Germany. He became a much-sought-after piano teacher. In 1888, he moved to Chicago, where he retired in 1926 at seventy-six. No evidence exists to suggest that he ever married. In late life his nearest kinsman was a nephew, Rev. Henry Foster of Savanna, Illinois. In his mid-90s James customarily walked a mile a day and played his piano regularly at his 7229 Rogers Avenue home. His social life consisted largely in his G.A.R. affiliations all during his 20th century years. He won scores of friends and knew hundreds of aging comrades, 99.66% of them older than he. Yes, Crugom knew their personalities well. Inevitably he came to miss them. At ninety-six he still had good eyesight and general health. James was admitted to Edward Hines, Jr., Veterans Hospital on Oct. 15, 1947; on March 15 he was discharged but returned ten days later, and there he died.[6] Among Illinois' final seven Union Army survivors, he was given military rites by the Rogers Park American Legion. During his last year James Crugom was acting Chaplain of the Illinois G.A.R.

John Hance Osteen

Dec. 22, 1856 – Sept. 24, 1948

"The Latest born of all known Civil War Veterans"

The latest born of all known Civil War veterans, "Uncle Hance" Osteen, of High Springs and Bell, Florida, goes down in American Studies for this unique distinction. Indeed, of all the youngster soldierlings, South and North, who single-digitly (under 10) contributed in a tangible way to the war effort, none are *known* to have arrived later into this life than he. Little Hance was all of 4 years 3 months 21 days old when Fort Sumter came under fire in the early dawn of that fateful 12th of April. He would live over eighty-seven more years or long enough to become one of Florida's final seven Old Rebs. Of these seven, three others—the nearby Keith Brothers and William A. Lundy (eldest & last of Florida's Rebs)—had also served on the homefronts locally as members of homeguard companies, vital boys-and-old-men paramilitary enclaves who were sometimes a veritable salvation for innocent, half-empty homes of women and children vulnerable to plunderings by scalawags, scoundrels, and looters—those so cowardly and undisciplined as to refuse allegiance to either of the great Causes—Confederacy or Union. Uncle Hance also shares laurels (at least in this study, if nowhere else!) with William O. N. Lea, of Hampstead, North Carolina in being the youngest on his inception of duty or upon initial service. *Ordinarily* (approaching *universally),* this datum or fact equated to a serviceman's date of enlistment. However, homeguardsmen were seldom accorded formal enlistments (paperwork), for paper was scarce and recording clerks scarcer. Rather, they were simply enrolled and/or sworn-in orally to serve minute-man fashion in their particular company. This sufficient-at-the-time practice "quite" inevitably militated against such a veteran's acquisition many decades later of a state (Confederate) pension. Proof of enlistment was *the* indispensable qualifying standard, short of hiring an attorney or orchestrating a special act of legislation. Regardless of eyewitness testimonials from former comrades and an applicant's own detailed account of his C.S.A. assignments, his request for a Confederate pension from the Florida (or any ex-C.S.A. State) State Pension Board was doomed to a denial pro forma, at least initially. Thus, many borderline cases (1920s & 30s) were repeatedly denied, while frequently those granted took several years "a-processing." A classic instance was that of Lake Charles, Louisiana's Auguste F. Saucier, of Company B, 7th Louisiana Cavalry, who at age 81 in April 1924, applied for his, and, after seventeen years of red tape ending in November 1941 when he was 98, was granted his first Confederate pension check (non-retroactive); poetic justice permitted him to collect on it until he died Jan. 1, 1949, at 105 years.[1] Uncle Hance Osteen's Application #A08946 was of *relatively* short duration, from Sept. 4, 1937, to approval June 4, 1941, "with pay from June 12, 1939."[2]

His Irish-English-German ancestry had settled in the southern seaboard states. Grandfather Shadrack A. O'Steen (1777-1854?) was a native North Carolinian. In 1841, his son, James A. O'Steen (Apr. 23, 1815-Feb. 5, 1877) married a girl from Camden County, Georgia— Miss Mary Ann "Polly" Markham (May 12, 1819-May 12, 1885), daughter of William Markham, a 1782 native of Prince George County, Virginia, and Mary Gorman, born in 1786 in Burke County, Georgia. John Hance was the fifth of their seven children—Ann Catherine "Kate" (Dec. 27, 1841-Mar. 18, 1912), who married John L. Beach (18361904); William Shade (Mar. 1, 1846-Mar. 7, 1936), who married Jane "Jannie" Polk; Whiney (1848-19 ?), who married Steve Parrish; J. Alfred "Hune" (1851-Dec. 13, 1927), who married (1) Cassie Conley and (2) L. Kinsey; and Leonard Franklin (Jan. 15, 1861Oct. 20, 1935), who married Agnes Martin (1861-1934). Grandfather Shadrack, at age 73 in 1850, living in James and Polly's southern Columbia County home, "Grampa'd" well all during his closing years, but Hance arrived too late to know him.[3] Hance was born three miles southeast of Old Fort White in southern Columbia County, about where Gilchrist and Alachua Counties meet (today). James and Polly moved in 1857 with their five children just a few miles southward into what would become northeastern Gilchrist County (remembering, however, that until 1925 Gilchrist was the western portion of Alachua County). Here, some dozen miles south of the Sante Fe River toward Bell, the lad matured early. Deer and turkey hunting and camping out on the ground about a campfire were favorite pastimes from his youth up. Of course, the Boys' War intervened and made for uncommon excitement while Hance advanced from age four to five to six. Most of his male relatives and acquaintances had gone off or "away" to fight for the Confederacy and states' rights, concepts too sophisticated for a five-years child. But certain awesome sounding tidings began to "register" on his callow consciousness—a skirmish at Palatka (3/27/63); captured by Federals—Jacksonsville (3/10/63); an action there (3/25/63), and a skirmish (3/29/63)—doings that kindled earliest stirrings of patriotism. A subdued though growing impetuosity in little Hance flamed anew with each flash of overheard war talk. His best hot line was via oldest brother (Wm.) Shade, 17, and an older leader in the local Santa Fe River Company of Underwood's Home Guards. Common county knowledge had it that some members were only nine, ten, eleven. By early summer 1863 this kid brother had waged a three-month barrage upon Shade (Shadrach), who at length, apparently by late July 1863, relented to allowing Hance, then

6 years 7 months, to learn a mail route done on horseback, an apprenticeship that began in early August 1863. We base this upon the veteran's own signed statement of Sept. 4, 1937, that "he actually performed the service and helped deliver the mail to the wives of Confederate soldiers from about the latter half of the year 1863 and continually to the end of said war..."[4] By his own handwritten statement at age eighty, J. Hance Osteen offered these details he would want us to include here:

> *...In 1863 my Father bought out a Ferry Boat. What is known as a Flat. At Old Fort White on Santa Fe River, where the older people had a fort in time of the Indian War. Later my Father James Osteen and my Elder Bro. W. S. Osteen built a new Flat. This was the latter part of 1863. During this time, there was a mail route established from Live Oak, Fla., to Fort Fannin, which was made on Horse Back. John Biley was the mail carrier. He would leave Live Oak Monday morning and come to the Ferry which my Father kept, and spend the night. Then Tuesday he would go on to Ft. Fannin and spend the night. Then Wednesday he would return back to the Ferry where my Father was and spend the night. On Thursday he would return to Live Oak. My Bro. Shade, which is W. S. Osteen would meet him at the Ferry and git the mail for the surrounding settlements an bring it to my Mother's, a distance of (8) eight miles. Then my Self an one of my Elder Bros. Elise {Alfred} Osteen would walk an run all over the Settle ments an deliver the mail to the Soilders {wives}, widows an there children. At times I would go with my Bro. Shade to meet the Mail Carrier an git the mail. an now as I haved past the age of 80 years an is not able to work much, I feel like I am due an desire some conderation, an iff the Board thinks I am due anything, I would like to have it.*
>
> *J. Hance Osteen*

Also, the specifics of where he performed his C.S.A. service are set forth in a June 30, 1938 deposition by Jane Polk (Mrs. W. Shad) Osteen, newly a widow, when she affirms, "I knew John Hance Osteen, and have known him ever since before the war, knew him as a small boy who, during the last two years of the war, assisted in delivering mail to Confederate soldiers, their wives, widows and families, that said service was performed in what is known as the Cow Creek Community near Mount Horeb Church in what is now Gilchrist County, Florida."

"The Santa Fe River component of Underwood's Home Guard were subject to military orders and subordinate to military authorities," according to Osteen, who asserted that "none of the boys had written enlistments." Confederate Mail Carrier Osteen's duties, on a weekly delivery basis, lasted some twenty months until April 1865. Humble role though it was, few full-fledged combatants could have taken their prescribed duties more seriously than this callow tyke. By mid-May 1865, the assorted boys of Underwood's Company in the Santa Fe River countryside disbanded. Most of them had four to seven more years yet ahead before they would reach full-grown manhood.

In fact, it was not until June 12, 1882, at Franklin, Florida, that Hance married. His bride was Miss Sarah Frances Elizabeth Hines (Nov. 4, 1862-Feb. 4, 1935), a native of Franklin Sink Territory "as known then" (in Gilchrist County *today*).[5] Her parents were W. Henry Hines, who died at Chickamauga, and the former Fannie Tompkins. The Osteens' five children were John Rufus, born Aug. 19, 1888; Grover Cleveland, June 9, 1893; Vander Bryan, Aug. 10, 1896; Ander Hampton, Feb. 4, 1899; and (Samuel) Dewey, Nov. 17, 1900. On their farm outside of Bell, Sarah and Hance raised cotton, corn and peanuts.

In his February 1973 missive from High Springs, Florida, A. Hampton Osteen assures us:

> *Daddy Hance was a strict but good father, firm in demands, sweet in personality, honest in dealings with his fellowmen, and a firm believer in God and Jesus, His son. He was proud of his Confederate duties and often recalled how "Whenever high water filled Santa Fe River, I swam with my horse to get the mail through, rain or shine, hot or cold." A Mason and member of Mt. Horeb Baptist Church, our Daddy was known too for his lighter side—as a fiddler much in demand for playing and calling at square dances. He loved horses. He was, too, a believer in "signs." "Boys," he'd say, "watch the moon and stars. They will tell you lots." Three of us five boys are living nearby today.*

In his Jan. 22, 1991 letter from High Springs, Arnold "Arnie" O'Steen, 53, passes along these thoughts from his father, "Dewey," who just celebrated his 90th birthday with a sizeable family gathering this past November:

> *Dewey, my Daddy, has many choice remembrances of Grampa Hance, who always taught his boys to be honest and not tend to anyone else's business and not let anyone tend to theirs. Hance loved politics, his church—Mt. Horeb Baptist, his Masonic lodge meetings (He reached the 32nd Degree). Dewey says, "Daddy and Mother took me to the Grand Lodge in Jacksonville when I was four in 1904. He represented Cherry Hill Lodge No. 12 in Fort White, as he was Master of it, still an active one today."*
>
> *John Hance farmed all his life and still had his four rows of crops alongside of mine {Dewey} up until his last two years or so—1946. His favorite foods were brisket stew, tomatoes fixed any way, corn bread, milk and clabber.*
>
> *His favorite hymns were "Amazing Grace" and "Dust on the Bible," the number he is playing during the taking of this 1947 photo of him fiddling. He chewed apple sun-cured tobacco, smoked a pipe some in his*

Florida News & Photo Service, Jacksonville, FL.

John H. Osteen, 92, in December 1947.

Florida News & Photo Service, Jacksonville, FL.

The latest-born Civil War veteran known—the youngest "Old Reb" at 92.

younger days. He played his fiddle at square dances. Back then, these were held at different folks' homes. He taught himself how to play the fiddle. He taught Singing School in several different churches in surrounding counties; he taught from the old Eight Note Book, *from* Christian Harmony, *and from* Temple Star Book.

What I (Arnie) remember Granddaddy most for was his politics (Democrat). I would help him tack up posters for different candidates. He would go to Masonic meetings and stay for days at a time...a Mason from 21 till he died. He always wanted me to join, but I've never been interested in it. I slept in the same room with him my first eleven years. He liked to sit by the fireplace in the winter and chew his tobacco and spit in the fire and listen to it sizzle. He bought my first little rocking chair for me to sit by him at the fireplace and rock. He gave me my first chewing tobacco. He loved to hunt deer, turkeys and foxes. He killed his last 10-point buck when 68. J. Hance and the other O'Steen (Old Reb Sim) were not directly kinfolk. The Confederate Stamp Alliance made Hance

Osteen an Honorary Colonel in the Confederate Air Force, late in life, which pleased him much.

Dewey, my dad, now approaching Grampa Hance's age has just joined a camp of the S.C.V.! He proudly wears the medal and goes to monthly meeting in Gainesville.

If the reader wishes to see excellent color photogravures of Arnie and Dewey Osteen, who died at 91, Dec. 6, 1991, (s)he need only to borrow a microfilm roll of *The Gainesville Sun* (Relax-Sec. D) for Sept. 29, 1990. Descendants today of Uncle Hance are justly proud of their Confederate heritage and his unique place in that heritage. Recognized and known or not, J. Hance Osteen may well have been the world's youngest living Civil War veteran to have served in a unit for an indeterminately long time, perhaps even for his entire post bellum life. There is little evidence or *none* at all to indicate that J.H.O. ever "traded on" or promoted himself with his remarkable distinction. He was too much a family man and focused upon others...and upon his favorite pet horse, Toby.[6] In fact, Hance never really admitted to being any less than eight years of age on his earliest C.S.A. service. As long as we refrain from doing the math (and he might be just as pleased if we did not do it), why then this benign myth may endure. Even so, our youthful Confederate mail carrier remains a tribute to an old-time truth formerly honored unsparingly (a outrance), though seldom, if ever given lip or pen service: when it came to eligibility for a chance to render *any* service however humble that would abet the momentous causes of the South and the North in the early 1860s, extreme juvenility scarcely knew *any* bounds.

The Keith Brothers

George Washington Keith (b. 1852)
William Thomas Keith (b. 1856)
James S. Keith (b. 1858)

They were natives of Holmes County in Florida's Panhandle. All three—each in his own turn—wanted to be in the C.S.A. All three were so young they had no hope of enlisting in a Florida regiment. Yet, they were scarcely to be denied.

George Washington Keith (Jan. 17, 1852-Nov. 7, 1951) was the eldest son of William Thomas (1822-1859) and Nancy Boutwell Keith [Paul] (1828-1900+). [We note that these youngsters were already fatherless *before* the war.] By the 1870 Census, Geo. W. was living with Jos. Allen Register; Wm. T., with the Prim family; Jas. S., with the Whitakers. The brothers married girls from these respective families.[1] George, 9 1/4, at Fort Sumter time understood rather well the whys and hows of the crisis. William Thomas Keith (Feb. 3, 1856-Oct. 27, 1949), age 5, had no memory of Florida's seceding but claimed to remember Fort Sumter. Like a younger brother, he approved of and emulated George's doings...and bided his time. As for little James S. Keith (Mar. 2, 1858-Feb. 7, 1931), age 3, at opening gun—well, he was so swaddled in innocence that the war would be nearly concluded before he "came to." By then, it was, practically, too late.

George W., on the brink of twelve, added exactly three years to himself (claiming 1849 as his birth year), and joined the West Florida Home Guard Company.[2] For some fifteen months George underwent drills with the W.F.H.G.'s and performed in their local defense of women and children at home from incursions of real or rumored marauders. Though no great glory attaches to his humble military role, we realize that dedicated youths like George enabled hundreds of sorely needed older "men-boys" to be available for battlefront service. Occasionally an older guardsman, ages 13-15, would "graduate" all trained to a C.S.A. regiment. Many decades later and for nearly six months G.W.K. would be our youngest known Civil War veteran.

On Apr. 10, 1873, George married Miss Caroline Register (1850-1932) of Holmes County. They had fifty-nine years together and nine children: Fannie Magee (Mrs. James C.) Jackson—4 children, 9 grands; James A. (b. 1875); Sarah Eliz. (Mrs. Geo. A. "Short") Register—1 child; Nancy Roxie

Jane Keith (1879-1954), who would be such a blessing as a caregiver to her aged father; George Henry (1881-1960), who married Dixie Register—1 child; Thomas Greenberry (1883-1934)—5 children by Alor C.; Margaret A. Lizer (Mrs. Elisha P.) Crutchfield (1885-1976)—3 children; John Alton Daniel (1888-1966)—3 children by Lena Frances James; Rosie Lee (Mrs. James E.) Collins.[3] For many years George W. was a constable and policeman in Graceville, his hometown. For twelve years he was deputy sheriff of Geneva County, Alabama, just a few miles to the northwest. He found time to socialize with comrades of the U.C.V. In 1917, with his escort, Thad Grace, he attended the highly successful 27th National U.C.V. Reunion in Washington, D. C. Again, twenty-one years later, he would join forty-seven Florida veterans to meet the Yankees at Gettysburg for a memorable week. George, by then, had been a member of his local Baptist church for as long as folks could recall. Two accidents in his late years were all that finally slowed him down. At ninety-five while roofing his house he fell and suffered bruises and shock. At ninety-seven he was struck by a ton-and-a-half truck. His recoveries were so remarkable that he achieved on his own soundness what most others could only dream of: he was granted an insurance policy making him eligible for hospital, surgical and death benefits. This, twenty years before Medicare! He remained a regular personality on the streets of Graceville.[4] In her July 26, 1971 note from Graceville, Ruby Lee Fowler (Margaret and Elisha Crutchfield's daughter), tells of his favorite pastime:

> *Grampa was interested in politics. His views were George Keith's as he had a mind of his own, and there was no changing it. I spent hours with him—I'd get on the opposite side and we would argue. He really enjoyed that. His mind was clear and he walked to town until about five months before he died at almost 100.*[5]

During his nineties his birthdays were gala family affairs with at least four generations always present. At 99, George became a member of a unique organization founded June 9, 1950, at the 5th Annual Mississippi Air Tour and headquartered at Vicksburg—The Confederate Air Force of the Planet Earth, Inc. As one of thirteen Confederate and six Union veterans, he received a life commission of "Colonel" from Kenneth E. Crouch, a historian and a staff member of *The Bedford (Va.) Democrat.* On a late fall day hundreds came to this C.S.A. ex- guardsman's rites at Antioch Free Will Baptist Church, where he was laid to rest in Antioch Cemetery, just over the Alabama line in Geneva County, to the north of Graceville. He left but one Reb in Florida—also in the Panhandle, William A. Lundy of Laurel Hill, who, at nearly 110 years in 1957, was one of the last three Rebs nationally.

William T. Keith goes down as one of *the* very youngest known and among the four or five *latest born* Civil War veterans. All during winter 1864 he envied George each day that guardsman left their fireside to report for duty, drill, instructions. By mid May, Billy-Tom had "worn down" the household and George to the point whereby to preserve a semblance of family harmony, it became attractive to allow the lad to "join" the West Florida Home Guard. And he did so about late May '64 at approximately 8 years 3 months. Going to and executing drills was awe-inspiring; performing assigned guard duty at bridges and ferries surely enhanced self-esteem and imparted vital purpose to being in the world for eight-year-old Billy-Tom Keith. Only the merest "handful" of youth did Civil War service at so early in life—*most* of them categorically little homeguardsmen Rebs—Wm. O. N. Lea, 6 1/2, of Hampstead, N.C.; J. Hance Osteen, 8 nearly, of High Springs, Fla.; F. L. Wall, 7 1/2, of State Road, N.C.; Benj. F. Williams, 7 1/2, of Louvale, Ga.; Edward Black, just over 8, of Hagerstown, Ind. (See Appendix A.)

William married Miss Elmira Victoria Prim (1856-1910) about 1876. Their children were Lennie (Mrs. J. Matt) Taylor (1876-1918),[6] Lizzie (b. 1878), Maston, Sam and William J. (1880). By his second wife Clyde or Clydie (1867-1921) there were four daughters—Bernice, Zorree, Rebecca Clark Newman, and Marynell.[7] His last wife (as of 2/26/23) was Willie Mae Barden (1875-1958). William led a full life of some sixty-five matrimonial years, raising hogs and cattle besides growing rice, corn, potatoes, sugar cane, velvet beans, peanuts, and a vegetable garden. He also maintained a large pecan orchard. One of his five children (at the time), Rebecca Clark (Newman) of Caryville, shares her Nov. 24, 1975 thoughts:

> *Daddy built the log house I live in today when he was very young. It is one of few such houses remaining in "the Wiregrass." Side rooms have been added to the original log structure. The stick-and-mud chimney has been replaced by a brick one and a new roof put onto the original stripping. People often stop to photograph my lived-in and loved log home here, northwest of Bonifay. Daddy belonged to Whitewater Missionary Baptist Church. His favorite scripture was "The Golden Rule" of St. Luke 6:31. He enjoyed just walking. He retired at eighty, used a cane about ten years, a wheelchair his last three. He was a warm, loving father to his family and to all others who knew him he was a helpful neighbor. He died in the Isagora Community and was buried at Whitewater Baptist Cemetery.*

W. T. Keith and G. W. Keith are entitled to a unique distinction: they were the last living brothers to have served in the War Between the States, for they handily eclipse (by 3 yrs. & 10 mos.) Alliance, Ohio's John (1846-1946) and Hiram Conrad (1849-1946) of Company A, 186th Ohio Infantry—last surviving brothers who had served in the Union Army. By sheer happenstance, we presume, John Conrad, the elder brother, and George W. Keith, the elder brother, each lived exactly 99 years 9 months 20 days!

George Washington Keith & William Thomas Keith.

"Uncle Tom" or "Wiregrass Tom" Keith, one of Florida's final quintet of Boys in Gray, was a true patriarch, for he left sixty grandchildren and a veritable host beyond them.[8]

It would appear that our third Keith brother, James S.—of Caryville (w.s.w. of Bonifay & a stone's throw from his native Holmes County)—occasions a few factualties or truths. Categorically, he was *the* latest born ever to apply for a Confederate (or Civil War) pension.[9] By the time the war was half over—April 1863, James had attained age 5 years 1 month...the first stirrings of patriotic impulses? By January 1864, aware of his brothers' guardsmanships, more especially Bill-Tom's effusive chatter over *his* newly shouldered W.F.H.G. duties, James *may have entertained fantasies* that his turn, too, would eventuate. Truthfully, time and the war "ran out" for "Jimmie."...probably *the* profoundest disappointment of his 73-year life. He never stopped admiring (or wanting for himself) the sublime persona of a Confederate. Scores of such boys ages 7-12, who craved this identity, likely *did* perform *briefly* supportive roles, chores, errands in 1864-5. Like so many of them fifty and sixty years later who applied for and were denied a Confederate pension, James also applied.[10]

James, 20, married Miss Mary Whitaker (1858-1916) on Dec. 5, 1878. Their six children were Nancy Missouri, (Mrs. John) Whitaker, 2 children; James Perry Keith (1883-1904) who married Doris—5 children; Ginny; Laura (1891); William "Will" (1894-1986); Mary "Mae"; Susan V. On Dec. 25, 1918, James married Hattie S. Curry (1875-1958).

James S. Keith, allegedly in Capt. Sam Grantham's Holmes County H .G. Company during October ' 63-April '65, *did* succeed (not without at least a mild protest) in obtaining his modest Confederate (Florida) pension—*the latest born ever to win one!* However, the writer, not subscribing to "the Grantham anthem" and in fairness to those thousands of slightly older homeguardsmen whose services are sufficiently documented, concedes (with reluctance, the reader may be sure), James' status as so borderline as to fall short of unqualified endorsement. This national study (1971-1997), *Callow Brave and True: A Gospel of Civil War Youth,* on the youngest who served, reveals prevailingly a Confederate sweep in the strategic category of latest born. Of these eight, *the* latest of the late to have enjoyed (?) a tangible Civil War role and the status of veteran, only Willie Bush was unknown. The other seven enjoyed their reputations as legitimate veterans of the War Between the States. (See Appendix A.)

Who today would in conscience deny them the cherished status—Blue-tinged or Gray—with which they went to their Maker? (Psalm 100:3)

Epilogue

Callow Brave and True is the concluding portion of a trilogy in Civil War biography. Each of these sub-studies is its own epic prose elegy, the first two being *The South's Last Boys in Gray* and *The North's Last Boys in Blue.*[1] Collectively, they represent a deep and, until now, fallow writing field of surpassing human interest elements. Taken together, these investigative reports comprise *Sunset and Dusk of the Blue and the Gray,* a 27-year endeavor. The 1400 + testimonials found throughout *SDBG* are based upon some 9000 querying letters to key source-persons all across America, perhaps three-fourths of whom are not living in late 1997. But *what* they have said shall live on. Their personal thought-donations *are* a reaffirmation of the elderly. Their offerings, whether primary or secondary source material, have supplemented official records from state and national archives.

The purpose of *CB&T* has been to liberate those identities who were our youngest Civil War patriots from the 130-year, passivity-fed inertia or grand maw/grand mal of ignorance that so often determines our too soon achieved and ultimate human condition/reward—OBLIVION. Begun at a late hour (100 + years after Appomattox C. H.) in 1971, a *comprehensive* investigation of the youngest had not been pursued with vigor, if at all; had not been explored as a thematic entity of book-length worthiness; had gone abegging. No longer do generations of Civil War enthusiasts and history-minded citizens have to go through life accepting journalistic judgments. How many *hundred* well-intentioned local newspapers during 1866-1944 boldly, naively proclaimed a youthful, "favorite-son" ex-enlistee living within or near their readerships as *the* Civil War veteran of tenderest age? Here, we have found that in nearly all cases the claim was not even remotely true or was an overstatement. Dearth of data abetted such flattering eye-catcher stories, for they flourished, sometimes unchecked, sometimes questioned by evidence shared on behalf of other claimants, "domino-effect" fashion. Familiarity with this present report will finally disabuse today's readers of the nearly-forgotten, long-standing myths their forebears entertained about who the very youngest veterans were--a funda*mental* goal of *CB&T.*

The writer affirms that the deeper significance of the largest looming name in this entire field—Johnny Clem—resides in the fact that he has served all these 130 + post bellum years as a smoke screen covering this whole topic; the American public and most Civil War scholars alike have preserved or promoted the gross illusion that he was the ultimate in child-soldiery. Clem must surely have personally become acquainted with scores of veterans who eclipsed him by lateness of their birth; he inevitably would have met a dozen or so among the 55,000 who attended the mammoth 1913 week-long Golden Battle Reunion of Blue and Gray at Gettysburg. Consulting our "Latest Born" tabulation, we realize Clem's name would not appear, even if this table were extended three more pages. But Clem does better in "The Youngest Who Served," placing among the dozen youngest in the Union Army (on this comprehensive though not definitive table), *IF Klem did leave home in May 1861 and succeed in his goal of joining up in the opening weeks of the conflict.* Hauntingly, this puzzler remains a mighty big IF. Clem's fast climb in the media of 1862-65 reflects how well he capitalized upon advantages—his exceptionally short stature, his almost baby-like face, his quick-wittedness, his flair for dramatics, his sense of heroics, his instances of actual heroism, his fortunate billets close to influential generals, and, not least, his lengthy, rather distinguished career in the Regular U. S. Army. Truthfully, the Clem mystique, more than any other single factor, has preserved for this writer the possibility of authoring *Callow Brave and True.*

Another discovery occasioned by this national report, a runner-up, for sure, to the Clem conun*drum* (What was the actual length of his *total* Civil War service, *enlisted or no*?), is the "mega-enigma" behind what ever became of Pvt. William "Willie" Johnston, of the Third Vermont Infantry, our youngest ever awardee of the nation's highest military decoration?

In summary, if we have erred in this study, let error lie in the realm of understatement rather than in overstatement. In "The Youngest Who Served" some 29 age ten or under are listed. Jimmy Dugan, much of his service with the Carlisle Barracks Band (Pa.), would surely have been *under* age eleven and placed here, had data on him permitted. In a few rare places—Cora E. Gillis' *Final Journal* (G.A.R.) being one of them—assertion is made that some 25 in the Union ranks were age ten or under. While 22 of the 30 here accounted for were Union personnel, probably no more than 16 of them were among that particular 25 (such listing likely never existed!), leaving, we calculate, as many as 9 unaccounted for—almost like MIA's.

Certain observations are noteworthy. *The* very youngest echelon—ages 6, 7, 8—tended to be valets or servant-waiters to their commissioned officer fathers; they usually served in their father's units, sometimes, too, with an older brother in the same regiment. We note this, for example, in young Byam's story. Mascots, markers, and some musicians quite often ranged from 8 to 11 years old, single digit ages admittedly rarer; the 9 to 15-year-olds performed individually and in regimental bands. Musicians 13 and up were expected to perform medical tasks, as surgeons' aides, like the 15-year-old James Lurvey at Gettysburg; grimly, they played muffled drums at funerals. While a *few* were spies, quite often those 13, 14, 15, "graduated" to bearing weapons (which worldwide *today* is the pathetic norm). Consulting geo-political current events, the once-romance of musicianal child-soldiering, manifestly popular in its 19th century heyday, has vanished in favor now of child weapon-bearers worldwide. The extent to which boys 12 to 16 made the ultimate sacrifice was perhaps somewhat greater than the general public might believe.

That they who fill the pages of this dissertation should make so strong a "showing" among the war's last survivors surprises none. This fact is but a carrying out of the Natural Law.

Orphanhood (loss of *one or both* parents), frequent enough among lilliputian militants as to seem a prerequisite, appears to have increased a youngster's chances of recruitment, perhaps to avoid loss also of the father, committed as he sometimes was to a military obligation; too, orphans, in running away, might the easier have employed aliases.

To achieve a sense of balance on behalf of several hundred Union Navy Apprentice Boys, 3rd Class Boys, and Boys 2nd and 1st Class, whose ages were ordinarily 12 to 14 years, we offer a study drawn from maritime Massachusetts (Appendix F). Of the 144 fully featured biographies set forth in the unabridged (unpublished) *CB&T*, ten belong to former sailor-boys. Our focus upon 55 Bay State naval volunteers lends a measure of depth to a salt-water truth: many *young* men chose shipboard duties. Let us realize too that as of Sept. 25, 1861, the Union Navy was authorized to enlist black sailors, that Federal vessels were spendidly unsegregated, that some 9,695 Afro-Americans served ably in the fleet, and that the bravery of eight of them was awarded a Naval Medal of Honor.[2] Shipboard photographs attest to the presence of very young-looking black sailors. Nathaniel M. Gwynne is believed the youngest black awardee of *the* Medal (Army). Proudly representing his famed 54th Massachusetts Infantry is its youngest private and last survivor, Rev. Eli George Biddle of Brookline.

The reader will notice that a goodly percentage of these child-militants served out rather lengthy tours for such tender years, and that a fair number performed for four years or nearly so, re-enlisting and emerging as young men by their ultimate mustering out. Appendix D calls to our attention their admirable record. Youngsters like Charlie Scott, of Johnson, Vermont, defying the odds, served three enlistments as beginning teenagers. However, in truth, many "kids" who tried to "get in" and didn't and scores of others who did succeed in donning a uniform only to find they were not equal to the severities of camp and field and marches...well, these "failures," though less researchable and of lower profile, *were* plentiful enough and less publicized. How easy to forget what we tend not to think about! Yet, several hundred probably served an aggregate of thirty or more duty months.

In closing, the writer, humbly recognizing his limitations, extends a "request for information" to anyone who has information on our A-to-Z candidates. Beyond these specific desirables he voices this apology for having omitted outstanding pre-teenagers who truly belong. Let us hope their identities will surface for inclusion in a future edition.

Request for Information

Well aware that numbers of standouts among those who were exceptionally young Yanks or Rebs are absent from this review, the writer issues this blanket invitation to all readers:

If you know of a youth age 13 or under who served in the Civil War in any contributing capacity, a worthy nominee for possible inclusion in a future edition, please share (nominate) that youngster by writing to:

Prof. Jay S. Hoar
248 Temple Road
Temple, ME 04984

After studying over some known personalities on whom information is inadequate, youngster-patriots who are highly worthy, the writer confesses the need for help on those below who merit attention. Learning (1) where and when death occurred, (2) the unit fought in, and (3) dates of birth and enlistment are the strategic initial data needed in most cases.

Beginning with these whose elusive lives (presently) seem most purposeful to de-mystify, we hope somebody can assist with amplifying missing data on any of the following:

A. **Dugan, "Jimmy"** (age 9 or 10?), bugle-boy in the Carlisle Barracks Band (cavalry depot in Pa.), who stood 3' 6", "could ride anything on four legs, sound all the calls, and marched a regulation 28" step at risk of splitting himself in two." {Wise & Lord}. Said to have been under fire. All papers on him, kept at USAM Hist. Institute, Carlisle, have, however, vanished, long since, erroneously given away to one of many inquirers. Basically, whatever happened to him?

B. **Claiborne, Felix G.**, 13 - 16, served in Co. B, 18th Inf., C.S.A. May 1861 to Dec. 1864 when he died or was killed. His father, Felix, was 1st Lt., Co. E, 38th Va. (?) F.G.C.'s final rank?

C. **Curry, Wm. E.,** 12, of the Key West Avengers (later Co. K, 7th Fla. Inf.), a drummer boy, of southern Florida.

D. **Hooks, J. C.,** 12. of Luray, Va., enlisted in Co. G, 14th Tenn. Cav., under Gen. Forrest. He chose this service after a Federal cavalry unit hanged him (with care) to extort info on Forrest's men, then within 50 miles. "J. C." wasn't seriously hurt. (See W. X. Broome story for parallel case.) Living in 1917.

E. **Tucker, H. B.,** of Bradenton, Fla., was only 86 in 1937 when he attended the 46th Reunion of the Florida U.C.V. His birth year-- 1850 or '51.

F. **Lamkin, Geo. S.,** born at Winona, Miss. 11/3/50, joined Stanford's Miss. Battery at Grenada 8/2/61 at age 11- 9- 0, then 5' 5"? He was living at 880 Adams Street, Memphis, Tenn., in 1904 and was 6' 4". He was badly wounded at Shiloh and injured at Chickamauga.

G. **Rush, Jacob,** of Orange, Calif., (Union), was listed as age 88 in mid-July 1938, on his return home from the Gettysburg Reunion, making his birth year 1850. Likely, age 13 on enlistment.

H. **Mosby, Charles F.,** 13, drummer boy of the Elliott Grays, 6th Va. Inf., and of Henderson's Hvy. Artillery, served the entire war. Quite often pictured as on p. 224 of *Time-Life's Arms and Equipment of the Confederacy.*

I. **McGuffin, Pvt. John T.,** 13?, (7/3/48 - 2/21/30) of Co. B., 52nd Va. Inf., is buried at Alone Community Cemetery, Rockbridge County, Virginia.

J. **Rhyne, Henry Stewart Foote** (1852 - 5/11/24), a native of Priceville, Miss., son of Henry and Sarah B. Rhyne, who in 1870 settled in Castroville, California, with other Itawamba County families. He died and is buried in San Jose. Served C.S.A. from his home county. Age 8 in August 1860. Itawamba County Census, p. 270.

K. **Maurice (1st Name? & last?),** 13, C.S.A., was a blind drummer of the 52nd Va.. at 1st Manassas.

L. **Ranson, Brisco,** 14, got severe sabre wounds at Brandy Station and was a prisoner at Old Capitol.

M. **Seddon,** C.S.A. Sec. of War, had a son so young he was unable to carry his gun on marches.

N. **Thompson, Fleming,** 13, enlisted Apr. '61 at age 13 to serve 48 months in 44th (Blythe's) Miss. Inf., retiring as Sergeant Major and served with his father, Maj. John C. Thompson. Source: *Confederate Veteran XVI* 1908, p. 585.

O. **Judd, Charles,** who served briefly at about age 10, with his brother P. S. W. Judd in their father's 106th N. Y. Infy. (See Judd story in my *N.E. Last C.W. Vets.*, 1976). Charles is traced to Chicago living in the 1890's.

P. **Tyler, John Bailey,** 12, of Chicago (later), (b. Frederick, Md. 1849-) was in Troop D, 1st Md. Cav., C.S.A.

Q. **Haigh, Charles T.,** 14, C.S.A. of Fayetteville, N. C., was killed at Spotsylvania.

R. **Lutz, George,** (Apr. 1849—age 77 in 1927) of the 22nd Mich. Inf., who was but age 14 at Chickamauga.

S. **Davis, Robert W.,** 14, of Florida, surrendered at Durham.

T. **Braddock, Chas. L.,** 13, C.S.A., of Petersburg, Va., was in Culp's Hill struggles at Gettysburg.

U **Young, William,** 11 +, of Detroit, Drummer, Co. G., 24th Mich. Inf., believed living in Detroit in 1900.

V. **Allen, Henry Clay,** 11 yrs. 7 mos. 20 days on his enlistment July 17, 1861, Co. B, 60th Ga., Evans' Brigade, Gordon's Div. , A.N.V., of Troop & Whitefield Counties (Fannin Guards). appointed 4th Crpl. Aug. '63. Wounded, left shoulder & arm fracture, perm. disabled, Spotsylvania 5/12/64.

W. **Bowden, Thos. W.,** B. 5/2/49 in Meriwether County, Ga. Enl. 9/10/61 at 12 yrs. 2 mos. Captured at Morris Island, S.C. 9/7/63. Of Co. E, 28th Ga. Infy. (Army of Tenn.). "The Invincibles." Surrendered, Greensboro, N. C. 4/26/65.

X. **Hamil, Robt. Etheridge.** Enl. at 12 yrs. 7 mos. on 5/16/62. Co. K, 62nd Ga. Transf. to Co. K, 8th Ga. Cav. 7/11/64. Paroled at Albany, Ga. 5/10/65. Died 6/10/1918 in Pike County . Green Cem.

Y. **Lt. Gen. W. J. Hardee's 16-year-old son,** ____________, was mortally wounded just after Bentonville in final campaign. Extent of his C.S.A. service?

Z. **Tyner, Geo. Winfield** "Pap," (1849 - 1949), of W. Monroe, La., a pvt., Co. C, 22nd (Consol.) La. Inf. Enl. at 15, at Mobile, Ala. Oct. 4, '64. Detailed as nurse in Hosp'l (Precise b. & d. dates? obit.?) Last lived in home of Geo. E.Tyner & wife. One of last 44 Rebs.

Appendix A

The Youngest Who Served

Age at Enlistment yr-mo-day	*Name*	*Unit*	*Date of Birth*	*Last Sunset*
6-6-0	Willie H. Bush	V.R.C., Elmira	9/21/1857	10/25/1938
6-5-20	Wm. O. N. Lea	*Greyhound*	9/17/1855	5/6/1928
6-7-17	John H. Osteen	Fla. Home Guard	12/22/1856	9/24/1948
7-7-9	Franklin L. Wall	Co. C, 21st N.C. Wilkes Co. H.G.	9/22/1856	12/28/1938
7-7-?	Benj. F. Williams	Stewart Co. H.G.	3/7/1854	8/26/1943
7-10-14	Charles Knecht	Benton Barracks Cadet Band	11/1/1853	1/18/1948
8-1-24	Edward Black	21st Indiana Inf.	5/30/1853	6/30/1872
8-3-15	Wm. Thomas Keith	West Florida Home Guard	2/3/1856	10/27/1949
8-9-0	Lewis H. Easterly	Co. G, 9th Ill. Inf.	11/17/1852	7/18/1943
8-11-29	Albert C. White	Co. D, 64th O.V.I.	11/15/1852	2/1/1928
9-0-22	Albert E. Tisdale	*USS Sabine*	8/12/1853	8/17/1906
9-0-29	Robert B. Tyler	*USS Racer*	3/12/1854	4/2/1941
9-6-?	"Tad" Lincoln	"Colonel"	4/4/1853	7/15/1871
9-7-0	Thomas L. F. Hubler	12th Ind. Inf.	10/9/1851	3/21/1913
9-8-11	Mancil V. Root	Co. B, 36th Wis.	6/18/1854	7/6/1929
9- 9-17	John J. Klem (Clem)	24th O.V.I.?	8/13/1851	5/13/1937
9-10-0	C. Perry Byam	Co. D, 24th Iowa	10/22/1852	2/7/1922
9-10+	Berry H. Binford	5th Ala. Cav. & Bertwell's 11th Cav.	10/?/1852	9/2/1889
9-11-0	John N. Fissell	Co. A, 45th Ohio	9/19/1852	9/1/1922
10-0-15	Wm. Lee Owens	Fla. Home Guard	3/26/1854	12/18/1942
10-3-19	Wm. Martin Purcell	Co. I, 19th Wis.	11/11/1851	11/8/1902
10-4-7	David Wood	6th Mo. Cav.	8/25/1851	3/9/1944
10-5-26	Geo. W. McDonald	Co. C, 65th Ill.	8/17/1851	2/6/1930
10-6-?	Susan H. Clayton	Nurse	9/13/1851	3/7/1948
10-6-10	James W. Harper	Fla. Home Guard	10/12/1853	4/29/1943
10-7-16	Gilbert Van Zandt	Co. D, 79th Ohio	12/20/1851	10/4/1944
10-9-?	Franklin D. Peck	Co. I, 12th N.Y. Inf. Co. I, 12th N.Y. Cav.	8/22/1850	10/4/1936
10-9-0	George S. Lamkin	Miss. Lt. Arty.	11/3/1850	?
10-9-20	James E. Powell, II.	25th Missouri	6/30/1850	6/29/1929
10-10-0	Charles Judd	106th N.Y. Inf.	10/?/1851	1910?
10-11-9	Charles E. Merrick	147th Ill. Inf.	3/4/1854	10/11/1943

Appendix B

The Latest Born Veterans

Date of Birth	Name	Unit	Date of Enlistment	Age at Enlistment yr-mo-day
1857				
9/21/1857	Willie H. Bush	V.R.C., Elmira	10/8/62	6-6-0
1856				
12/22/1856	John H. Osteen	Fla. Home Guard	8/8/63	6-7-17
9/22/1856	Franklin L. Wall	Co. C, 21st N.C. Wilkes Co. H.G.	5/1/64	7-7-9
2/3/1856	Wm. Tho. Keith	West Florida Home Guard	5/18/64	8-3-15
1855				
9/17/1855	Wm. O. N. Lea	*Greyhound*	3/7/62	6-5-20
1854				
6/18/1854	Mancil V. Root	Co. B, 36th Wis.	2/29/64	9-8-11
3/26/1854	Wm. Lee Owens	Fla. Home Guard	4/10/64	10-0-15
3/12/1854	Robert B. Tyler	*USS Racer*	4/10/63	9-0-29
3/7/1854	Benj. F. Williams	Stewart Co. H.G.	10/?/61	7-7-?
3/4/1854	Charles E. Merrick	147th Ill. Inf.	2/13/65	10-11-9
1853				
12/30/1853	Nimshi Nuzum	W. Va. Home Guard	1/11/65	11-0-12
11/1/1853	Charles Knecht	Benton Barracks Cadet Band	9/15/61	7-10-14
10/12/1853	James W. Harper	Fla. Home Guard	4/22/64	10-6-10
8/12/1853	Albert E. Tisdale	*USS Sabine*	9/3/62	9-0-22
5/30/1853	Edward Black	21st Indiana Inf.	7/24/61	8-1-24
4/4/1853	"Tad" Lincoln	"Colonel"	10/?/62	9-6-?
3/4/1853	Frank Ironmonger	16th Va. Inf.	11/?/64	11-8-5
2/3/1853	James V. Brannen	3rd Pa. Arty.		10-?
1/8/1853	William H. Wall	Co. C, 21st N.C.	5/1/64	11-3-23
1852				
12/5/1852	Reg. F. Nicholson	*USS St. of Georgia*	3/?/64	11-5-?
11/17/1852	Lewis H. Easterly	Co. G, 9th Ill. Inf.	8/20/61	8-9-0
11/15/1852	Albert C. White	Co. D, 64th O.V.I.	11/14/61	8-11-29
10/29/1852	James Scholls, Sr.	C.S. Marines	2/24/64	11-3-26
10/22/1852	C. Perry Byam	Co. D, 24th Iowa	8/22/62	9-10-0
10/?/1852	Berry H. Binford	5th Ala. Cav. & Bertwell's 11th Cav.	9/?/64	9-10+

Appendix C

Soldierboy Casualties

Name	***Unit***	***Description***
John E. Andrew	Co. C, 79th OVI	Wounded, Peachtree Creek.
Thos. C. Bartow	Co. F, 125th Pa. Co. M, 20th Pa. Cav.	Prisoner of war.
Samuel M. Bennett	Co. K, 25th N.C. Inf.	Wounded, March, 1862.
Billy Bethune	Co. K, Ga. Inf.	Died of wounds, age 15.
Edward Black	21st Ind. Inf.	Captured, wounded.
Frederick Blake	*USS Canadaigua*	Died of disease, age 16.
Michael Burns	Co. C, 11th Mass. Inf.	Wounded, Gettysburg, age 15.
Charles Chapman	Co. A, 1st U.S. Inf.	Died of wounds, Hatcher's Run, age 16.
Felix G., Claiborne	18th Va. Inf..	Died of wounds, age 16.
John Lincoln Clem	Co. C, 22nd Mich.	Captured, 1863. Wounded, Atlanta Campaign, 1864.
Joel Closson	Co. A, 14th Maine	Died of wounds, Ship Island, Miss., age 13.
Joseph N. Coburn	Co. E, 3rd Mass. Cav.	Died of wounds, 8/17/64, age 15.
B. R. Crossthwait	Co. C, 2nd Misouri Inf.	Died of wounds, Corinth, Miss., 10/4/62, age 16.
James Crugom, Jr.	Co. D, 1st Wisc. Inf.	Wounded, 10/8/62.
David Frakes Day	Co. D, 57th OVI	Wounded, Shiloh, Vicksburg. Medal of Honor recipient.
Wm. H. Dennison	Co. C. 25th Mich. Inf.	Died of disease, 1/16/63, Bowling Green, Ky., age 15. Buried Nashville Nat'l. Cem.
F. B. DeWitt	Co. C, 121st OVI	Prisoner of war.
Henry Clay Durham	Co. A, 156th N.Y.	Died of disease, Baton Rouge, 7/8/1861, age 13.
John C. Elmendorf	Co. F, 20th NYSM	Died of disease, 6/8/61, age 12.
Joseph H. Estes	Co. G, 13th Miss. Inf.	Wounded, Malvern Hill, age 15.
Charles H. Gardner	Co. A, 8th Mich. Inf.	Died of wounds, Knoxville, Tenn., 12/21/63, age 15.
Daniel Thos. Greene	Co. B, 31st Ga. Inf.	Prisoner of war.
Cyrus Hanks	Co. G, 120th N.Y.	Died of wounds, Petersburg, Va., 10/5/64, age 16.
Chas. Carter Hay	45th & 15th Ala.	Wounded, Atlanta, age 13.

Robt. H. Hendershott	Co. C, 9th Mich. Co. B, 8th Mich.	Wounded, captured, 12/13/62.
Wm. Frank Hopkins	Co. I, 32nd Va.	Wounded, 9/30/64.
Patrick Howard	Co. A, 1st Vt. Hvy. Art.	Died of wounds, Weldon R.R., 6/25/64, age 15.
Orion P. Howe	Co. C, 55th Ill.	Wounded, Vicksburg. Medal of Honor recipient.
Geo. N. Huntington	N.Y. Inf.	Wounded, 10/19/64.
Edwin F. Jemison	2nd La. Inf.	Died of wounds, Malvern Hill, 7/1/62, age 16.
Silas E. Kennedy	Ala.	Wounded, Shiloh, age 13.
Charles E. King	Co. F, 49th Pa.	Died of wounds, Antietam, age 13.
John Dixon King	Co. F, 1st Tenn. Inf.	Captured, Cheat Mt.
Zachary Lawrence	Co. H, 4th Iowa Inf.	Died of Measles, 5/20/64, age 16. Chattanooga Nat'l Cem.
Wm. O. N. Lea[1]	CSS *Greyhound*	Wounded & captured, 5/7/62, age 6.
Eddie Lee	1st Iowa Inf.	Died of wounds, Wilson's Creek, 8/11/61, age 13.
Thomas G. Libby	Co. A, 1st Me Hvy Art.	Wounded, Petersburg, age 16.
Tom McCammon	5th Miss. Inf.	Died of wounds, Franklin, 11/30/64, age 15.
Clarence McKenzie	13th N.Y.S.M.	Died of wounds, 6/11/61, age 12.
Wm. D. McMillan	Co. K, 51st N. C.	Wounded, Ft. Harrison, 5/14/64, Bermuda Hnd., 7/25/64, Drewry's Blf., 9/29/64, age 16.
Egbert Maranville	Co. B, 2nd Vt. Inf.	Wounded & captured, Petersburg, 3/27/65, age 16.
Stephen Mauer	Co. I, 30th Mass. Inf.	Wounded, 10/19/64.
Charles W. Mendell	Co. E, 32nd Maine Co. E, 31st Maine	Wounded & captured, 7/30/64. Died of disease, 9/8/64, age 16.
Harlow Miller	Co. F, 82nd N.Y.	Died of wounds, Gettysburg, 7/2/63, age 16.
Wm. Montgomery	155th Pa.	Died of wounds, Appomattox, 4/12/65, age 15.
Charles Morrison	Co. E, 32nd Maine Co. M, 31st Maine	Died of disease, 9/1/64, age 16.
Wm. M. Nelms	Co. H, Lowery's Regt.	Died of wounds, 1865, age 16.
Wm. E. T. Ogletree	Co. E, 34th Ala. Co. C, 8th Ga. State Gds.	Wounded & captured, Covington, Ga. 7/23/64
Frederick D. Painter	2nd Conn. Hvy. Art.	Died of wounds, Cold Harbor, 6/1/64, age 14.

Wm. Palmer	Co. H., 111th Pa.	Died of wounds, 12/21/61, age 15.
Geo. B. Payne[2]	w/ J.H. Morgan	Wounded, 1863, age 15.
John W. Phillips	Co. A, 28th N. C. Enlisted at age 14	Wounded & captured, Spotsylvania, 5/12/64.
Andrew J. Pool(e)	Co. F, 25th Tenn.	Wounded (amputation), age 16, Murfreesboro, 12/31/62.
Mancil V. Root	Co. B, 36th Wisconsin	Wounded, Wilderness, May '64, captured, Deep Bottom, 8/17/64, age 10.
Charles W. Scott	Co. L, 1st Vt. Art. Co. I, 28th Mass.	Wounded, Cold Harbor, 6/3/64.
Julian A. Scott	Co. E, 3rd Vt.	Wounded, White Oak Swamp. Medal of Honor recipient.
Thomas E. Shamp	Co. E, 123rd O.V.I.	Prisoner, died 6/25/63, age 15.
Isaac Sharp	Co. G, 1st Ohio Cav.	Wounded, Lovejoy Sta. Sabre Charge, 8/20/64.
Ansel N. Skillin	Maine	Died of disease, 1863, age 13.
Elnathan H. Smith	Co. E, 3rd N.J. Inf.	Died of wounds, Petersburg July 1864, age 15.
Cyrus F. Snell [3]	Co. C, 19th Maine	Died of wounds, Wilderness, 6/12/64, age 16.
Abram Springsteen	Co. I, 63rd Ind.	Wounded, 5/4/64. Captured & escaped, 11/29/64.
Jimmy Taylor	C.S. Flag-bearer	Died of wounds, Gaines Mills 6/28/62, age 16.
Jesse J. Templeton	Co. K, 105th Pa. Inf.	Died of disease, 3/26/62, age 16.
Bev. W. Thornton	Co. I, 46th Ga. Inf.	Died of wounds, Cold Harbor 6/27/62, age 14.
Albert E. Tisdale	USS *Sabine*	Wounded, Jan. '63, age 9.
Charles L. Towle, Jr.	Co. F, 3rd Maine Co. I, 17th Maine	Died fo wounds, 1865, age 15.
Wallace N. VanCor	Co. G, 17th Vt.	Wounded, Cold Harbor, age 16.
Emmett M. Waller	13th Tenn. Inf.	Wounded & captured, Murfreesboro
Oscar Wetherald	Co. K, 40th Indiana	Died of disease, 12/6/64, age 14.
Wm. E. Whittinghill	Co. B, 4th Ky. Inf.	Prisoner at Andersonville
James W. Winn	Co. H, 25th Ga.	Died of wounds, Franklyn, 11/30/64, age 16.

1 Probable youngest wounded, *either side,* during the war.

2 Kendall A. Payne, orig. source, of Greenville, Miss.

3 His brother, Walter Scott Snell, 20, was also killed on June 29th, just 17 days later, near Petersburg. {Source: Ellen Wheelock, Oakland, Maine}.

Those Youngest Who Served Longest

Name (age)	Unit	Dates of service	Length of service (mos.)
Israel Broadsword (13)	Troy, Kan. Home Guards 51st Missouri	1859 - 65	65
Henry Doll (14)	USS *Hartford*	1862 - 67	60
Abraham J. Palmer (13)	Co. D, 48th N.Y. Inf.	1861 - 66	57
Franklin D. Peck (10)	Co. I, 12th N.Y. Inf. Co. I, 12th N.Y. Cav.	1861 - 66	50
Michael Burns (13)	Co. C, 11th Mass. Inf.	1861 - 65	50
Thos. L. F. Hubler (9)	Co. A, 12th Ind. Inf.	1861 - 65	49
Willie Johnston (11)	Co.D, 3rd Vt. Inf.	1861 - 65	49
Chas. F. Emerson (13)	Co. G, 15th Maine Inf.	1862 - 66	49
James Johnson (13)	Co. A, 7th La. Inf. USS *Portsmouth*	1863 - 67	49
Robert L. Morelock (14)	Co. F.,3rd Tenn. Inf.	1861 - 65	48
John R. Dimock (12)	USS *Sabine*	1864 - 68	48
Wm. F. Hopkins (11)	Co. I, 32nd Va.	1861 - 65	47
Flem C. Thompson (13)	Blythe's Co., 44th Miss.	1861- 65	47
Chas. E. Mosby (13)	Co. I, 6th Va. Inf. Henderson's Hvy. Arty.	1861 - 65	47
Charles Carter Hay (11)	Co. H, 15th Ala. Co. C, 45th Ala.	1861 - 65	47
John F. P. Robie (13)	Cos. A & F, 8th N.H.Inf.	1861 - 65	46
Thos. W. Daniel (12)	Cos. E & D, 9th Ga. Inf.	1861 - 65	46
Patrick F. Brannan (13)	15th Ala. Inf.	1861 - 65	46
Alfred L. Bennett (13)	USS *Monitor* USS *Jackson*	1861 - 65	46
Ira Stormes (15)	2nd Wis. Cav.	1861 - 65	46
John Dixon King (11)	Co. F, 1st Tenn. Inf.	1861 - 65	46
James R. Barrow (12)	Co. B, Cobb's Legion	1861 - 65	45
John W. Meek (?)	Co. H, 2nd Texas Inf.	1861 - 65	44
William H. Horsfall (14)	Co. G, 1st Ky. Inf. Co. K, 4th U.S. Inf.	1862 - 66	43
Eddie Black (8)	21st Indiana Inf. 1st Indiana Hvy. Art.	1861 - 65	43+

Alonzo D. Pigman (14)	Co. I, 32nd Kentucky Orderly to Gen. Millin	1862 - 65	43
David F. Day (14)	Co. D, 57th O.V.I.	1862 - 65	42
Geo. B. Payne (13)	Co. I, 4th Ky. Cav. J. C. Breckinridge's Courier	1861 - 65	42
Nathaniel H. Sledge (12)	Co. K, 13th Ga.	1861 - 65	42
Wm. Albert Kiney (15)	Co. G, 5th Ky. Mtd. Inf.	1861 - 65	42
Henry A. Horton (15)	Co. E, 31st Mass. Co. A, 2nd Vt.	1861 - 65	42
Lansford W. Noyes (14)	Co. I, 54th Ill.	1861 - 65	42
Theodore D. Parker (16)	42nd, 55th & 41st Ills.	1861 - 64	41
Nathan M. Gove (11)	3rd N.H. Inf.	1861 - 65	41
Luther B. Harris (16)	4th Vermont	1861 - 65	41
Charles D. McNeill (13)	Co. H, 4th Ga. Inf.	1861 - 65	41
Emmett M. Waller (13)	13th Tenn. Infy. Forrest's Cav.	1861 - 65	41
Francis B. DeWitt (12)	Co. B, 46th O.V.I. Co. C, 121st O.V.I.	1861 - 65	40+
Holt Collier (?)	Co. H, 9th Texas Cav.	1861 - 65	40
Martin Purcell (10)	Co. I, 19th Wis. 36th Wis.	1862 - 65	40
Benj. F. Williams (8)	Commissary Wagoner	1861 - 65	40
Orion P. Howe (14)	Co. C, 55th Ill.	1863 - 67	39
Geo. S. Lamkin (11)	T.J. Stanford's Bty., Miss. Lt. Art.	1861 - 65	39
Calloway Beetes (13)	Co. B, 3rd E. Tenn. Inf.	1862 - 65	38
Austin Case (16)	75th N.Y. Inf.	1861 - 64	38

Appendix E

Those Youngest Who Earned The Nation's Highest Decoration— The Congressional Medal of Honor

Name	*Unit*	*Location & age (yr-mo-day)*	*Date of Award*
William Johnston	Co. D, 3rd Vt. Inf.	Peninsula Campaign 11-11-19	9/16/63
John E. Anglin	USS *Pontoosuc*	Fort Fisher 14-2-18	6/22/65
Orion P. Howe	Co. C, 55th Ill. Inf.	Vicksburg 14-4-20	5/19/63
Oscar E. Peck	USS *Varuna*	Forts Jackson & St. Philip 14	?
James Snedden	Co. E, 54th Pa. Inf.	Piedmont, Va 14-8-16	9/11/97
Nathaniel Gwynne	13th Ohio Cav.	July 28, 1864 15-0-23	1/27/65
John Cook	4th U.S. Artillery	Antietam 15- 1- 0	6/30/94
Joseph Henry Shea	Co. K, 92nd N.Y. Inf.	Chapin's Farm, Va. 15-1-12	Mar. '66
Robinson B. Murphy	Co. A, 127th Ill. Inf.	Atlanta 15-2-17	July 22, 1890
Wm. H. Horsfall	Co. G, 1st Ky. Inf.	Corinth, Miss. 15-2-18	Aug. 17, 1895
Julian A. Scott	Co. E, 3rd Vt. Inf.	Lee's Mills, Va. 16-2-0	Feb. '65
David Frakes Day	Co. D, 57th O.V.I.	Vicksburg 16-2-0	1/2/95
George Hollat	USS *Varuna*	Forts Jackson & St. Philip 16	4/3/63
James Machon	USS *Brooklyn*	Mobile Bay, Ala. 16	12/31/64
Geo. Wm. Schmal	Co. M, 24th N.Y. Cav.	Paine's Cross roads, Va. 16	5/3/65
Johann Christopher	Co. B, 9th N.Y. Inf.	Camden, N.C. 16-7-0	1/7/95
Delano Morey	Co. B, 82nd O.V.I.	McDowell, Va. 16-9-24	8/14/93

Appendix F

Massachusetts Lads Who Served in the Union Navy

As a leading Northern maritime state, the Commonwealth of Massachusetts supplied an impressive number of youngsters under age fifteen, perhaps some 40% of those from New England, which contributed nearly two-thirds of the Union Navy personnel. This study, gleaned from Volumes VII and VIII of *Massachusetts Soldiers, Sailors and Marines in the Civil War (1933 & 1935),* confirms that many of our youngest combatants went to sea, that they commonly served six months up to three years. Their duties often included deck seamanship, messing, carrying powder bags, being messengers, and being apprenticed toward an eventual rating.

The federal policy, until late February 1864, of no military service credits for enlistments in the U. S. Navy was especially severe upon the New England maritime states. Massachusetts, Connecticut, Rhode Island and Maine, for example, were compelled to fill their entire assigned quotas by Army enlistments, regardless of how many of their sons might have served aboard vessels doing their part at sea. Some 22,360 Bay Staters had enlisted in the Naval Service between Apr. 13, 1861 and Feb. 24, 1864, when this injustice was partly rectified by Section 9 of the Act of Congress approved on that date. Governor John A. Andrew personally took a lead in bringing about this far more just policy. (Vol. VIII, p. 534).

Name	*Age at enlistment*	*Vessel(s)*	*Dates of service*	*Length of service*
Charles A. Alexander	12	USS *Ohio, Macedonian*	12/62-3/63	3 mos.
Enoch F. Anderson	14	USS *Rhode Island, Sasscus, Vanderbilt, Suwanee*	9/64-12/67	38 mos.
Asa B. Baxter	14	USS *South Carolina*	9/61-?	
Frederick Blake	14	USS *Canandaigua* Died onboard	6/62-10/64	27 mos.
Edward A. Cambridge	14	USS *Cumberland, Minnesota*	10/60-5/62	18 mos.
John Carney	14	USS *Ohio*	10/61-10/62	12 mos.
Lewis Cass	14	USS *Ohio, Guard*	3/65-2/68	36 mos.
Richard Castello	14	USS *Ohio, Canandaigua*	7/62-5/65	34 mos.

Fernando C. Cate	14	USS *Ohio,* *Macedonian*	11/62-3/63	4 mos.
		Iron Age, *Cherokee*	6/63-7/65	25 mos.
Frederick A. Churchill	14	*Ohio Kingfisher,* *Daiching, T.A. Wood,* USS *Saratoga*	9/61-10/64	37 mos.
Charles W. Cole	14	USS *Ohio*	4/62-9/62	5 mos.
Charles E. Collins	14	USS *Ohio,* *Sabine, Wabash*	8/64-4/65	7 mos.
James Connolly	14	USS *Ohio,* *Mercedita,* *Galena*	4/63-4/65 Deserted 6/64, apprehended 2/65.	24 mos.?
Francis H. Couers	14	USS *Ohio,* *Housatonic, Colorado,* *Gertrude, Preston*	7/62-8/65	37 mos.
Samuel P. Cutter	14	USS *Ohio, Relief,* *Jamestown*	3/64-10/65	19 mos.
Thomas E. Day	13	USS *Ohio,* *Minnesota*	4/61-4-64	36 mos.
Patrick J. Donahue	13	USS *Sabine, Wabash,* *Hartford, Vermont*	7/64-8/68	49 mos.
James Dutcher	14	USS *Ohio,* *R. R. Cuyler*	7/62-9/62	2 mos.
Charles O. Farmer	14	USS *Geo. Mangham,* *Commodore Read*	7/63-7/65	24 mos.
Thomas F. Fitzmaurice	14	USS *Paul Jones* Died onboard	3/65-9/67	30 mos.
Henry E. French	13	USS *Osceola, Ohio*	2/64-7/65	17 mos.
Nehemiah Getchell	14	USS *Ohio,* *Rhode Island*	7/64-6/65	10 mos.
Thomas Gibson	14	USS *Housatonic,* *Nantucket, St. Louis*	7/62-5/65	34 mos.
George Gilbert	14	USS *Ohio,* *Minnesota*	11/62-8/64	21 mos.
Coono C. Graff	13	USS *Ohio*	9/62-9/70	96 mos.
William A. Hammond	14	USS *Ticonderoga,* *Maumee*	11/63-6/65	19 mos.
Michael Harney	14	USS *Ohio,* *Macedonian*	8/62-8/63	12 mos.
Robert E. Harvey	14	USS *Ohio,* *Susquehanna*	5/61-6/63	13 mos.
Richard Hennessy	13	USS *Niagara,* *Hartford, Richmond,* *Kickapoo*	10/63-7/65	21 mos.

William A. Henry	14	USS *Rhode Island, Constellation, National Guard, Casco*	6/62-1/65	31 mos.
Halsey H. Hicks	14	USS *Hendrick Hudson, Savannah, Supply*	11/63-6/68	52 mos.
Henry Horne	14	USS *Ohio, Macedonian*	8/62-3/63	6 mos.
George E. W. Ide	14	USS *Kensington, Pink, Savannah*	12/61-2/65	39 mos.
Martin James	14	USS *Ohio*	3/63-5/63	3 mos.
Patrick Kincey	14	USS *North Carolina, Princeton, Powhattan, Brooklyn, Richmond*	10/61-11/64	37 mos.
Edmund S. Knight	13	USS *Ohio, Macedonian*	11/62-3/63	4 mos.
Marcus Lindbury	14	USS *Ohio*	3/64-6/64	3 mos.
Edmund Maloney	14	USS *Ohio, Young Rover*	8/61-11/62	15 mos.
Wm. D. Maurer	13	USS *Ohio, Fort Donelson*	5/64-6/65	13 mos.
John McGrath	14	USS *Ohio, Colorado, N. Carolina, Princeton, Pawtuxet, Vermont, Huntsville, Tonawanda*	11/62-3/67	48 mos.
Michael McGrath	14	USS *Ohio*	3/64-1/65	10 mos.
John S. McGraw	14	USS *Onward, Sacramento*	1/64-8/65	19 mos.
William McHugo	14	USS *Ohio, Penobscot, Mystic*	3/62-3/65	36 mos.
James Merrill	14	USS *Colorado, Cayuga*	7/62-7/65	36 mos.
Frederick E. Nelson	14	USS *Ohio, Macedonian*	12/62-3/63	2 mos.
John O'Brien (also John Brine)	14	USS *Ohio*	11/63-12/63	1 mo.
George C. Patterson	14	USS *Huron, Nahant, Vermont, New Hampshire*	1/62-1/65	36 mos.
Patrick Power	13	USS *Ohio, Hendrick Hudson*	8/63-8/65	24 mos.
Manuel Rosario	14	USS *Kearsarge, Tahoma, Wampanoag*	3/65-3/68	36 mos.

Oliver E. Sadlier	14	USS *Massasoit,* *Rhode Island*	2/64-2/65	12 mos.
Daniel Shehan	14	USS *Mississippi,* *Portsmouth,* *Colorado, Pocahontas*	5/61-7/63	26 mos.
John Sullivan	14	USS *Ohio*	3/64-1/65	10 mos.
George F. Taylor	14	USS *Ohio,* *Sabine*	5/61-2/63	20 mos.
Frank W. Townsend	13	USS *Ohio,* *Niagara,* *Savannah*	7/63-7/64	12 mos.
Joseph H. Hoffman	14	USS *Shamrock* U. S. Marine Corps	4/62-7/69	72 mos.

Appendix G

Chronology of Successive Tenures of the Youngest in the Union Army

Like most people who have not mulled this issue over at some length, I, too, assumed, when talking of the youngest soldierboy, that we would be referring to one person only, an individual. But soon the realization hits us—the distinction of being "youngest of all" couldn't be held for long by any one youth since every person continues to age.

Take, for example, Tommy Hubler of Warsaw, Indiana. In the opening week of the war, from the day of his enlistment at age 9 years 7 months, Tommy appears to have held this elusive distinction...until some other extremely young enlistee came along, which happened to be Eddie Black, of Hagerstown, Indiana, who that July 24th at age 8 years 1 month 24 days held the distinction until Charles Knecht, "youngest ever," joined 50 days later and held his place his entire enlistment.

Because Secretary of War Stanton decreed a moratorium in 1864 on preteenagers being accepted for duty, this table appears distressingly incomplete. Joseph Fissell likely could not have been "Youngest" for longer than a few months. Who could have been between Fissell and Root remains a mystery.

Such as it is, I offer this first attempt at a unique chronology. To not attempt it would amount to an egregious omission from a study purporting to be authoritative upon those who were the youngest to serve in our "Lachrymal Extravaganza."

Name (date of birth)	***Unit***	***Age (yr-mo-day) & date at Enlistment***	***Age & date at end of service***	***Time as "Youngest" & (total length of service)***
James E. Powell (6/30/50)	Valet to his father	10-9-13 4/12/61	11-9-9 4/8/62	7 days (*)
Tho. L. F. Hubler (10/9/51)	12th Indiana Inf.	9-7-? 4/19/61	13-8-? 6/25/65	3 mos., 5 days (49+ mos.)
Edward Black (5/30/53)	21st Indiana Inf.	8-1-24 7/24/61	9-3-12 9/11/62	10+ mos.** (44 mos.)
Charles Knecht (11/1/53)	Benton Barracks Cadet Band	7-10-14 9/13/61	8-2-7 1/8/62	3 mos., 26 days (Same)
Joseph N. Fissell (9/19/52)	45th Ohio Inf.	9-11-0 8/19/62	12-8-? 6/15/65	17+ mos. (33+ mos.)
Mancil V. Root (6/18/54)	36th Wis. Inf.	9-8-12 2/29/64	11-4-? 7/12/65	11+ mos. (16 mos., 13 days)
Charles E. Merrick (3/4/54)	147th Ill. Inf.	10-11-10 2/13/65	11-10-16 1/20/66	6+ mos.*** (11 mos., 7 days)

*Powell had actually been in "service" with his father for over two years when Ft. Sumter was attacked.
**Black was "Youngest" twice—before and after Knecht's enlistment. This total accounts for both times.
***Merrick's time as "Youngest" was all post-war, but is included here since his enlistment began during the war.

Notes

John Converse Elmendorf

1. Steward R. Osborne's letter of 7/7/94. Quotes are traceable to John's father Peter, chiefly, and to Col. Pratt. Also, Dyer, *A Compendium of the War of the Rebellion,* 1959, 1412. The Ulster Guards (3 mos.) had duty at Annapolis and Baltimore until mustered out 8/2/61.

Clarence David McKenzie

1. New York *Times,* June 13, 1861, 8.
2. Luther Goodyear Bingham, *The Little Drummer Boy, Child of the 13th Regiment, N.Y.S.M., & Child of the Mission Sunday School* (Boston: Henry Hoyt, 1862) 30.
3. *Ibid.,* 31.
4. *Ibid.*, 29.
5. New York State Archives. "McKenzie, Clarence D.", Record of Military Service.
6. Bingham, 51-59.
7. Bingham, 67.
8. Bingham, 79.
9. New York *Times,* June 13, 1861, 8.
10. Bingham, 131.
11. J. W. Carnahan, *History of the Easel-Shaped Monument, etc.* (Chicago: Dux Publ. Co., 1893), 335. Note: Young McKenzie is mentioned briefly in Francis A. Lord & Arthur Wise*'s Bands and Drummer Boys of the Civil War,* 106.

Charles Edwin King

1. William A. Frassanito, *Antietam: the Photographic Legacy of America's Bloodiest Day* (New York: Scribners, 1978), 192.
2. (Photographic Query from Jay S. Hoar), *Daily Local News,* West Chester, Pa., 11/23/1995.
3. Frassanito, *Antietam,* 194.
4. Dyer, *Compendium,* 1590.
5. Dennis C. Roussey, "A War, a Drummer Boy, and a Search for a Grave," *Daily Local News,* West Chester, 4/8/1985, 5.
6. Frassanito, 195.
7. Bowles, Henry H. Service Record & Grave Registration, Maine State Archives, Augusta, Me. Ex-private Bowles, a native of Machias, who belonged to Burnham Post 50, G.A.R., died of cancer of the stomach and was buried at Cherryfield's Pine Grove Cemetery, Lot 109, on 6/7/1916.
8. Roussey, "Family Learns Silver Spoons Rich in History," *Daily Local News*, 4/8/85, 10.
9. Roussey, 10.
10. Roussey, 5. Here we learn that Pennell King died in Nov. 1902; Adaline, in 1900; that they rest in Green Mount Cemetery in West Goshen Township; that a daughter Adda M., 3 yrs. 10 mos., died Sept. 17 (!), 1864, and is with her parents; finally, that Charley is not there.

Henry Clay Durham

1. Dyer, 1463.
2. Again, we are indebted to Seward R. Osborne, of Olivebridge, NY, for bringing H. C. Durham into this study, where he surely belongs.
3. The writer will certainly "look up" Durham the next time he is in Baton Rouge, a place he has never yet been to! That is the intention.

Charles Howard Gardner

1. Jonathan Robertson, Adj.-Gen., Compiler, *Michigan in the War,* Rev. Ed., Lansing: W. S. George & Co., 1882, 291.
2. LeRoy Barnett, Archivist, Michigan Historical Center, Dept. of State, Lansing, *Michigan Volunteers, 1861-1865,* 56. Also, Helen H. Ellis' Review of "Robertson's *Michigan in the War* in *Michigan History* [Geo. S. May, Ed.], Vol. 50, No. 2, June 1966, 183.
3. Dyer, 1285.
4. Robertson, 292.

Frederick D. Painter

1. *History of the Second Regiment C. V. Heavy Artillery* written by Captain James N. Coe, late of Co. H, 192. Connecticut State Archives.

2. Coe's *History,* 173.
3. Dyer, *Compendium,* 1007.
4. Coe, 173.

Edward Black

1. Dyer, 743, 1110-1111.
2. Allen Wade Mount, Sr., of Prairie Village, Kansas, and Miss Viola Black, a niece to the young soldier, have both labored to preserve the documented history of their illustrious kinsman and his place in the war. The writer expresses his appreciation to Bob Hansen, publisher of *The Hagerstown Exponent;* to James P. Hartig for a copy of "Edward Black, Drummer Boy: 1832-1982, A Sesquicentennial Story, "*Hagerstown Exponent,* March 1982; and to Lavonne Stall, Director of the Historic Hagerstown Museum. Finally, my thanks to Scott F. Lacey of Hagerstown, Ind.

Zachariah Taylor Lamb

1. Named after John Huie (b. 1808), original captain of Co. G, 44th Georgia, who served March to Dec. 5, 1862, resigning for being over age and in declining health. [Source: Charlie Lott, of Winston, Ga., and Camp 165, S.C.V., Carrollton].
2. See C. Perry Byam and James Crugom for examples of the presence of *both* a father and an older brother.
3. Zachariah T. Lamb's Company Muster Roll of Apr. 1, 1864, "Pay due from enlistment." Marked as present. Pay fm 1/18/64 to 3/31/64 was $26.40.

Nathaniel McL. Gwynne

1. Dyer, *Compendium,* 1480.
2. Reichley, "Youthful Civil War Hero Identified as Civilian," *The Annals,* Dec. 1985, Vol. 8, No. 2, 33.
3. Dyer, 1480.
4. *Kansas City Star,* Nov. 10, 1985.

William "Willie" Johnston

1. Stephen M. Carr, "Some Interesting Citation Details Developed," 52. Papers from Medal of Honor Society, Alexandria, Va.
2. T. S. Peck, Adj.-Gen. Compiler, "Officers and Enlisted Men of Vermont Awarded Medals of Honor," *Revised Roster of Vermont Volunteers in the War of the Rebellion,* Montpelier, 1892, 741.
3. Albert G. Chadwick, *Soldiers' Record of the Town of St. Johnsbury, Vermont, in the War of the Rebellion,* 1861-5, St. Johnsbury, 1883, 95.
4. Other youths enlisted from St. Johnsbury. Cpl. Wm. H. Orne, 16, in Co. C, 3rd Vt., who carried a weapon most of 6/1/61-2/18/62 before his discharge for disability; youngest townsman to carry a musket was Patrick Howard, 14, of Co. A, 11th Vt. Repeatedly rejected solely for his youth, he enlisted 12/7/63, was in six battles, and fell mortally wounded on the Weldon RR skirmish line. His older brother John perished in Andersonville. Charles H. Brown, 15, served in Co. A, 11th Vt., also during 11/21/63-8/25/65, along with Samuel Marden, 16, in this same unit until Sam was killed 6/23/64, not far from Pvt. Howard (above). Turrell E. Harriman, 15, of Co. C, 8th Vt., also of St. Johnsbury, during 12/3/61-6/28/65 got 3 promotions up to Orderly Sergeant.
5. Dyer, 902-4, 1650.
6. E. B. Long, *Day by Day,* 235-6. Also on 7/1/62, a quietly momentous presidential signature approved the Federal Income Tax which became operative, the 1861 measure failing. $600 to $10,000 was 3%, higher income was 5%.
7. Edward T. Fairbanks, *The Town of St. Johnsbury, Vermont: A Review of 125 years to the Anniversary Pageant, 1912* (1914), 281-82.
8. G. G. Benedict, *Vermont in the War,* 140-1. Also, W.H.B.J.'s statement 5/3/89 at La Junta, Colorado, Veterans Home. Other comparable accounts abound. See Maj. Otis F. R. Waite, *Vermont in the Great Rebellion* (Claremont, NH: 1869), 287-8.
9. Willie Johnston, Drummer, M & D roll of Veteran Volunteers One 20 V. R. C. "Return" reports him as on a second furlough for Feb.-Mar. 4, 1865, and a return to the Regimental Brass Band duty afterward.
10. Dyer, 1650.
11. G. Clifton Wisler has written a children's fictional treatment based upon our Willie's army career—*Mr. Lincoln's Drummer,* 1995, "scrupulously"? researched. Wisler has Willie age 10 (?), furloughing to visit his mother? (step-mom), for example. "all par-

ticulars unraveled!" If so, why not tell the world what became of the real life hero? It *would have been* a great service to America to have mentioned *the deep on- going mystery* of Willie's ultimate fate.

N.B. My indebtedness to Raymond Collins, Alexandria, Va., a key member & savant of the Medal of Honor Society...I herein now acknowledge. George Parsons, too, of Crystal River, Fl., has been supportive. Also, J. R. "Bob" Powell, of Metairie, La., a "Willie" sleuth/enthusiast, deserves credit.

Berry H. Binford

1. Chris Edwards and Faye Axford, *The Lure and Lore of Limestone County,* Tuscaloosa, Al., 199.
2. "Berry Binford Dead—The Eventful Career of a Man Who Joined the Confederate Army When 9 Years Old," *Alabama Courier,* 9/12/89, [in *Limestone Legacy* Vol. 4, #1, Oct. 1981].
3. A copy of this rare (& believed unpublished) original manuscript was sent to Prof. Hoar, May 6, 1994, by Charles W. Post, Jr., (former Cmdr., Camp #1479 Granbury's Texas Brigade, S.C.V.), who lives at Spring, Texas, and who pretty much single-handedly has made Binford's rightful appearance in this study possible. Hence, my thanks, lastingly, to him.
4. Vasser manuscript, 15.
5. Vasser, 57-8.
6. Vasser, 64.
7. Vasser, 68. "He strove for the extrication of the South from all the troubles entailed by the war. As brave a soldier as he was, his greenest laurels are those he won in civil service to the South as legislator, educator, orator, diplomat.
8. Vasser, 73.
9. *Limestone County, Alabama, Cemeteries,* Vol. III, *Athens City and Additions,* Limestone County Historical Society, 1979, 19.
10. *LCAC,* Vol. III, 72.

Julian A. Scott

1. *The* most traveled of anyone who served in the American Civil War, Wm. H. Jackson, is a pioneer in photography; his fame is assured these hundred years since as our "Photographer of the Far West" while place names for him abound, e.g. Jackson Hole, Wyo. (See *North's Last Boys in Blue,* if and when published*!)*
2. By act of Congress Dewey was exempted from compulsory retirement and never did retire, holding the special rank "Admiral of the Navy." (See last note for Reginald F. Nicholson). See also Murat Halstead's *Life and Achievements of Admiral Dewey: from Montpelier to Manila* (Chicago: Our Possessions Publishing Co., 1899), 87-88.
3. Robert J. Titterton, "Julian Scott: Special Agent to the Eleventh Census:" [Thesis Presented to Faculty of the Graduate College of the University of Vermont] May 1993, 23.
4. *Roster of Vermont Volunteers in the War of the Rebellion,* 87.
5. Dyer, *Compendium,* 1704.
6. Dyer, 1705.
7. *Roster of Vermont Vols.,* 265. Also Dyer, 1648.
8. The first six Medals of Honor, earned but four days earlier, were awarded to Union soldiers who daringly stole the Confederate locomotive "The General" at Big Shanty, Ga., wreaking strategic rail destruction along the Georgia-Tennessee RR line.
9. Vance Hartke, *Medal of Honor Recipients 1863-1973* (Washington, D.C., GPO, Oct. 22, 1973), 219.
10. "Absent detached serv in gen'l Hosp. As nurse. Harrison's Landing from July 19/62."
11. *Roster of Vermont Vols.,* 741.
12. *Roster of Vermont Vols.,* 449.
13. MSSM in CW, Vol. III, 258.
14. Abby M. Hemenway "Heroic Adventure," *Vermont Historical Gazette,* Vol. II, Burlington, Vt., 1871.
15. Military Record, Pvt. Charles W. Scott, Nat'l Archives & Records Admin., Wash., D.C.
16. Charles' matrimonial details surfaced in conversation with Robert Titterton (8/15/95), whose book *Julian Scott: Artist of the Civil War and Native America (1996)* is being published by McFarland & Co. in Jefferson, N.C.
17. Obit. *News and Citizen,* Morrisville, Vt., May 15, 1901, 5.
18. Titterton, "Sketchbook," *C.W.T.I.,* 60.
19. Titterton, *Julian Scott: Special Agent,* Chap. 1.
20. Titterton. People often addressed Scott as "Colonel," for he frequently served the in-

terests of the G.A.R., the Society of the Army of the Potomac, and Drake's Veteran Zouaves, with whom he held honorary membership.

(William) Martin Purcell

1. Richard B. Purcell (grandson), "Hero of the Nineteenth—Martin Purcell, Drummer Boy of the Potomac," *The Republican and Leader,* n.p. Fri. Mar. 1, 1901. Also, the name Martin Pursel appears on rolls of Co. I, 19th Regt., Wis. for Mar-Apr. 1863 with rank of Musician, his pension papers (Certif. #605,005 of 7/27/1901.)
2. Dyer, *Compendium,* 1681.
3. Haskell, enlisted May '61, became 1st Lt. in 6th Wis. (Iron Brig.) & aide to Gen. John Gibbon. When the 36th was to organize, Gov. Salomon promoted Major Haskell to Colonel to be its C. O. Haskell is noteworthy for his posthumous booklet *The Battle of Gettysburg* (from a letter to his brother).
4. Capt. Wm. H. Hamilton, of Spring Green, Wis., had enlisted in Oct. '61 in the 6th Battery, Wis. Lt. Art. "He was promoted (after losses in field ranks by the 36th) to Major, and to Lt. Col. and was the 36th's C.O. in the Grand Review. Wm. A. Bolgrien's letter of 9/26/1996—President, Beloit Historical Society & of the Rock County C.W.R.T.
5. Dyer, 1687. This source says the 36th mustered out in Louisville, Ky. Chptr XLIV, p. 834 of *The Military History of Wisconsin* by E. B. Quiner, 1866, says Jeffersonville, Ind. (w. side of Ohio R.) The 36th Wis. Vols. lost 157 in killed, 230 wounded in action, 185 by disease & 179 of diseases while Confederate prisoners.
6. R. B. Purcell (of Hendersonville, N. C.)
7. *Ibid.*
8. A marriage notice appeared in *Beloit Free Press,* 12/25/1873.
9. "Decl. for an Orig. Invalid Pension, 3/3/1890, Madison, Wis., (Nat'l Archives).
10. *Beloit Free Press,* 12/31/1881; & 1/4/1882.
11. Pension Papers #605,005 of Jan. 6, 1899. Supt. of Cemeteries Jim Ferry's letter & record of 6 burials Lot 183, Oakwood Cem. Beloit—9/28/96.
12. *Beloit Daily News,* Nov. 10, 1902. Thanks to Joyce (Mrs. Gerald) Monroe, Beloit.
13. "In Army at Ten," *Beloit Daily News,* 11/10/02. "Beloit Man, Who died Saturday Served All Through Civil War, Though Only Regularly Enlisted a Year and Four Months."

N.B. We are indebted to Marion Martin Pliner (Fort Dodge, Iowa). Richard B. Purcell (deceased)'s sister Janet married Marion's father's brother, Robert A. Martin. "I was told by Uncle Robert that after Janet died in 1983, he had given some Martin Purcell artifacts to the Historical Society in Beloit." Ltr. of 10/25/1994. Much credit goes to Wm. A. Bolgrien and to Alan and Maureen Gaff, of Fort Wayne, Ind. Alan is the author of *Brave Men's Tears: The Iron Brigade at Brawner Farm* and three other books.

Albert E. Tisdale

1. Hoar, "Almosts," in NLBB.
2. "Almosts," NLBB.
3. *Civil War Naval; Chronology,* I-31.
4. Nat'l Archives Pension Record Certif. #12,348, (Docket #52,048) of 2/6/1899, 3.
5. Pension Papers, 5/15/99, 8, 14. Conclusions in Albert's favor confirming his loss of sight as due to his shipboard injury were summarized: 1st, Strabismus at his age is very unusual, except from injury; 2nd, A dislocated lens at that age is very unusual, except from injury; 3rd, Retinitis and choroiditis are very unusual at such an age...except from injury; 4th, We seldom get such a group of symptoms as presented in this case, except when due to some injury.
6. Pension Record, Certif. #12,348 (Docket #52,048 Appeal), 2/6/99, 1 - 2.
7. Ltr. from James E. Fahey, Archivist, Military Div. History Research and Museum, 143 Speen St., Natick, Mass., 12/21/1990. "There's no mention of Tisdale in *MSSM in CW (Naval)* nor in Porter's *Naval History of the Civil War;* no mention in *O.R.* (navies)." Note: This is explicable for Tisdale's being credited to Connecticut on enlistment rather than to Mass., as he was then already living in Norwich, his hometown.
8. *Boston Sunday Post,* 7/1/06.

C. C. Hay

1. C. C. Hay, "Boy Company of the 45th Alabama," *Confederate Veteran X,* 1902, 353.

Also, his "About Another Youngest Soldier," *CV IX*, 1901, 352.
2. E. B. Long, *Day by Day*, 682.
3. *CV, X*, 1902, 354.
4. *CV, X*, 354.
5. This large statement is among CCH's Confederate Pension application papers notarized 7/5/1907 by J. P. Crawford, N. P., and sent to the writer by Hunter Phillips of Gadsden, Al., c. 1992.
6. Roster of Company "C" 45th Ala. (Presented by C. C. Hay).
7. Paraphrased from *Brief Historical Sketches of Military Organizations Raised in Alabama During the Civil War* (Ala. State Dept. of Archives & History), 1966, 656-7. Also, *Confederate Military History*, Vol. VII, 1899, 196-7. An indicator of the success of the 45th Alabama at Spring Hill is reflected in musician Abram F. Springsteen's capture here 11/29/64. (See Springsteen).
8. *CMH, VII*, 197.
9. C. C. Hay "Boy Company" *CV X*, 353-4. Supplied by Charles Sullivan of Perkinston, Ms.
10. We thank Hunter Phillips, of Gadsden, Al., for this late information.

Thomas L. F. Hubler

1. "The Youngest Drummer Boy," *Warsaw Daily Times*, Sept. 24, 1883.
2. Thomas Stephen Neel's letter to the Kosciusko County Historical Society from New London, Ohio, Sept. 1, 1983.
3. Dyer's *Compendium of the War of the Rebellion*, Vol. III, 1122-3.
4. *Ibid.*, 1123.
5. "Thomas Hubler Passes Away," *Warsaw Daily Times*, Mar. 22, 1913, 1.
6. "Society to Honor Youngest Soldier," *Times-Union*, Warsaw, In. May 27, 1978, 19. My particular appreciation goes to Doris L. Camden of Warsaw, In., for her supportive researches and genealogical "trench work."

James Lawrence Scholls Sr.

1. Entire credit for Scholls' identity and researches on him, his brother William, and his father Jacob goes to David M. Sullivan, of Rutland, Ma., a proven Civil War scholar of many original published articles excerpted from his forthcoming books, *An Illustrated History of the U. S. Marine Corps* and *An Illustrated History of the Confederate Marine Corps*. We are indebted to Mr. Sullivan for the details and much of the composition of this feature. Sullivan affirms that the maximum effective strength of the C.S.M.C. at any one time was 539 officers and men, as far as available records disclose.
2. Source: Granddaughter Ethel Marthine Scholl's application for membership in the D.A.R., herself a daughter of James L. Scholl, Jr. and 1909 native of Pensacola, Fla.
3. Register of Enlistments in the Regular Army, National Archives Microfilm MZ33. David M. Sullivan's "The Confederate Marines of Pensacola," *Pensacola History Illustrated* Vol. 2 Fall 1987, No. 4, 12, 16.
4. *Ibid.*, 17.
5. *Ibid.*, 17.
6. *Ibid.*, 18. Also, Sullivan's Wm. H. Scholls Note 2 on p. 21 that cites a Mar. 22, 1862 Order from Flag Officer French Forrest to Lt. Cmdg. V. Morgan of Frigate *United* (CONFEDERATE) *States*.—Forrest's Papers, Accession 2206, Southern Historical Collection, Univ. of N. C. at Chapel Hill.
7. *Ibid.*, 18. Sullivan accounts for William's key place in the Scholls saga—William returned to Pensacola, married Prudence A. Williams, of Pineapple, Fla., had a 25-year career there as a harbor pilot until July 1, 1890, when, at age 42, he enlisted in the United States Navy! He rose to Chief Master at Arms, serving on USS *Franklin, Louisiana, Pontiac, Georgia* and at the Naval Training Station at Newport, R. I. After sixteen enlistments of exemplary conduct and high proficiency, Chief Scholls retired Mar. 4, 1920, six weeks beyond age 72! After retiring to Orlando, William finally berthed at the U. S. Naval Home in Philadelphia. (Nat'l Personnel Records Center, St. Louis, Mo.)
8. NA, RG 45, Entry 426, Muster Rolls and Pay Rolls of Marine Detachments of the Confederate States Navy, Nat'l Archives.
9. The Florida State Archives, Dept. of State (R. A. Gray Bldg.), has a Sept. 8, 1921 letter of testimonial to James L. Scholls' presence at Appomattox written in behalf of Mrs. Rosa L. Scholls (then seeking her Confederate Widow's Pension) by Charles W.

Forum, an Assistant Secretary & Treasurer of Pensacola's Consolidated Grocery Company, to a Mr. Sinclair Weeks, Secretary, State Pension Board, Tallahassee, Fla. Significant points are made about J. L. S.'s service:

Mr. W. H. Scholls, who is now in the U. S. Navy, served with Jas. L. Scholls in the same company with him up to the surrender at Appomattox. Mr. Robert Simpson states that he was not in the same company but enlisted about the same time...and knows positively that Jas. L. Scholls served up until the surrender at Appomattox, having been associated with him immediately thereafter.

Mr. Scholls did not feel that during his lifetime he should accept a pension, but since his death his widow is in need of this assistance. [from Sullivan's findings]

10 "Robert Walter Scholls was a Federal Census taker for the 1900 Census," reports David Sullivan (11/19/93), "a fact I found quite by accident while going through that document. I noticed his name in the upper right corner of one of the pages. What became of him after that, I do not know."

11. Sullivan, "Confederate Marines at Pensacola, etc.," 21. J. L. Scholls Note 8 and Widow's Pension Claim, Application 22023, Form E "Affidavit to be Made by Comrade."

C. Perry Byam

1. C.P.B. C777 494 "Wm. W. Byam's Deposition A", p. 6, 10/29/08.
2. "A horrible occurrence is related as having transpired in the family of E. C. Byam, a former resident of this county [Fayette], well known to nearly all our citizens. While he was absent from home, his little daughter fell from a fence and was taken up for dead. She was buried before his return. He was so grief stricken as to feel that he could never be content until he had looked once more upon her sweet face. The body was taken up and the coffin opened, when it was discovered that it lay on its face and that the hands were both clutched full of hair, giving unmistakable evidence that the child was buried alive." From "Buried alive"—*The West Union Gazette, The Iowa Northwest,* Nov. 8, 1868, 3.
3. "Deposition A", 7.
4. Dyer, 1174-5.
5. C. P. B. on 12/6/06 in an 8-page letter to the Commissioner of Pensions wrote at length of a chronic diarrhea condition acquired in the war, citing some six doctors who had tried various attempts at a cure—some radical, like opium, alcoholic medicines, or severe enough remedies "to make a nervous wreck out of me." (Pension Records)
6. C. P. B. 12/6/06, 4.
7. One awkward brief episode in Perry's life made news, "Perry Byam in Trouble," *Fort Dodge Messenger,* 1/29/1891. On Jan. 28, 1891, he was arrested in Chicago for swindling. *The Chicago Times* "particulars" [not quite verbatim, here, for brevity] stated:

C. Perry Byam, "the youngest soldier of the Rebellion" and Harry Hart, formerly a wealthy Board of Trade man, were briefly locked up in the West North Avenue Station for an extensive land swindle in operation a short time.... Hart was the tool—the man who actually negotiated exchanges from his 4th floor 177 LaSalle Street office.

Daily, scores came by to see about exchanging their stock of goods for "desirable lots" he was offering. After striking a bargain, Hart made out papers and notified his superior that the transaction was advanced enough for a chattel-mortgage to be placed. An office rule was to give a man the full value in land of the price he set upon his business. As a matter of form, Byam and Hart sent an examiner to the place to be bought, who always reported the business was worth all that was asked for it, creating good feelings...it was a woman who ended things, one of Byam's dupes.... She had met Byam in St. Paul. Believing he was single and would redeem his promise of marriage, she consented and came with him to Chicago, where they took up quarters off Humboldt Park, near Byam's home. When, three days ago, she found he was married with several children, at 886 Humboldt Ave., she went to the police. [It was *some time* before this affair "blew-over," and, no doubt, Perry had some explaining to do at home. Likely, this untoward event accounts for, at least initially, C.P.B.'s being enamored with the far West Coast.]

8. C 777 494, Form 3-173, 1/4/1899 & 8/8/1901.
9. *The Tacoma News Tribune,* 2/9/1922. A 1" obit. Pat Clemons, of Montesano, Wash., offers (5/8/1997), "I called the Whiteside Chapel in Elma, Washington, to see if Charles Byam's name was listed in their burial records, but he was not. There are no Byams in the area phone book. He, perhaps, left McCleary, Washington, sometime after 1922." Also, "Youngest Soldier Dies," *Fort Dodge Chronicle & Messenger,* 2/10/22, 16. Another 1" obit. [No mention of place of burial.]
10. C. P. B.'s Pension File 777 494.

    N.B. Marion Martin Pliner, of Fort Dodge, gets high marks for her offerings on Byam. She notes (11/12/1994), "Great-Grandmother Elizabeth Kimball Martin had a sister Nancy Kimball Moore, who died in 1859 just after a daughter was born. A notice in *The Cedar Valley Times* (7/26/1860) announced (that Nancy's widowed husband) 'Martin Moore was married by Rev. E. C. Byam to Miss Mary Lavicy Webb at the residence of her father in Marion Township on the 24th' "

Joseph N. Fissell

1. Joseph Fissell's Death Certificate, File No. 438895, Primary Reg. Distr. No. 8227, Cincinnati, Ohio, Sept. 4, 1922. Two errors are noteworthy in this document: the date of birth is given as Sept. 1, 1851. His age is stated as 71. Joe's mother's name appears here as Katherine, though elsewhere it is usually with a C.
2. Dyer, 1517-18.
3. Notice of his funeral service *did* appear in the *Cincinnati Enquirer,* Sept. 3, 1922, 5. The Public Library of Cincinnati & Hamilton County assures the writer (8/31/93) "We could find no additional mention of his death in all the local papers during Sept. 1 - 5, 1922."
4. Joseph Fissell's Certificate of Discharge June 12, 1865. His age is stated here as 12 years. [from John F. Fissell].
5. Dyer, 1518.
6. Son John A. (Aug. 23, 1840-Mar. 1, 1913) married Frances Kirkendall 3/15/66 and by 1880 had three children. Son George H. married Alice Brown 5/17/66 and farmed on Darby Creek in Muhlenberg Twp. and by 1880 had six children. In the 1900 Census for Circleville, John and Frances had seven children (5 living); his sister Adaline, 32, was a schoolteacher, while John himself, 59, was Register Clerk at the Post Office; Son George, 55, was grocery clerk and Alice, 46, was a mother of ten, all living. John A., like Joseph, died of a cerebral hemorrhage. Son Wesley, a retired carpenter, died Dec. 29, 1914, at age 76. Son James, 64 and single, died of consumption May 14, 1906. Alice, 55, George's wife, died Dec. 6, 1902, of apoplexy. Joseph's sister Adeline F. Shook died Jan. 8, 1945, at age 97.

Albert Corydon White

1. Instances of boys ages 12 or 13 adding as many as five or six years to themselves to be set down as age "18" are known. One such fellow was George Ney Lockwood (Oct. 15, 1851-Sept. 28, 1945) of Los Angeles and Co. K., 9th Mich. Cavalry.
2. Dyer, 1526. Also, see Corydon E. Foote.
3. Pension Application Affidavit, Oct. 16-21, 1905.
4. List of Persons Assessed & Exempt a Poll Tax in the Town of Ware May 1, 1897, 40.
5. Pension Application Form 3-447 of Oct. 16, 1905.
6. Death Certificate, Pasco Cty, Fla., District #3805?, Precinct #38565, Registered No. 43, Apr. 11, 1928.
7. This statement from Mr. Wiley is recorded in Howard C. Aley's *A Heritage to Share: The Bicentennial History of Youngstown and Mahoning County, Ohio, 1975,* 193, under the heading "*Ladies Home Journal* credits Youngstown with 2nd Youngest Civil War Soldier." It comments further:

    Burch's *Directory,* first issued in 1886, lists Elias Wright as a restaurant, sample room, and billiard room operator at 105 W. Federal Street.

    N.B. The writer wishes to thank Tom Molocea, of Boardman, Ohio, for this (above) excerpt forwarded from *A Heritage to Share.* Further, the writer deeply appreciates the early photograph taken on Albert's first day in his new uniform, a picture sent to him by Larry Stevens, of Newark, Ohio, this image being found in *The Story of Sherman's Brigade,* Alliance, Ohio: Press of the Daily Review, 1897, 598, a history written and published by Wilbur F. Hinman "Late Lt. Colonel, 65th Ohio Regt., and author of the humorous and well received, long-time column "Corporal Si Klegg and his Pard," that thousands of Union Army veterans read in *The National Tribune-The Stars and Stripes,* printed from 1877 on at 44 G St., N.W., Wash., D. C.

William Orlanda Neubold Lea

1. S. A. R. Applic. Form (Rev. 1980) for John Stephen Avery (b. 11/5/59), son of Lowell & Reba Miller Avery (b. 1933, at Hackleburg, Ala.).
2. Elizabeth Avery Godwin's strategic "out of the blue" letter of 5/3/92 from Wilmington, NC, has made possible Lea's appearance in this report. She is Lowell's daughter.
3. Sarah Bernard's father was Daniel Bernard, a sergeant in NC's Continental Line (Amer. Rev.), a shoemaker, farmer, "and a Jew, according to his headstone," reports Lowell. "His wife was Mary Flores, whose father, Thomas Flores, was the first goldsmith/jeweler in Wilmington in the early 1770s. This means W. O. N. Lea's father was Jewish if he chose to be. I have other Jewish ancestry and am a Reformed Jew," reports Lowell.
4. *Charleston Daily Courier,* Apr. 15, 1861, 1. "Cmdr. Hartstein, naval officer at this port, sent a messenger to Major Anderson informing him that the ISABEL was at his command and waiting to take him off—to New York, if agreeable—and that, if he wished to go, he had better take advantage of the tide. Major Anderson accepted..." See also, "Death of an Old Pilot," *Charleston Daily Courier—Confederate States of America,* Thurs., July 25, 1861. "Capt. W. P. Lea, Sr., one of the oldest pilots of this city and for a number of years engaged as pilot on the steamer ISABEL, running between this port and Havanna, died on Wednesday at his residence here. Capt. Lea was widely known and highly esteemed...."
5. Lillian M. Moone, Director, Blandford Cemetery. City of Petersburg, Va. (letterhead) "Also recorded as Soldier."
6. There were several *Greyhounds* in Confederate service, as several states had their own Navy! Along the s.e. coast were hundreds of small vessels that sailed to Bermuda to purchase munitions and private supplies for the people, not usually for the government. In Pender Co., NC, were two ports (then)—Rick Inlet and old Topsail Inlet or McWilliams Landing & Scottsville. Most such vessels were hastily built, low in the water, 40' to 80' in length, carrying cotton & tobacco. Craft in Ga. & Fla. traded with the Bahamas. They were not usually registered; sometimes they were re-named and often flew English, German, Dutch or Mexican flags. Charles E. Lea, uncle to W.O.N., owned *Zig Zag* out of Charleston, a vessel not recorded in history books, but so well known in Charleston that an alley is named for it in the best residential section. The homes of W.O.N.L.'s father & grandfather are standing today in Charleston—in upper middle class areas. (L. S. Avery).
7. Marriage License No. 39, Dec. 6, 1883.
8. Lowell S. Avery letter, 10/27/96.

James E. Powell II

1. Offered by Granddaughter Jeanne Canty and supplied by Donna B. McAllister of Caratunk, Maine.
2. "The Powell Papers"—probable source, James I's Military Record and writings of Lena B. (Mrs. Malcolm) Merrill, a longtime Caratunk resident..
3. The writer *wants* to believe that, although James Sr., did leave home without any financial arrangement, the Army, knowing Lt. Powell was a married family man (the presence of Jimmy made it evident), would have required Powell to have made a token quarterly allowance to the wife and mother, up to their 1860 divorce. But this desideratum is not easily established.
4. Donna Bigelow McAllister, "A Boy Goes to War," *Morning Sentinel,* 1 M, Waterville, Maine, May 1 & 2, 1993. Mrs. McAllister and Major Timothy Bigelow (Benedict Arnold Expedition of 1775) have a common ancestor.
5. The 13th Missouri Vols. was formed largely from Home Guard Battalions of Majors Peabody, Van Horn, and Berry. The 13th

guarded a portion of the line of the Hannibal and St. Joseph R.R. until ordered to Lexington in late August. The 25th Missouri was sent to Gen. Grant and brigaded in McKean's Brigade, Prentiss' Division, Everett Peabody, its colonel; Van Horn, its Lt. Col.; Powell, its Major.

6. Dyer, 1332.
7. This passage, almost verbatim, is the writer's more tightly written version than wording in the O.R.
8. Written 106 years, to the day, after Great-grandfather's death. As of this date (4/6/1968), Maj. Powell's burial site is still undetermined. Burial records at Shiloh National Military Park and Cemetery have been checked, also those at Corinth, Miss., and Jefferson Barracks, Mo., but none shows him listed. Adjutant General's offices at Jefferson City, Mo., and Washington, D.C., have no burial record for him. I now have an inquiry out to the Chief of Support Services, Att: Headstone Branch, Memorial Div., Dept. of the Army, Washington, D. C. (Lena B. Merrill, Caratunk, Maine.)
9. Whether James II (Jimmy) ever received back pay due him from the Government for military service, is not clear from the various papers relating to this aspect of the pension applications on file. His mother DID apply for her son's back pay, but it would hardly appear that it was granted, since $20 per month pension for 3 sons would not seem adequate to have covered any extra for his services as a waitor on the battlefields to his father." (The Powell Papers).
   Junior's services to his father were roughly equivalent to what Body Servants in the Confederate Army often did for their owner-family's son(s), and *many* of these blacks drew "Class B" Confederate pensions later. J.S.H.
10. Coburn (Mar. 22, 1803-Jan. 4, 1885), a wealthy lumberman-surveyor of great executive ability, grew up in Skowhegan and was instrumental in the completion of the Somerset & Kennebec R.R. Of strictest integrity, a bachelor and Republican, he was elected a Civil War governor of Maine, 1863-64. Waterville's Coburn Classical Institute was renamed in his honor, as a recipient of his philanthropy.
11. "Powell Family Group" sheet (Powell Papers).
   N.B. We are also indebted to Mrs. Artie Heald of Solon and Harold Sterling of Falmouth.

Mancil V. Root

1. Official Service Record of Augustus Root, State Historical Society of Wisconsin, Madison, Wis. Age 40 on enlistment, Augustus was later reburied at the National Cemetery-Vicksburg, Miss., in Sect. F, Grave #673. (from Roll of Honor, Vol. #24, 97.
2. Official Service Record of Wilber M. Root, State Hist. Soc. of Wis.—"Official Notice—War Department May 19, 1892, received 5-23-92, decides that charges of desertion against Wilber M. Root, Co. C, 4th Wisconsin Cav. are erroneous and notation to that effect has been made on Official Records, War Dept." (These Remarks, most accommodatingly transcribed in the handwriting of Harold L. Miller, Reference Archivist, State Historical Society of Wisconsin, on Mar. 16, 1993)
3. Enlistment Papers—Mancil V. Root, Musician, mustered-in at Camp Randall, Madison, Wis. [State Hist. Soc. of Wis.]
4. "M. V. Root, Youngest Veteran of the Civil War, Dies of Injuries," *Cedar Rapids Gazette & Republican,* July 7, 1929, 1, 3.
5. Dyer, 1687.
6. "Original Discharge, presented by Adjutant General's Office 4-29-1889, [indicates] this soldier to have been discharged 7-12-65 at Jeffersonville, Indiana, etc." [State Hist. Soc. of Wis.]
7. *Cedar Rapids Gazette & Republican,* July 8, 1929. Funeral notice states "services were held today," and that he was born in Cleveland, Ohio. My appreciation to Norman Erickson of Cedar Rapids for his liaison support, June-July 1990, shortly following my viewing of M. V. Root's Pension Claim File at the National Archives Building.

George William McDonald

1. H.R. 820 Resolution that claimant's name [George W. McDonald] be placed on the pension roll at the rate of $30 per month. Rept. 741. Recorded Mar. 24, 1921 *Congr. Record,* Ltr. Fm. Invalid Division Apr.. 4, 1921. Pension Claims Folder #1,187, 491. Nat'l Archives, C 2628 945.

2. G. W. McDonald's Pension Folder—"Declaration for Original Invalid Pension—Special Act (Form 6-1897) Apr. 13, 1921.
3. Pension folder C 2628945.
4. Dyer, 1075.
5. An Oct. 10, 1930 copy of Mrs. Elizabeth B. McDonald's Death Certificate, Regis. Dist. No. 3107 Form V.S. No. 30B Evanston, Ill.
6. Directive (Copy) to Initiate $50 monthly pension fm Chief Clerk A. D. Wilkinson Approved Mar. 3, 1921 Pvt. No. 116 3/19/21.
7. G. W. MacDonald's Death Certificate Series No. 23, Regis'd No. 3819, Chicago. Filed 2/7/30 Sealed 10/14/30. As also "Supplemental Report: Correction of Death Record" (Ref. 3819-23)—Item No. 2 should read George William McDonald. Oct 14, 1930.
8. Cmdr. Chas. O. Brown's letters of 4/23/30 & 10/14/30—Pension Folder.
9. Selden M. French's 10/18/30 deposition notarized by John B. McDonald.
10. Pension C 2628 945 (same as #6)
11. G.W.M.'s Death Certif. (See Note 7)
12. See Note 8.
13. See Note 9.

My deep appreciation goes to Robert M. Coch of Flat Rock, Mich., who kindly disclosed to me the identity of G.W. M. pictured on p. 48 of *Illustrated Roster of the Department of Illinois G.A.R., 1914.*

Abram Furman Springsteen

1. "Eventful Life of Pioneer Is Ended," *Indianapolis Star,* Sept. 26, 1909.
2. *Ibid.*
3. "R. E. Springsteen, Former Postmaster 10 Years, Dies," *Indianapolis Star,* Mar. 3, 1931.
4. "Youngest Soldier of Union Army, Who Lived Here, Dies," *Indianapolis Star*, *Jan. 22, 1930.* [Indiana Biography—Indianapolis—Marion County Public Library].
5. *Ibid.*
6. *Sixty-Third Regiment Indiana Volunteers,* 593. [Indiana Regiments in the Civil War]. My gratitude to Jerry Wildenhaus, who is sleuthing the lives of all who served in the 63rd Indiana.
7. Dyer, 1133.
8. "Youngest Soldier" [Same as Note 4].
9. This letter was an original written by Abram and sent among many others to the writer from a fat file of his Federal employment records kept these 60 years at the Office of PersonnelManagement, OPF/EMF Access Unit, P. O. Box 18673, St. Louis, Mo 63118.
10. Visalia, California, happened to be the hometown of that state's eldest Civil War veteran, John "Scotty" Martin of Co. H, 79th New York Infantry, who died there Oct. 28, 1942, at age 111 years 11 months 4 days.
11. "Sixty-Third Holds Reunion," *Covington* (Indiana) *Friend,* Aug. 25, 1911, 4. [My appreciation to Jerry Wildenhaus, Dayton, Ohio.]
12. "Veterans of the 63rd Meet in Reunion," *Covington Friend,* Aug. 23, 1912, 1. [Again, we are indebted to Jerry Wildenhaus, who is attempting to account for what happened to each one who ever served in the 63rd Indiana Vols.]
13. The Shortridge letter was among many papers in Springsteen records at St. Louis, Mo.

Walter Xonpher Broome

1. Their first three children—Amy Jane "Amy," 1828-1898; Wm. Alexander, 1829-1905; Nancy "Nannie," b. 1830—were native S. Carolinians, while their fourth, Eliza C. "Leggie," 1834-1863, was a Mississippian. Nancy Robinson was a daughter of Alexander, Sr., the surname sometimes found spelled Robison. We are indebted to Dorothy A. Coleman (Mrs. James) Brewer (grt. Granddaughter of John Mathew B., Walter X's oldest sibling by their father's second wife, Betsy), of Raymond, Miss., for *all* genealogical data.
2. From *History of the Utica Baptist Church.*
3. Walter, both his wives and many Broomes of the next several generations are buried in the nearby Henry Easterland Family Cemetery located off Carpenter St. behind the Lena Price Breeden home. This ground today is better known as the Broome Cemetery, since only Broomes and their descendants are in marked graves. Mathew donated land in 1852 for Utica's school.
4. Some sources, however, affirm (Henry) Alonzo to have died at Petersburg, Va., in defense of Battery Gregg. Also, another son, William, in Co. K, 1st Miss. Lt. Art'y., was captured at Port Hudson.

5. It is not known if Cammie was married to a Howard earlier. (The Hinds County marriage license gave her name as Clifford Cammie Howard.). Cammie died in New Orleans and is buried there. (Dorothy Coleman Brewer Papers).
6. Lamar G. Broome (Oct. 1996) is an honorary comrade of an SCV camp in Vicksburg and on 5/9/1929 became a duly elected member of the Children of the Confederacy, Col. S. B. Thomas Chapter, Miss. Div. of the U. D. C. His sister, Dorothy Nell B. Pittman, lives in Metairie, La.
7. The near hanging of W. X. B. serves to remind us of a parallel case that ended in martyrdom—that of David Owen Dodd executed 1/8/64 at Little Rock, Ark., by Federal authorities. The story is in *Confederate Veteran,* X, 1902, 353.

   N.B. My appreciation to Scott Bubier of West Farmington, Maine, for his liaison effectiveness. My thanks to Gene (Mrs. Martin H.) Schroll of Vicksburg for her support.

Franklin D. Peck

1. Death Certificate Register No. 44, Michigan Dept. of Health, Division of Vital Statistics, October 7, 1936.
2. Dyer, 1410.
3. Dyer, 1378.
4. "Special Schedule—Surviving Soldiers, Sailors and Marines, and Widows" S. D. 4; E. E. 95; Michigan, 3 (c. 1890).
5. As of April, 1999, Peck's matrimonial and family life are known to the writer, who has reached Barbara Berry. Further details may be at the National Archives and will be useful in the event of a later edition of CB&T.

John Lincoln Clem

1. Mercedes Rodriguez, *The Drummer Boy John Lincoln Clem: The Civil War Years*—A (Master's) Thesis, Dept. of History, San Jose State Univ., June 1974, 6.
2. *Ibid.*
3. Classic instances of orphanhood, whether single or double, among soldierling musicians are Andrew Burke, Harry S. Duffield, Michael Burns, Geo. W. McDonald, R. B. Tyler, and James Crugom, to name a few of the more obvious. *Orphan,* tantamount to being a nuisance word like *invaluable,* is a child who has lost *either* or both parents.
4. Rodriguez, 14.
5. Capt. Robert E. Bassler, USN (Ret.) in "The Drummer Boy of Shiloh and Chickamauga," *The Royal Arch Mason,* 337-9, 350, offers, "He made his way to Columbus, Ohio, and attached himself to the 24th Ohio Volunteers. His stay was brief. Finding an uncle in the outfit, he knew his dream of soldiering would come to an abrupt conclusion if he were discovered."
6. *Official Roster of the State of Ohio in the War of the Rebellion* Vol. III, *21st-36th Regts- Infantry,* Cincinnati, 1886, 160 [Co. H, 24th O.V.I.] An overwhelming majority of surnames in this unit are pre-eminently German—J.S.H. Also, *Alphabetical Index,* 3106.
7. Dyer, 1291.
8. *Ibid.,* 1507.
9. Rodriguez, 6.
10. *Ibid.,* 30, Note 81. Interview with Clem's niece, Anita Sanderson, in Alexandria, Va., (8/12/1973), suggested that the boy's early drinking habit was "good for a laugh," but that, at length, Gen. Thomas, learning of this delinquency, called Johnny into his tent and asked point blank, "Do you want to be a man or go to the dogs?" Whereupon, reportedly the answer came, "General, I want to be a man." And he reformed from that moment, never again resuming the practice.
11. An aprocryphal story goes that upon the loss of his drum, he picked up a musket and cartridges from a dead soldier and began shooting at his foes. Clem never acknowledged this. It would seem unlikely for his small size and the fact that he was *already* nearly exhausted. See Rodriguez 41, Note 99.
12. *Official Roster,* etc., Vol. III, 140.
13. Greg Pavelka of Yankton, S. D., a Clem scholar, believes Clem first took up with the 22nd Michigan at Newark, Sept. 5-6, '62 by entraining with them there on their way from Cleveland to Covington, Ky. He builds a respectable case in *CWTI* (one of extremely few to do so) in his candid "Where Were You, Johnny Shiloh?" Jan. 1989, 35- 41.

14. Also, one may often read a consistent error "of the second magnitude" found in almost any article presenting the 1913 Joint 50th Reunion at Gettysburg—namely, Clem is extolled as youngest present. Even his name—*the* most famous Civil War Youth—gets convoluted. A classic instance is Elizabeth Lewis' "Reunion at Gettysburg," *Gettysburg Magazine,* July 1991, 127, "...while Colonel John N. Clemens, who ran away at age 10 to become the Drummer Boy of Shiloh," was youngest at 61." The 1913 pool was 55,000+ veterans! Some dozen *or more* of the 1845 veterans at Gettysburg 25 years later were of greater youth than Clem. For openers, See R. B. Tyler, b. 3/12/54, Benj. F. Williams, Frank Ironmonger, 3/4/53, and Nimshi Nuzum, 1/30/53.
15. This phraseology goes at least as far back as *Michigan in the War,* compiled by Jonathan Robertson, Adj. Gen., Lansing, Mich., 1882, 428. "In the 22nd was the waif Johnny Clem, who had straggled from his home with an Ohio regiment...the first that is known of this little wanderer of ten summers—small enough to live in a drum—he is beating the long roll for the 22nd. Although a mere child, he had learned all sorts of tricks from the soldiers, and did not fully yield obedience to all orders. One morning Colonel Doolittle (of 18th Mich.) heard a musket report in the vicinity of the camp, and, desirous of learning the cause, hurried out among the bushes and there found Johnny and his victim, a hog, nearby. "John," says the Colonel, "don't you know that it is against orders to kill hogs?" "*I know it. But, Colonel Doolittle, I don't intend to let any rebel hogs bite me!*"
16. Dan Clancy, *"Newark's Drummer Boy is Hero," Columbus Dispatch,* Columbus, Ohio, Oct. 4, 1959, 2 D. Displayed here are ten wartime poses of Johnny, Nos. 1 and 8 looking cherub-like; #7, "wearing a cut-down uniform of Gen. Grant's" after being made a Sgt.' #8 displaying a drum harness (M. Brady photo), wearing a dress uniform newly tailored in Chicago that he posed in while on furlough in Newark in '63; #4 holding rifled musket he used to shoot a C.S.A. colonel; #5 standing beside a regular sword that's nearly shoulder high in '64; #6 sporting a new special uniform with wide pants stripes & Sgt. chevrons paid for by Newark ladies; #10 wearing custom fitted sword.
17. Rodriguez, 48.
18. *The Washington Post* (2/20/1927) carried a reference to an alleged incident—"Eight years following *the* incident, when Clem was a 2d Lieutenant stationed at Fort Brown, Texas, he chanced to meet a prominent lawyer from Brownsville. The two began to reminisce on their Civil War exploits. Upon Clem's mentioning he had shot a Confederate colonel at Chickamauga, the lawyer exclaimed, 'So *you* are the damned little devil that did it!' the lawyer was the colonel Johnny had shot. (Note 117 on p. 50 of Rodriguez's Master's Thesis). [The pointless anonymity effectually discredits (routs) this STORY!—J.S.H.
19. Pavelka, *C.W.T.I.,* 39.
20. *Ibid.*, 40.
21. Rodriguez, 52, Note 126.
22. *Ibid.,* 52.
23. *Ibid.*, 53, Note 128.
24. "General Clem 'Captured' by Four Women While Home on Furlough, in War Time..." "*Licking County Advocate,* Oct. 9, 1915, (from Licking County Hist. Soc. 3/13/1996). Helen King (Mrs. Edward) Spangler of Coshocton; Libbie Sprague (Mrs. John) Hamilton who is living; Mary Warner (Mrs. Fred H.) Wilson; and Mary Ocheltree (Mrs. A. R.) Kennedy were pictured with Clem.
25. This more serious wound is mentioned in Arthur Budd's "The Drummer Boy of Chickamauga," *The Newark American Tribune,* n.d. (in JLC Coll., Newark, O.)
26. Rodriguez, 55, Note 134.
27. *Ibid.*, 58, Note 139 (condensed)—Once, while in charge of a squad sent out to apprehend cattle thieves, he trailed them to the Mexican Border. The bandits crossed the Rio Grande and then made insulting gestures to the American soldiers. Lt. Clem chased them across the Border. Officially, he was reprimanded for thoughtless actions by his Dept. Commander, Gen. E. O. C. Ord, but penciled in the margin was "Good boy, Johnny. Do it again."
28. Though Clem converted from Catholicism to Episcopalianism, his daughter took the

veil of the Carmelite Order. As Sister Anne, she resided many years at a convent in Reno, Nevada.

29. Pavelka, 41.

Casper Androus Ricks

1. *History and Genealogy of the Ricks Family in America,* Section V, 598-603, sent 3/30/91 by Bob Hill, of Lufkin, realtor & grt.-grt.-grandson of C.A.R.
2. Miriam Havard Tatum, "About an Editor, C. A. Ricks," *River Road: Remembering, Angelina Free Press,* Diboll, Texas, (year?).
3. Bob Hill affirms, "I have been unable to find any record of his attending school in Natchitoches, La., but I've found nothing to say he didn't either. Nor can I find any record of a Major Harry Porter, who was provost marshall at New Orleans; I am told there is no record of a Camp Werton as a prison at or near Indianapolis." Further, the writer is indebted to Bob Hill, of Lufkin, for an excerpt of the 1850 Census for the City of Louisville, County of Jefferson, Kentucky, p. 159 [by Wm. P(?)reston Sohustou], establishing John W. Ricks as Casper's father.
4. An Apr. 4, 1991 letter from Gladys (Mrs. Carl G. T.) Liese, of Lufkin (a non-relative).

N.B. My appreciation to Geneva Raley, great-granddaughter, of Orange, Texas, for 1928 and 1937 news clippings; also, to Mr. George Ricks of Lufkin. My thanks to Joe Murray of *The Lufkin Daily News.*

We are indebted to DeLois Broussard, of Port Neches, for her patience, clarifications and long-standing support in bringing this family history off and giving it due placement here.

Thomas W. Daniel

1. The Ninth Georgia Infantry Records copies forwarded to the writer by John Rix Seibert II, Sept. 21, 1993.
2. W. J. Ingram's Witness Deposition in R. P. Daniel's Pension Application, Cartersville, Bartow County, Ga., Apr. 18, 1902.
3. Sara Dunway, of the Georgia, Division, U.D.C. , wrote John Rix Seibert II on Feb. 22, 1990, "There are no complete records on Southern Crosses of Honor." Nor do service or S. C. of Honor records for any of these four Daniel veterans appear to be in the holdings of the National Headquarters of the U. D. C. in Richmond, Va. Hence, we are fortunate today for the initiative and the research that have gone into this offering from John Rix Seibert II of Akron, Ohio.

Willie H. Bush

1. "Dr. A. K. Bush Is Dead," *Chehalis Valley Vidette,* 11/21/1902. This reveals that at least one high-ranking Union general was aware of both father and son. Willie declined, wishing to follow A. K. B.'s interests, wherever they led.
2. *Ibid.*
3. Dyer, 1121.
4. Dyer, 1112. *Vidette* 11/21/02.
5. *Vidette,* A. K. B. obituary.
6. Mark M. Boatner III, *The Civil War Dictionary,* 1959, 870. Originally (Apr. '63) the name Invalid Corps coincided with "Inspected-Condemned" stamped on worn-out government equipment & animals, hence the name was officially altered to VRC in Mar. '64. Its units consisted of officers and men unfit for full combat duty but who could perform limited infantry service. Those who could handle a weapon were in the 1st Bn. for guard duty. The worst crippled formed 2nd Bn. and were nurses and cooks around hospitals. [6 cos. of the 1st Bn. & 4 fm the 2nd Bn. made a Regt. in the Corps after Sept .'63].
7. *Vidette,* 11/21/02; also *Montesano Vidette,* 10/27/38.
8. The 11th Regiment Invalid Corps (later V.R.C.) org. at Elmira as early as Oct. 10, 1863. It was mustered out by detachments June 29 thru Nov. 23, 1865. At Elmira's Woodlawn National Cemetery rests dust of 2,963 C.S.A. prisoners, 322 Union veterans, 1000 WWII veterans.
9. My primary deep appreciation goes to Robert Coch, of Flat Rock, Michigan, who on Oct. 10, 1995, enclosed a photocopy of a c.d.v. of Willie Bush from the collection of Mark Weldon, of Fort Wayne, to whom I am indebted for the identity of Mick Kissick, of Albany, Indiana, who had purchased an original c.d.v. of both W.H.B. *and* A.K.B. from a pawn shop some years ago. Kissick kindly shared a photo of Willie "blown up"

from his c.d.v. *and* a fragment from A.K.B.'s Pension Record (disclosing Montesano, Washington).

10. Copy of a Mar. 10, 1866 pension application (#98,775) stamped July 2, 1897, at Pension Office.
11. In A. K. B.'s Pension Record is a Jan. 5, 1903 witnessed statement by the widowed 2nd wife Julia that her husband had "also served as 2nd Lt. in 2nd U. S. Art. from Mar. 14, 1867 to Feb. 28, 1869." ...one of very few times/places this post bellum tour of duty appears to be mentioned.
12. We are indebted for data & articles supplied by Charles H. Fattig, of McCleary, Washington, and the McCleary Museum, who sedulously "dug" for and supplied source stories on the Bushes. Further, a large thanks must go to Alex Goff, creative nonfictionist, for his ground-breaking featurette on Willie in the 3/28/97 *Olympian,* and to Steve Willis, of McCleary, for his liaison efforts.
13. *Vidette,* 5/31/1895.
14. *The Chehalis Valley Historian* Vol. 14 No. 1 Spring 1997, 2.
15. "Monte Pioneers Fifty Years Wed," *Vidette,* 5/3/1935.
16. *South-western Washington,* etc. (Pacific Publishing Co.), Olympia, 1890, 157. *The Vidette* for 10/27/38 (obit) cites "the fish war of 1887 that resulted when Grays Harbor was invaded by the "gill netters" of Astoria, "the kingfishes of the Columbia Rr. fisheries," as W. H. B. termed them, to whom the local trap fishermen then "played a very second fiddle." In a battle on the lower harbor, word was that two gill netters were killed and 1 badly wounded. Sheriff Bush, with a 15-man posse arrested 13 men who were in a bunkhouse in Aberdeen—part of 19 the grand jury indicted—the whole episode remarkable for lack of violence.
17. *Vidette,* 10/12/1933; 5/11/1933.
18. *Vidette,* 6/7/1912.
19. *Vidette,* 10/12/1933.
20. "They're Back at the Old Press Again," *Montesano Vidette,* 10/12/1933; 1/27/1983.

Nimshi Nuzum

1. Hoar, *South's Last Boys,* 46.

Reginald Fairfax Nicholson

1. Somerville, son of Maj. A. A. and Helen Bache (Lispinard) Nicholson, was appointed Midshipman June 21, 1839, and passed Midshipman July 2, 1845; he was promoted to Lt. Commander July 16, 1862, to Commander Jan. 2, 1863, to Captain June 1870, and to Commodore January 1880. He retired in April 1881. *Who was Who in America,* Vol. 1 (5th pr.), 898. He was also a brother of A. F. Nicholson, of the U. S. M. C. (*Army & Navy Register,* 6 May 1905). My appreciation to Alice S. Creighton, Head, Special Collections Dept., The Nimitz Library, U. S. Naval Academy, Annapolis, Md.
2. *Dictionary of American Biography,* Vol. 13, New York: Scribner's, 1934. 508-9. In the War with Spain, William was on Gen. Sanger's staff as a major and chief ordinance officer. He commanded the 11th Cavalry in Mexico during Pershing's expedition. In World War I he commanded the first training camp at Camp Meade. He distinguished himself in the Avocourt sector, the Meuse-Argonne offensive, and in the Bois Belleu-Cote sector until the Armistice.
3. *Civil War Naval Chronology 1861-1865* (Washington: Naval History Div., Navy Department, 1971) II-57 & II-74.
4. Adm. Evans retired, after sailing the Great White Fleet around the world, on Aug. 18, 1908.
5. New York *Times,* Dec. 20, 1939.
6. If we recall Lt. George Dewey, who had served extensively under David Farragut in the Union blockade, to whose eyes Capt. Malancthon Smith entrusted the nighttime conning of his powerful USS *Mississippi* past Forts Jackson and St. Philip—Dewey, who, for his victory at Manila Bay (May 2, 1898), (1) received the public thanks of Congress, (2) was awarded the special rank of "Admiral of the Navy," and (3) was made exempt from compulsory retirement and *never* did retire until his death Jan. 16, 1917, then we realize that Admiral Dewey himself was second only to Nicholson in being the last active duty Civil War officer, thus conferring upon Gen. Clem third place. But Dewey, like Robley Evans, already held an officer's commission, as a Civil War sailor.

Dr. Robert Blake Tyler

1. The brilliant orator-statesman James Cabell Breckinridge (1821-1875), a native of Lexington, Ky., and a major (3rd Ky. Vols.) in the Mexican War, was nominated in June 1860 at Baltimore for president by the Seceding Delegates (one of two Southern splits) of the Democratic Party. Ironically, the Breckinridge platform avowed to carry slavery into the Territories at any cost. He helped organize the provisional government of Confederate Kentucky. In November 1861 he was made a brigadier general under Albert S. Johnston and served well at Shiloh. Defending Vicksburg, he was promoted to major general. In Jubal Early's raid on D. C., Breckinridge was a division commander at Murfreesboro and Cold Harbor. He was *the* most popular man in Kentucky during 1868-1875.
2. *Civil War Naval Chronology 1861-1865,* 111-118.
3. *American Naval Fighting Ships,* Vol. IV, 132.
4. *Ibid.,* 521.
5. Benj. Franklin Williams (Mar. 7, 1854-Aug. 26, 1943) of Louvale, Ga., a Reb, was next to youngest at Gettysburg's Diamond Reunion.
6. Dr. Tyler's sixty-five years in medicine remind us that *the* Civil War veteran who piled up the longest medical practice was Bethel, Ohio's "Dean of American Physicians," Dr. William Eberle Thompson (July 6, 1835-Feb. 19, 1940) who doctored from 1860 to 1940, a little matter of eighty years.

William Lee Owens

1. Wm. L. Owens' Pension Record, Florida State Archives, Tallahassee, Fla.
2. *Ibid.*
3. Dyer, 631, 695.
4. Worthy of note in George Reddick's letter is this further comment: "My Uncle Henry W. Reddick, was in the C.S. A. '61 to '65 and reached age 99 years when he died. He is interred at the same Early Cemetery at Niceville as Wm. L. Owens is, but has no flag." [The writer apologizes for omitting Mr. Reddick from his *South's Last Boys in Gray* (1986).]
5. Hoar, *SLBG,* 41, 45, 532.

James W. Harper

1. Confederate Pension Records Section, Florida State Archives,Tallahassee.
2. Hoar, *SLBG,* 46.

Lewis Henry Easterly

1. John Alexander Logan (Feb. 9, 1826-Dec. 26, 1886) was born in Jackson County, Il., the son of Dr. John and Elizabeth Jenkins Logan. In 1862, he was Brig. Gen. of Illinois Volunteers.
2. Dyer, 1047.
3. This description fits the *Sultana* disaster of Apr. 27, 1865, about 60 miles north of Memphis. Some 1647 humans lost their lives, nearly all of them weakened prisoners just liberated. *If* this *was* Baughman's vessel, then we can categorically pronounce *him* the last survivor of that most tragic sea disaster. Previously (16 years earlier, 1972) the writer had understood that Wm. Norton, 87, of Darrowsville, Ohio, who died Dec. 30, 1928, was the last survivor. Baughman died Apr. 14, 1942, at 95—Co. B., 58th Ohio.
4. David Easterly closed his 1976 letter by adding, "My wife Flora and I ate dinner in Farmington, Maine, at the Exchange Hotel. She had sold Walk-Easy Shoes and arch supports in Maine. She and her companion, Ruth Thompson, from North Carolina, had rooms at Senator Margaret Chase Smith's parents' home and she wanted to visit them again, but they were not at home."
5. *Los Angeles Evening Express,* May 1, 1930.
6. Ronald T. Clemmons, "Away Out West in Dixie," *Confederate Veteran,* July-Aug. 1989, 28. Trinidad's Wm. Messer (Aug. 4, 1848-Aug. 20, 1941) was there with Easterly to greet the 35 Old Reb stalwarts.
7. *Gunnison News Champion and Gunnison Republican,* July 22, 1943, 1-2.

Note: I wish to express my appreciation to Ruth (Mrs. James) Stell of Gunnison and to Mrs. Olive R. Gifford, Circulation-Reserve Librarian at Western State College, Gunnison (retired 1982) for their support. Finally, Mrs. Gifford, in her Aug. 8, 1989 letter from Gunnison enables us to round out our story as follows:

David Howard Easterly
July 17, 1891-July 5, 1989

Born on the original homestead ranch (Ohio Creek), David *was* the youngest of five. After high school he attended two years of Agricultural College at Fort Collins, now Colorado State University. In 1915 he married Veta M. Marshall of another pioneer Gunnison family. Their three children were Irva M. Tunstall, Karl H., and Verald Lewis Easterly. In 1924 they moved to Detroit, where David was a tool and die maker for the Model A Ford. But in 1929 events returned them to Gunnison. In World War II Veta, 48, died. David repaired ships at the Navy yards at Pearl Harbor. He married Flora Hallowell of Gunnison in August 1943 in Hawaii. David worked for Coleman Motors in Littleton, Colorado, the post-war years. In retirement he and Flora traveled widely. At 97, Flora died July 30, 1981, David then ending a 66-year "matrimonial marathon." He was a life member of the I.O.O.F. from 1919 on and a longtime and eldest parishioner of St. George's Episcopal Church.

David (namesake for his father's Uncle David who died at Shiloh), who has this summer died 124 years after the Civil War ended, leaves a posterity of 3-5-4-2...and rather few remaining Real Sons of Union Army veterans.

Gunnison Country Times, Aug. 2, 1989, 2.

Benjamin Franklin Williams

1. McLeod's interview is told under the heading "Ran Yankees Two Miles But Was Leading Them.": Biographic data here discloses Atlanta, Ga. Confederate B. Mar. 1853. Stewart Co."
2. In her Nov. 4, 1991 letter from Dept. Of Archives & History, Atlanta, Ga., Charlotte Ray reported: "I have not been able to locate the birth and death dates for Benj. Fr. Williams. I checked various Civil War indices and did not find anything. You could write the Georgia Vital Records at 47 Trinity Ave., Atlanta, requesting his death certif. Copy."
3. As early as 1976, while pouring through data identifying Georgia's last Confederate pensioners of the 1940s county by county (at 330 Capitol Ave., S.E.), I learned of one Benjamin Franklin McCoy, of Atlanta, who served in Co. A., 19th Georgia Infy., and died June 29, 1942, at age 89...extremely young to have died so late! For months in 1985 I was haunted by a suspicion that McCoy and Williams quite possibly might be the same Old Reb.
4. Confirmation of Sgt. R. B. Hooper as a soldier of the American Revolution may be found in H. E. Terrill and S. R. Dixon's *History of Stewart County, Georgia,* Vol. I, 434; in Flora Hooper Collier's *Hooper Genealogy—A Southern Branch,* 6, 13, 23, 199, 201; in National Archives, Record Group No. 15A (No. S-16418), Wash., D. C.; in the D. A. R. Patriot Index, 341. Richard B. Hooper, 107, is believed buried in an unmarked grave at Armor Cemetery, the Brooklyn-Louvale Community (*Stewart County History, Vol. II)* east of town.
5. Mary Galloway, President of Cordele Chapter 793, U. D. C., accompanied the Pilchers and the writer on 6/5/84 visiting the gravesite of "Daddy" & Effie Bush at Fitzgerald's Evergreen Cem. entirely surrounded by huge magnolias. Mary was instrumental & crucial to my research on John C. Fenn (1846-1948), 19th Ga. Cav., buried so. of Cordele. *South's Last Boys in Gray, 344-6.*
6. John A. Shierling, Sr., ex-prisoner at Rock Island, walked, caught rides, and begged food until he reached home. Walking with him were Thos. Jeff. Sherman, George Hallidy, and Will Overly.
7. A roll dated Oct. 16, 1864, Petersburg, Va., shows N.J.W. present. Lillian Henderson, *Roster of the Confederate Soldiers of Georgia 1861-1865,* Hapeville, Ga., Longino & Porter, Inc., 1964, 333.
8. "Funeral Services for Benjamin F. Williams held Sunday, Aug. 29," *The Stewart Webster Journal,* Sept. 2, 1943.
9. Finally, in her 9/4 & 9/16/1996 letters from Savannah, Ga., Lucile Wilson (Mrs. Ralph A.) Jackson, 72, daughter of Robena or "Bena," offers: "I believe Grandfather has his father's uniform on in the picture I'm sending. B. F. W. lived with us where my father's ice cream company was in Americus awhile and in Tybee in 1936. I have a sister, Joanne W. Boop, of Riverdale, Ga., and a brother, Harry F. Wilson, in Pompano Beach, Fl. Grace (Mrs. Herman) Gips) in

Houston, Tx., says her father (my Uncle Bass) told her stories from the war and that Tobe, at one time, considered settling in Texas and even went out there *briefly* in the 1870s."

Charles E. Merrick

1. Charles E. Merrick's Military Record— C 257 5785; Cert. No. 245 839; Applic. No. 403, 558.
2. Dyer, 1102. Also, Illinois Federal Census Report—1860 & Illinois State Archives Civil War Service Report.
3. "Notes with the G.A.R., " *The Washington Times,* Wash., D. C., Sept. 23, 1936, 2. Death Certificate, Distr. No. 1992; Registrar's No. 714—M 620, Los Angeles.

David Wood

1. Frances and Dorothy Wood, *I Hauled These Mountains in Here,* Caldwell, Idaho: The Caxton Printers, Ltd., 1977, 14.
2. Wood's Independent Company [Kansas Rangers] was a synonym for his Independent Battalion of Missouri Cavalry (Union Rangers, Co. A), afterward Sixth Regt. Missouri Cavalry, Co. G. Wm. Frayne Amann, *Personnel of the Civil War,* Vol. II, 1961, 164.
3. *I Hauled,* 14-18.
4. *Ibid.,* 18, 19.
5. *Ibid.,* 23
6. *Ibid.,* 183-4. Dave Wood took out ads in *Solid Muldoon* and, overall, held to a life friendship with Dave Day. At least once, however, (1886) this relationship was strained. A temporary anthracite coal shortage precipitated Day into threatening to set up a rival freight line from Denver to Ouray. Wood's rates were the lowest available, including those of the Denver & Rio Grande RR. (238, 240, 242).
7. *I Hauled,* 274.
8. *Ibid.,* 324. Arthur Osbourne Ridgway (1870-1953), a Lawrence, Kansas, native and engineering consultant for western railroads; author of eight books.
9. Mark Tooley, "End of an Era: The 75th Reunion at Gettysburg," *The Gettysburg Magazine,* July 1, 1992, 120.
10. The five youngest at Gettysburg in 1938 were: Robert B. Tyler of Joplin, Mo., b. March 12, 1854; Benj. Fr. Williams of Louvale & Decatur, Ga., b. Mar. 7, 1854; Chas. E. Merrick of Los Angeles, b. March 4, 1854; Nimshi Nuzum of Fairmont, W. Va., b. Dec. 30, 1853; Frank M. Ironmonger, b. Mar. 4, 1853.

Gilbert VanZandt

1. VanZandt's Military Record, National Archives, Wash., D. C.
2. "Civil War Drummer Boy—Gilbert VanZandt of K. C. Mo.," *Kansas City Star,* June 7, 1929, 60.
3. *Kansas City Star,* 60.
4. "Gilbert VanZandt, " *The San Francisco Chronicle,* Oct. 20, 1901, 145.
5. *Chronicle,* 145.
6. Hoar, "Edward A. Paddock," *The North's Last Boys in Blue.* The Union Army's second tallest man had been David Van Buskirk, 6' 10 " of Indiana. Pat Bane of Green County, Pa., and the 22nd Pa. Cav., who exceeded seven feet, was the tallest in the Northern forces, while the tallest Reb was Henry C. Thurston, 7' 7", of Bonham, Texas. Thurston served in the Texas Rangers and in Co. I, 4th Mo. Cav. He fought at Elkhorn Tavern [Pea Ridge], was wounded at Poison Springs, Ark., and during Gen. Price's Missouri Raid, was grazed by a bullet atop his head. *Civil War times Illus.,* No. 1974, 42. See also Hoar, *The South's Last Boys in Gray,* 426-7. The tallest man was Robert Wadlow, 8' 11", of Alton, Ill. He died at age 22 in 1940. "Tallest Man Had a Big Heart" by David Fox , *Kennebec Journal,* Augusta, Me., Sept. 8, 1984, 10.
7. *Kansas City Star,* 61.
8. 1860 U. S. Census of Clinton Co., Ohio—Liberty Township (P. O. Port William). Taken 6/29/1860, p. 28, Reel 95.
9. "VanZandt, Gilbert—Death," *Kansas City Star,* Oct. 5, 1944, 146.
10. Hoar, *North's Last Boys* ("Jonathan Hollingsworth").
11. *Chronicle,* 145.
12. *Star,* Oct. 5, 1944, 146.
13. "Youngest Union Soldier," Ripley's *Believe It or Not* once featured Gilbert VanZandt.

The Wall Brothers

1. Hester B. Jackson, *Surry County Soldiers in the Civil War,* Charlotte, N.C., 1992, 414.

2. Holland D. Warren, *Warrens and Related Families of North Carolina and Virginia* (Wall Family), 1990, 360.
3. Warren, 362. Also, "Family Record—Burrel(l) T. Wall/Elizabeth 'Betty' Carter."
4. Jackson, 180-2.
5. Surry County Genealogical Assoc., *The Heritage of Surry County, North Carolina,* Vol. II, (Family Histories—Helen Wall #643), 1994, 390.
6. *Heritage of Surry,* Vol. II, (Fam. Hist.-Michael Grant Wall #646).
7. Hoar, *SLBG,* 47-8.
8. *Heritage of Surry,* Vol. II, M. Grant Wall #646, 391-2.

   Other sources: William Hastings Wall Death Certif. No. 12600, Registr. Dist. No. 86-50, Certif. #26, 4/13/1945.

   N.B. The writer pays special thanks to Tanya Morrisett of Ithaca, N.Y., and to Betty H. Fletcher of State Road, N.C., supportive descendant kin. With Barry Price, Hoar also enjoyed a pleasant late-morning visit at the agrarian home of Dale and Eloise Wall in rural Dobson on May 29th 1996, strawberries then much in season!

Charles Knecht

1. This nom de guerre may be found early in Twain's sardonic satire "The Private History of a Campaign That Failed." Samuel L. Clemens was a 2nd LT. in the Confederate Army for two whole weeks in 1861 before skedaddling to Nevada, where he rode out much of the war on the staff of the *Virginia City Enterprise.* Twain's entire family were staunchly pro-Union. The essential irrationality and abysmal idiocy of war are *tren*chantly articulated in one of the literary world's (& Twain's) most uncompromising reductios ad absurdums ever.
2. Benton Cadets—Independent Company Infantry was organized at St. Louis, Mo., Sept. & Oct., 1861. Fremont's Campaign in Missouri September to November 1861. Duty at Rolla till Jan. 1862. Mustered out Jan. 8, 1862. Dyer's, 1340. (Apparently Charles served out his Company A's entire tour, after all).
3. "Just for the record" it might prove illuminating to share a Mar. 24, 1983 reply from A. A. Schatz, Director, Administrative Service, Dept. of Veterans Benefits, V. A., Washington, D. C. 20420:

   Dear Mr. Hoar: RE: Civil War pension record of Charles Knecht

   Veterans Administration records for Charles Knecht, identified by File number XC 2634 460, were retired to the Federal Archives and Records Center in Suitland, Maryland. Personnel from the Center informed us that these records were lost. We conducted a nationwide search for Mr. Knecht's records to no avail. If we are able to locate his records in the future, we will notify you. I apologize for any inconvenience this may cause you.
4. Out of curiosity [What wrote this study!], fifteen years later the writer wrote to The Ozarks Methodist Manor to learn "How long after my contact with Mr. Roster did this grand old man live?" In her Aug. 24, 1987 reply, Ethelyn French, Office Manager, supplied Mr. Roster's dates. It is *noteworthy* that Wm. H. Roster also lived to age 94 and was within 65 days of attaining his friend's final age. "Bill" Roster has a daughter, Wilma Roster, who lives at the Manor now.
5. Diana Jenkins, Libn., James Mem. Library, St. James, Mo., ltr. 7/13/1991.
6. His pallbearers were William H. Roster, Sherman Bishop, Dr. F. J. Towell, Paul Winter, Otta Backer, Wm. T. Copeland, & W. W. Jackson, altn. Knecht's survivors were his widow; a niece Hanna Gregory; four nephews—Ted Herman of Creve Coeur, Mo.; Ernie Fisher, St. Louis; Adolph Herman, Kansas City, Mo., and Louis Herman, St. Louis, and a sister-in-law, Clara Kendall of St. James.

Susan Haines Clayton

1. *Medford Mail Tribune,* Mar. 8 & 9, 1948.
2. Grace E. Andrews, "Only Living Civil War Nurse, Mrs. Sue Clayton, in 95th Year of Adventurous Life," *Ashland Daily Tidings,* Ashland, Ore., Dec. 18, 1945.
3. (There is a strong likelihood that during 1869-75 the young Mrs. Clayton may have met) Mary Ann Ball Bickerdyke (July 19, 1817-Nov. 8, 1901), a native of Mount Vernon, Ohio, a super-human, who was the most widely beloved and most energetic nurse of the Civil War. She schooled four

years at Oberlin College and trained for nursing under Dr. Reuben Mussey in Cincinnati. In April 1847 she married Robert Bickerdyke. In 1856 they moved to Galesburg, Ill., where he died in 1858. Mrs. Bickerdyke, with $500 worth of supplies put at her disposal, began her immense task in regimental hospitals at Cairo, Ill. She was in nineteen battles with Armies of the Ohio, the Tennessee, and the Cumberland. Highly efficient, she ministered to men on the fields, at the operating tables, from diet kitchens often superintending hospitals, until Mar. 20, 1865. She was a particular favorite of Generals Grant and Sherman. She established army laundries. In 1867 she started a movement that encouraged ex-soldiers to go west. By her influence about 300 families migrated to Kansas, she herself settling in Salina. She died in her son's home at Bunker Hill, Kansas, and was buried at Galesburg, Ill.

Allen Johnson, ed. *Dictionary of American Biography,* II, 237-38.

4. This feature appeared in *Oregon Historical Quarterly,* Summer 1983, Vol. 84, No. 2, 206-210.

James Crugom, Jr.

1. James Crugom, Sr., Service Certificate 71591-5, State Historical Society of Wisconsin, Madison, Wis. May 15, 1991. Also, *Wisconsin Volunteers,* 219.
2. James Crugom, Jr., Service Certificate 71591-6, State Historical Society of Wisconsin, Madison, Wis., May 15, 1991.
3. Dyer, 1673.
4. Charles O. Brown Pension Record C 2513 379, Applic. No. 1273405.
5. G. Nawrocki, Chief, Med. Admin. Service, V.A. Hospital, Hines, Ill. Sept. 24, 1973.

John Hance Osteen

1. Hoar, *SLBG,* 361.
2. J. Hance Osteen's Florida C.S.A. Pension File (#A08946).
3. The 1850 Columbia County, Georgia, Census Record (from Aleene Markham Havird, of Lake City & from (Samuel) Dewey Osteen—Mt. Horeb Baptist Church Cemetery Records).
4. Pension File #A08946, 9/4/1937. Also, officially, Florida House Bill No. 1015, an Act Granting a Confederate Pension 6/4/1941.
5. Marriage Certif. copy. Married by D. C. Beach, J. P. Witnesses: Mr. & Mrs. W. W. Hines, Mr. & Mrs. J. A. Osteen, Mrs. Fannie Hines, Henry Hines.
6. Karen Voyles, "A Son of a Son of the South," *The Gainesville Sun,* 1D, 9/29/1990.

N. B. The late discovery of Willie H. Bush of Montesano, Washington, certainly an *unknown* of plausible veteran status, never drew a pension based on his Civil War service, which "J. Hance" did achieve. The writer feels that the opening statements of this Osteen profile should be allowed to "stand."

The Brothers Keith

1. Frances L. Keith, great-granddaughter of Geo. Wash. K. of Tallahassee, offers (10/28/96), further, "The three boys' mother Nancy later married a James Paul. Tradition says that Mr. Paul would not let her keep her children.
2. Hartman, "Home Guard and Miscellaneous Units," *Biographical Rosters,* 2148... "Keith, George W. (b. 1/17/49 [sic] Holmes Co.) has the comment "Does not appear on any rolls..." [The question arises—How extensive (sparse) could clerical work have been in various H. G. companies? Who kept such records, or had sufficient time to?]
3. Frances L. Keith (b. 1937)—Daughter of Martha M. Margie Marshall and George Allen Keith, a son of John A. D. Keith (& wife Lena F.), a son of Geo. Wash. K.—her letter of 2/21/94 with her "Descendancy Chart," 1-4. Her document is the soundest genealogical study available, the only record that offers accurately the birthdates of all three brothers.
4. *Graceville News,* Graceville, 1/24/46; 1/23/47; 1/30/49; 1/25/51.
5. *SLBG,* 460-1.
6. Frances L. Keith, "Descendancy Chart."
7. Some source(s) say(s) he had 14 children by his first two wives.
8. *SLBG,* 394-5.
9. A Florida CSA Pension File #A10405 for James S. Keith contains 18 sheets of documents evidencing his lifelong seriousness about his idealized service in Capt. Sam Grantham's H. G. Company created in late

summer 1863 in Holmes County. These papers reveal that controversy attended the application (1927). Pre-datings of James' birth abound—02 Mar. 1850; 4 Mar. 1850; 1851. A sheet notarized 12/16/30 & signed by Geo. W. Keith states, "James S. Keith, my brother, was born Mar. 2, 1856." (Likely a typo, for the middle brother, Wm. Thomas K. had just been born some 27 days earlier!) G. W. K. goes on to clear the air by asserting, "He was entirely too young. He never served in Grantham's Company of H. G.'s. James always acknowledged himself as the youngest Keith brother. He likely did know these older boys as he names them over in his 7/9/29 letter "...remembers in his H. G. Company, G. W. Lewis (b. 4/27/49); H. L. Lolley (b. 4/12/50); Thos. C. Keith; Sam F. French, J. B. Webb; John & Aaron Mattox; J. A. Forehand; Wm. M. Forehand (b. 8/1/48); N. B. Clancey; Jas. Leavins. He mentions M(adison) L(evi) Bowlin (*SLBG,* 249) but not as a Grantham H. G. comrade.

Sam Grantham, who led most of the boys in the preceding paragraph and others, "had not served in any war, but Mr. Martin Brett and Mr. Bethley Mattox, who had been in the Indian War, drilled the Company regularly at Brett and Lockley's Mills in Holmes County. They guarded river and creek crossings and protected communities from raiders (deserters)." A10405 papers.

10. Several #A10405 (State Archives, Tallahassee) sheets record that "J.S.K. enlisted on 8 Sept. 1863 in Capt. Grantham's Home Guard of Fla. and served till the close of the war." ...that he received a pension from Florida (Certif. No. 8799) as of Oct. 5, 1927 until his death. Initially, James' widow, Hattie S. Keith's pension was denied for her marriage having been on Dec. 25, 1918, due to a provision in the Gen. Pension Law that to be entitled a Confederate widow must have married prior to June 1, 1917.

N. B. My appreciation to Jas. B. Hayward, Cmdr. Camp 1282, SCV, of Brandon, FL. My thanks to Ralph W. Webb of Chipley and to James L. "Jimmy" Harrison of Palmetto, FL, who sent archive data confirming another George Keith as in Co. K, 11th Fl. Infy., as of March '63 but who died in Richmond, Va. of rubeola (measles) 6/25/64.

Epilogue

1 *The North's Last Boys in Blue*, to date, remains an unpublished manuscript.

2 *Black Soldiers in the Civil War* (coloring bk.), Bellerophon Books, 1994.

Bibliography

This is not a definitive listing of all books/journals consulted. Still others may be found in the respective notes where newspapers are documented.

Aley, Howard C. *A Heritage to Share: The Bicentennial History of Youngstown and Mahoning County, Ohio: Youngstown and Mahoning County, Ohio, from Prehistoric Times to the National Bicentennial Year.* Youngstown: Bicentennial Commission of Youngstown and Mahoning County, OH, 1975.

Baxter, Elizabeth. *Historic Ogdensburg: Founded in 1749, Incorporated in 1817.* Ogdensburg, NY: Ryan Press, 1977.

Benedict, G. G. *Vermont in the War: A History of the Part Taken by the Vermont Soldiers and Sailors in the War for the Union, 1861-5.* Burlington, VT: Free Press Association, 1886-1888.

Bingham, Luther G. *The Little Drummer Boy, Child of the 13th Regiment, N.Y.S.M. & Child of the Mission Sunday School.* Boston, MA: Hoyt, 1862.

Carnahan, J. W. *History of the Easel-Shaped Monument and a Key to the G.A.R. and Its Co-Workers.* Chicago, IL: Dux Publ. Co., 1893.

Chadwick, Albert G. *Soldiers' Record of the Town of St. Johnsbury, Vermont, in the War of the Rebellion, 1861-5.* St. Johnsbury, 1883.

Civil War Naval Chronology. (Naval History Div., Navy Dept.), Washington, D.C. 1971.

Clemmer, Gregg S. *Valor in Gray.* Staunton, VA: Hearthside Publ. Co., 1996.

Coe, Capt. James N. *History of the Second Regiment, Connecticut Volunteer Heavy Artillery.* n.d.

Confederate Veteran (the original magazine of the U.C.V.) "Extensive Use."

Crute, Jos. H., Jr. *Units of the Confederate States Army (Kentucky).* Midlothian, VA; Derwent Books, 1987.

Davis, Wm. J., Ed. *The Partisan Rangers of the Confederate States Army.* Louisville, KY: G. G. Fetter Co., 1904.

Downey, Fairfax. *Fife, Drum & Bugle*. Ft. Collins, CO: The Old Army Press, 1971.

Dyer, Frederick H. *A Compendium of the War of the Rebellion* 3 Vols., NY: Yoseloff Publ., 1959.

Echoes of Glory: Arms and Equipment of the Union (Editors, Time-Life Books), Alexandria, VA, Time-Life Books, 1991.

Ewen, David. *Great Men of American Popular Song: the History of the American Popular Song Told through the Lives, Careers, Achievements, and Personalities of its Foremost Composers and Lyricists from William Billings of the Revolutionary War to the "Folk-Rock" of Bob Dylan.* Englewood Cliffs, NJ: Prentice-Hall, 1970.

Fairbanks, Edward T. *The Town of St. Johnsbury, Vermont: A Review of 125 Years to the Anniversary Pageant, 1912.* St. Johnsbury: The Cowles Press, 1914.

Frassanito, William. *Antietam: The Photographic Legacy of America's Bloodiest Day*. NY: Scribner, 1978.

Garofalo, Robert & Mark Elrod. *A Pictorial History of the Civil War Era Musical Instruments and Military Bands.* Charleston, WV: Pictorial Histories Publishing Co., 1985.

Gillis, Cora E. *Final Journal of the Grand Army of the Republic, 1866-1956.* Washington, D.C: GPO, 1957.

Grand Army of the Republic, Department of New York, Personal War Sketches of the Members of Bidwell-Wilkeson Post #9, of Buffalo. 1897.

Grand Army Review. Vol. 4, No. 1, Boston, MA, June 1888.

Harwell, Thos. F. *Eighty Years Under the Stars and Bars.* 1947.

Hartke, Vance. *Medal of Honor Recipients 1863-1973.* Washington, D.C.: GPO, 1973.

Hay, Chas. C. *The Complete Romantic and Dramatic History of Cleburne and His Flag.* n.d.

Hemenway, Abby M. "Heroic Adventure," *Vermont Historical Gazette,* Vol. II, Burlington, VT, 1871.

Henderson, Lillian. *Roster of the Confederate Soldiers of Georgia 1861-1865.* Hopeville, GA: Longino & Porter, Inc., 1964.

The History and Genealogy of the Ricks Family in America (Sect. V, pp. 598-603). Revised Ed. 1957.

History of Butts County, Georgia. Atlanta, GA: Cherokee Publ. Co., 1978.

Hoar, Jay S. "Albert S. Twining." *Beyond Memos.* Farmington, ME: U.M.F. Printery, Spring 1993.

______ "Gettysburg's Last Surviving Soldier: James Marion Lurvey," *Gettysburg Magazine*. No. 16. Dayton, OH: Morningside House, Inc., Jan. 1, 1997.

______ *Montana's Last Civil War Old Soldiery*. Farmington, ME: U.M.F. Printery, 1984.

______ *New England's Last Civil War Veterans*. Arlington, TX: Seacliff Press, 1976.

______ *The North's Last Boys in Blue*. (Unpublished manuscript.)

______ "Susan H. Clayton, American Lady, 1851-1948," *Oregon Historical Quarterly*. Vol. 84, No. 2. Portland, OR. Summer 1983.

______ *The South's Last Boys in Gray*. Bowling Green, OH: Popular Press at Bowling Green State University, 1986.

______ "Thomas L. F. Hubler," *Beyond Memos: Journal of the U.M.F. Faculty*. Farmington, ME: U.M.F. Printery, Spring 1992.

Hull, Susan R. *Boy Soldiers of the Confederacy*, NY: Neale Publ. Co., 1905.

Huxford, Folks. *Pioneers of Wiregrass, Georgia*. Vol. 6, s.n. 1951?.

Illustrated Roster of the Department of Illinois, G.A.R., 1914.

Jackson, Hester B. *Surry County Soldiers in the Civil War*. Charlotte, NC: 1992.

Jensen, Les. T*he 32nd Virginia Infantry*. {Virginia Regimental Series} Lynchburg, VA: H.E. Howard, Inc., 1990.

Johnson, Adam R. *The Partisan Rangers of the Confederate States Army*. Louisville, KY: G.G. Fetter Co., 1904.

Journal of the 75th National Encampment, G.A.R., Columbus, Ohio Sept. 14-19, 1941. Washington, D.C.: GPO, 1942.

Journal of the 78th National Encampment, G.A.R., Des Moines, Sept. 10-15, 1944. Washington, D.C.: GPO, 1946.

Journal of the 81st Annual Encampment, Dept. of Minnesota G.A.R.

Lawrence, Vera Brodsky. *Music for Patriots, Politicians, and Presidents*. New York: Macmillan, 1975.

Livingston, Joel T. *History of Jasper County, Missouri*. Chicago, IL: The Lewis Publishing Co., 1912.

Long, E. B. *The Civil War Day by Day: An Almanac 1861-1865*. Garden City, NY: Doubleday, 1971.

Lord, Francis A. & Arthur Wise. *Bands and Drummer Boys of the Civil War*. New York, NY: T. Yoseloff, 1966.

McCormick, Hugh D. *Confederate Son*. Winchester, VA: Shenandoah Univ. Civil War Institute, 1993.

McLeod, Martha N. *Brother Warriors: Reminiscences of Union and Confederate Warriors.* Washington, D.C.: The Darling Printing Co., 1940.

Massachusetts Soldiers, Sailors and Marines in the Civil War (all vols.) Norwood, MA: Norwood Press, 1930's.

Nine, Wm. G. and Ronald G. Wilson. *The Appomattox Paroles April 9-15, 1865.* 4th Ed. Lynchburg, VA: H.E. Howard, Inc., 1989.

Official Roster of the State of Ohio in the War of the Rebellion, 1861-1866. Akron, OH: Werner Co., 1886.

Payne, Brook. *The Paynes of Virginia.* 2nd Ed. Harrisonburg, VA: C.J. Carrier Co., 1990.

Proceedings and Official Reports of the 81st Annual Encampment of the Department of Illinois G.A.R. Held at Rockford, Ill. June 6-9, 1947.

Quiner, E. B. *The Military History of Wisconsin.* Chicago, IL: Clarke & Co., 1866.

Reichley, John. "Youthful Civil War Hero Identified as Civilian," *The Annals* (Medal of Honor Historical Society). Vol. 8, No. 2. Dec. 1985.

Revised Roster of Vermont Volunteers in the War of the Rebellion. (T.S. Peck, Adj.-Gen., Cmplr.), Montpelier, VT. 1892.

Rodriguez, Mercedes. *The Drummer Boy John Lincoln Clem: The Civil War Years.* Master's Thesis, History Department; San Jose State University, 1974.

Rudolph, Col. Jack. "The Children's Crusade," *Civil War Times, Illustrated.* Harrisburg, PA: May 1982.

Sobel, Robert & John Raimo. *Biographical Directory of the Governors of the United States, 1789-1978.* Westport, CT: Meckler Books, 1978.

Sullivan, David M. *An Illustrated History of the Confederate Marine Corps.* (1998?)

Tatum, Miriam H. "About an Editor, C. A. Ricks," *River Road: Remembering, Angelina Free Press.* Diboll, TX: n.d.

Terrill, H.E. & S.R. Dixon. *History of Stewart County, Georgia.* Vol. I. Columbus, GA: Columbus Office Supply Co., 1958.

Titterton, Robert J. "A Soldier's Sketchbook," *Civil War Times Illustrated.* Harrisburg, PA: Sept.-Oct., 1991.

_____ *Julian Scott: Artist of the Civil War and Native America.* Jefferson, NC: McFarland & Co., 1996.

_____ *Julian Scott: Special Agent to the Eleventh Census.* Graduate Thesis, Graduate College of the University of Vermont, 1993.

Townsend, David G. *The Seventh Michigan Volunteer Infantry: The Gallant Men and Flag in the Civil War 1861 to 1865.* 1993.

Waite, Maj. Otis F. R. *Vermont in the Great Rebellion.* Claremont, NH: Tracy, Chase & Co., 1869.

War of the Rebellion: Official Records of the Union and Confederate Armies. Series I, Vol. 52, Part I, Supplement. Washington, D.C.: GPO, 1989.

Westbrook, Sgt. Robert S. *History of the 49th Pennsylvania Volunteers.* Altoona, PA: Altoona Times Print, 1898.

"When Soldier Boys Meant BOYS," *Fort Dodge (Iowa) Messenger,* August 9, 1961.

Wiley, Bell Irvin. *The Life of Billy Yank.* New York, NY: Doubleday, 1971.

Wood, Frances & Dorothy. *I Hauled These Mountains in Here.* Caldwell, ID: Caxton Printers, Ltd., 1977.

Yeary, Mamie. *Reminiscences of the Boys in Gray, 1861-1865.* Dayton, OH: Morningside House, Inc., 1986.

Professor Hoar kneels beside David Morrison's grave at the Soldiers' Home Cemetery in Washington, D.C. Morrison was an uncle of the author's grandmother.

About the Author

The recognized authority on our last and eldest veterans of the War Between the States, Prof. Hoar has now explored a longstanding, unsettled issue from "The Boys' War." He has pioneered his way to comprehensive answers to such haunting questions as—How young were the youngest soldierboys? Who were the latest born? Who were the youngest at enlistment? Was Johnny Clem the youngest in the Union Army? Could there have been more than one youngest on each side? Did they too sacrifice their lives in any appreciable numbers? For the first time we may know these elusive answers. Until Prof. Hoar came along, no scholar had yet been able to unravel these mysteries or shed light broadly upon these long kept secrets, topics of pre-eminent human interest.

Prof. Hoar has synthesized widely scattered fragments of data; he has cooperated with a veritable network of strategic Americans {See Acknowledgements} to bring off this original contribution to American Studies. This book is a bible that lays down gospel truths about the child-soldiery who were our sincerest patriots of all. Even the noted Bell Irvin Wiley in his *The Life of Billy Yank,* admitted with a tone of reluctance, "It is possible that boys even younger than twelve marched in the Union ranks, though the writer is not able to state this as a positive fact . . . The claim to the distinction of being 'the Youngest Yank' seems impossible of establishment."

Jay S. Hoar was educated at Rangeley High School, the University of Maine (Orono), and at Middlebury College (M.A. 1964). A U.S. Navy veteran (1956-60), he has taught for 38 years in Maine high schools, at the Maine Maritime Academy, and at the University of Maine at Farmington. He teaches nonfiction writing, grammar, sea masterpieces, Maine writers, and Civil War literature. He has been for 12 years published regularly in *Confederate Veteran Magazine.*